THE ICONOGRAPHY OF
ISLAMIC ART

THE ICONOGRAPHY OF ISLAMIC ART

STUDIES IN HONOUR OF ROBERT HILLENBRAND

Edited by Bernard O'Kane

Edinburgh University Press

Transferred to digital print 2015

Edinburgh University Press Ltd
22 George Square, Edinburgh

Typeset in Trump Mediaeval by
Iolair Typesetting, Newtonmore and
printed and bound by CPI Group (UK) Ltd, Croydon, CR0 4YY

A CIP record for this book is available from the British Library

ISBN 978-0-7486-3367-8 (paperback)

*This publication has been made possible with the support of the
Iran Heritage Foundation and the Altajir World of Islam Trust.*

Contents

CONTENTS

vi

Preface

In 1972 in the library of the British Institute of Persian Studies, the director approached a refugee from the hippy trail who was poring over Donald Wilber's architectural magnum opus. Sensing a neophyte who needed a guiding hand, he advised the traveller, if he wished to pursue his interest in Islamic architecture, to contact Robert Hillenbrand at Edinburgh University.

This happy accident led me to the portals of that university where Robert had just begun his teaching career, taking over the post of Byzantine art from David Talbot Rice. His route to Islamic art, as with many in our field, had been equally circuitous. Were it not for the vision and tenacity of his father, his family would not have been able to escape East Germany in the aftermath of the Second World War. Robert, having read English at Cambridge University, gave up a civil service career to work towards his doctorate at Oxford on the tomb towers of Iran, and, on the strength of several publications, began his teaching career even before it was finished. Juggling a new career in teaching with the completion of a doctorate in another subject while raising a small family is a dependable recipe for stress, yet I can affirm that no trace of this was evident to his students.

An extended fieldtrip in Iran is an excellent way to know one's travelling companions, and at the end of two months in the hot summer of 1973 it says much that my respect for Robert's kindness, humour, generosity and even temper was deepened. I, and others of my family, have been fortunate to have been the recipient of hospitality at the home of Robert and his wife Carole many times, where Robert's abilities to whip up a tasty meal at short notice have greatly impressed. Robert's recording of the thanks he owes to brothers, parents, wife and daughters in his book, *Islamic Architecture*, mirrors his warm family life, which has made such visits a privilege indeed.

Islamic art is a vast field. The study of it in recent decades has blossomed to the extent that specialisation has become the norm. This must have been a temptation to one who was initially teaching in a different field, but has been successfully, and spectacularly, resisted. His contributions in 1973 on the Umayyads to the *Propylaen Kunstgeschichte* already reveal a strong interest in iconography. His seminal article on 'La Dolce Vita in Early Islamic Syria' and numerous others on Umayyad art followed.

In 1977 Robert curated in Edinburgh one of the largest exhibitions of illustrated Persian manuscripts ever held, accompanied by a comprehensive catalogue. Combining his interests in the art of the book and the meaning of works of art, his article 'The Iconography of the Shah-nama-yi Shahi' was a major examination of a neglected aspect of this manuscript. He delivered the Kevorkian lectures in New York on the Great Mongol *Shahnama*, another monograph in the making that is eagerly awaited.

There are few scholars who have the intellectual breadth that is reflected in Robert's prize-winning survey, *Islamic Architecture*, published in 1994. Its text is informed by his extensive travels in virtually all of the countries under discussion. One reviewer expresses better than I can one of the book's strongest points: '[his] arguments are incisively presented in a prose which is never less than lucid, and which occasionally achieves an eloquence that mesmerises'.

This lucidity and eloquence informs all of his publications, and is one of the characteristics that make his lectures such a pleasure. This is reflected in the visiting professorships that he has held at Princeton, UCLA, Bamberg and Dartmouth College, and of course in his award of a chair in Islamic art at Edinburgh University in 1989.

Robert's service on the councils of the British School of Archaeology in Jerusalem, British Research in the Levant and the British Institute of Persian Studies should not go unmentioned. With his guidance, the massive two-volume work on Ottoman Jerusalem has been produced. Under his Vice-Presidency, the British Institute of Persian Studies has seen itself transformed once more into a vital institution of research.

Iconography has been one of Robert's enduring interests, and it is with appreciation for his contributions to the field that this book is offered. This tribute fortunately finds Robert in the prime of his scholarly capacities. We have much to look forward to in the way of monographs on the Dome of the Rock, Iranian tomb towers, the Great Mongol *Shahnama*, Ayyubid Jerusalem and Saljuq architecture, a list that once again emphasises the versatility and vitality of his scholarship, which has ranged from the Umayyads to the Qajars, and from Spain to India.

Illustrations

Plates

Between pages 112 and 113

Between pages 208 and 209

Contributors

Sylvia Auld
University of Edinburgh

Marianne Barrucand
University of the Sorbonne, Paris

Sheila S. Blair
Boston College

Jonathan M. Bloom
Boston College

Barbara Brend

Anna Contadini
School of Oriental and African
Studies, University of London

Abbas Daneshvari
California State University, Los Angeles

Géza Fehérvári
Tareq Rajab Museum, Kuwait

Barbara Finster
Bamberg University

Finbarr Barry Flood
New York University

Oleg Grabar
Instiue of Advanced Study,
Princeton

Ulrike al-Khamis
Royal Scottish Museum, Edinburgh

Marcus Milwright
University of Victoria

Bernard O'Kane
American University in Cairo

B. W. Robinson
Victoria and Albert Museum, London

Avinoam Shalem
Ludwig-Maximilians University,
Munich

Raya Y. Shani
Hebrew University of Jerusalem

Rachel Ward

Acknowledgements

My suggestion of a festschrift for Robert was met with great enthusiasm by Nicola Carr of Edinburgh University Press. Subsequently Eddie Clark and Ann Vinnicombe have similarly worked towards producing a high-quality book.

To the Iran Heritage Foundation and the Altajir World of Islam Trust goes many thanks for their generous subvention which made it possible to include colour plates. My chief thanks goes to the authors whose own concerns for quality are manifest in their research and who responded so readily to the call to honour Robert Hillenbrand, to whom this book is dedicated. Their wide-ranging contributions mirror his own interests in iconography and his mastery of so many areas of Islamic art.

CHAPTER ONE

Birds and Blessings: A Kohl-pot from Jerusalem[1]

Sylvia Auld

From the earliest days of Islam, birds appear in every area of art. This short chapter cannot hope to encompass a subject which would be more suitable as the topic for a book. It will concentrate instead on a small object it has proved disconcertingly difficult to locate.[2] The little pot illustrated in Figures 1–4 was discovered in the suq in Jerusalem in the winter of 1966. In those days, many such objects could be found, brought in by pilgrims who stopped in the city on their way to or from Mecca. Many paid for the journey by selling

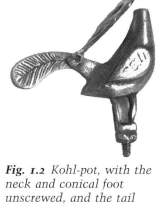

Fig. 1.2 *Kohl-pot, with the neck and conical foot unscrewed, and the tail bent forwards. The inscription read as* al-madīna *is on the wing.*

(Private collection, photograph © S. Auld.)

Fig. 1.1 *Kohl-pot (mukḥula), side view, showing the inscription read as* al-mukarrama *on the wing.*

(Private collection, photograph © S. Auld.)

Fig. 1.3 *Kohl-pot, showing the component parts, including the shaft (mirwad).*

(Private collection, photograph © S. Auld.)

Fig. 1.4 *Kohl-pot, front view, showing the line of solder.*

(Private collection, photograph © S. Auld.)

semi-precious stones, artefacts and jewellery. Because of this, it is difficult to be sure of the provenance of such an object, particularly when in universal use. The kohl-pot (*mukhula*, pl. *makāhil*[3]) in question is unusual, however, not only because of its form, that of a bird, but also because of its metal content. It is cast in brass, covered in a thin layer of nickel.[4] Neither of these is a precious metal, and their use to make the pot, together with the very clumsy way it was made, underlines its everyday nature. The woman who sold the little kohl-pot in the Jerusalem suq was not from a rich family. Even more telling is the fact that the black substance used for the eye cosmetic, which is still sticking to the shaft, consists of iron oxide rather than a more expensive compound.

Kohl *(al-kuhl)* is used to outline the eyes, and sometimes as an eye unguent. The term is usually translated as antimony trisulphide (Sb) and the primary source in the medieval period was Iran. However, *kuhl* is synonymous in the sources with *surma* and *ithmid* and it was rare that it denoted antimony.[5] Moreover, contrary to the general view, not even in ancient Egypt was the eye paint made with an antimony base (which is highly poisonous) but rather it consisted of a paste made of galena, pyrolusite, brown ochre and even malachite, among other minerals. The cosmetic paste was ground as finely as possible in a special vessel, which had a spout with which to pour the thinned cosmetic into a narrow-necked kohl-pot.[6] In the medieval period, these were usually of glass. The paste was applied to the eyes by a stick called a *mirwad*. It is this stick that in our pot is attached to the neck of the bird, which unscrews to reveal the 2.5cm-long spatula-like shaft (Figure 1.3). The pot itself stands overall 12cm high and is 9cm from the tip of the beak to the tail.

The body of the bird was cast in two sections, probably in sand,[7] and then soldered together (Figure 1.4). The surface is pitted in the way typical of sand-casting; this is particularly noticeable on the underside of the conical foot. A line of solder is clearly visible, running along the back and belly of the bird. The two halves form a cavity in the croup for the cosmetic paste. The legs terminate in a solid base, scored across by a single indentation. This detail is strongly reminiscent of the way the 'foot' of the finial of the kohl stick (described below; British Museum inv. no. 1909 2–16 59) is treated. From this a screw emerges, which is attached to a conical foot decorated with two concentric rings. A separate movable 'tail' is attached by means of a pin (Figure 1.2). The tail is fan-shaped, and is pierced by two crescent-shaped and twelve circular holes,[8] six (originally seven) of which are arranged round the scalloped upper section and five of which run across the width of the tail (Figure 1.4). The middle circle at the apex of the fan is broken, probably through frequent contact with the neck. It is difficult to see why the second tail should be movable; while it would be possible to balance the stopper in one of the pierced holes, this would offer little security because the movement renders it insecure as a resting place.

Details are engraved into the body metal. There are inscriptions on both wings (Figures 1.1–2) and the fixed tail has a central line, from which successive strokes emerge to form the traditional 'feathers' or 'spear' design of Palestinian embroidery.[9] Not only the movable second tail but also the 'crown' on the head of the bird identify it as a peacock, *ṭāwūs* or *ṭāwwūs* in Arabic.[10] There are several instances of similar birds associated with kohl-pots, but I know of no other example where the bird forms the container itself. One kohl-stick with a peacock finial is illustrated in *The Arts and Crafts of Syria*;[11] although in the catalogue the bird is described as being 'perhaps a sunbird,' it is almost certainly a peacock. Abbas Daneshvari[12] trawled through the literary texts in search of peacocks, and produced an illuminating study on their meaning. Of particular interest to our question, he asserted (p. 58) that the peacock has a specific association with the sun. Indeed, in medieval Persian literature, the sun is called on occasion *ṭāwūs ātish parr*, 'peacock with wings of fire.'[13] Daneshvari pointed out that the peacocks on the segmental niche in the tomb tower Kharragan I, which was the main focus of his study, appear in discs 'of radiating light.' Frick's[14] investigation of possible sources for decorative motifs drew attention to the link with the Yazidis in Syria. These people, who originated in Kurdistan, were by 1200 settled in Syria, Egypt and Persia; one centre was in the north of Syria. Considered to have incorporated elements of Zoroastrianism, Manichaeanism and Nestorian Christianity into Islam, Frick suggests that the popularity of the peacock as a motif was related to the prime importance in the hierarchy of angels of the Malak Ta῾ūs (*sic*), the 'Peacock Angel' (p. 234). This esoteric interpretation is, however, far removed from the function of our humble kohl-pot and can be safely ignored here.

Other examples of kohl-sticks have peacock finials. A collection donated by Rabino to the British Museum sometime before 1909 includes three such (inv. nos. 1909 2–16 59, 1909 2–16,50 and 1909 2–16 53). They are all of a dark metal, either bronze or oxidised brass, and measure approximately 3–4 cm in height. Probably from Iran and dated to the twelfth–thirteenth centuries, they resemble in casting technique and appearance the small three-dimensional birds that are frequently attached to incense burners and lamps.[15] That there is a continued association from this early period of peacocks with cosmetics is proved by a faceted cylindrical kohl-pot of some 7cm in height with an integral chain, probably dating to the sixteenth–seventeenth centuries (British Museum, no number). Its stopper has a finial in the shape of a peacock with a double tail. It is possible that the kohl-stick did not originally belong to the pot, although both appear to be made of oxidised silver. Finally, this time securely provenanced to Kirman, there is a small brass peacock in the Sykes collection (British Museum, inv. no. 1921–2–20). Its head is quite different in appearance, for its beak is almost raptor-like; but it is 'crowned' and the upright tail is the closest I have seen to the kohl-

3

pot which is the subject of this chapter. On the basis of the examples just described, I think ours may be Iranian and 'modern,' that is twentieth century in date.[16] There is no question but that the pot is modern because of the use of nickel, and the Iranian connection would be consistent not just with the objects in the British Museum, but also because of the continued use of peacocks as a motif in later pieces,[17] and an association with 'the Peacock Throne.'[18] The tail in particular had royal or paradisiacal connections in the tradition of the Sassanian dynasty.[19]

On the face of it, a peacock seems a suitable shape for an object used to hold make-up because the root *t w s* carries the primary meaning of 'to adorn or beautify.'[20] Thus *tāsa* is translated by Lane as 'he was, or became, beautiful' and *tatāwwasat* as 'she adorned herself [as though she made herself like a *tawwūs* or peacock]'. Another subsidiary word (*tūwās*) is related to phases of the moon, in particular at the time of change, for example 'one of the nights of the last part of the [lunar] month.' *Tāʾūs* in the dialect of Syria carries the meaning 'a goodly, or beautiful man' and in the Yemen of 'verdant land, wherein, or whereon, is every kind of plant, or of flowers, in the days of spring.' Wehr's more up-to-date dictionary gives *mutawwas* as 'ostentatiously made up' or 'ornate.'[21]

There are two inscriptions. On one wing (Figure 1.1), when the bird is facing to the left, the letters *a l m k r m* can be quite clearly seen; there is also a final flourish. If it is correct to interpret this final 'tail' as *taʿ marbūta* (and it is almost certainly right to do so[22]) the word should be read as *al-mukarrama*, 'the honoured.'[23] The root consonants are associated with *al-karīm* (the generous). The word has connotations which lie outside the purely religious, but if it is right to see the little kohl-pot as coming from Mecca, as the argument below explains, then it brings *baraka* from that holy place to its owner.

The inscription on the opposite wing, visible when the bird is facing to the right, is more difficult to decipher because the surface is badly pitted (Figure 1.2). Although perhaps due to wear and tear, it is more likely that the casting mould itself was deficient. With a good deal of uncertainty, a tentative reading might produce *al-madīna*, the city. This reading depends on identifying ambiguous pits in the surface of the metal as deliberate dots above and below the letters. It is common enough to place the second part of a word or phrase on a line above and a little to the left of the first letters. The two sides of the pot read in conjunction would thus give *al-madīna al-mukarra-ma*, the epithet for the holy city of Mecca. There seems to be no connection between the inscriptions and the practical purpose of the pot,[24] but it is reasonable to assume that the kohl-pot was originally bought in Mecca as a souvenir of the *ḥajj*; it would thus be doubly auspicious for not only would it bring *baraka* from its place of purchase but also in the inscriptions on its wings. This does not help with the place of manufacture, however, for many such objects are imported into the city for sale to pilgrims.

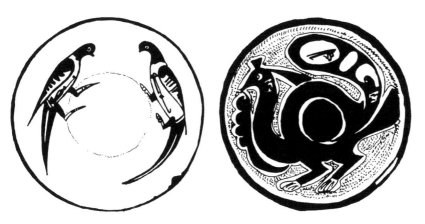

Fig. 1.5 (left) *Bowl with two confronted long-tailed birds, each with the word* baraka *within its body, Iran 10th century. Freer Gallery of Art, Washington, DC, inv. no. 56.1.*

(Drawing © S. Auld.)

Fig. 1.6 (right) *Bowl with peacock, Mesopotamia 9th–10th centuries, Brooklyn Museum, Acc. no. L.63.9.23.*

(Drawing © S. Auld.)

Kohl, thought to originate from Egypt, was used not merely to add emphasis to the eyes of both men and women, but also to act as a shield against the evil eye. There is an additional link through the bird-form of the pot and this idea of warding off evil; Penrice draws attention to the form of the root *ṭāra* 'to fly' and the generic noun *ṭa'ir* (birds) in the active participle *ṭā'ir* 'a flying thing, an omen, and especially an evil one.'[25] He continued *tat'aīra* or *aṭa'īra* had the meaning 'to augur evil, draw an evil augury from,' which is perhaps a residue of the pre-Islamic method of prediction by means of animal entrails.

While birds in Islamic art are commonplace from the earliest period, peacocks are comparatively rare. In Arabic lore they were of no interest because they were considered inauspicious;[26] elsewhere, and particularly in Iran because of the Sassanian tradition, they do occur in art. Early examples are found in tenth-century Mesopotamian tin-glazed earthenware with lustre decoration, one of which is currently in the Freer Gallery of Art (Figure 1.5).[27] The bird is characteristically represented in profile with a second tail, and a plumed 'crown' on its head. The bowl in Figure 1.5 carries an inscription that is repeated in the body of each bird; it reads *baraka*, 'blessing'; other similar bowls read *baraka li-ṣāḥibi*, (blessing to the owner) and *'izz* (glory) (Figure 1.6). Oliver Watson drew attention to the connection with textiles where birds in roundels are a frequent feature;[28] other textiles are decorated with bands of inscriptions of the type known in Arabic as *du'ā*, a prayer formula invoking God's blessing. There is, for example, a Persian silk textile in the Treasury of Aachen Cathedral,[29] where two peacocks' heads are framed by a 'halo' surrounded by typical Sassanian 'pearls' (Figure 1.7).[30] The border of the bowl published in *Treasures of Islam*, no. 199, confirms the identification of the species as a peacock for it consists of a series of 'eyes.'[31] The representation of the bird in profile seems to have become the norm, perhaps under Sassanian influence.[32] A cast bronze ewer allegedly from Daghestan in the Hermitage Museum, St Petersburg, has two large peacocks on its body, confronting each other to

Fig. 1.7 Persian silk textile with peacocks, Treasury of Aachen Cathedral.

(Drawing © S. Auld.)

5

either side of a fleshy palmette. Crowned and with tail feathers decorated with the characteristic 'eyes,' the identification of the species is incontrovertible.[33] An eight-sided money vessel in the Iran Bastan museum is decorated with a series of oval cartouches,[34] each with a bird in profile with three erect tail feathers. Although uncrowned, these too may represent peacocks. An anonymous illustration of the assembly of the birds in a copy of the *Mantiq al-Tayr* of 1493 in the Bodleian Library in Oxford[35] shows the peacock in profile in the foreground. He has the characteristic trailing tail covered with 'eyes,' a short second tail and a plume of feathers on his head. Perhaps under western influence, later birds are shown with their tail displayed;[36] another, rather awkwardly, is shown still in profile but has its tail feathers fully displayed. This last example appears in a painting attributed to Fa'iz Allah showing a view of a palace with gardens and fountains.[37] There are also (rare) incidents of free-standing peacock statuettes. A base-metal aquamanile in this form has inscriptions in Arabic and Latin.[38] They read 'amal 'Abd al-Mālik al-naṣrānī (work of 'Abd al-Malik the Christian) and *opus Solomonis erat* (work of Solomon), which is interesting because of the connection between the biblical king and the peacock, discussed below. Barbara Brend believed that the figure was made in Sicily or Spain in the eleventh or twelfth century CE. The bird has a triple crown and an open tail; its beak and head, however, resemble a raptor and are reminiscent of, say, the ewer signed by Sulayman, dated 180/796–7, in the Hermitage Museum, St Petersburg.[39] Peacocks also appear on ivory objects from Spain, for example on a casket made for Subh, the mother of a son of al-Hakam II.[40] They also seem to have been popular in Mughal India, interestingly in view of the connections with Iran. Mark Zebrowski[41] devoted a chapter in his study to what he called 'an exotic menagerie,' many of which are free-standing peacocks in the guise of containers for oil, water and incense. One large free-standing steel peacock in the British Museum also has a fully-opened hinged tail displayed and it too has a triple crown. This last example dates to nineteenth century Iran. The body and tail of the bird are engraved with figural scenes and inscriptions with some gilding; the eyes are set with turquoise.[42] Rachel Ward identified the figures in a lotus-shaped medallion in the centre of the tail as 'Ali, the first Shi'ite imam, and his two sons, Hasan and Husain. 'Ali, his face veiled, is shown on a hexagonal dais above two lions, and a domed kiosk appears above his head in the apex of the medallion. Jinns, deer and birds surround the group, and a border of inscriptions encircles them.

It seems, then, that the peacock may have had a particular resonance within the Iranian psyche, despite the fact that the role of the peacock in Islamic literature is not always favourable. For example, the Saljuq poet Nizami warned against a preoccupation with outward appearances, holding up the peacock as an example: 'Do not judge a peacock by the colour of its feathers and the manner of its flight for, like the cat, he too has an ugly cry.'[43] In particular the peacock's role in seducing Adam and Eve into eating the forbidden fruit and thus introducing the Devil into Paradise was never forgotten.[44] This can be demonstrated by Farid al-Din ʿAttar's *Mantiq al-Tayr*, written sometime in the second half of the twelfth century CE, where the peacock is listed in the opening invocation as one of those chosen to search for the simurgh. The link with Paradise is confirmed in the poem, for the bird is immediately introduced as 'once of paradise / who let the venomous, smooth snake entice [his] instincts to its master's evil way / and suffered exile for that fateful day'.[45] The peacock is described as 'splendidly arrayed / In many-coloured pomp; this he displayed / As if he were some proud, self-conscious bride / Turning with haughty looks from side to side.'[46] The bird's excuse for not accompanying the hoopoe on the quest was 'How could I seek the Simorgh [*sic*] out when I / Remember paradise?'[47] The peacock is, then, immediately identified as both vain and proud, believing that his personal experience of paradise puts him above his fellows. The hoopoe in reply warns 'These thoughts have made you stray / Further and further from the proper Way.'[48] The peacock has been blinded by the beauty of the 'palace' to set it above 'Him who fashioned it and all the earth.'[49] This point is underlined by the associated story in the text, which is about Adam. Why, asked a novice, was Adam forbidden to remain in Paradise? The reply is that 'The man whose mind and vision are ensnared / By heaven's grace must forfeit that same grace / For only then can he direct his face / To his true Lord.'[50] Jalal al-Din Rumi was scarcely more flattering about the bird. The peacock is exhorted in the *Mathnawi* (5:574) 'do not tear out thy feathers, but wean thy heart from pride in them.' In the same book (648) the bird replies 'Needs must I tear them out . . . These gorgous plumes which only tempt my pride.'[51] It is possible to see behind the choice of a peacock as a kohl-pot a memory of these medieval texts, which issue a warning to the user of the sin of vanity and the mistake of setting external beauty in the place of the Creator.

On the other hand, Annemarie Schimmel drew attention to lines by Khaqani, who died in 1199. These read 'From the cheeks and the face and the tresses you have / got a peacock and a paradise and a serpent together,' which she glossed as 'the cheeks are radiant and colourful like a peacock, a bird usually connected with spring and Paradise owing to its dazzling beauty.'[52]

Birds in general seem to have had a connection with cosmetics from an early period. James Allan drew attention to a type of small Persian toiletry dish in the form of a bird, with a flat lip and projecting head, wing and tail[53] in the Keir Collection,[54] which suggested to him an Egyptian connection. He also cited a kohl-bottle in the form of a bird with its head missing,[55] listed in the *Survey of Persian Art*, which, because it is in the round, he sees as being more typically Islamic, falling into a similar group as the aquamaniles, oil-lamps and incense-burners in three-dimensional zoomorphic form.[56] Eva Baer illustrated a similar phial to the one illustrated in the *Survey*, also in the shape of a bird with its head missing, from the Fogg Art Museum;[57] a complete example with its stopper is in the Victoria and Albert Museum, London (Figure 1.8).[58] Assadullah Souren Melikian-Chirvani, warning against the assumption that the receptacle was used to hold scent because of a lack of definitive evidence, described the head as being 'attached to a long rod, the square section tapering to an oval section and then gradually flattening and curving up; the tip, shaped like a spatula, was possibly actually used as such'. He does not, however, offer an alternative theory to explain its original use. The decoration of the bird, inlaid in silver, is particularly interesting. The tail is decorated with a 'scale-pattern', as Melikian-Chirvani described it, but this can be interpreted plausibly as 'peacock eyes'. The head is uncrowned. The inlaid figural decoration is related to astrology. There are running quadrupeds, figures on a throne with dragon heads, which are grasped by the neck, a goat, addorsed birds, and so on, all of which are associated with star signs.[59] Peacocks too were linked to cosmological imagery. As well as being a solar symbol (see below), the tail of the bird was sometimes associated with celestial bodies, for example the moon, Mercury and Jupiter, while the bird itself had life-giving water, spring and fertility connotations.[60] These associations in turn may have led to the idea of the bird having apotropaic power. If the eye is seen as 'the mirror of the soul' then it would seem logical to protect it from harm by ringing it with a cosmetic taken from a potent symbol.

Peacocks as a decorative motif may have originated in the west, despite their eastern provenance. There was an ancient belief that the flesh and feathers of a peacock do not decay. This led to the peacock becoming a Christian symbol for Christ's Resurrection;[61] in Islam too, as we have just seen, the peacock is closely associated with Paradise.[62] As such, the bird features in scenes of the Nativity and Annunciation in Christian art.[63] The Hellenistic association with Dionysos, a *typos* for Christ, may have added depth to the identification with eternal life.[64] This may in part explain the frequent

Fig. 1.8 *Bird-shaped metal flask in the Victoria and Albert Museum, London (no number).*

(Drawing © S. Auld.)

appearance of peacocks at the Byzantine church of St Polyeuktos dedicated by the princess Anicia Juliana in sixth-century Constantinople,[65] where not only did they appear in a prominent position in the main entablature, but also 'each exedra accommodated five large peacocks, their tails outspread, necks and heads carved in the round, their feet in high relief on short pedestals'. There is evidence to suggest that the eyes of these birds were inlaid with green glass, and that the marble was originally painted in vivid colours.[66] The strong Sassanian influence on the sculpture at St Polyeuktos adds further evidence to a Persian connection, but the main association is through the biblical Solomon, for the first forty-one lines of a poem in praise of the benefactress were carved around the nave of the church. These included the lines 'She alone has conquered time and surpassed the wisdom of renowned Solomon, raising a temple to receive God, the richly wrought and graceful splendour of which the ages cannot celebrate.'[67]

There are problems about the traditional biblical connection between peacocks and Solomon, however. A single reference to the plural Hebrew word *tukkiyim*, believed to derive from the Tamil word *tokei*, is found in 1 Kings 10:22 and 2 Chronicles 9:21; it is translated in the King James Authorised Version as '. . . every three years once came the ships of Tarshish bringing gold, and silver, ivory, and apes, and *peacocks*' (my italics); modern scholarship suggests that a more accurate translation of the word is 'baboons'.[68]

Although the peacock does not appear in person in the Qur'an, birds are associated in general with Solomon. Qur'an 21:78 speaks of the wisdom bestowed on Solomon, who was taught the language of the birds (27:16), and on David, causing the 'mountains and the birds to join with David in our praise'. Three Suras describe praise as one of the main functions of birds: Qur'an 24:41 ('Do you not see how God is praised by those in the heavens and those on earth? The very birds praise Him as they wing their flight . . .'), Qur'an 34:10 ('We said: "Mountains, and you birds echo his [David's] song of praise"'), and Qur'an 38:17 ('We made the mountains join with him [David] in praise evening and morning, and the birds, too, in all their flocks'). The other function of birds is to demonstrate the overarching power of God, who mustered birds and jinn into an army in support of Solomon (27:17) and of the Prophet (105:1). Indeed, the very flight of birds, sustained only by God, proves His power and is a sign to true believers (16:79, 67:19), and promises their ultimate resurrection (6:36), as in Christian symbolism. Certain species of birds are named – the hoopoe (*hudhud*) (27:19) as a messenger, and quails (*salwā*) as food in the desert (2:57, 7:160, 20:81), proof of God's bounty. The name of the *hudhud* carries its own secret, for it echoes the name of one of the twenty-eight prophets named in the Qur'an (Hud, heading Sura 10), which extols the believer to seek forgiveness and to return to God and, in verse 6, asserts that 'There is not a creature on the earth but God provides its sustenance. He knows its dwelling and its resting-place.'

Birds fulfil a specific role in Islam. One of the reasons for taking up the theme for this festschrift paper is that they convey a blessing (*baraka*). From the earliest days of Islam, birds appear as a decorative feature,[69] part of the classical heritage.[70] The cockerel and eagle in particular enjoyed a special status in Sassanian iconography, where they are shown beribboned to denote royal status,[71] and often with a pearl, plant stem or tassel dangling from their beak. From these early years, the birds seem to fall into two groups; these represent sun birds and moon birds, the hunter and the hunted, the underlying iconography relating to the image of the ruler as the supreme hunter, but it is outside the parameters of this chapter to deal with the imagery in detail.

At Khirbat al-Mafjar, these images of power are prominently displayed throughout the palace complex. The message is encapsulated in the famous mosaic in the *dīwān*, where to the right of the tree of life a lion subdues a doe. Directly above, there are winged horses (a moon symbol) on the pendentives and, above them, there is a frieze of quails at the base of the dome. Over and above the reliance on Sassanian precedents,[72] this position underlines the relationship of the birds to the vault of heaven, the abode of the holy.

Beyond the Qur'anic role of praise-singer, there may be another side to quails. In Arabic they are *salwa*; other meanings of the same root letters *sīn lām wāw* are 'consolation', 'comfort' and 'fun'. The birds are a visual pun. This is not surprising when it is recalled that the patron of Khirbat al-Mafjar liked nothing better than a joke and a good party.[73] In more serious vein, the Qur'an tells of God's gift of manna and quails in the desert (2:57, 7:160, 20:81), just as the Exodus story in the Hebrew Bible tells how the birds were provided by God to feed the children of Israel. A biblical gloss[74] underlines the double nature of their appearance for 'God's sending of quails to feed the Israelites in the wilderness is viewed both as a blessing (Exodus 16:9–13; Psalm 105:40) and a judgment (Numbers 11:31–34; Psalm 78:26–31).' Perhaps, then, as in other cultures, quails in early Islam had the additional meaning of a 'solace sent by God'. Their special status seems to have continued, for these small plump birds (or others very similar in appearance) feature frequently on metalwork, often round the base or at the mouth of a vessel.[75] The association, too, of birds with augury or omen may account for their appearance at an opening or entrance.[76] Their presence may act as a talisman to withstand evil, or even as a barrier against poison.

Birds seem to appear either as themselves, as a simile, or as representatives of the heavenly bodies. There is, for example, a series of twelfth-century ewers from Herat where birds appear in the round[77] at the top of the body; their elevated position and the associated iconography underlines their cosmological significance. In more linear form birds adorn the great Mamluk Baptistère de St Louis, which was signed by Muhammad ibn al-Zayn and made c. 1300. This has a frieze of curiously fish-like birds inlaid around its upper rim. Perhaps their fish-like form as well as the position at the top of the basin is a reference to the so-called 'fish-pond ornament' of the *chishma-yi nūr*, or Fount of Light, where the heavens are depicted as a pool filled with creatures. An analysis of these beings identifies them with the Arabic names of the fixed stars and constellations, many of which bore the name of birds, fish and animals.[78] Birds appear elsewhere on the Baptistère. Water-birds, far more naturalistically portrayed, are dotted about in the landscape behind the wide band of human actors on the exterior of the bowl. These water-birds may also refer to the concept of the heavens as a pool of light. Similar birds are found by themselves in a whorl, connected by the neck, in the base of Mamluk bowls,[79] in a frieze,[80] as incense burners,[81] or in medallions; sometimes ducks appear as the prey of a raptor,[82] which may be a reference to their identity as a moon creature.

Elsewhere too a frieze of birds carries an astrological meaning. There is no space to give a catalogue of the many examples, but two well-known appearances are on the so-called 'Bobrinski bucket' (559/1163)[83] and on the penbox made by Mahmud ibn Sunqur (680/1281).[84] On the Bobrinski bucket confronted pairs of birds circle the outer lip and appear again in the lower frieze on the body among the huntsmen,[85] and on the pencase they fly in pairs on the inside of the lid, in association with personifications of the planets. The celestial iconography on the pencase continues on the outside of the lid, where three groups of four symbols of signs of the zodiac appear, each in its domicile, while on the base of the box pairs of huntsmen confront two-headed planet-eating dragons. The base is framed by a frieze of flying birds; their wings touch and they form a diaper pattern against scrolling stems. A similarly astrological connotation accompanies the appearance of birds as terminals on a frieze of zoomorphic script on a penbox from Iran or Afghanistan dated 607/1211,[86] and on the Wade Cup.[87]

Birds do not only appear in friezes. They are also shown either alone, in pairs, or in association with other animals – as part of the landscape, as it were, as on the Baptistère, or more clearly in manuscript painting, for example the *Shahnama* of Sultan Ibrahim, where, in a landscape painted in gold and silver, the species include cranes,[88] ducks and indeterminate flying birds.[89] Birds shown in a landscape are commonly the local varieties – ducks, geese, pigeons, and so on. It was the Mongols who introduced eastern species into Arab and Persian iconographies, and these included the Chinese phoenix (*sīmurgh*).[90] These exotic creatures are first recorded in Iran in the company of other oriental breeds such as parakeets, swans and parrots. Here peacocks feature as an imported species from India. The association as a non-native, romantically strange creature may explain the inclusion of a peacock among the birds seeking the *sīmurgh* in 'Attar's masterpiece.

Finally we have reached the key question of this chapter. Beyond the association of birds with the celestial, is there a deeper, hidden message for the initiated, even in our ordinary little kohl-pot?

Winged creatures have been associated from the earliest recorded periods with the idea of the heavens.[91] Fair enough then, to carry the association further, and to group together the creatures of the air with the celestial bodies, as has already been suggested. But beyond this, there grew up a concept of winged creatures which were able to defy the laws that tie the other inhabitants of the world to its surface. There are multiple examples of winged victories – cupids, angels, creatures of the air, which are celestial and not confined to the sublunar laws of mortification of the flesh.[92] Mention has already been made to the belief that the flesh of the peacock does not decay, and that the 'eyes' of its tail feathers represented the all-seeing eye of the Creator. From the tenth century CE this concept of the bird as auspicious, close to God, is underlined by what I think is a significant detail. A group of Samanid ceramic bowls bearing a single – sometimes a pair – of long-tailed birds with the word *baraka* inscribed within their bodies (Figure 1.5) has already been mentioned. Over a dozen examples exist. It is necessary to look closely to identify the inscription hidden within the bird's body. The secret quality of the message adds a mystical dimension; it is as though the blessing must be deliberately sought before it can be revealed (Plate 1).

There are other clues in this association of bird and spirit/bird and soul. In Arabic the soul or vital spirit (*nafs*) is associated with something precious, highly prized (*nafīsa*), and with the idea of air or breath (*tanaffus*, respiration). The soul is associated with the breath of life and is the essential constituent of a being.[93] It may be fanciful but there would seem some logic in the idea that there is an association with a winged creature, and it is therefore of particular interest to discover that the word for the action of a cock is *nafasha*, to swell out, puff up, or to ruffle the feathers.[94] This too is another sort of visual pun for, of course, the letters *sīn* and *shīn* are distinguished only by three additional dots.

Annemarie Schimmel identified various species that were thought to be particularly appropriate images of the bird as a spiritual being.[95] The pigeon crooning *kū-kū* ('Where? Where?') is searching for God; in Turkish she cries *hū-hū* ('He! He!'). The stork, a migratory bird which builds her nest at the highest point of a village (often the minaret), with her cry of *laq laq*, from which the Arabic name of the bird is taken (*laqlaq*), attests *al-mulk lak, al-ʿizz lak, al-ḥamd lak* ('Thine is the kingdom, Thine is the power, Thine is the praise'). In about 1200 CE, Sanaʾi invented a *Litany of the Birds* (*Tasbīḥ al-ṭuyūr*), where the cry of each bird is interpreted in a religious sense. These ideas permeated medieval mystical thought and poetry, culminating in ʿAttar's *Mantiq al-tayr*. The underlying thesis is that, just as it takes a great master to penetrate the depths of the soul, the language of birds can only be understood by a true master. Indeed, the hoopoe acted as a messenger between Solomon and Bilqis Queen of Sheba as well as guide to those seeking the mystical *sīmurgh* in *Mantiq al-Tayr*. When Solomon/Sulaiman (Qur'an 27:16) and Bilqis go in search of the magical *sīmurgh*, they are led by the hoopoe through seven valleys. ʿAttar puts into the mouth of the hoopoe the introductory words 'My purposes are heaven-sent; / I keep God's secrets, mundane and divine, / In proof of which behold the holy sign/*bismallah* etched for ever on my beak.'[96] The explanation for the name of the *sīmurgh* is because thirty birds undertook a pilgrimage through seven valleys in search of a goal. When they had accomplished their mission, they found that they themselves were the goal – the divine *sīmurgh*.

There can be little doubt that in the world of Islam, as elsewhere, folk tales contain vestiges of medieval belief. It is perhaps not so surprising after all that the little kohl-pot with which this chapter began should be in the form of a peacock. It carries hidden within its body a black substance. Over and above this 'secret', it carries in its very form a long history of traditional associations. But here, in this chapter, it carries with it a wish for all things good for a generous master cast in the best medieval mould.

Notes

1. Robert and Carole Hillenbrand have been my friends and colleagues for many years. Without them I would not have stepped onto the slippery slope of looking at and behind things Islamic. Robert is the sort of inspirational teacher who forces a student to trust his or her own mind, encouraging the belief that ignorance is not necessarily a sign of stupidity, and a little work clarifies any problem. I am so deeply grateful for his patience and wisdom that it seems impudent to submit this short piece in recognition of all the support and patience we, all of his students, have received over the years. But I do so dare, and offer it with love.

2. It is a measure of the affection with which Robert Hillenbrand is regarded that a large number of people have willingly given their time to trying to unravel the puzzle. In alphabetical order these include James Allan, Graeme Auld, Sheila Blair, Michael Burgoyne, Sheila Canby, Carole Hillenbrand, Ulrike al-Khamis, Venetia Porter, Jennifer Scarce, James Tait and Sheilagh Weir. Thanks are due to all of them, and to the editor too for his suggestions.

3. Edward William Lane, *Manners and Customs of the Modern Egyptians* (New York, 1973), 37–8.

4. The metal content was analysed by the Royal Museums of Scotland. It was a surprise to discover that nickel was used, not tin as anticipated. It was equally surprising to discover that the black substance still visible on the spatula was liquid iron oxide (ink) instead of the usual antimony. A brief report by Dr James Tait of the Royal Museums of Scotland forms the appendix to this chapter. I am most grateful to him for his interest and time.

5. E. Wiedemann (J. W. Allan), 'Al-Kuhl', *Enclycopaedia of Islam*, 2nd edn (henceforth *EI* 2), 5:365–7.

6. See Géza Fehérvári, *Islamic Metalwork of the Eighth to the Fifteenth Century in the Keir Collection* (London, 1976), no. 18.

7. For a brief description of sand-casting in Palestine, see Jehan Rajab, *Palestinian Costume* (London and New York, 1989), 133. For a fuller

description of the technique, see Herbert Maryon, *Metalwork and Enamelling* (New York, 1971), 216–18. I am grateful to Dr Michael Burgoyne of Historic Scotland for his confirmation of the method of casting.

8. It is likely that these pierced details have additional connotations. The number twelve is associated with the calendar year. On the crescent, see Richard Ettinghausen, '*Hilal* Part ii', *EI* 2, 3:381–5. Crescents feature in talismanic jewellery, sometimes in association with birds. See *Ya kafi, Ya shafi, The Tawfik Canaan Collection of Palestinian Amulets* (Birzeit, 1999), nos 77. 89, 90, 104, 119 and 125, and Shelagh Weir, *Palestinian Costume* (London, 1989), 194–5, for example.

9. See Weir, *Palestinian Costume*, 115; and Grace M. Crowfoot and Phyllis M. Sutton, 'Ramallah Embroidery', *Embroidery* (March 1935), pl. XI, nos 11 and 20. Leila El Khalidi, *The Art of Palestinian Embroidery* (London, 1999), 92, calls this pattern 'acanthus' (*sabāla*).

10. Blue peacock, *Pavo cristatus*, belonging to the same Phasianidae family as the pheasant (*Phasianus colchicus*). Both were 'originally jungle birds from India, from which they must have been imported to Persia, since [they] were probably introduced from Persia to Athens by Pyrilampes, a friend of Perikles', according to Nan Dunbar, *Aristophanes Birds* (Oxford, 1995), 165, no. 102. It appears that while serving as an envoy to Persia, Pyrilampes was given the peacocks, which he was later accused of using as a bribe. In Aristophanes's time, the peacock was so rare in Greece that people travelled from Sparta and Thessaly to Athens to see the birds exhibited by Pyrilampes's son on the first day of each month. In Greek, the bird is called *taos*. Dunbar adds that this name, 'of unknown derivation, must, like the bird itself, have come from the east'. Arabic was a little uncertain where to put this root of Greek origin, hence the two spellings *ṭā'ūs*, under *ṭā', hamza, sīn* and *ṭāwūs*, under *ṭā', wāw, sīn*. I am indebted to Carole Hillenbrand for her grammatical expertise here. See too F. Viré and Eva Baer, 'Ṭāwūs', *EI* 2, 10:396–7.

11. Collection Antoine Touma and Linden-Museum, Stuttgart: Johannes Kalter, Margareta Pavaloi and Maria Zerrnickel, *The Arts and Crafts of Syria* (London and New York, 1992), 234, fig. 591 left. The displayed tail feathers indicate that it is probably a peacock.

12. Abbas Denshvari, *Medieval Tomb Towers of Iran: An Iconographical Study*, Islamic Art and Architecture, 2 (Lexington, KY, 1986), 46–62.

13. 'See the peacock with wings of fire in the azure heavens, from whose fanning the world has turned into a golden ornament': ibid, quoting Khaqani, *Divan*, ed. A. ʿAbd al-Rasuli (Tehran, 1978), 188.

14. Fay Arrieh Frick, 'Possible Sources for some Motifs of Decoration on Islamic Ceramics', *Muqarnas* 10 (1993), 231–40.

15. See, for example, Arthur Upham Pope and Phyllis Ackerman, *A Survey of Persian Art* (reprinted Ashiya, 1981) vol. XIII, pls. 1283B, 1209 B and D. There are too many similar examples to list here. The association of birds with incense or light is to be expected in view of the link with the heavens from which light radiates and to which incense rises.

16. Jennifer Scarce, who has a particular interest in all things to do with dress and cosmetics, suggested to me that the kohl-pot might be from the Gulf. The close association between Iran and the Gulf states does not need to be underlined and such a provenance would be consistent with the object being sold in Jerusalem by a pilgrim either on the way to or from Mecca.

17. See, for example, a 'Kubachi' ware dish of the sixteenth century in Copenhagen, Kjeld von Folsach, *Isamic Art: The David Collection* (Copenhagen, 1990), 119, no. 166.

18. For example, see *Tahkt-i tā'ūs* made for Fath ʿAli Shah in c. 1215/1800, in the Gulistan Palace, Tehran: Pope and Ackerman, *Survey*, vol. VIb, 2657–8; XIII, 1479.

19. Viré and Baer, 'Ṭāwūs.'

20. Edward William Lane, ed. Stanley Lane-Poole, *Arabic–English Lexicon* (London, 1874), Book 1, pt 5, 1899.

21. Hans Wehr, *Dictionary of Modern Arabic*, ed. J. Milton Cowan (Wiesbaden, 1961).

22. Both Carole Hillenbrand and Sheila Blair, whose joint expertise in deciphering inscriptions is beyond question, have reassured me that this is so.

23. 'Témoignage d'estime,' Reinhart Dozy, *Supplément aux dictionnaires arabes* (Leyden and Paris, 1927), 2:468; Venetia Porter was the first to make this suggestion. Dr Porter, in a communication dated 13 November 2001, wrote that the kohl-pot 'reminds me of ones I used to see in Syria, especially with the pierced tail'. Unfortunately she has no further details.

24. There are many such objects. A seventeenth-century bowl (*jām*) in the Victoria and Albert Museum, for example, (inv. no. M.718–1910) has an inscription which begins 'He that holds the bowl in his hands / For ever hold Jam's Kingdom . . .' while a torch-stand (*mashʿal*) has a *ghazal* by Fahmī Kāshānī which begins 'O Candle like the butterfly in awe of You I die / About Your Head I turn' (Assadullah Souren Melikian-Chirvani, *Islamic Metalwork from the Iranian World 8th–18th Centuries* (London, 1982), 327, 343; nos. 148 and 159).

25. John Penrice, *A Dictionary and Glossary of the Koran* (Old Woking, repr. 1971), 93.

26. This belief, stemming from the legend that it was the peacock which introduced Satan in Paradise, is discussed below. See Viré and Baer, 'Ṭāwūs,' 396.

27. E Atıl, *Ceramics from the World of Islam* (Washington, DC, 1973), 27, no. 7, inv. no. 54.16. Other examples are published in *Treasures of Islam*, ed. T. Falk (Geneva, 1985), 211–12, nos 199–200. See too, among other examples, a bowl on loan to the Brooklyn Museum (no. L.63.9.23) published as no. 262 in *The Arts of Islam* (London, 1976), 217, and others in the Freer Gallery of Art, Washington (Atıl, *Ceramics*, 23, no. 5, inv. no. 66.27) and the Victoria and Albert Museum, London (published in *Islamic Pottery, 800–1400* (London, 1969), no. 40). Both of these last examples show peacocks carrying a fish in their beaks. The Metropolitan Museum, New York, has a lustre-painted bowl with confronted peacocks, facing each other across a palmette; Fletcher Fund, inv. no. 64.134, illustrated in Ernst J. Grube, 'The Art of Islamic Pottery', *Metropolitan Museum of Art Bulletin* (February 1965), 209–28, pls 3–4.

28. Oliver Watson, 'Ceramics,' in *Treasures*, ed. Falk, 211, no. 199. Blessings also appear on textiles in the form of prayers. I am grateful to Sheila Blair for drawing my attention to this in her article 'A Note on the Prayers Inscribed on several Medieval Silk Textiles in the Abegg Foundation', *Islamische Textilkunst des Mittelalters: Aktuelle Probleme* (Riggisberg, 1997), 129–37.

29. Illustrated in colour in Martin Harrison, *A Temple for Byzantium* (London, 1989), pl. 166.

30. See too a Sassanian textile fragment (with what may be a peacock) in the Textile Museum, Washington, DC, inv. no. 73.724 published by Prudence O. Harper, *The Royal Hunter* (New York, 1978), 137, no. 61. Abbas Daneshvari, *Medieval Tomb Towers in Iran: An Iconographical Study* (Lexington, KY, 1986), 46, n. 104, lists other examples of textiles and ceramics with peacocks. These include examples of Sassanian and Buyid silks, and ʿAbbasid, Samanid, Ayyubid and Saljuq wares.

31. Falk, *Treasures*, 211.

32. Birds were customarily shown in profile; see, for example, Harper, *The Royal Hunter*, 62, no. 19; 63, no. 20; 64–5, nos. 21 and 77, no. 26 for silver objects decorated with birds, or 117, no. 49 for a stucco fragment of a quail. For later examples, see Viré and Baer, 'Ṭāwūs', figs. 1, 2 and 5.

33. Published by Ulrike al-Khamis, 'An Early Islamic Bronze Ewer Re-examined', *Muqarnas* 15 (1998), 9–19, where the role of the bird as a symbol of paradise or resurrection is briefly discussed on 12–13.

34. See Melikian-Chirvani, *Islamic Metalwork*, 192–3, pl. 87a. It is worth noting that the change in angle at each facet is marked by a vertical stem with a paired-leaves or feather motif. There can be confusion about the identification of a peacock because the mythical senmurv was sometimes shown with a peacock-like tail. However, to my knowledge a peacock was always shown with a 'crown', while the senmurv was not.

35. Elliot 246 fol. 25b, copied by Naʿīm al-Dīn al-Shīrazī, published as plate 81 in B. W. Robinson, *Persian Drawings from the 14th through the 19th Century* (Boston and Toronto, 1965), 109.

36. Viré and Baer, 'Ṭāwūs,' fig. 3, showing a detail from a frontispiece of Farid al-Din ʿAttar's *Mantiq al-tayr* painted about 1600, currently in the Metropolitan Museum of Art, New York.

37. Mughal, painted in Faizabad, India, in c. 1765; The David Collection, Copenhagen, no. 46/1980, illustrated in Folsach, *Islamic Art*, 66, no. 52.

38. Musée du Louvre, Paris, inv. no. MR1569, published in Barbara Brend, *Islamic Art* (London, 1991), pls 42, 67.

39. Hermitage Museum, St Petersburg, inv. no. NP-1567, illustrated in Rachel Ward, *Islamic Metalwork* (London, 1993), 46, pl. 31; Jonathan Bloom and Sheila Blair, *Islamic Arts* (London, 1997), 122, fig. 67; and recently published in *Earthly Beauty, Heavenly Art: Art of Islam*, ed. Mikhail B. Piotrovsky and John Vrieze (Amsterdam, 1999), 226, no. 199.

40. An ivory, probably from Madinat al-Zahra, dated 353/964, National Archaeological Museum, Madrid, illustrated in Brend, *Islamic Art*, 58, pl. 33.

41. Mark Zebrowski, *Gold, Silver and Bronze from Mughal India* (London, 1997), 94–101.

42. British Museum, inv. no. OA 1912.7–16.1 (89cm in height), illustrated in Ward, *Islamic Metalwork*, 121, pl. 96.

43. Nizami, *Sharaf-name*, ed. V. Dastgardi (Tehran, 1936), 256, quoted by Daneshvari, *Medieval Tomb Towers*, 51.

44. For examples, see Daneshvari, *Medieval Tomb Towers*, 52.

45. The translation is taken from Farid ud-Din Attar, *The Conference of the Birds*, tr. Afkham Darbandi and Dick Davis (Harmondsworth, 1984), 30–1, lines 649–52.

46. Ibid., 39, lines 825–8.

47. Ibid., 39, lines 828–9.

48. Ibid., 39, lines 830–1.

49. Ibid., 39–40, lines 832–3.

50. Ibid., 40, lines 849–52.

51. From the translation by Reynold A. Nicholson, *Rūmī Poet and Mystic (1207–1275)* (London, 1950), 70, 72.

52. Annemarie Schimmel, 'The Celestial Garden', in *The Islamic Garden*, ed. Elisabeth B. Macdougall and Richard Ettinghausen (Washington, DC, 1976), 20.

53. J. W. Allan, 'The Nishapur Metalwork', in *Content and Context of Visual Arts in the Islamic World*, ed. Priscilla Soucek (University Park, PA and London, 1988), 1–7.

54. See Fehérvári, *Islamic Metalwork*, no. 107, pl. 36a.

55. Pope and Ackerman, *Survey*, vol. XIII, pl. 1312B, where it is described as a twelfth or thirteenth-century 'ampula'. The form seems to be that of a pigeon.

56. There are many examples; see for instance Fehérvári, *Islamic Metalwork*, 107–22, nos 27–49. For an overview, see Eva Baer, *Metalwork in Medieval Islamic Art* (Albany, NY, 1983), esp. ch. 2, pls 20, 41–2.

57. Fogg Art Museum, Harvard University, inv. no. T.L.16838.1, Baer, *Metalwork*, pl. 47. She cites a further example in the Metropolitan Museum of Art, no. 24.47.6.

58. Unnumbered; see Melikian-Chirvani, *Islamic Metalwork*, 122, no. 50, where the object is described as from 'Khorasan, second half of twelfth century'.

59. For comparable images, see Willy Hartner, 'The Vaso Vescovali in the British Museum', *Kunst des Orients* 9 (1973–4), 99–130, and D. S. Rice, *The Wade Cup in the Cleveland Museum of Art* (Paris, 1955). In point of fact, the lid and body of the 'Vaso Vescovali' are not originally from the same object; for good colour reproductions, see Ward, *Islamic Metalwork*, pls 57, 73. For a discussion on a detailed astrological interpretation, see Sylvia Auld, 'Characters Out of Context: The Case of a Bowl in the V. & A.', in *Shahnama: The Visual Language of the Persian Book of Kings*, ed. Robert Hillenbrand (Aldershot 2004), 99–116; and (unpublished conference paper given at Edinburgh in 1995) 'Arabesques and Talking Heads: Another Look at the *Waq-Waq*'.

60. Daneshvari, *Medieval Tomb Towers*, 56–8.

61. See Engelbert Kirschbaum et al., *Lexikon der Christlichen Ikonographie* (Rome, 1971), 3:410–11; and *The Oxford Dictionary of Byzantium* (Oxford, 1991), 3:1611–12.

62. Daneshvari, *Medieval Tomb Towers*, 53–4, where al-Jahiz, Jalal al-Din Rumi, Shams Tabasi, Muffaddal ibn Saʿd al-Mafarrukhi, Abu'l-Nasr al-ʿUtbi and al-Rawandi *inter alia* are quoted in support of his thesis.

63. James Hall, *Dictionary of Subjects and Symbols in Art* (London, revised edn, 1974), 238. See too George Ferguson, *Signs and Symbols in Christian Art* (London, Oxford and New York, 1961), 23. The examples are too many to cite, but see Carlo Crivelli, *The Annunciation*, National Gallery, London, where a peacock sits above the Virgin, or Fra Angelico/Fra Filippo Lippi, *Adoration of the Magi*, National Gallery of Art, Washington, DC (Kress Collection), where a peacock sits on the roof of the stable. A pair of peacocks confronting the Tree or Fountain of Life, or the Chalice of the Eucharist, were known in the early church; see, for example, Heather Child and Dorothy College, *Christian Symbols* (London, 1971), fig. 2 and, singly, fig. 92.

64. A pair of peacocks in the round with outspread tails, each straddled by the figure of the young Dionysos, were excavated at Serapaion at Memphis in Egypt. Jean-Philippe Lauer and Charles Picard, *Les statues ptolemaîques du Serapeion de Memphis* (Paris, 1955), 194–209.

65. Martin Harrison, *A Temple for Byzantium* (Austin, Texas, 1989).
66. Ibid., 121–2.
67. Ibid., 34.
68. *The Eerdmans Bible Dictionary*, ed. Allen C. Myers (Grand Rapids, MI, 1987), 807–8. I am indebted to Graeme Auld for this reference and the supporting literature.
69. Umayyad period at Khirbat al-Mafjar, Mashatta and Qusayr Amra in the Jordan Valley; they also appear in Umayyad metalwork. The so-called Marwan ewer is but one example with a spout in the form of a cockerel. In addition to the raptor ewer signed by Sulayman and discussed below, an acquamanile in bird-form of roughly similar date is held at St Catharine's Monastery, Sinai.
70. Quails, for example, feature in Coptic textiles. See a linen and wool fragment dating to fourth–fifth-century Egypt with a quail, in the Benaki Museum, no. 222 (cover, catalogue entitled *Coptic Textiles* (Athens, 1971)).
71. See Harper, *Royal Hunter*.
72. For the appearance of quails (or guinea fowl) on Sassanian silver objects, see Harper, *Royal Hunter*, 63, no. 20: silver-gilt roundels in the Römisch Germanisches Zentralmuseum, Mainz, each with a bird in profile.
73. See Robert H. Hamilton, *Walid and his Friends: An Umayyad Tragedy*, Oxford Studies in Islamic Art 6 (Oxford, 1988).
74. *Eerdmans Bible Dictionary*, ed. Myers, 865.
75. For example, the Vaso Vascovali, London, British Museum, 1950.7.25.1, ill. in Baer, *Metalwork*, 180, fig. 154.
76. In classical Greece and Rome, the flight and entrails of birds were read in an attempt to ensure an auspicious outcome; Cicero's *de divinatione* II, tr. William A. Falconer (Cambridge, MA, 1959), I, ii, 225; x, 241; xv, 253–7, for example. A panel over the east portal of the palace of Sitt Tunshuq in Jerusalem (Michael H. Burgoyne, *Mamluk Jerusalem* (London, 1987), 485–504, pl. 48.1–2) terminates in bird-finials. A ninth-century Tulunid section of sycamore frieze in the Museum of Islamic Art, Cairo, no. 6280, illustrated in *Arts of Islam*, 282–3, may also have originated from a similar position.
77. The Tiflis ewer dated 1180–1200, for example, which has addorsed raptors around the top of the body, or two similar examples in the British Museum and others in the Metropolitan Museum of Art and the State Hermitage Museum, St Petersburg; for illustrations, Pope and Ackerman, *Survey*, vol. XIII, pls 1322–3, 1325–6.
78. See Paul Kunitzsch, *Untersuchungen zur Sternnomenklatur der Araber* (Wiesbaden, 1961).
79. On the lid of a cylindrical brass box made for Badr al-Din Lu'lu in 631–59/1233–59, London, British Museum, inv.78.12–30; see Baer, *Metalwork*, 76, fig. 56, 173, fig. 147 and 174, fig. 148 (British Museum, inv. no. 1884).
80. Frieze on a Persian-Mongol bowl, New York Metropolitan Museum of Art 91.1.581 (Baer, *Metalwork*, 190, fig. 164).
81. Incense-burner in the form of a duck, Khurasan or Afghanistan, twelfth century, New York, Metropolitan Museum of Art, inv. no. 1972.87 (Baer, *Metalwork*, 59, fig. 42).
82. For example on a candlestick, perhaps from Mesopotamia, thirteenth century, Cairo Museum of Islamic Art, inv. no. 15.121 (Baer, *Metalwork*, 168, fig. 142).

83. State Hermitage Museum, St Petersburg, no. IR-2268, made in Herat.

84. British Museum inv. no. OA 1891.6-23.5.

85. Which names not only the craftsman, owner and patron, but also the date: 'Ordered by 'Abd al-Waḥīd, worked by *ḥājib* Mas'ūd ibn Aḥmad *the decorator of Herat, for its owner the brilliant khwāja* Rukn al-Dīn, pride of the merchants, the most trustworthy of the faithful, grace of the pilgrimage and the two shrines, Rashīd al-Dīn 'Azīzī ibn Abu'l-Ḥusain al-Zanjānī, may his glory last – Muḥarram 539/December 1163.'

86. Washington, Freer Gallery of Art, acc. no. 36.7, see Eva Baer, *Islamic Ornament* (Edinburgh, 1988), fig. 84.

87. Cleveland Museum of Art, published by Rice, *Wade Cup*; and Baer, *Islamic Ornament*, fig. 85; and see other examples in Baer, *Islamic Ornament*, figs 86 and 87.

88. In Korean, Chinese and Japanese iconography, cranes denote good luck.

89. Shiraz c. 1435, Ouseley Add. 176, f. 3a, Bodleian Library, Oxford. For a coloured illustration, see Basil Gray, *Persian Painting* (London and Basingstoke, 1977), 100.

90. Tiles in the British Museum, almost certainly from Takht-i Sulaiman, show alternating dragons and *sīmurgh*s. Images of the *sīmurgh*, a magical bird that is born again from fire, became particularly popular under the Timurids, see a *Shahnama* fragment from Tabriz, c. 1370, Hazine 2153, f. 231, Topkapi Saray Library, Istanbul. See too Thomas W. Lentz and Glenn D. Lowry, *Timur and the Princely Vision: Persian Art and Culture in the Fifteenth Century* (Washington, DC, 1989), 192–5, cat. nos 91, 93, 95–6.

91. Winged cherubim, for example, were introduced into Israelite cosmology from neighbouring ancient Near Eastern mythologies. Their appearance in reliefs and statues occur in Aleppo, Carchemish, Byblos and Taanach; ivories from Nimrud also depict winged creatures with human features reminiscent of the sphinx. See *Eerdmans Bible Dictionary*, ed. Myers, 204.

92. In the Roman period, for example, the apotheosis of an emperor took the form of a winged being. See apotheosis and decursio on the base of the column of Antoninus Pius, c. 161, Vatican Museum, or apotheosis of the Hadrianic Sabina in the Palazzo dei Conservatori, Rome.

93. See Annemarie Schimmel, *Deciphering the Signs of God* (Edinburgh, 1994), *passim* but particularly 184–5.

94. Wehr, *Dictionary*, ed. Cowan, 986.

95. On the bird-soul in general, see Schimmel, *Deciphering the Signs of God*, 26–8.

96. (Tr.) Afkham Darvandi and Dick Davis, *The Conference of Birds* (Harmondsworth, 1984), 32 lines 689–92. On the role of the hoopoe as a mystic messenger, see Belinda Hunt, 'An Exploration of the Hoopoe (*Upupa epops*) as a mystic symbol'. Unpublished MA thesis (London, June 2001).

Appendix

National Museums of Scotland
Conservation and Analytical Research
Analytical Research Section Report AR 02/04
XRF analysis of a metal kohl-pot (C&AR No. 10688) dated 22.1.02

Introduction
A small white-metal pot in the shape of a bird was submitted by Dr Sylvia Auld for analysis to determine the composition of the alloy. The presence of a spatula with remnant black material suggests the artefact was a kohl-pot. The black material was also analysed to determine whether its composition was consistent with kohl.

Method
X-ray fluorescence
The artefact was analysed using non-destructive energy dispersive X-ray fluorescence (XRF). No surface preparation was possible and as this is a surface technique the analyses may not be representative of the interior metal if surface alteration has occurred (e.g., during deposition, burial, daily use or wear). As the XRF system used is an air-path system, only elements above potassium can be detected. Further details of the method are given below.

Results and Discussion
The pot was analysed by XRF in four separate areas. All gave the same basic compositional information:

FI25000B on the left-hand wing of the bird shows that the basic metal is the copper-zinc alloy brass (Cu and Zn) with small amounts of tin (Sn) and lead (Pb), the latter probably to help in casting. The analysis shows that the silvery plating on the surface is a layer of nickel (Ni). FI25001B on the other wing is similar, as are FI25002B and FI25003B on other areas, showing slightly less nickel where the plating is worn. The inside of the base (FI2502) shows slightly more zinc and less tin, presumably because this surface remains more as cast and probably did not have a smooth finish. Manganese (Mn) also appears as a trace here, possibly due to contamination but there was insufficient time to examine this aspect further.

The spatula has black material attached to its surface. FI25004B (fig. 1.9) shows that the spatula is brass like the rest of the pot, but the black material is iron (Fe) rich. Traditionally, kohl is composed of either lead oxide (galena) or antimony. However, some modern kohl is composed of carbonaceous material and carbon would not be detectable by XRF. The analyses hence suggest that either the black material is not kohl or it is an iron-rich, possibly carbonaceous, kohl. X-ray diffraction of a small amount of the black material would be required to determine whether this was a black iron compound (such as the iron oxide magnetite) and whether carbonaceous material was present.

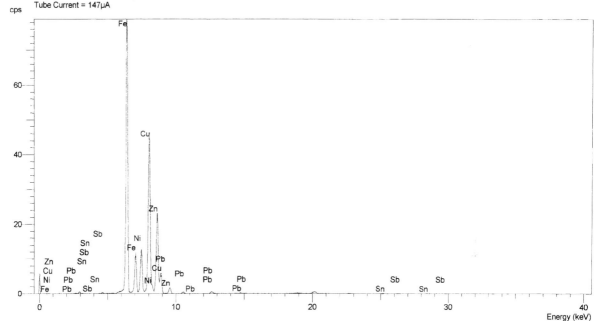

Fig. 1.9 Kohl-pot, XRF spectrum (No. F125004B) of the spatula and black compound, undertaken by the Royal Museums of Scotland, Edinburgh.

The presence of nickel plating indicates that this artefact must post-date the invention of nickel plating in the late nineteenth century. It is possible, but seems very unlikely, that the nickel plating could have been applied later to a brass body made earlier.

The analyses are qualitative from unprepared surfaces and cannot be used to derive the alloy composition accurately. Abrasion of the surface to remove the plating and analysis of interior metal would be required to obtain an accurate quantified composition for the brass. Comparison with analyses of similar material of known provenance and date would be required to obtain more definite information on the provenance and date of this pot.

Conclusions

The artefact is composed of nickel plated brass (the copper-zinc alloy). The presence of nickel plating indicates an origin no earlier than the introduction of nickel plating in the late 19th century. The black material on the spatula was an iron compound. Traditionally kohl was either galena (lead oxide) or antimony. Hence the black material is either not kohl or is an iron-rich, possibly carbonaceous, form of kohl.

Note on X-ray Fluorescence Method

The analysed area was irradiated with a primary X-ray beam produced by a Rhodium target X-ray tube. The primary beam was collimated to give an area of about 4mm x 2mm. Secondary X-rays were detected with a silicon (lithium) solid state detector. The detection limit varies depending on the elements, matrix and analytical conditions, but is typically in the range of 0.05%–0.2%. The XRF system used was an Oxford Instruments ED 2000 with Oxford Instruments software ED 2000SW version 1.31.

Spectra were collected under the fixed conditions 'Old XRF' which uses a voltage of 46kV with no filters to ensure detection of a wide range of elements. As the analytical technique used has a limited penetration depth, the reported compositions may not be representative of the bulk of the alloy if there is a chemically distinct surface layer.

CHAPTER TWO

Remarks on the Iconography of the Medieval Capitals of Cairo: Form and Emplacement

Marianne Barrucand

The 'head' or 'crown' of the column or pillar (*ra's* or *tāj al-rukn*), the capital is an architectural element that attracts the sight and holds the attention of the viewer. The works of Christian Ewert and Patrice Cressier have proved that their form in the hypostyle halls of the Umayyad Mosque at Cordoba and the mosque of Sidi Uqba at Qayrawan was significant.[1] There the emplacement of certain specific types of reused capitals was due not to chance but to give a hierarchy to space; they therefore possess, aside from their formal qualities, an ideological value, that is an iconographic message for the community of the faithful. How does the question of forms and their signification relate to the medieval capitals of Egypt? Even today one is still dazzled by the splendour of outstanding Proconesian marble capitals in the courtyard of the mosque of al-Azhar, and it is difficult to imagine that Muslims of the Fatimid days were not similarly impressed. They would probably also have noticed, as we can, that most of the capitals are of Christian origin. The wealth of the Fatimid caliphs at first sight excludes the explanation of economising, since if necessary they could have borne the cost of making new ones. Did the Muslim patrons prefer to salvage these spectacular remnants of an overturned past to signify the dominion of their faith and their power? Are capitals of a specific type found in certain places rather than others? If so, what message do they carry? Did the employment of reused capitals suppress or on the contrary stimulate the creation of new types? Can one see an evolution of the forms of capitals and their signification between the first Friday mosques in Egypt and those at the apogee of Mamluk architecture in the fourteenth century?

The works written up to now on medieval capitals in Egypt have been essentially by specialists in early Byzantine art; they have far from exhausted the possibilities on the subject.[2] Here we will first present the different types of reused capitals, then describe the new forms and finally try to establish their emplacements. The fundamental question remains the links between the types of capitals and their place in the building, and the eventual evolution of these links.

Typology

Reused capitals

The most common type in religious architecture in Cairo is the Corinthian capital with two acanthus crowns, most frequently of the 'soft' type, sometimes of the 'spiny' type (sometimes mixing both types), and occasionally of the 'Asia Minor' type.[3] These capitals (Figure 2.1) have four large corner leaves that emerge from the upper crown and are placed beneath the volutes. They do not have enveloping leaves and the helices are usually absent. This is the most common type of reused capital in mosques. But the canonic Corinthian capital, conforming to the Vitruvian model, with its two rows of acanthus, its stalks, calices and enveloping leaves, its volutes and helices, is not entirely absent (Figure 2.2). Other reused types are mainly divided between the smooth-leaved Corinthian capital with one or two crowns (Figure 2.3), the composite capital, the Pergamon capital with its crown of grooves emerging from an acanthus zone (Figure 2.4), and rarely, the Ionic capital. One also finds capitals with protomes (Figure 2.5) and eagles (Figure 2.6) or crosses (Figure 2.7) in place of the abacus flower. A capital with a grotesque is found in the

Fig. 2.1 Corinthian capital with two crowns of eight acanthus leaves each, with a corner leaf under the four volutes. Mosque of al-Salih Tala'i', courtyard arcade.

(Photograph © M. Barrucand.)

Fig. 2.2 Classical
Corinthian capital with
two acanthus crowns, with
volutes, helices, calices and
enveloping leaves. Mosque
of al-Azhar, courtyard
arcade.

(Photograph © M. Barrucand.)

Fig. 2.3 Corinthian capital
with two crowns of smooth
leaves. Mosque of al-Salih
Tala`i´, courtyard arcade.

(Photograph © M. Barrucand.)

Fig. 2.4 *Pergamon capital (with two zones, a row of grooves above an acanthus crown). Mosque of al-Azhar, main prayer hall, west side, first arcade from courtyard.*

(Photograph © M. Barrucand.)

mosque of al-Salih Tala'i (Figure 2.5).[4] But the impost block capital with vine decoration, so characteristic of Coptic architecture, was not among the reused types.

Some of the reused examples are imported Proconesian marble ones that were sculpted at Constantinople; others, imported in large blocks, would have been worked, or at least finished off, by local craftsmen at Alexandria. It is at Alexandria and its region that one finds the closest parallels to the reused Cairene examples.[5]

Ptolemaic capitals are rare; they were esteemed in some Mamluk mosques such at that of al-Maridani (1338–40) but seem to be absent from earlier ones (Figure 2.8).[6] However, sculpted Pharaonic blocks were reused from the Fatimid period onwards, but mostly in less visible locations.[7]

New Capitals

New capitals, that is, those sculpted specifically for a building, probably appear for the first time in the mosque of Ibn Tulun. These

26

Fig. 2.5 *Capital with two zones, with protomes of eagles and a grotesque. Mosque of al-Salih Tala`i`, courtyard arcade.*

(Photograph © M. Barrucand.)

stucco capitals are often considered as descendants of the Corinthian capital,[8] but with their barely noticeable swelling, their absence of volutes, helices and acanthus, and with the appearance of the vine that clings tightly to the bell-body of the capital, they diverge radically from classical categories. Their Samarran origin is obvious and has often been commented on.[9]

Were any newly designed capitals used in Fatimid mosque? It appears to me that one can establish a formal evolution from Constantinopolitan Corinthian capitals imported in the fifth-sixth centuries, through locally made Egyptian pre-Islamic capitals, to certain capitals of the prayer hall at al-Azhar (end of the tenth century) and finally to some capitals of the courtyard of al-Azhar (first half of the eleventh century). These last are made of marble and are large[10] good quality examples that are neither Byzantine nor Coptic (Figure 2.9).

27

Fig. 2.6 *Capital with two crowns of smooth leaves, with an eagle in place of the abacus flower. Mosque of al-Azhar, courtyard arcade.*

(Photograph © M. Barrucand.)

Fig. 2.7 *Classical Corinthian capital with a cross in a crown of laurels in place of the abacus flower. Mosque of al-Azhar, courtyard arcade.*

(Photograph © M. Barrucand.)

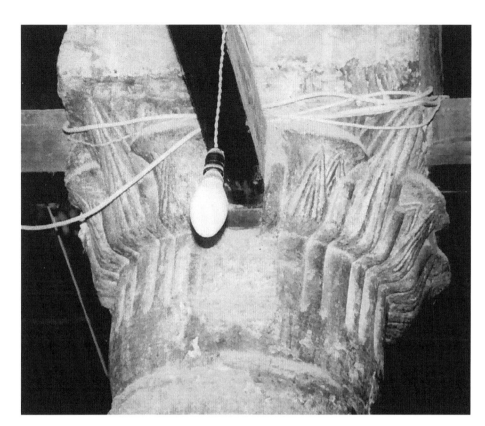

Fig. 2.8 Ptolemaic capital. *Mosque of al-Maridani, prayer hall.*

(Photograph © M. Barrucand.)

Fig. 2.9 Corinthianising capital with four acanthus leaves. Mosque of al-Azhar, arcade, 12th century.

(Photograph © M. Barrucand.)

Their initial model was the Corinthian capital with one or two acanthus crowns, with a corner leaf placed beneath each of the four volutes (Figure 2.1). These capitals have one or two complete crowns, and even though there are irregularities, each crown has about eight leaves. From this type of Corinthian capital arose two 'Corinthianising' types, which are seen already among the capitals of St Menas and those of the great mosque of Qayrawan.[11] They are first the capital with two crowns of four leaves each and, second, the capital with four corner leaves which cover the whole of the body. The two crowns of the first type can be further divided into three groups:

1. The eight leaves are on two distinct levels; the four corner leaves at the upper level emerge from the interstices of the lower leaves which are oriented in the middle of the faces (Figure 2.10 left-hand capital).
2. The leaves, overlapping and uniform, constitute a form of thick sheath from which the four corner volutes emerge (Figure 2.11).
3. The ensemble of eight leaves is set back from the base of the capital; the four lower central leaves are small enough to permit the upper corner leaves to emerge between them from the lower level. This group has two variants: one in which the central lower leaves are truly lower (Figure 2.12), another in which they are extended to the same height as the corner leaves (Figure 2.13).

Fig. 2.10 Two Corinthianising capitals; on the left with eight acanthus leaves on two crowns; on the right with four acanthus leaves. Mosque of al-Azhar, prayer hall on west side.

(Photograph © M. Barrucand.)

Fig. 2.11 *Corinthianising capital; the eight acanthus leaves are joined in a sheath. Mosque of al-Azhar, main prayer hall, east side, second arcade from courtyard.*

(Photograph © M. Barrucand.)

Fig. 2.12 *Corinthianising capital with eight acanthus leaves forming two crowns. Mosque of al-Azhar, main prayer hall, east side, second arcade from courtyard.*

(Photograph © M. Barrucand.)

Fig. 2.13 Two
Corinthianising capitals
with eight acanthus leaves
around a crown. Mosque of
al-Azhar, prayer hall on
west side.

(Photograph © M. Barrucand.)

For all of these series of two rows of four leaves the central leaves are placed before the corner leaves, overlapping them slightly. In almost all of these capitals, the upper lobes of the corner leaves are substituted for volutes.

The latter trait is also characteristic of the four-leafed capital which appeared in medieval times, particularly in Tunisia, but also in Egypt (Figure 2.10 right-hand capital, Figure 2.9). The four leaves, which spread out over the body, may be adjoined in a naturalistic manner, but more often their meeting engenders abstract geometric forms. This type was found quite frequently in churches and was often reused in hypostyle Fatimid mosques. But it is also found, in more carefully finished examples, among the large capitals of the arcades of al-Hafiz from the beginning of the twelfth century, where the simplified form, close to that of an impost block, the flat modelling, the transformation of the lobes and shoots of the acanthus into scallops and comma and eyelet forms, and the flattening of the central stems, all differentiate them from earlier work and suggest they were a contemporary design for this monument. On these capitals the leaves are treated as independent units and meet only in an abstract manner, or sometimes by means of a horizontal moulding or a projecting angular one. This type of capital continued to evolve in Mamluk architecture; it is still found in the complex of al-Ghawri.

The reused smooth-leaf capital itself engenders a medieval type, notably in the mosque of Sultan Hasan, where the mihrab is flanked by two pairs of gilded examples (Figure 2.14).

Muqarnas capitals seem to appear in Egypt in the Mamluk period. In the mosque of Sultan Hasan (1357–61) they occupy a prime spot (Figure 2.15). Present in Syria in the Ayyubid period, for example in the courtyard of the Firdaus madrasa (1235–6) at Aleppo,[12] and used from the fourteenth century on even in Nasrid architecture, muqarnas capitals become commonplace in Mamluk architecture after the mosque of Sultan Hasan.

The bulbous capital (or 'bell-capital') on the other hand, is an older Cairene type; in a very simple rounded form, usually smooth, it was often used as a base. Common in the Arab and Iranian worlds, it flanks Fatimid mihrabs, from those of Friday mosques[13] to those of the little wooden portable mihrabs,[14] ranging from those of al-Mustansir at the mosque of Ibn Tulun (Figure 2.16) to the wooden mihrab of al-Amir, originally in the mosque of al-Azhar (Figure 2.17), to the triple stucco mihrab of the shrine of Ikhwat Yusuf.[15] The mihrab of the mausoleum of al-Salih Najm al-Din Ayyub also has this type of capital, here finely carved with an allover pattern.[16] The type continued in the Mamluk period often in mihrabs (Figure 2.18)[17] and

Fig. 2.14 Two capitals with three crowns of smooth leaves, derived from composite capitals. Mosque of Sultan Hasan, mihrab of the prayer hall.

(Photograph © M. Barrucand.)

33

Fig. 2.15 Muqarnas capital.
Mosque of Sultan Hasan,
corner of mausoleum.

(Photograph © M. Barrucand.)

especially on *dikka*s (Figure 2.19). It was also used for the tribunes in some Coptic churches in Cairo.

This overview of new and reused capitals leads to several conclusions: the reused capitals are distinguished by their classical rather than by their Coptic traits. The Coptic communities around Alexandria and Cairo, and those further south, also used these classical capitals, but more selectively. It was these Corinthian capitals which furnished the greatest number of *spolia*, acanthus leaves being their only vegetation. Capitals taken from Pharaonic monuments remained exceptional and only appeared in later periods.

The Corinthian capital without stalks, calices and enveloping leaves, often without interior helices, but with four corner leaves supporting volutes, gave rise to the creation of a new derivative, the Corinthianising capital with either eight leaves on two levels or with only four corner leaves at one single level, and this development was probably already before the Islamic conquest. These two types also

Fig. 2.16 (opposite) *Mihrab of al-Mustansir. Mosque of Ibn Tulun.*

(Photograph © M. Barrucand.)

34

Fig. 2.17 *Mihrab of al-Amir, made for the mosque of al-Azhar. Museum of Islamic Art, Cairo.*

(Photograph © Museum of Islamic Art, Cairo.)

Fig. 2.18 *Bulbous capital. Mihrab of the mosque of al-Ashraf Barsbay at Khanqah.*

(Photograph © M. Barrucand.)

appeared in other regions, at the same time, notably in Tunisia,[18] and proved to be long lived.

The bulbous capital, quite different from the classical or classicising types, survived long in Cairo. Its basic simplicity did not lend itself to enormous variations, although these could be expressed in rounded or angular volumes, through differing proportions of the globular bass and the splayed upper part, and through the presence or absence of relief decoration.

Placing

The placing of these capitals are not due to chance: in the Fatimid period the smaller reused capitals, of mediocre execution, are

37

Fig. 2.19 Dikka. *Mosque of Sultan Hasan.*

(Photograph © M. Barrucand.)

common at the sides of the main prayer halls and in the hypostyle areas to the sides of the courtyard of the mosque of al-Azhar. Reused capitals are more numerous, but there are some carefully carved contemporary Corinthianising ones, which were specifically made for their location. The central nave and the courtyard arcades have capitals that are both larger and more carefully executed. But even if the principal axis of the mosque, from the entrance to the mihrab, is accentuated by the domed bay at the entrance to the prayer hall and the groups of triple columns on each side of the central bay on the wider sides of the courtyard, this axis is not further underlined by symmetry of the capitals beyond it. Evidently the architect wanted to emphasise this axis, thus creating a hierarchy of spaces. But even if it seems that the column, understood as an ensemble including base, shaft and capital, was seen as useful in organising space, this did not extend to the symmetrical placing of capitals.

The use of paired capitals apparently corresponds to the demands of symmetry at close quarters or to the availability of certain groups of capitals at the moment of their installation, but not to a deliberate choice of similar elements to give a visual emphasis to key locations.

All of the capitals of the courtyard arcades of al-Hafiz, whether

Corinthian or Corinthianising, are of particularly fine work. The remains of red paint on several of these capitals makes it possible that they were gilded. The bulbous capitals of the mihrabs, in contrast, are more modest. They are based on Samarran models, and ultimately on their Sassanian prototypes, as opposed to the classical acanthus of the courtyard and prayer hall which evoke a classical Mediterranean world. This latter, even if prestigious, was apparently thought unsuitable for the ornamentation of the most sacred spot of the building, the more oriental type seeming more appropriate for the mihrab, unlike the great mosque of Qayrawan and the Ibn Tulun mosque with their rich Byzantine capitals flanking the sacred niche. The preference given to classical rather than Coptic or Pharaonic echoes in Fatimid buildings designed to receive the community of the faithful at Friday prayer brings an association on the one hand with ideas of beauty, brilliance and riches and on the other with the pre-Islamic classical Mediterranean heritage. Was this association designed to evoke a native Egyptian continuity of art and architecture, somehow perennial, one above politics and religion? Why then avoid Pharaonic references? It is more likely the symbol of a new power that had annexed and recycled the works of the previous power, conquered but still considered particularly prestigious.

For the Ayyubid period few hypostyle monuments have been preserved in Cairo; more detailed research must be undertaken to evaluate the taste of patrons and their master masons. The Mamluk period remains largely faithful to the interpretation of the form of the capitals: Corinthian spolia and Corinthianising capitals adorn the arcades of the courtyards and the naves, with bulbous capitals being reserved for mihrabs.

The complex of Sultan Hasan (1357–61), comprising a Friday mosque, four madrasas and a mausoleum, was a prestigious edifice which produced several innovations in the form and usage of capitals. The newest type, muqarnas ones, set off spectacularly the façade of the mausoleum and the main portal, as well as the entrance to the minbar (Figure 2.20). Corinthian and Corinthianising columns are used mainly in secondary locations such as the windows of the mausoleum and the arcades of the entrance corridor (Figure 2.21). Capitals with smooth leaves, a faint echo of their classical prototype, flank the mihrab of the prayer hall (Figure 2.14). Their derivation from a pagan model borrowed from antiquity seems to have been forgotten or to have become acceptable for the most sacred location. The mihrab of the mausoleum nevertheless has two pairs of capitals, one of Pergamon type, the other bulbous but with bevelled edges (Figure 2.22). The *dikka* has more conventional bulbous capitals (Figure 2.19).

In the time of Sultan Hasan, the forms of the capitals are more varied than in the previous examples, with the sculpture work- shops no longer limiting themselves to repetition of the same type.

39

Fig. 2.20 (opposite) *Minbar. Mausoleum of Sultan Hasan.*

(Photograph © M. Barrucand.)

Fig. 2.21 *Two Corinthian capitals with two crowns of acanthus leaves, with a corner leaf under each volute, one Corinthianising capital with four corner leaves. Mosque of Sultan Hasan, window of mausoleum.*

(Photograph © M. Barrucand.)

Fig. 2.22 *Polygonal bulbous capital and Pergamon capital. Mihrab of the mausoleum of Sultan Hasan.*

(Photograph © M. Barrucand.)

There are innumerable formal and decorative innovations. The desire for new and spectacular effects seems to have replaced the traditional association of the sacred place, the mihrab and the modest bulbous capital. The most dazzling effect is expressed in the most up-to-date capital type, the muqarnas, used for the most conspicuous areas.

Notes

1. Christian Ewert, *Forschungen zur almohadischen Moschee. I: Vorstufen,* Madrider Beiträge 9 (Mainz, 1981); Patrice Cressier, 'Les chapiteaux de la Grande Mosquée de Cordoue (oratoires de ʿAbd al-Rahmân I et ʿAbd al-Rahmân II) et la sculpture de chapiteaux à l'époque émirale', *Madrider Mitteilungen* 25 (1984), 257–313, pls 36–72; *Madrider Mitteilungen* 26 (1985), 216–81, pls. 72–82. Ewert suggests that the placement of the capitals and columns of the Great Mosque of Qayrawan evokes the plans of the Dome of the Rock and the mosque of al-Aqsa.
2. R. Kautzsch, *Kapitellstudien* (Berlin, 1936); H. G. Niemeyer, 'Wiederverwendete spätantike Kapitelle in der Ulmâs-Moschee zu Kairo,' in *Mitteilungen des Deutschen Archäologischen Instituts Abteilung Kairo* 18 (1962), 133–46, pls. XXVIII-XXXV; P. Pensabene, *Elementi architettonici di Alessandria e di altri siti egiziani,* Repertorio d'arte dell'Egitto Greco-Romano (Rome, 1993); P. Pensabene, 'La decorazione architettonica, l'impiego del marmo e l'importazione di manufatti orientali a Roma, in Italia e in Africa (II–VI d.C.)', in *Societa romana e impero tardoantico. Le merci gli insediamenti,* ed. A. Giardini (Rome, 1986), 3:285–429, 825–42; H. -G. Severin, 'Beispiele der Verwendung spätantiker Spolien. Ägyptische Notizen', in *Studien zur spätantiken und byzantinischen Kunst F. W. Deichmann gewidmet,* ed. Otto Feld and Urs Peschlow (Bonn, 1986), 101–8, pls 16–21; H. -G. Severin, 'Auswärtige Einflüsse in der Architektur und Baudekoration des spätantiken Ägypten und die christliche Sakralarchitektur im mittelalterlichen Ägypten unter muslimischer Hoheit', *Madrider Beiträge* 24 (1996), 92–107, pls. 26–7; H. -G. Severin, 'Konstantinopler Bauskulptur und die Provinz Ägypten', in *Spätantike und byzantinische Bauskulptur. Beiträge eines Symposiums in Mainz, Februar 1994,* ed. U. Peschlow and S. Möllers (Stuttgart, 1998), 93–104, pls 29–33. A. Pralong, 'Remarques sur les chapiteaux corinthiens tardifs en marbre de Proconnèse', in *L'acanthe dans la sculpture monumentale de l'Antiquité à la Renaissance,* colloque, Sorbonne, octobre 1990, Comité des travaux historiques et scientifiques (Paris, 1993), 133–46; A. Pralong, 'Recherches sur les chapiteaux corinthiens tardifs en marbre de Proconnèse', unpublished doctoral thesis, 4 vols., Sorbonne University, Paris I, 1997; A. Pralong, 'La typologie des chapiteaux corinthiens tardifs en marbre de Proconnèse et la production d'Alexandrie', *Revue Archéologique* (2000) (no. 1), 81–102; A. Pralong, 'Les chapiteaux de la mosquée El-Omari de Beyrouth: remploi et fabrication', in *Utilis est lapis in structura: Mélanges offerts à Léon Pressouyre,* Comité des travaux historiques et scientifiques (Paris, 2000), 313–27. P. Grossmann, 'Wiederverwendete spätantike Kapitelle aus der Moschee von Bahnasâ', *Damaszener Mitteilungen* 11 (1999), 185–90.
   See also the studies, older but still relevant, of Ernst Kitzinger, 'Notes

on Early Coptic Sculpture', *Archaeologia* 87 (1938), 181–215, pls. 67–77; E. Drioton, *Les sculptures des Coptes du Nilomètre de Rodah*, Publications de la Société d'Archéologie Copte. Bibliothèque d'Art et d'Archéologie (Cairo, 1942); E. Drioton, 'De Philae à Baouît', in *Coptic Studies in Honour of Walter Ewing Crum. The Bulletin of the Byzantine Institute* (Boston, 1950), 443–8, pls 12–15; F. W. Deichmann, 'Zu einigen spätantiken Figuralkapitellen', in *Rom, Ravenna, Konstantinopel, Naher Osten. Studien zur spätantiken Architektur, Kunst und Geschichte* (repr. Wiesbaden, 1982), 255–68, pls 25–7; V. Rondot, 'Note sur six chapiteaux composites réutilisés dans la mosquée al-Yûsufî à Mellawi', *Annales du Service des Antiquités de l'Egypte* 70 (1984–5), 143–9, 3 pls; V. Rondot, 'Sur le voyage de sept chapiteaux d'Antinoé vers le Caire', *Annales Islamologiques* 25 (1991), 240–3, 2 pls.

The relationships of medieval Islamic art of the near east with the antique heritage have been the object of several important studies: J. M. Rogers, 'A Renaissance of Classical Antiquity in North Syria (11th–12th centuries)', *Annales Archéologiques Arabes Syriennes* 21 (1971), 347–61; Terry Allen, *A Classical Revival in Islamic Architecture* (Wiesbaden, 1986); Ernst Herzfeld, 'Damascus – Studies in Architecture', *Ars Islamica* 9 (1942), 1–53; 10 (1943), 13–70; 11/12 (1946), 1–71; 13/14 (1948), 118–38. For the classical heritage in the medieval art of Egypt, see especially Hasan ʿAbd al-Wahhab, 'al-Athar al-manqula waʾl-muntahila fiʾl-ʿimara al-islamiyya', *Bulletin de l'Institut d'Egypte* 38/1 (1955–6), 243–83; Viktoria Meinecke-Berg, 'Spolien in der mittelalterlichen Architektur von Kairo', in *Ägypten. Dauer und Wandel. Symposium anlässlich des 75 jährigen Bestehens des Deutschen Archäologischen Instituts Kairo* (Mainz, 1985), 131–42. For the classical heritage in Fatimid architecture, see Marianne Barrucand, 'Les monuments fatimides et leur décoration à l'époque de la fondation de Bâb Mardûm: la question des héritages classiques', in *Entre el Califato y la Taifa: Mil anos del Cristo de la Luz, Actas del Congreso International* (Toledo, 1999), 153–67, and Marianne Barrucand, 'Les chapiteaux de remploi de la mosquée al-Azhar et l'émergence d'un type de chapiteau médiéval en Egypte', *Annales Islamologiques* 36 (2002), 37–75.

3. I use the definition of Annie Pralong in 'Remarques', 134–5, or Annie Pralong, 'La typologie', 85: 'la différenciation . . . des deux feuilles [d'acanthes molle et épineuse] réside dans la façon dont est traité l'espace qui sépare chacun de ses lobes. Dans la feuille d'acanthe molle . . . la séparation est matérialisée par un intervalle étroit, profondément creusé, au tracé le plus souvent coudé à mi-parcours, tandis que dans la feuille d'acanthe épineuse . . ., elle s'agrandit au point de prendre une forme circulaire ou ovale, toujours fortement creusée, et d'imposer aux digitations voisines un tracé arrondi et des pointes acérées.' I would like to thank Annie Pralong here for her interest in these capitals, for her constructive and incisive criticism, and for being such a warm and patient colleague. She herself intends to prepare a corpus of these spolia. Regarding the acanthus, see *L'acanthe dans la sculpture monumentale de l'Antiquité à la Renaissance*, Actes du colloque d'octobre 1990 à la Sorbonne (Paris, 1993).

4. Cf. Severin, 'Konstantinopler Bauskulptur',, pl. 29, 4–5.

5. For Saint-Ménas, see G. et H.-G. Severin, *Marmor vom Heiligen Menas*, Liebighaus Monographie 10 (Frankfurt, 1987), figs 29–32; for comparable capitals of the region of Alexandria, see Pensabene, *Elementi*,

417–8, figs. 473, 477, 479; the precise provenance of most of these capitals is still unknown.

6. The Ottoman mosque of Fakahani, built on the site of a Fatimid mosque, uses, besides the sculpted doors, late antique capitals taken undoubtedly from the earlier Fatimid edifice; where the four Ptolemaic capitals of the Ottoman building came from remains unclear. For comparable Ptolemaic capitals reused in a mosque, see Rondot, 'Note sur six chapiteaux', pls II-III; Rondot, 'Sur le voyage', pl. XXIII.

7. See especially the mosque of al-Hakim, for which see K. A. C. Creswell, *The Muslim Architecture of Egypt*, 2 vols (Oxford, 1956–9) (henceforth *MAE*), 1:65–106, but Creswell does not seem to have paid particular attention to the Pharaonic reuses. See n. 2 above: H. Abd al-Wahhab and V. Meinecke-Berg. The walls and gates of Badr al-Gamali and the Ayyubid period as well as their Mamluk restorations use fragments with Pharaonic sculptures, for an analysis of which by a specialist of Pharaonic art, see Jean-Pierre Corteggiani, 'The Site: From the Primeval era to the Arab Invasions', in *The Glory of Cairo: An Illustrated History*, ed. André Raymond (Cairo, 2002), 15–55, particularly figs. 4–7, 14, 35–7.

8. K. A. C. Creswell, *Early Muslim Architecture*, 2nd edn, 2 vols in 3 parts (Oxford, 1969), 2:327–60.

9. Most sources on Islamic art history follow Creswell on this.

10. It has rarely been possible, up to now, to take measurements. For the courtyard columns the total height is around 3.55m; the capitals take up 42–6cm of this and the impost block is around 60cm.

11. See Noureddine Harrazi, *Chapiteaux de la Grande Mosquée de Kairouan*, 2 vols (Tunis, 1982). For St Ménas, see Severin, 'Beispiele'; Pensabene, *Elementi*.

12. Yasser Tabbaa, *Constructions of Power and Piety in Medieval Aleppo* (University Park, PA, 1997), fig. 153.

13. The usual affirmation (following Creswell) that they are Mamluk restorations seems to me to need verification; they could be either Mamluk capitals which copy the bulbous form of the originals or Fatimid capitals. The undoubtedly Fatimid mihrabs have the same bulbous capitals; see notes 14–15.

14. See in this regard Klaus Brisch, 'Beobachtungen zu einer kleinen Holztafel mit Mihrab', in *Aus der Welt der Staatlichen Museen an der Schwelle der achtziger Jahre*, ed. Werner Knopp (Berlin, 1983), 59–70; Sandrine Linxe, Recherches sur les petits "mihrâbs portatifs" en bois d'époque fatimide', unpublished masters thesis, Paris IV-Sorbonne, 1998.

15. *MAE*, 1: pl. 118.

16. Ibid., 2: pl. 40.

17. Mamluk mihrabs with bulbous capitals: numerous examples are reproduced in *The Mosques of Egypt from 214 (641) to 1365 (1946)*, 2 vols (Giza, 1949) and in *MAE*, vol. 2 (e.g. the complex of de Baybars al-Gashankir, the mosque of amir Husayn, the complex of amir Qarasunqur, the mosque of al-'Amri at Qus, the mosque of Aqsunqur, the complex of al-Ashraf Barsbay at Khanqah, the mausoleum of al-Ashraf Barsbay, the mosque of Qadi Yahya on al-Azhar St., the complex of Qaytbay, the complex of Qijmas al-Ishaqi (Abu Hariba), the mosque of Khayr Bak, the complex of al-Ghawri).

18. Cf. Georges Marçais, *L'Architecture musulmane d'Occident* (Paris, 1954), 104, fig. 59; 105, fig. 60; 342, figs. 214–15.

CHAPTER THREE

A Mongol Envoy

Sheila S. Blair

Robert Hillenbrand and I met, mentally, over the Mongols. We have long been close friends and colleagues, but our intellectual contacts are deepest when dealing with the arts of the Ilkhanids. Robert's university is home to two of the finest manuscripts that have survived from the period, the copy of al-Biruni's *Athar al-baqiya* produced in 707/1307–8 and part of the Arabic version of Rashid al-Din's *Jami' al-tawarikh* produced in 714/1314–15. Robert and I also share an abiding interest in the third great manuscript of the period, the Great Mongol *Shahnama*. No wonder, then, that my frequent visits to his city have often stimulated lively discussions about the development of painting in this seminal period. Because of our shared bond, I dedicate to him this chapter on the iconography of an Ilkhanid painting showing a royal procession, now detached from its original manuscript and mounted in an album in Berlin (Plate 2).[1]

I write this study for several reasons. First, the painting shows how art history can illuminate history, as the details of the painting inform us about protocol during the period of Ilkhanid rule in Iran and West Asia during the late thirteenth and early fourteenth centuries. Second, detailed study of the iconography helps confirm the date of this detached painting and thereby its companions once mounted in the same album and another in Istanbul (H. 2153).[2] Third, comparison of this scene to similar ones in later copies of the text shows how the iconography was modified over time and therefore helps us to understand the process of copying, both within a single manuscript and between traditions.

The scene, drawn on paper in black ink and heightened with a thin coloured wash, centres on a mounted figure. At least three specific attributes – the parasol over his head, his plumed and feathered hat and the folding stool on the nearby horse – immediately identify him as a Mongol ruler. The parasol, used as early as the ninth century BCE and spread across Asia from Egypt to Han China, had long been an attribute of royalty in Iran.[3] Under the Achaemenids it had been an ensign of rank, used to shelter and honour the sovereign. Many of the door jambs at Persepolis, including the northern and southern entrances to the main room of the Council Hall, have low relief carvings showing the king under a parasol.

The idea of the protective shade cast by the parasol was incorporated into Islamic protocol. Rulers from Abbasid times were considered 'God's shadow on earth' (*zill allāh fī'l-ard*).[4] Mamluk rulers also used this title,[5] as did their contemporaries, the Ilkhanids in Iran.[6]

The parasol was also a royal attribute of the Mongols. Textual sources, such as Marco Polo, mention the parasol as an attribute of rank.[7] Visual sources also show how important the parasol was for the Mongols. It was depicted over the head of important figures, both legendary and historical, in paintings made for both the Ilkhanids and the Timurids. For example, Kay Khusraw sports a parasol when he meets Rustam in a painting from a 'small' copy of the *Shahnama* (Minneapolis Museum of Art 51.37.11). So does the Timurid prince and bibliophile Baysunghur b. Shah Rukh in the double-page frontispiece to the copy of the *Shahnama* made for him (Tehran, Gulistan Library).[8]

The rider's hat in the detached painting (Plate 2) also identifies him as a Mongol ruler. It has a long flap down the back and is decked with several plumes, two large owl feathers and three long eagle feathers. This type of hat was commonly depicted in the Ilkhanid period, particularly in the detached pages that are now mounted in albums in Berlin and Istanbul (Figure 3.1). These paintings show that the number of eagle feathers was significant: typically the enthroned ruler wears a hat with three eagle feathers, whereas the flanking attendants wear hats with only one. In the detached painting showing the procession, two figures wear hats with three eagle feathers: the main figure under the parasol and the bearded figure on whom he gazes behind him on the viewer's right. The parallel number of eagle feathers suggests that the bearded figure might also be a prince. There was an inflation in eagle feathers (or perhaps a decrease in their iconographic significance) in later Ilkhanid times: the enthroned ruler in the frontispiece to a copy of the *Mu'nis al-ahrar* transcribed at Isfahan in Ramadan 741/February-March 1341 sports a hat with seven eagle feathers.[9]

The ruler in the detached painting of the procession is accompanied by a pair of horses carrying the royal stool. The folding stool, technically known as a *faldstool*, was already known in both Middle Kingdom Egypt and contemporary Mesopotamia. The Romans elevated it to a seat of honour as the *sella curulis* of the republican magistrates and later the campstool of the Roman emperors (*cella castensis*).[10] Like the parasol, the folding stool was imported to China by Han times, where it became known as the 'Barbarian Bed' (*huchuang*). First used on campaign or for informal seating in a garden or the country, it became an accepted piece of house furniture in the Sui and Tang periods. The method of using it evolved similarly, from sitting with crossed legs to letting the legs hang down. In China it

46

Fig. 3.1 *Right half of a double-page enthronement scene. 35.5 × 30cm.*

(Istanbul, Topkapı Palace Museum, H2153, fol. 148b.)

was eventually replaced on formal occasions by the rigid frame chair (*yi*), though it remained common as a princely seat among the Mongols and Tartars.[11]

This type of folding seat was used by princes and other important members of the court in the Islamic lands as well.[12] It is shown in many enthronement scenes painted during the Ilkhanid period. In the detached enthronement scene in Istanbul (Figure 3.1), for example, the prince on the bottom right sits on a folding stool, perhaps indicating that he is more important than the other princes and therefore the heir-apparent. The stool was also used as a table for the royal turban or crown, as shown by contemporary paintings such as 'The Death of Mahmud b. Sabuktagin' from the copy of Rashid al-din's *Jami' al-tawarikh* done in 714/1314–15[13] and 'Gulnar Coming to Ardashir's Pillow' from the copy of the Great Mongol *Shahnama* painted a generation later.[14]

Ipşiroğlu, who first published the detached painting along with others in the Diez albums in Berlin,[15] identified the scene as a princely procession. Michael Rogers went one step further, noting the similarity between the detached painting and another miniature in a later copy of the *Jami' al-tawarikh* in Paris, in which the scene was entitled 'Hulegu Travelling Under a State Umbrella' (Plate 3).[16] Blochet, the first to study the Paris manuscript, believed that it was contemporary with the composition of the text and dated it to the fourteenth century,[17] but on stylistic grounds other scholars generally date the manuscript a century later.[18] Francis Richard has further narrowed the manuscript's dating and provenance by identifying the author of a poem glorifying Baghdad inscribed on the double-page painting (fos. 180b-181a) showing the tomb of Ghazan Khan.[19] The poem is signed by Sayf al-din al-Vahidi, whom Richard identified as an artist in the atelier of the Timurid prince Baysunghur and author of an elegy on the prince's death composed in 837/1434.[20] The Paris manuscript can thus be localised securely to Herat and dated c. 1425.

The Paris manuscript is not the only copy of Rashid al-Din's *Jami' al-tawarikh* with a painting of Hulegu's procession. The same scene is also illustrated in another copy of the *Jami' al-tawarikh* now in the Asiatic Society of Bengal (Figure 3.2). First published by Basil Gray, this manuscript too is without colophon, but is generally attributed to the late fourteenth century.[21] Rührdanz called attention to the similarity of these three scenes (the detached painting in Berlin and the two in the Paris and Calcutta manuscripts), noting the similar compositions with rider, parasol and attendants, and therefore identified the scene in the detached painting as Hulegu at the head of an army.[22]

Close comparison of the text in Rashid al-Din's *Jami' al-tawarikh* with the iconography of the detached painting pinpoints the scene as Hulegu leading his army against the castles of the Assassins. The text around the painting in both the Paris and Calcutta manuscripts comes from the section of Rashid al-Din's world history dealing

Fig. 3.2 '*Hulegu Moving to Attack the Assassins*'.

(Calcutta, Asiatic Society of Bengal, D31, fol. 55b.)

with the Ilkhanids of Persia.[23] The section opens with the history of the dynasty's founder, Hulegu. Like the biographies of other successors to Genghis Khan, that of Hulegu is divided in three parts: the first part treats the ruler's family, the second part relates the events leading to his enthronement, and the third part discusses his conduct and character. The first part usually contains a genealogical table and is accompanied by small paintings of the khan and his wife, whereas the second part is illustrated by larger, often double-page illustrations. Some show the ruler enthroned with his wife and surrounded by his family. The detached page in Istanbul (Figure 3.1), for example, is the right-half of such a double-page scene, with seven sons standing to the right of the ruler's throne, the same number of sons that Hulegu had. Other large illustrations show significant events in the

49

ruler's life, such as the double-page paintings of Hulegu's taking of Baghdad and of Ghazan's tomb in Tabriz.

Most of Hulegu's biography is devoted to his battles, beginning with his conquests over the Assassins. Following a period of exchanges, Hulegu realised that further negotiations were useless and would do nothing to intimidate the Assassin leader Rukn al-din Khwarshah. Therefore, on 10 Sha'ban 654/2 September 1256, the Ilkhanid ruler Hulegu mounted in Bistam and set out for the lands and castles of the Assassins. He ordered his troops to ready themselves: the right wing was to proceed via Mazandaran, the left wing via Khwar and Simnan, while Hulegu himself rode at the centre with 10,000 warriors.

The detached scene in Berlin (Plate 2), like that in the two later manuscripts, illustrates this event of Hulegu setting out to destroy the Assassins. Hulegu is shown mounted in the centre; the bearded figure to his left (shown on the right of the picture), also wearing a hat with three eagle feathers and the direct focus of the mounted figure, may be his son and heir Abaqa, who accompanied his father on his campaign to Iran along with his younger brothers Yoshmut and Taraghai.[24] The key to identifying the scene is the pedestrian on the left. Rogers already noted his unusual costume: the bearded figure wears a tall, pointed and fringed hat, a short tunic with wide belt supporting two pouches with tassels of yak-tail, crossed garters on his shins, and shoes quite distinct from the boots worn by the other figures. In his left hand, he holds a staff; his right hand is held out upturned.

Rogers thought that the pedestrian was beating a drum held against his stomach and therefore argued that he was a shaman, leading a funeral procession and beating the drum either to scare away onlookers, lest they be killed as part of the khan's funeral or more generally to keep the affair secret. Rogers related the shaman to Palladius's statement, based on Chinese sources and repeated by the eminent Soviet scholar V. V. Bartold, that the funeral procession of a dead khan was preceded by a (female) shaman leading a horse with richly decorated saddle by its bridle. In this case, however, Rogers noted that the shaman was male and the single horse was turned into a less than impressive pair of horses, which were not led but rather walked beside the ruler.

Rogers's reasons for identifying the scene as a funeral procession were mistaken, however, for the object between the pedestrian figure's hands is not a drum. Oval in shape, it is pierced above the centre with a hole for a cord by which it is attached to the figure's body. It must therefore be a *pāīza* (Chinese *p'ai-tse*, Mongolian *gerege*), a type of passport or safe-conduct pass. According to contemporary descriptions, this tablet of authority was made of wood, silver, or gold and embellished with a tiger or gerfalcon at the top, depending on the rank and importance of the holder.

The *pāīza* was carried by an envoy or official travelling on government business called an *ilchi*.[25] The Mongols had long been insistent on the sacrosanct status of their ambassadors. The Khwarzamshahs' murder of an envoy, for example, helped precipitate Genghis's invasion of Iran. In order to facilitate communication through the vast empire, in 634/1234 during the reign of Ogedai, the Mongols had set up an official communication system known as *yam*. It was derived from the system used by the Khitan in China, who had also issued silver tablets to their envoys.[26]

Marco Polo was particularly impressed with the Mongol system of communication and left a long description of it.[27] A system of highways radiated from the capital at Khanbalik (modern Beijing) to all provinces. Posting stations were spaced twenty-five miles apart to provide a ready supply of horses. In times of need, riders, often in teams, were dispatched, equipped with a *pāīza* in order to speed travel. Tightening their belts and swathing their heads, they set off post-haste. As they approached the next station, they sounded a horn so that fresh horses were readied and the riders had only to remount and continue. In this way, they could cover as much as 200 or even 250 miles per day. Along with these equestrian stations, Marco Polo mentioned others spaced at three-mile intervals for runners, each manned by a clerk who noted the times of arrival and departure. The messengers, who wore large belts set with bells so that they could be heard from afar, ran in relays. As soon as the first man reached a station, another runner was waiting to take whatever the first was carrying, plus a note from the clerk.

Not all authors painted such a rosy picture of the Mongol communication system, perhaps because of differing purposes in writing their accounts. Whereas Marco Polo was intent on describing the wonders of the east, the vizier Rashid al-Din wanted to glorify his ruler's reforms and hence emphasised how the system had been abused under the early Ilkhanids and was therefore ripe for reform. According to Rashid al-Din, everyone – from wives, princes, and camp officers to leopard keepers and equerries – thought it essential to use an envoy. The roads became clogged, the envoys rapacious and the people resentful. Further, many bandits masqueraded as envoys. As a result, real envoys were often prevented from doing their business. All these problems led Ghazan to lay down reforms to curtail such abuses.[28]

In addition to texts mentioning the *pāīza* worn by envoys and government officials, a few *pāīza*s have survived. They vary in shape and decoration. One excavated from the lands of the Golden Horde, the collateral line of Mongols descended from Genghis's eldest son, Jochi, and rulers of southern Russia (Figures 3.3–4), is close in shape to the one depicted in the painting. Rectangular with rounded ends, it has a hole two-thirds of the way up. The top part is fashioned with the stylized face of a dragon so that the hole falls between the creature's yawning jaws. The lower part is inscribed vertically in the traditional Uighur-Mongol script.[29]

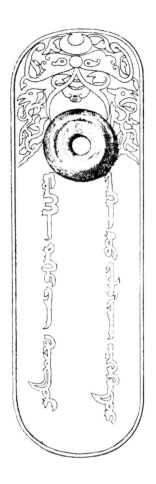 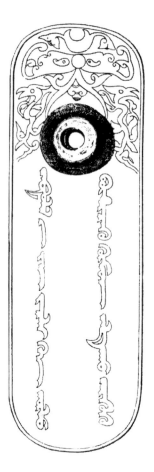

Figs 3.3–4 *Silver* pāīza *excavated near the Dnieper in the lands of the Golden Horde. 28 × 9cm.*

(St Petersburg, Hermitage Museum, ZO-295.)

Other *pāīzas* are attached by a ring at one end. Several found in China are pear-shaped. The triangular section at the top is decorated with the face of a dragon similar to the one on the excavated *pāīza*, and the round body is inscribed vertically in Phagspa, the square, box-like script developed by the Tibetan Buddhist monk and adopted by the Mongols under Khubilai.[30] One made of iron inlaid with silver (Figure 3.5) is in the Metropolitan Museum;[31] a similar example is in the Kansu provincial museum.[32]

A third type of *pāīza* (Figure 3.6) dates from the reign of the Ilkhanid ruler Abu Saʿid (r. 1317–35).[33] It is rectangular in shape, like the *pāīza* from the Golden Horde, but scalloped at the end with the ring, like the Chinese examples. One side of the silver-plated copper plaque is decorated with a walking figure. In his right hand he carries a roll; in his left he holds a three-pronged stick, which resembles the three-pronged spear (*nīza*) depicted in the copy of the *Mu'nis al-ahrar* made in 741/1341.[34] The *pāīza* is inscribed in the regular Uighur-Mongol script with the names of the Ilkhanid ruler Abu Saʿid and the petitioner Tudagha the vizier (*ḥājib*).[35] It is also stamped with the seal of a certain individual named Qutlugh Tegin, whom Quchani tried to connect with someone of the same name buried in 777/1375–6 in the Shah-i Zinda cemetery outside Samarqand.[36] This *pāīza*, therefore, seems to represent the type of personal patent that became widespread under the Ilkhanids and was so deplored by Rashid al-Din.

Fig. 3.5 *Iron* pāīza *with silver inlay. 18 × 11.5 cm.*

(New York, Metropolitan Museum of Art, 1993.256.)

53

Fig. 3.6 Silver-plated copper
pāīza *from the time of Abu*
Sa'id. 7 × 12cm.

(Tehran, National Museum of
Iran.)

The pedestrian in the detached painting (Plate 2) resembles the one
depicted on the Ilkhanid *pāīza* (Figure 3.6). Each figure wears a
pointed hat. The figure in the detached painting holds his hand open,
but the one depicted on the Ilkhanid *pāīza* carries a rolled object in
his right hand, perhaps the clerk's note or permission mentioned by
Marco Polo or the patent or treaty that the emissary was dispatched
to convey.[37] Each figure carries a long implement over his left
shoulder. The one in the painting with a crooked end may be a
special staff, perhaps related to one of the implements of war mentioned and illustrated in the copy of the *Mu'nis al-ahrar* made in 741/
1341. In addition to the three-pronged spear (*nīza*) and dart (*khisht*),
the illustrations show an ox-headed mace (*gurz*), a wooden club with
a crook at one end (*nāchakh*), and an ax with polylobed blade
(*tabar*).[38]
    As opposed to the figure on the Ilkhanid *pāīza*, the figure in the
detached painting is an official envoy. His status is underscored by
the pouches with tassels of yak-tail hanging from his belt. Tassels of
yak-tail were another attribute of royal authority for the Mongols.

Genghis, like the Turkish Khans before him, adopted a standard (*tugh*).[39] His comprised a pole with nine white yak tails dangling from its head. Nine was considered a sacred number, and other commanders had similar but less elaborate standards.[40]

Tassels made of yak-tail are regularly depicted in official Mongol paintings. For example, a hanging scroll showing Khubilai and his wife Chabi hunting includes tassels of yak-tail hanging from the bridles of the royal couple's horses (Figure 3.7). This scroll, which is remarkable for its minutely observed details of costume and equipage, is signed and dated in the lower left by Liu Kuan-tao in 1280. A native of the Chung-shan district near the capital Ta-tu (Beijing), the artist was known as a competent painter of religious subjects, figures and animals as well as landscapes in the manner of Kuo Hsi. In 1279, the year before he painted this scroll, the artist was awarded a position in the Imperial Wardrobe Service, thereby ensuring his

Fig. 3.7 *Detail of a hanging scroll painted by Liu Kuan-tao in 1280 depicting Khubilai and his wife Chabi hunting.*

(Taipei, National Palace Museum.)

intimate knowledge of courtly dress. In official portraits like this one, the Chinese artist trained in the academy was required not only to present a recognisable likeness of the royal figures, but also to include accurate details of imperial regalia which symbolized the emperor's exalted status.[41]

The painter of the detached painting in Berlin (Plate 2) included the pedestrian because of the surrounding text, which is now missing. It mentions repeatedly that Hulegu sent emissaries to Khwarshah, ruler of the Assassins, to sue for peace. The line just below the same scene in the Paris manuscript (Plate 3) mentions that when Hulegu set out, emissaries (iljiyan) were sent in advance to announce that the expedition was in motion and that if Khwarshah would come out from his stronghold, he would be pardoned.[42] The envoy's outstretched hand presumably represents the offer of peace.

The specificity and accuracy of the envoy's dress in the detached painting, notably the similarity between the representation of the paīza and actual patents and details of his dress and implements, means that the unidentified artist knew and had seen a real paīza-bearing envoy. Such specificity confirms the suggestions by Rogers and Rührdanz that the detached album paintings come from an early copy of Rashid al-Din's Jami' al-tawarikh and are therefore datable to the opening decades of the fourteenth century. Their attributions stand in contrast to others, notably by Karamağarali and Gray, who argued that the detached paintings should be dated to the late fourteenth century because of their large format. In this case, however, iconography trumps format, for, as Rührdanz showed, different sizes of illustrations were used to illustrate different parts of Rashid al-Din's text and increased size was not, therefore, indicative of a later date. These detached paintings, then, probably come from a manuscript of volume one of Rashid al-Din's *Compendium of Chronicles* that is contemporary with the Arabic copy of the second volume done in 714/1314–15 and now divided between Edinburgh University Library and the Nour Collection in London.[43]

Comparing the detached painting to the same scene in copies of the *Jami' al-tawarikh* made in the second half of the fourteenth century (Figure 3.2) and the first half of the fifteenth (Plate 3) explicitly shows how Persian painters simplified iconography over the course of a century. The Calcutta page (Figure 3.2), unfortunately badly damaged, shows the same scene, but with more figures and less specific iconography. The artist again depicted the mounted Hulegu under a parasol. This time, however, the ruler is flanked by two courtiers: the one to the right carries the parasol, while the one to the left bears a standard with a yak-tail. To the right behind the ruler is a group of eight courtiers. They comprise four Mongols (identifiable by their hats with owl feathers but no eagle feathers), three guards (identifiable by their hats with wide brims), and one foot soldier at the rear who wears a hat with long earpieces.

To the left in front of the mounted ruler are two envoys on foot.

They may represent the pairs of envoys often dispatched on official missions or simply be an inflation in the number of figures in the painting. They both wear tall and pointed hats, but these are now melon-shaped and have no fringe. The envoy on the left has a binding around the waist and loins, perhaps the remnants of a strap to affix the *paīza*. The envoy on the right has something hanging from his waist.

In addition to the three main groups found in the Ilkhanid original, the artist of this painting has added a fourth component: a man with a hound on a leash in the foreground. This group replaces the pair of horses, one with the royal stool, in the Ilkhanid original. The inclusion of this detail may reflect the memory of a lost original or another generalised attribute of royalty. From Marco Polo's account, we know that hounds were another royal prerogative. The keeper of the hounds occupied an exalted position at court, and often wore a special livery.[44] The silk scroll depicting Khubilai and Chabi (Figure 3.7) hunting also includes a royal hound painted off to the right of the roayl figures, as do many other paintings of Mongol princes from the Yuan period.[45]

The scene in the Paris manuscript done c. 1425 (Plate 3) shows a more simplified composition. Hulegu rides in the centre under his parasol flanked by two mounted attendants, the one on the right carrying the parasol and the one on the left carrying a standard with a yak-tail. Now, however, both attendants as well as the central figure in the right group wear the princely hat with one eagle feather. The pedestrian on the left repeats many of the features of the Ilkhanid envoy. He is bearded and wears a tall, melon-shaped hat, short tunic with a belt, leggings and shoes. The *paīza*, however, is missing. He seems to hold a roll in his right hand, but his left hand is empty, though poised as if to hold a standard. Details of the robes are similarly confused: the envoy, as well as two of the attendants, wear the gold-embroidered robe that was typically associated with the court and worn by Khubilai in the hanging scroll. The most obvious change is the dog, which is now unleashed and lopes along in the foreground.

Analysing the iconography of the Mongol envoy in the detached painting in Berlin (Plate 2) and comparing it to later copies shows the importance of studying the original image. Copies are much less exact in iconography. Reproductions too often obscure salient details, which may be the key to identifying an image, and thereby lead to mistaken conclusions. Studying the original is particularly important in the Mongol period, when the image become a major source to illuminate written history, for this is the time when Persian painting came of age. Only by knowing the original are we able to identify the figures in the later copies. As Robert Hillenbrand would be the first to agree, a close look at iconography pays substantial rewards.

SHEILA S. BLAIR

Notes

1. First published in M. Ipşiroğlu, *Saray-Alben: Diez'sche Klebebände aus den berliner Sammlungen* (Wiesbaden, 1964), ill. 13, pl. X, fig. 14, and recently in Linda Komaroff and Stefano Carboni, (eds), *The Legacy of Genghis Khan: Courtly Art and Culture in Western Asia, 1256–1353* (New York, 2002), no. 23, fig. 68.
2. For the 49 paintings in Berlin, Diez album A, fos. 70–2, see Işpiroğlu, *Saray-Alben*, Group II, and David J. Roxburgh, 'Heinrich Friedrich von Diez and His Eponymous Albums: Mss. Diez A. Fols. 70–74,' *Muqarnas* 12 (1995), 112–36; for the four pages in the Topkapi Library in Istanbul, H2153, see Beyhan Karamağarali, 'Camiu't-tevarih'in bilinmiyen bir nüshasina air dört minyatür', *Sanat Tarihi Yilliği* (1966–8), 70–86, and Filiz Çağman and Zeren Tanındı, *The Topkapi Saray Museum: The Albums and Illustrated Manuscripts*, ed., expand. and tr. J. M. Rogers (Boston, 1986), nos. 43–4.
3. Eleanor Sims, 'Čatr', *Encyclopaedia Iranica*, (Costa Mesa, CA 1993) 5:77–9.
4. Ignaz Goldziher, *Muslim Studies (Muhammedanische Studien)*, ed. S. M. Stern, tr. C. R. Barber and S. M. Stern, 2 vols (Chicago, 1971), 2:67.
5. Max van Berchem, *Matériaux pour un Corpus Inscriptionum Arabicarum I: Egypte 1*, Mémoires de la mission archéologique française au Caire 19 (Cairo, 1894–1903), 368.
6. Lutfallah Hunarfar, *Ganjīna-yi Āthār-i Tārīkhī-yi Iṣfahān* (Tehran, 1350/1977), 116.
7. Marco Polo, *The Travels of Marco Polo*, tr. and ed. Ronald Latham (London, 1958), e.g., 121.
8. Both cited in Sims 'Čatr'.
9. Marie Lukens Swietochowski and Stefano Carboni, *Illustrated Poetry and Epic Images: Persian Painting of the 1330s and 1340s*, exh. cat. (New York, 1994), esp. 12–13.
10. Otto Kurz, 'Folding Chairs and Koran Stands', in *Islamic Art in the Metropolitan Museum of Art*, ed. Richard Ettinghausen (New York, 1972), 299–314.
11. C. P. FitzGerald, *Barbarian Beds: The Origins of the Chair in China* (South Brunswick and New York, 1965).
12. It occurs, for example, in the frontispiece to the *Kitab al-Aghani* of 615/1218–19, illustrated in Richard Ettinghausen, *Arab Painting* (Geneva, 1962), p. 65.
13. David Talbot Rice, *The Illustrations to the 'World History' of Rashid al-Din*, ed. by Basil Gray (Edinburgh, 1976), no. 64.
14. Geneva, Musée d'art et d'histoire 1971–107/3a; illustrated in Oleg Grabar and Sheila Blair, *Epic Images and Contemporary History: The Illustrations of the Great Mongol Shah-Nama* (Chicago, 1980), no. 40.
15. See n. 1 above.
16. Note added to V. V. Barthold and J. M. Rogers, tr., 'The Burial Rites of the Turks and the Mongols', *Central Asiatic Journal* 14 (1970), 195–227.
17. E. Blochet, *Les Enluminures des manuscrits orientaux, turcs, arabes, persans* (Paris, 1926), 75–88.
18. See, most recently, the bibliography in Francis Richard, *Splendeurs persanes: manuscrits du XIIe au XVIIe siècle* (Paris, 1997), no. 40.
19. Ibid.

20. Francis Richard, 'Un des peintres du manuscrit *Supplément Persan 1113* de l'Histoire des Mongols de Rašid al-dīn identifié', in *L'Iran face à la domination mongole*, Bibliothèque Iranienne 45, ed. Denise Aigle (Tehran, 1997), 295–306.

21. Basil Gray, 'An Unknown Fragment of the '*Jāmiʿ al-Tawārīkh*' in the Asiatic Society of Bengal', *Ars Orientalis* 1 (1954), 65–76.

22. Karin Rührdanz, 'Illustrationen zu Rašid al-dīn's *Taʾrīḫ-i Mubārak-i Ġāzānī* in den berliner Diez-Alben', in *L'Iran face à la domination mongole*, Bibliothèque Iranienne 45, ed. Denise Aigle (Tehran, 1997), 295–306.

23. According to Thackston's arrangement, it is volume III of the modern division. For a translation, see Étienne Quatremère, *Raschid-Eldin: histoire des Mongols de la Perse: texte persan, publié, traduit en français accompagnée de notes et d'un mémoire sur la vie et les ouvrages de l'auteur*, repr., 1836 (Amsterdam, 1968), 181–95, and Rashid al-Din, *Jamiʿuʾl-Tawarikh: Compendium of Chronicles; A History of the Mongols*, Sources of Oriental Languages and Literatures 45, tr. W. M. Thackston (Cambridge, MA, 1998), 482–4.

24. Ibid., 480.

25. David Morgan, 'Elčhī', *Encyclopaedia Iranica*, (Costa Mesa, CA, 1993) 8:344–5.

26. David O. Morgan, *The Mongols*, (Oxford, 1986), 105–7.

27. Marco Polo *Travels*, 150–5.

28. Rashid al-Din, *Jamiʿuʾl-Tawarikh*, 714–18.

29. Illustrated in Morgan, *Mongols*, 105, and Komaroff and Carboni, *Legacy of Genghis Khan*, no. 154, fig. 34. This shape had also been used for pre-Mongol examples in China, as in the one in the Hebei Provincial Museum with a Khitan inscription made under the Liao dynasty (907–1125), illustrated in Komaroff and Carboni, fig. 70. A similar rectangular *pāīza*, but with one rounded and one square end, is also shown on a mounted figure in another illustration of a Mongol travelling that was probably cut from the same manuscript and is now mounted in the same album in Berlin (Komaroff and Carboni, *Legacy of Genghis Khan*, no. 22, fig. 39).

30. For the various scripts used by the Mongols, see James Bosson, 'Scripts and Literacy in the Mongol World'' in *Mongolia: The Legacy of Chinggis Khan*, ed. Patricia Berger and Terese Tse Bartholomew (New York, 1995), 88–95.

31. Illustrated in ibid., 33, fig. 5; Lauren Arnold, *Princely Gifts and Papal Treasures: The Franciscan Mission to China and its Influence on the Art of the West* (San Francisco, 1999), 21, fig. I-8; and Komaroff and Carbonie, *Legacy of Genghis Khan*, no. 197.

32. Illustrated and discussed in Morris Rossabi, *Khubilai Khan: His Life and Times* (Berkeley, 1988), 160, fig. 12.

33. ʿAbdallah Qūchānī, 'Pāʾīza', *Mirāth-i farhangī* 17 (Summer, 1997), 42–5.

34. Swietochowski and Carboni, *Illustrated Poetry and Epic Images*, 2f and 3a. Quchani compares the weapon to the three-pronged dart (*khisht*) depicted on another page (Princeton University Library, 94G) from the same copy of the *Muʾnis al-ahrar* (4c), but this weapon is shorter.

35. Interestingly, Abu Saʿid revived the traditional Uighur-Mongol script for his name, along with a new Ilkhanid calendar, on coins issued in the 1330s; see Sheila S. Blair, 'The Coins of the Later Ilkhanids: A Typological Analysis', *Journal of the Economic and Social History of the Orient* 26/3 (1983), Type F and plate X, fig. 12.

36. Quchani, 'Paiza'.
37. The mounted figure in the detached painting similar to the one discussed here (Komaroff and Carboni, *Legacy of Genghis Khan*, no. 22, fig. 39) also carries a roll.
38. Swietochowski and Carboni, *Illustrated Poetry*, fig. 4e.
39. C. E. Bosworth, 'Tugh', *The Encyclopaedia of Islam*, 2nd edn, 10:590. The Tughluqids, the line of Delhi sultans who ruled the Indian subcontinent in the fourteenth century, derived their name from the commander Ghiyath al-Din *tughluq* (the bearer of the standard).
40. E. D. Phillips, *The Mongols: Ancient Peoples and Places* (London, 1969), 40. I thank Morris Rossabi for answering my queries about the *tugh*; he informs me that the Museum of History in Ulan Bator has a *tugh* made of horsehair that reputedly belonged to Genghis.
41. Wen C. Fong and James C. Y. Watt, *Possessing the Past: Treasures from the National Palace Museum, Taipei* (New York, 1996), 270–1, and pl. 138.
42. My thanks to Karin Rührdanz for identifying the exact placement of the painting in the text, which is not visible in the reproduction.
43. For reproduction of all the paintings in the section in Edinburgh, once thought to date from 707/1306–7, see Rice, *Illustrations to Rashid al-Din*; for reproduction of the section in the Nour collection and the collation of the whole manuscript, see Sheila S. Blair, *A Compendium of Chronicles: Rashid al-Din's Illustrated History of the World* (London, 1995). There (93–9), however, I dated the detached pages to c. 1330. I think this date should be revised to c. 1315.
44. Marco Polo, *Travels*, 142.
45. Nancy Shatzman Steinhardt, 'Yuan Period Tombs and their Decoration: Cases at Chifeng', *Oriental Art* (1990/1991), 198–221.

Chapter Four

Almoravid Geometric Designs in the Pavement of the Cappella Palatina in Palermo

Jonathan M. Bloom

Robert Hillenbrand has been fascinated by the wonderful painted muqarnas ceiling of the Cappella Palatina in Palermo for many years, and he – like many other scholars – views it as a distant if somewhat incoherent reflection of the type of ceiling that might once have decorated the Fatimid palaces in Cairo.[1] In anticipation of his eventual publication of the many hours he spent meticulously studying the ceiling, I offer him this short chapter about another aspect of the building, namely the twelfth-century opus sectile pavement that lies underneath the magnificent ceiling he has admired so much (Figure 4.1). While the chapel has long been thought to represent an outpost of metropolitan Fatimid art in the central Mediterranean region, I will show that the design of the pavement has much in common with contemporary geometric designs from the western Islamic lands and suggest that we might profitably look to the Almoravid arts of Spain and Morocco for additional sources for the Norman-Islamic arts of twelfth-century Sicily.

The Cappella Palatina

The Cappella Palatina in Palermo is the palace church built by the Norman King Roger II (b. 1111; r. 1130–54). The chapel was consecrated in 1140, but it is likely that its rich marble, mosaic and painted decorations were not completed until some time later. [2]The building is typically dated to the period 1130 to 1142, but the most recent scholarship suggests that the building was begun somewhat later, probably in the late 1130s. Work on the decoration of the sanctuary began in the early 1140s (the mosaic in the apex of the dome is dated 1143), then progressed downwards and outwards to the outer limit of the sanctuary by the mid-1150s, yet the decoration remained incomplete at the time of Roger's death in 1154.[3]

The present building consists of three parts: a columnar nave separated from two aisles by ten granite and cippolino columns

Fig. 4.1 *Palermo, Cappella*
Palatina, general view of
the interior.

(Photograph: Alinari/Art
Resource.)

which support a magnificent wooden ceiling of carved and painted muqarnas; a tripartite vaulted sanctuary on the east raised four steps above the level of the nave; and a Norman throne raised on five steps at the west end of the nave, opposite the sanctuary.

Artisans – presumably Greeks from Byzantium – decorated the ceilings and walls of the sanctuary with mosaics and marble revetments following the Middle Byzantine canon of showing Christ Pantokrator surrounded and supported by angels, archangels, prophets and evangelists. The mosaics on the three apses and chapel walls differ somewhat from Byzantine conventions, while the narrative mosaics of the nave differ even more strongly, as they depict Old Testament scenes in several registers. These stylistic differences, combined with documentary and other types of evidence, led William Tronzo to interpret the building dynamically as it was changed to meet the differing needs of King Roger II and his successors.

The Pavement

The pavement of the Cappella Palatina is one of the best-preserved opus sectile floors from the twelfth century. Opus sectile, a technique in which various coloured stones are cut in shapes and fitted together to form geometric designs, is an ancient paving technique that enjoyed great favour in medieval Byzantium and Italy. It differs from mosaic, or *opus tesselatum* – with which it was often combined, in the larger size of the stone pieces used and the consistently abstract nature of the designs. The Cappella Palatina pavement is comparable to other pavements known from Rome and Latium, or southern Italy and Sicily, but the pavements of the latter regions are not nearly as well known as those of the former.[4] Apart from the few pages Tronzo devoted to it, the building's pavement has never been the subject of a detailed publication, despite its remarkable state of preservation.[5]

Covering over 300 square metres (the nave, side aisles and transept together measure about 25 metres long and 12.5 meters wide), the pavement is conceived as a series of panels that exactly reflects the divisions of the chapel's structure into nave, aisles, choir and transept. Bands of white marble and narrow opus sectile strips between the bases of the columns that support the vaults delineate a large single panel under the dome of the choir, two nearly square panels in each of the transept arms, four rectangular panels in each of the aisles and three large rectangular panels in the nave (Figure 4.2). All of the panels contain one or more relatively large disks of dark-red porphyry or dark-green serpentine breccia, obviously sliced from some ancient columns, which have been arranged in singletons, pairs, triplets, rows or quincunxes. Six of the panels (that under the choir dome, the easternmost in the north aisle and the four in the south aisle) bear curvilinear twist patterns (Plate 4), while the rest of the panels are decorated with angular interlace designs (Plate 5).

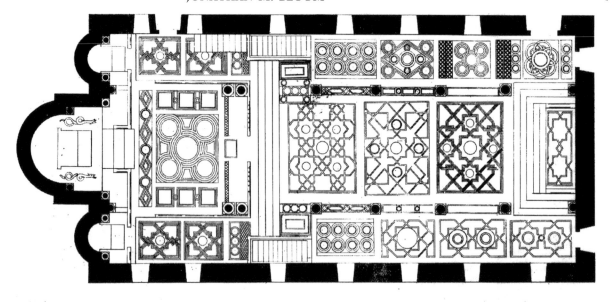

PIANTA DELLA CAPPELLA DEL REAL PALAZZO

Fig. 4.2 *Palermo, Cappella Palatina, plan of the pavement (south is at the top).*

(Photograph: after Serradifalco.)

The strapwork designs on the curvilinear panels circumscribe and connect the stone disks with sinusoidal (**S**-shaped) bands, while the angular strapwork designs create irregular polygons, including eight-pointed stars, **Y**-shapes and irregular octagons, in which disks are set. In both types of designs, however, mosaic micropatterns of triangles, hexagons, checkerboards, hexagrams and interlocking circles fill the median strip of the strapwork bands as well as the background of or interstices between the panels. Most of the panels do not contain more than one repeat of the geometric design – the exceptions are the westernmost two panels in the north aisle and the easternmost panel in the nave – and in all cases the regular and apparently infinite geometric design has been modified at the edges of the field so that the strapwork bands turn back and reconnect with each other rather than continuing infinitely. The only representational designs on these pavements are the snakes depicted to either side of the main altar and a small panel depicting addorsed lions on either side of a schematised tree at the entrance from the nave to the choir.[6]

In addition to the porphyry and serpentine breccia disks, the pavement is predominantly worked from three types of stone: white cipollino streaked with grey, yellow to orange giallo antico and a fine-grained white limestone. The bands that separate the panels are made of cipollino, as are the main strapwork bands in the decorative panels; all five types of stones are all used to make the mosaic micropatterns, presumably indicating that trimmings from the larger pieces were

64

frugally saved and used elsewhere. In some areas of the pavement there are also disks of pink and green marble and rectangular panels of pink and grey-white marble. Red glass is also occasionally used in the micropatterns.

Although it has been restored and repaired over the centuries, the pavement essentially preserves its original design, which must date from a single campaign during Roger's reign. A sermon delivered by Philagathos, Roger's court homilist, for the feast of Saints Peter and Paul sometime in the late 1140s or early 1150s indicates that the pavement already existed by that date, for Philagothos said that the floor was 'adorned with pieces of marble colored like flowers, truly like a spring meadow except for the fact that flowers wither and die, and this is a meadow that will never wither but will last forever, preserving in itself an eternal spring'.[7] The Austrian Byzantinist Otto Demus originally tried to explain the differences between the curvilinear and rectilinear designs as the product of differences in date, namely that the curvilinear designs were earlier and the rectilinear ones were later. Tronzo convincingly demonstrated, however, that the pavement had to have been laid in a single campaign, so Demus's hypothesis cannot stand.[8]

Comparable, but not identical, pavements of opus sectile are found in the nave of the church of St Mary's of the Admiral in Palermo, which was built and decorated in the 1140s. There the pattern consists of two concentric squares that are connected by a continuous strapwork band which outlines and connects a series of porphyry and breccia disks set between the squares (Figure 4.3). Depictions of vases and plants occupy the interstices between the disks; a quincunx of disks fills the interior of the inner square.[9] An entirely different type of pattern is found in the pavement in the choir of the Cathedral of Monreale (Plate 6), which has been dated somewhat later in the century. Here the quincunx patterns in Palermo have given way to a 'free ranging rectangular interlace' of irregular octagons linked together like chain mail to form a pattern of octagons 'dotted with porphyry and marble disks . . . as if the earlier format had been subjected to a process of blending and unification'.[10]

Several features of the Cappella Palatina pavement have been linked to contemporary Byzantine art. The primarily curvilinear strapwork patterns, for example, are paralleled in the opus sectile pavement of the twelfth-century Pantokrator Monastery in Istanbul, where a continuous strapwork fillet connects and encloses circular and rectangular elements arranged in a quincunx (Figure 4.4). The depictions of snakes and lions at significant places on the floor of the Cappella Palatina have been linked to apotropaic or symbolic figures also found on earlier Byzantine pavements. Tronzo, however, was unable to determine whether the curvilinear designs derived directly from Constantinople or from Byzantine-influenced pavements produced elsewhere in central Italy. Several of the individual micropatterns of the Palermo pavement have also been linked to designs

Fig. 4.3 *Palermo, St Mary's of the Admiral, pavement.*

(Photograph: after Tronzo, ill. 25.)

Fig. 4.4 (opposite) *Istanbul, Pantokrator Monastery, plan of pavement.*

(Photograph: after Eyice.)

found in Roman pavements dating from the first half of the twelfth century, although several other distinctly Roman features, such as the patterned rectangles and the alignment of disks along the nave's axis, are not found in Sicily.[11]

Nearly a hundred years ago, the French writer Émile Bertaux suggested that the rectilinear designs in the Cappella Palatina pavement derived from Islamic art, a logical conclusion considering the frankly 'Islamic' character of the ceiling directly above the pavement.[12] Dorothy Glass and then Tronzo agreed that the rectilinear patterns do have a distinctly 'Islamic' look, but they were unable to find exact parallels in Islamic pavements, although they found similar patterns in Islamic architectural decoration, citing a range of sources from the Maghak-i Attari mosque in Bukhara to the Qarawiyyin mosque in Fez.[13] Tronzo also noted similarities between these rectilinear patterns and numerous objects of Islamic craftsmanship either made in Sicily or imported there, such as the wooden doors and other architectural fittings that once decorated the Norman buildings of Palermo.[14] For example, a wooden panel datable to the twelfth century in the Galleria Regionale della Sicilia in Palermo (Figure 4.5) is decorated with strips of grooved lath and intricately carved panels in the shape of eight-pointed stars, arrows and other polygons laid to create a geometric strapwork design based on a 45° grid.[15]

66

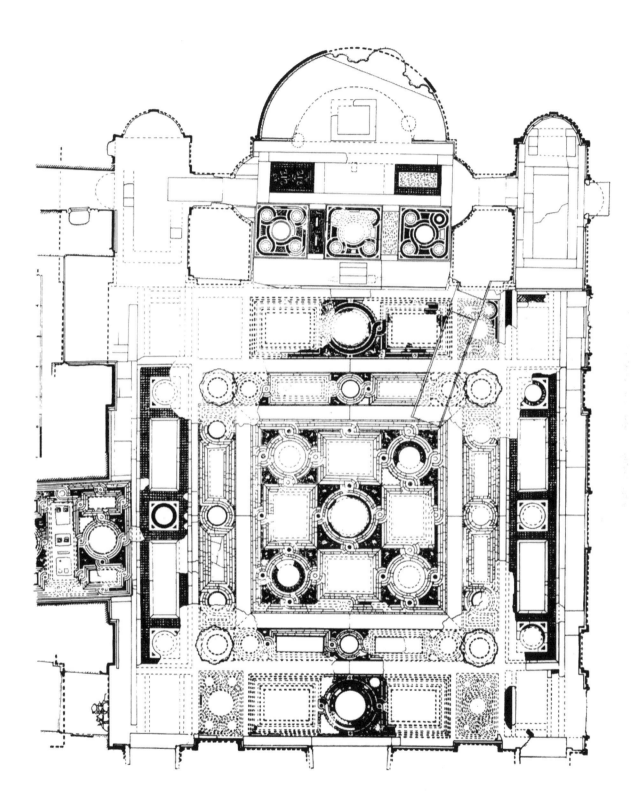

Fig. 4.5 *Wooden panel, 12th century, Galleria Regionale della Sicilia, Palermo.*

(Photograph: after Tronzo, fig.—29.)

Despite the differences between the curvilinear and rectilinear types of interlace, there are important points of similarity between them. Both types of patterns are executed in the same techniques, and both are organised around configurations of disks in a quincunx, an arrangement that was one of the staples of Italian floor design, although it was largely unknown in Islamic art.[16] Tronzo surmised, 'only one conclusion seems possible: the designer of the pavement was either an Easterner or Byzantine-trained, that is to say, steeped in Byzantine practice and approach'.[17]

Scholars generally agree that medieval pavements were customarily designed to serve the rituals, movements and processions that took place on them.[18] Byzantine pavements, in contrast to medieval Roman ones, were very carefully designed to reflect the architecture above, as at the twelfth-century Pantokrator monastery in Constantinople, where the pavement perfectly mirrors the vaults that once stood above. The individual panels at the Cappella Palatina fit neatly into the spaces defined for them by the architecture, and Tronzo believed that the distribution of curvilinear and angular pavement patterns was not accidental but planned, as the two types were employed more or less separately in different sections of the floor. Curvilinear patterns dominate in the sanctuary and the south aisle; angular patterns dominate in the transept arms, the north aisle and the nave. This division, Tronzo believed, was designed to emphasise the greeting ceremony with *proskynesis* (Greek: ritual greeting) that the audience-hall chapel was designed to serve.

Origins of the Geometric Designs

It is quite clear that curvilinear twist designs around quincunxes derive from a long tradition of Roman, Byzantine and medieval Italian pavements. It seems equally clear, as Bertaux remarked a century ago, that parallels for rectilinear designs should be sought in Islamic art, particularly that of Fatimid Egypt, a region whose connections to Sicily appears to need little or no explanation. Within a few months of the Fatimid conquest of North Africa in 909, a Fatimid governor had been sent to replace the Aghlabid governor in Sicily, and from the middle of the tenth century until the middle of the eleventh and the beginning of the Norman conquest, members of the Kalbid family served as governors for the Fatimids. The removal of the Fatimids from North Africa to Egypt in 972 meant increased freedom of action for the Kalbids, who nevertheless remained firmly loyal to their distant overlords.[19] The Norman conquest of Sicily, which was accomplished between 1061 and 1091, brought Sicily back into the mainstream of European politics. Roger II, the most illustrious of the Norman rulers, had to struggle not only against German and Byzantine aggression but also against the Fatimids' successors in North Africa, where Norman expeditions attacked and held various coastal cities. Meanwhile Roger pursued a policy of détente with the Fatimids of Egypt, continuing commerce in grain and other commodities.[20]

The geometric designs on the pavements appear to be distinctly 'Islamic', yet it has been difficult to find exact or even close parallels for them in contemporary Fatimid art. From the tenth to the mid-eleventh centuries, Fatimid artists in Egypt primarily used vegetal and epigraphic motifs for architectural decoration; geometric patterns, which are known in Fatimid art from the late tenth century, were initially subservient to the vegetal elements, but began to play an increasingly important role – though never to the exclusion of vegetation and epigraphy – at the end of the eleventh century in such monuments as the wooden minbar made in Syria in 1091–2 for the shrine of al-Husayn at Ascalon, now in the Haram al-Khalil at Hebron. Geometric interlace designs do not really appear in Egyptian art until somewhat later, as on the well-known wooden mihrabs of Sayyida Nafisa (1145–6) and Sayyida Ruqayya (1154–60), both now in the Museum of Islamic Art in Cairo. In any event, purely geometric designs – such as those found on the pavement at Palermo – are extremely rare in Fatimid art, where geometry was always combined with vegetal ornament.

The mihrab of Sayyida Nafisa (Figure 4.6), for example, has two geometric patterns. That on the niche itself consists of interlocking eight-pointed stars and polygons delineated by narrow strapwork bands which are interlaced with vegetal arabesques. The design, carved into a solid piece of wood, is based on a $45°$ grid, and it apparently continues beyond the borders of the niche itself. The interlaced radiating design on the face of the mihrab is based on a $60°$ grid; it is constructed out of separate pieces of lath and intricately carved polygonal panels fitted together with tongue-and-groove joints to create a design of six-pointed stars and interlocking bands. Like the carved pattern on the niche, this marquetry pattern makes no concession to the epigraphic frame that surrounds it. The part of the pattern we see is like a piece cut out of an infinite wallpaper design.[21]

The history of Islamic ornament, especially its geometric component, has not yet been chronicled in an entirely satisfactory fashion, perhaps because it is such a difficult subject to write about.[22] Purely geometric designs, in which repeated combinations of lines and curves alone form the 'subject matter', seem to have two sources in Islamic art. One is derived from the geometric subsidiary and border motifs used in the late antique and early Byzantine decoration of the Mediterranean basin. The mosaic floors and stucco wall and balustrade panels of the eighth-century palace at Khirbat al-Mafjar near Jericho, for example, present a virtual catalogue of the types of late antique geometric patterns known in early Islamic times which have been transformed into the subject matter of the decoration.[23]

Another strand of geometric ornament appears somewhat suddenly in the decorative arts of Iran and Central Asia in the tenth and eleventh centuries. It has recently been proposed that this strand,

Fig. 4.6 *Mihrab of Sayyida Nafisa. Museum of Islamic Art, Cairo.*

(After David-Weill, pl. XIV.)

characterised by intricate and angular strapwork designs, was linked
to the emergence of Sunni 'Ashari modes of thought in tenth-century
Baghdad, but there is no contemporary monumental evidence to
either support or disprove the hypothesis. This 'geometric mode'
was supposedly linked to the Sunni revival of the eleventh and
twelfth centuries and resisted by Fatimid and Spanish Umayyad
patrons of the arts until their Ayyubid and Almohad successors
eventually accepted Sunni orthodoxy and the associated mode of
ornament.[24] Unfortunately this seductive theory does not fit the
facts, for not only have we seen already that geometric strapwork
ornament appears in Fatimid art, but this same type of ornament is
also found in the Almoravid (i.e. pre-Almohad) art of Islamic Spain –
and perhaps even in late Umayyad art as well.

The major monument of Almoravid art in Spain is the wooden
minbar formerly in the Kutubiyya mosque in Marrakesh, Morocco.
The enormous minbar, standing 3.86 metres high, was ordered in
1137 by the Almoravid sultan 'Ali ibn Yusuf (1106–43) for the
Almoravid congregational mosque in Marrakesh. An inscription
on the minbar itself states that it was made in Cordoba. It was then
shipped in pieces to Morocco and assembled in Marrakesh. Soon after
the minbar was installed in the Almoravid mosque, the Almohads
took the city, destroying the building and transferring the minbar as a
trophy to their own new mosque in the same city, which eventually
came to be known as the Kutubiyya or Booksellers' mosque.[25]

The wooden frame of the Kutubiyya minbar is completely envel-
oped in a web of extraordinary carved and inlaid decoration, which
represents the full range of Almoravid design and the finest of its
craftsmanship. The minbar's triangular flanks are decorated with an
interlace pattern generated from eight-pointed stars and coordinated
exactly to the height and depth of the minbar's steps (Figure 4.7). The
pattern employs strapwork bands, worked in marquetry of bone and
coloured woods, which cross and twist around each other, forming a
continuous mesh of I-shaped elements and creating a regular pattern
of stars and irregular polygons in the interstices. The infinite design
of the field has been modified at its edges, where the pattern meets
the inscription band. The strapwork bands are not simply cut by the
edges but turn back on themselves and connect so that the under-and-
over pattern is maintained logically. The inscription band, the letters
of which are worked in African blackwood outlined with bone strips,
is displayed against a marquetry ground made of thousands of small
tiles, about 9mm square, which have been pierced and filled with four
tiny blocks of reddish wood and a black paste.

On the flanks finely carved wooden panels in the shape of stars,
elongated hexagons and Y-shaped units have been inlaid in the
interstices between the bands to create a continuously decorated
surface in which the underlying carcass is invisible.[26] The wooden
panels are carved with an amazingly rich variety of largely vegetal
designs; the strapwork bands consist of strips of different coloured

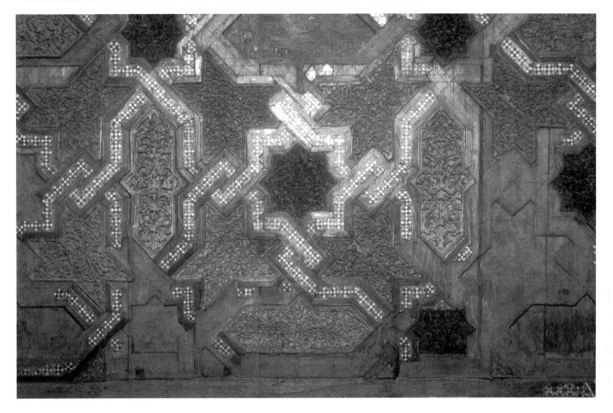

woods surrounding a median strip of marquetry micropatterns made of tiny bone and wooden elements glued together in repeated quincunxes.

Thus, the patterns found on the Kutubiyya minbar are much more similar to those found on the pavement of the Cappella Palatina in Palermo than they are to those in contemporary Fatimid art. Common features include the accommodation of the strapwork bands to the enclosing frame, the use of the 45° grid and the mosaic/marquetry micropatterns down the median strip. The relationship between these two styles is even clearer when one compares the chain-link pattern on the slightly later floor of the presbytery of Monreale Cathedral (see Plate 6) with the type of pattern found on the minbar's flanks. What some scholars had thought to be a 'blending and unification' of the earlier format now appears to be a purer and more nuanced understanding of the principles of Almoravid geometric design.

Before rushing out to discover new connections between Marrakesh and Palermo, however, let us recall that the Kutubiyya minbar was not made in Marrakesh but in Cordoba, once the capital of the Umayyad caliphate in the west and the unquestioned centre of its visual culture. The extraordinary quality of the Kutubiyya minbar indicates that it was not a one-off creation ordered by uncouth Almoravid patrons but the product of a continuous workshop tradition going back at least to the tenth-century minbar of Cordoba and

Fig. 4.7 *Minbar from the Kutubiyya mosque, Marrakesh, detail of decoration.*

(Photograph: J. M. Bloom.)

73

the exquisite carved ivories of Cordoba and Madinat al-Zahra.[27] The carving of the panels on the Kutubiyya minbar is comparable to if not finer than that found on the finest of the Cordoban ivories and shows that the imagined decline of the Cordoban craft industry after the fall of the Umayyads in the early eleventh century is just that – imaginary. That the Cordoban craftsmen prefabricated the minbar for shipment suggests that other pieces – whether large boxes or small chests – might have been similarly made for export. Although all that survives today are mostly provincial reflections on which to base our analysis, we can be sure that throughout the eleventh century and into the twelfth, arts and crafts of the highest quality continued to be produced in Cordoba.

Relations between Norman Sicily and the Almoravids

The unexpected similarities discovered between geometric designs from Almoravid Spain and Norman Sicily suggest that one should look at other examples of Almoravid and Norman-Islamic art and culture to see if other parallels exist. If so, they may revise our understanding of the diffusion of artistic ideas in the medieval Mediterranean basin. The Arab-Norman art of Sicily is routinely compared to and derived from the arts of Fatimid Egypt. The rectangular muqarnas vault of the Cappella Palatina, for example, is normally thought to represent a local survival of a kind of ceiling that no longer exists in Cairo. Muqarnas vaults appear suddenly throughout the Maghrib around 1135.[28] Apart from a few muqarnas elements in the Qubbat al-Ba'adiyyin in Marrakesh (which was the ablution pavilion of the mosque for which the Kutubiyya minbar was made) and the Great Mosque in Tlemcen, Algeria, the muqarnas vaults in the Qarawiyyin Mosque in Fez seem to spring out of nowhere: they are extremely well designed and attain a degree of elegance and beauty which would rarely, if ever, be matched, even in the more famous vaults in the Alhambra. Where did the muqarnas come from?

No early muqarnas survives in Tunisia, but some large plaster muqarnas elements datable to the late eleventh or early twelfth centuries have been found in the ruins of the Qasr al-Salam and the Manar palace at the Qal'a of the Bani Hammad, the palace-city in the mountains of Algeria that was the Hammadid capital for about a century and a half.[29] Archaeologists have reconstructed these elements as the supports for a dome – but not the dome itself – over the entrance to a palace. Scholars also hypothesise that there must have been several other muqarnas vaults at the Qal'a, although none has actually survived. The Qal'a was abandoned for the city of Bone on the Mediterranean coast, and it is imagined that more elaborate muqarnas vaults would have been constructed there, although none has survived there either. It is presumed that these imagined vaults would have provided Roger's architects with the inspiration for the muqarnas ceiling of the Cappella Palatina.

In any event, no rectangular muqarnas vaults like those in the Cappella Palatina are known in the central or eastern Islamic lands, and it has long been acknowledged that the closest parallel to the muqarnas ceiling of the Cappella Palatina is found neither in Egypt or even in those parts of North Africa closest to Sicily, but at the Qarawiyyin mosque of Fez, Morocco. At the Qarawiyyin mosque, a series of muqarnas vaults (Figure 4.8) covers the central aisle of the mosque, which was extensively renovated between 1132 and 1142–3. Inscriptions in the large rectangular muqarnas vault as well as in the square muqarnas vault over the mihrab state that they were ordered by the Almoravid sultan ʿAli ibn Yusuf ibn Tashfin and completed in 1137, or roughly at the same time as the Cappella Palatina.[30] This connection, however, has normally been seen as irrelevant, because it was imagined that the muqarnas technique diffused east to west, from Egypt across North Africa to Tunisia, Algeria, Morocco and finally to Spain. According to this model, Sicilian muqarnas would have derived, if not directly from Egypt, from one of the Fatimid successor principalities in North Africa with which the Normans had contact. Despite the presence of some evidence for muqarnas in Algeria, Tunisian evidence is entirely lacking and the Egyptian evidence is too late.[31]

Western Islamic elements in the design of the Cappella Palatina pavement suggests that the traditional diffusionist model for the building's muqarnas ceiling may also be wrong and that connections should be sought in the western Islamic lands. However, just as the Kutubiyya minbar should be understood as a product of Cordoba, not Marrakesh, the sophisticated muqarnas vaults at the Qarawiyyin mosque in Fez must also be understood as the product of a tradition developed or nursed not in the provincial cities in Morocco but in the metropolitan centres of Spain, even though early Spanish muqarnas ceilings are entirely lost.[32]

A third example of a possible artistic connection between Sicily and the Islamic west is the enigmatic Palermo casket (Figure 4.9), an ovoid wooden box in the treasury of the Cappella Palatina. Measuring 40 × 23 × 39cm, the box has an elliptical base and an elongated hemispherical lid. Incrusted with ivory and a black substance, with traces of red and green, and decorated with a series of figural roundels between bands of poetry inscribed in naskh script, themselves enclosed by decorative bands or geometric ornament, the casket is quite unlike the carved or painted ivory boxes ascribed to Sicily and has traditionally been attributed to Ayyubid, or late twelfth- and early thirteenth-century, Egypt.[33]

Ugo Monneret de Villard, who published this object, found confirmation of this attribution in the long history of incrustation in Egypt, although he could find no close Egyptian parallels to the techniques on the Palermo casket. He did, however, find a rough parallel to the distinctive technique of decorating the box with tiny square tiles drilled and filled with mastic on a piece of woodwork

Fig. 4.8 *Qarawiyyin mosque, Fez, muqarnas vault in the prayer hall.*   (Photograph: after Terasse, fig. 28.)

Fig. 4.9 Wooden box
incrusted with ivory.
Palermo, Cappella Palatina,
Treasury.

(Photograph: after Gabrielli and
Scerrato, fig. 159.)

showing a falcon attacking a hare discovered at Edfu and dated to the
eleventh century, but the Egyptian work is rather coarse.[34] A much
closer parallel is found on the minbar from the Kutubiyya mosque,
where the wooden frame is similarly incrusted with thousands of
comparable tiny tiles, which are used to provide backgrounds to the
main designs.[35] No similarly decorated caskets or articles of furniture
survive from Almoravid Spain, but there is no reason to believe they
were not made. Could the Palermo casket be Spanish rather than
Egyptian?

An exploration of the relations between Sicily and the western
Mediterranean is beyond the scope of this brief article, but it seems
that in our haste to draw connections between Sicily and Fatimid
Egypt we may be overlooking connections between Sicily and Spain.

One of the most important figures at the court of Roger II was the *sharif* Abu 'Abdallah Muhammad al-Idrisi, who had been born of a noble family in Ceuta, Morocco, in 1100. Descended from both the 'Alawi Idrisids, claimants to the caliphate who had ruled the region around Ceuta from the late eighth to the late tenth century, and the Hammudids, the former rulers of Malaga who had migrated to Ceuta in the eleventh centuries, al-Idrisi travelled widely in Morocco and Spain and even ventured as far as southern France and the English coast. Around 1138, or exactly the time when Roger was constructing the Cappella Palatina, the king invited al-Idrisi to Palermo, ostensibly as protection from his enemies, and commanded al-Idrisi to construct a world map and write a commentary on it. The original map is lost, but the book, known variously as *Nuzhat al-mushtaq* (*Pleasant Journeys*) or the *Book of Roger*, made the author famous.

The irony is that al-Idrisi was not a geographer and had little prior knowledge of geography or cartography; the reason for Roger's invitation was to further his own political objectives, which included the conquest of North Africa and Islamic Spain and the establishment of Norman hegemony over the western Mediterranean. After some unsuccessful attempts to gain a foothold in North Africa, Roger conquered Djerba in 1134; Tripoli in 1145; Mahdiyya in 1147; Sousse, Sfax and Gabes in 1148; and Bone in 1153. Al-Idrisi's impressive genealogy, which went back to the prophet Muhammad as well as to the former rulers of Malaga, made him a possible pretender and potential puppet ruler for some new state Roger planned to establish in the conquered territories.[36]

The study of the arts of the western Islamic lands during this period is hampered by the paucity of surviving documents. The wholesale destruction of artworks of the Almohad period – whether religious or secular – by later rulers in Spain and Morocco does not mean they were never made at all. The similarities between the few surviving examples of Almoravid art and the pavement of the Cappella Palatina, its muqarnas ceiling, and the casket suggest that the connections between Norman Sicily and Almoravid Spain and Morocco may have been stronger than previously imagined. Conversely, the connections with Fatimid Egypt may have been less important than once thought. These similarities also show that in the study of the artistic history of the medieval Mediterranean world, although the shortest distance between two points is always a straight line, human geography is far more important for understanding how art and ideas travelled.

Notes

1. Robert Hillenbrand, *Islamic Art and Architecture* (London, 1999), 68.
2. Roberto Cotoneo, 'Palermo II, 2 (ii)', in *The Dictionary of Art*, ed. Jane Turner (London, 1996), 23:844–5.

3. William Tronzo, *The Cultures of his Kingdom: Roger II and the Cappella Palatina in Palermo* (Princeton, 1997), 29.

4. Ibid.; Dorothy Glass, *Studies on Cosmatesque Pavements*, British Archaeological Reports, International Series (Oxford, 1980); Paloma Pajares Ayuela, *Cosmatesque Ornament* (New York, 2001).

5. Tronzo, *Cultures*, 29–37.

6. Ibid., 33–4.

7. Ibid., 30.

8. Ibid., 34.

9. Ibid., 32–3 and fig. 25.

10. Ibid., 37.

11. Ibid., 33, notes 17–18; Glass, *Studies*.

12. Tronzo, *Cultures*, 34.

13. Glass, *Studies*, 4 and n. 15.

14. Tronzo, *Cultures*, 35.

15. Giovanni Curatola, *Eredità Dell'Islam* ([Venice], 1993), no. 86.

16. Tronzo, *Cultures*, 36.

17. Tronzo, *Cultures*, 37.

18. Tronzo, *Cultures*, 99–100.

19. Aziz Ahmad, *A History of Islamic Sicily*, Islamic Surveys (Edinburgh, 1975), 25–40; Clifford Edmund Bosworth, *The New Islamic Dynasties: A Chronological and Genealogical Manual* (Edinburgh, 1996), 33.

20. Ahmad, *Islamic Sicily*, 48–58.

21. K. A. C. Creswell, *The Muslim Architecture of Egypt* (Oxford, 1952–9), I: pls 120c, 121a.

22. In the meantime, see Eva Baer, *Islamic Ornament* (Edinburgh, 1998); Oleg Grabar, *The Mediation of Ornament*, A. W. Mellon Lectures in the Fine Arts, 1989 (Princeton, 1992), ch. 3; Gülru Necipoğlu, *The Topkapi Scroll: Geometry and Ornament in Islamic Architecture* (Santa Monica, 1995), ch. 6.

23. R. W. Hamilton, *Khirbat al-Mafjar: An Arabian Mansion in the Jordan Valley*, with a contribution by Oleg Grabar (Oxford, 1959).

24. Necipolu, *Topkapi Scroll*, ch. 6. Most recently, see Yasser Tabbaa, *The Transformation of Islamic Art during the Sunni Revival* (Seattle and London, 2001), ch. 4: 'The *Girih* Mode: Vegetal and Geometric Arabesque'.

25. Jonathan M. Bloom et al., *The Minbar from the Kutubiyya Mosque* (New York, 1998).

26. Jonathan M. Bloom, 'The Minbar from the Kutubiyya Mosque', in Bloom et al., *The Minbar*, 7.

27. Bloom, 'Minbar', 23.

28. Henri Terrasse, *La Mosquée al-Qaraouiyin à Fès* (Paris, 1968), 31–4.

29. Lucien Golvin, *Recherches archéologiques à la Qal'a Des Banû Hammâd* (Paris, 1965), 125–7; L. Golvin, 'Les plafonds à muqarnas de la Qal'a des Banū Õammåd et leur influence possible sur l'art de la Sicile à la période normande', *Revue de l'Occident Musulman et de la Méditerranée* 17/1 (1974), 63–9.

30. Terrasse, *La Mosquée al-Qaraouiyin*, 31–4.

31. Jonathan M. Bloom, 'The Introduction of the Muqarnas into Egypt', *Muqarnas* 5 (1988), 21–8.

32. Terrasse, *La Mosquée al-Qaraouiyin*, 31; 'Mukarbas', *Encyclopaedia of Islam*, 2nd edn.

33. Ugo Monneret de Villard, *La cassetta incrostata della Cappella Palatina di Palermo*, Monumenti Dell'arte Musulmana in Italia (Rome,

1938); Francesco Gabrieli and Umberto Scerrato, *Gli Arabi in Italia: cultura, contatti e tradizioni* (Milan, 1989), fig. 159.

34. *Trésors fatimides du Caire*, exh. cat., 28 April–30 August 1998, Institut du Monde Arabe (Paris, 1998), no. 10.

35. Bloom et al., *The Minbar*.

36. S. Maqbul Ahmad, 'Cartography of al-Sharif al-Idrisi', in *Cartography in the Traditional Islamic and South Asian Societies*, The History of Cartography 2, ed. J. B. Harley and David Woodward (Chicago, 1992), 156–74; Jonathan M. Bloom, *Paper before Print: The History and Impact of Paper in the Islamic World* (New Haven, 2001), 150.

CHAPTER FIVE

A Kingly Posture: the Iconography of Sultan Husayn Bayqara

Barbara Brend

To see the Timurid world in action we naturally turn to pictures. The majority available to us are illustrations to literary epics and romances, and a minority only shows purported history or the contemporary scene. However, the documentary evidence of literary illustrations is not to be discounted since the artists, having rather few extraneous pictorial sources, must have modelled their pictures largely on the world around them. Conversely, though pictures showing contemporary events or emblematic of the status of a patron would not have carried conviction if they strayed much from an accurate portrayal of actions and paraphernalia, they may, nevertheless, have been moulded into an iconography that seeks to convey a message. It is thus legitimate to search pictures of real subjects for elements that go beyond reportage, and to supplement our information by reference to pictures of fictional happenings.

One of the most notable depictions of the contemporary world to have come down to us is the double-page frontispiece of a *Bustan* of Sa'di, copied for Husayn Bayqara in Rajab 893/June 1488 (*adab fārsī* 908, National Library of Egypt, Cairo), which shows the sultan in a setting of courtly carousal (Plates 7–8).[1] It may be hard for us to tell what here is realism and what convention, but the patron was surely in a position to dictate how he was to be presented. A signature has been erased from the right-hand page, but the picture is almost certainly the work of Mirak. His status as head of the royal library accords with the execution of a royal frontispiece, and details of the treatment match with 'The King of Egypt and the Pauper' in the *Mantiq al-tayr* of 892/1487 (63.210.28, Metropolitan Museum of Art, New York; Figure 5.1), which Melikian-Chirvani has shown to be his work.[2] Mirak was celebrated not only as a painter but as an illuminator and a designer of monumental inscriptions, and the latter skills are evident in his painting. In the frontispiece his palette favours gold and blue, with turquoise-green, some whitish and some dark colours.[3] The conjunction of gold and blue, frequently seen in

Fig. 5.1 '*The King of Egypt and the Pauper*', Mantiq al-tayr, *63.210.28. Metropolitan Museum of Art, New York. Fletcher Fund.*

illumination, carries a latent symbolism of sun and sky, and this is made explicit in the inscriptions here portrayed. On the left-hand page (Plate 7) a pavilion bears a calligraphic frieze which sees the golden brickwork of a castle given an added lustre by the sun. It is natural to interpret the sun as meaning Husayn Bayqara[4] and on the adjacent tentage the metaphor is confirmed in a more iconographic manner. The sultan's titles with his name in gold are contained in a *shamsa* in the middle of an awning placed behind a tent of domical, trellis type.[5] Seen with a small portion obscured by the curved roof of the tent, the *shamsa* is surely meant to represent a rising sun.

Allied to the use of colour, composition has been very carefully judged. Both pages have octagonal courtyards viewed over a barrier. On the left-hand page a solid, dark wall contrasts with a flooring of pale rectangular tiles; on the right-hand page (Plate 8), a white railing is less easily distinguished against a floor of pale hexagonal tiles, rimmed with blue. As a result there is both unity and hierarchy: the eye is drawn – as though by a floodlight – to the left-hand court; the right-hand court – seen as though in a more diffused light – is clearly secondary. Whether Husayn Bayqara's architect had in fact abandoned the traditional red railings – perhaps in a gesture towards silver?[6] – is more than we know, but his painter was certainly able to deploy the idea to build the meaning of the picture. A more important departure from the norm is the fact that Husayn Bayqara is placed on the left-hand side of his double page. Though a western viewer may take a short cut to him, a Timurid would presumably progress in according to his reading direction from the right, so that the effect for him would be unusually dynamic. In the centre of the left-hand page and framed by the tent and awning, Husayn Bayqara stops the eye, since he faces right, and is backed on the left by the pavilion. Before Husayn Bayqara a loose circle is formed by courtiers, musicians, singers and attendants carrying flasks. One man has been overcome by the effects of music, wine, or both. The right-hand court echoes – or better, preludes – the left-hand, but at a less refined level. It also contains a circle of figures; the majority are engaged in ensuring the supply of drink, and one inebriate is being assisted away. The principal figure is seated in the upper left of the circle; his location is approximately equivalent to that of Husayn Bayqara, but subtly less balanced; perched rather uncomfortably on a small dais, he wears a blue robe and a fur-trimmed cap. The round face is evidently a portrait, and it seems that this must be the sultan's eldest son, Badiʿ al-Zaman. The curious isolation, tense figure and averted face suggest that the painter was already aware of bad relations between father and son, a state of affairs that would be confirmed by the latter's rebellion in 902/1496–7.[7]

The intoxicating delights of music and wine are evidently a theme of the picture: as well as being distinctly real, they may, as often in poetry, refer to a state of mystical enlightenment. Two groupings on the extreme right may also carry a symbolic significance. In making his approach, the Timurid viewer might have half noted in the lower right of the right-hand page (Plate 8) an incident past which he was privileged to skirt: a man denied entrance by a gatekeeper with a rod. This vignette may simply illustrate the exclusivity of the court. However, the man excluded or repulsed wears dark clothing, and the fact the he falls back into the margin gives him considerable emphasis. It may thus be that he betokens sorrow or misfortune, which could legitimately be 'banished' from a court. This conceit might then be seen as a forerunner to those informing pictures which show the Mughal Jahangir shooting poverty or his foe Malik ʿAmbar.[8] The scene at the gate is balanced visually by another in the upper right. In this an Indian vina player sits beside an Indian woman who is exercising her skill in distilling.[9] Whether these figures have a particular significance is not clear, but in general terms they indicate the power of Husayn Bayqara's court, which can attract or acquire foreign specialists. The groups of the upper and lower right mark the base of a horizontal, isosceles triangle whose apex is Husayn Bayqara.

Husayn Bayqara wears the colour which may be described as turquoise-green; though not exclusive to kings, it often carries royal connotations (Plate 7). Brighter than any jade available to the Timurids, it is probably to be associated with turquoise(*fīrūza*), and hence victory and prosperity (*fīrūzī*). It is used for Timur and his son ʿUmar Shaykh in illustrations incorporated into the *Zafarnama* copied in 872/1467–8 (John Work Garrett Collection, Johns Hopkins University, Baltimore), which I should date to the 1460s.[10] The colour occurs with varying degrees of emphasis in other royal portraits and depictions of kings from literature.[11] Husayn Bayqara kneels on the left of a carpet facing a young man in blue, who is also kneeling.[12] Amid all the activity of the court he is strikingly in command of himself and of the proceedings. It is probably by intention that he is drawn to a slightly larger scale than the other figures, but this might also result if the figure were taken from a pre-existing model. Evidently a portrait, the face has slanting eyes, and a jaw-line squared up by flesh and a fringe beard.[13] He proffers a rose to the young man, who, overcome with bashfulness, has to be urged to accept: the balance of power between the two is evidently different from that of the literary *topos* in which the older admirer is disdained by a proud youth. Husayn is also shown holding a rose in a double-page picture in the *Gulshan Album* (Gulistan Palace Library, Tehran), in which he is taking his ease in a garden surrounded by his women.[14] The sultan here appears some years younger than in the *Bustan* frontispiece, but it may be suggested that this double page might perhaps have been designed for a *Gulistan* of Saʿdi, which the *Bustan* would follow as a companion-piece. These two instances of flower-holding may mean simply that Husayn Bayqara chose to be depicted as a lover of flowers. That in itself would demonstrate a new departure in portraiture, since, if I am not mistaken, no previous ruler of Iran had declared such an interest in such a manner. There may, however, be an international influence at work. Probably in 1479–80, and thus before the Persian double pages, the Ottoman Mehmed II had been depicted holding a nosegay of roses (H. 2153, 10a, Topkapı Sarayı Kütüphanesi; Figure 5.2); the Ottoman portrait is related to a portrait in oils of Mehmed II, attributed to Gentile Bellini, who was in Istanbul at this period.[15] The Bellini does not include a rose, nevertheless, those shown in the Topkapı picture clearly derive from

Fig. 5.2. Mehmed II, 10a, H. 2153.

(By permission of Topkapı Sarayı Müzesi Müdürlüğü.)

a European model. Portraits in which the sitter holds a token, sometimes a flower, are in fact more characteristic of Netherlandish painting, as for example the *Man with Pinks* of about 1430 by a follower of Jan van Eyck.[16] It thus appears likely that, whether by way of the Ottoman court or independently, the European conception of a portrait with a flower had reached the court of Husayn Bayqara.[17]

A yet more important departure from previous Timurid portraiture is the fact that Husayn Bayqara is kneeling. We know from historians of the Timurids that a protocol of postures and gestures was observed for important encounters, and it is clear that the subservient posture of kneeling would not be adopted unthinkingly.[18] Illustrations to works of literature bear this out. Rulers kneel in exceptional circumstances only: Iskandar from respect when he visits a holy hermit, and from respect and necessity when he comforts the dying Dara.[19] Persons of lesser status must often kneel. Iskandar Sultan's *Anthology* of 1411 (Add. 27261, British Library) has a king, travelling incognito, who kneels as he shares the throne of a Fairy Queen, since he is there at her invitation, while a servant kneels to offer a dish, in spite of the obvious inconvenience.[20] Holymen may also kneel, as the same manuscript shows.[21] The normal sedentary postures for a ruler are three. Whether enthroned or on a carpet, he may be cross-legged, or use a variation on this with one knee raised, or when enthroned he may drop one bent knee sideways, while the other foot is pendant. In the early fourteenth-century *Jami' al-tawarikh* and the Great Mongol *Shahnama* the third posture predominates.[22] Illustrations incorporated into the Khvaju Kirmani *Khamsa* fragment of 798/1396 (Add. 18113, British Library) suggest that Jalayirids sat cross-legged on the throne.[23] The first two postures are applied to Timur in the *Zafarnama* copied in 1436, though he kneels to mourn Muhammad-Sultan;[24] and in the *Zafarnama* copied in 1467–8 he is shown enthroned in the third posture. Similarly, pictures that are certainly, or almost certainly, contemporary representations of Baysunghur, show the prince cross-legged or with one knee raised.[25] Ulugh Beg, accompanied by kneeling wives, is cross-legged (46.26, Freer Gallery of Art, Washington, DC; Figure 5.3). This is also the posture of princes identified as the Turkman Pir Budaq and Sultan Khalil, and later the Uzbek Shibani.[26]

Husayn Bayqara does not kneel in the *Gulshan Album* picture, instead, in the intimate company of his women, he reclines with one knee raised. However, he does kneel in two other pictures. One is a single-figure drawing of the sultan in mature age, reserved against a background of turquoise-green (1958.59, Harvard University Art Museum; see Plate 9); mounted with a Safavid attribution to Bihzad, this is probably datable about 1490.[27] Since the figure is presented without a setting, the kneeling posture must have been selected as either characteristic or appropriate, or both. The other picture, which is earlier, is more complex, and more may be deduced from it. Soudavar has identified a folio in the Art and History Trust Collection as showing the coronation of Husayn Bayqara in March 1469 (Figure 5.4).[28] Husayn kneels on the throne platform but below the actual throne, he is accompanied by a child, presumed to be Badi' al-Zaman, and facing him is a kneeling cleric, whom Soudavar identifies as Qazi Qutb al-Din Ahmad. On the throne is an object that Soudavar identifies as a cushion embroidered with the Profession of Faith. Soudavar sees the position of Husayn in relation to the Profession as referring to the concept of the sultan as the Shadow

Fig. 5.3 (opposite) *Ulugh Beg and court, 1946.26. Freer Gallery of Art, Smithsonian Institution, Washington, DC.*

(Courtesy of the Freer Gallery of Art, Smithsonian Institution, Washington, DC.)

86

Fig. 5.4 *Coronation of Husayn Bayqara. Art and History Trust Collection.*

(Courtesy of Abolala Soudavar.)

of God. While this may be so, it seems likely that the element of assertion in this claim is here less important than that of humility. The position below the throne also recalls the presumably calculated restraint of Timur, who did not adopt a rank above amir and *gūragān*. The new sultan's position in Herat was exceedingly insecure: he had come to power in an opportunistic move on the death of Abu Saʿid, and in 1470 he was to lose control of the city for a period and be obliged to recapture it.[29] The message of the 'Coronation' is surely that Husayn Bayqara, kneeling like Iskandar before a holyman, is the legitimate ruler since his power is ratified by the religious authority. But does the picture record an event or display a calculated iconography? The item bearing the Profession of Faith – with which Husayn is associated by the sap-green of his gown – could as easily be read not as a cushion, but a large block of jade. The cushion or jade would have had to be part of a pre-existing regalia, since either could hardly be made in the two days since Husayn's acquisition of the city. Did the object really exist? It seems quite as likely that we are being presented with a concept rather than a record, and that already at the outset of the reign a clever artist is designing an iconography for the sultan.

The artist in question must surely be Mirak.[30] The dutifully kneeling figure of the 'Coronation' suited the need of a particular moment, but in the 'King of Egypt and the Pauper' of the *Mantiq al-tayr* Mirak appears to modify the meaning of the posture.[31] The fictional king, who is not precisely Husayn Bayqara since he is younger, but who wears turquoise-green, kneels, though on his throne. Demonstrating a point of Sufi thought, he condemns to death, for an insufficient commitment to love a pauper, who perforce also kneels. The king does not need to kneel here, but his posture, alert and disciplined, implies his perfect control of the scene. This picture leads the way to the *Bustan* frontispiece and the *gravitas* of the single-figure portrait. In these the kneeling posture of the sultan implies that he continues to be on good terms with the ʿulama or the powerful Sufi orders, but it also insinuates a secular authority; the impression conveyed is that Husayn is very competent to rule. Though rooted in traditional etiquette, the new posture may also owe something to Europe, for the Timurids may well have assumed that the subject of a bust portrait was kneeling – the question of how to dispose of the legs had evidently been a problem for the painter of Mehmed II.

Clerics or Sufis, often kneeling, are important in two other pictures in the *Bustan* and also in illustrations added in 901/1495–6 for Badiʿ al-Zaman to a *Khamsa* of Navaʾi,[32] but the possibilities offered by the new dignity of the posture are more fully exploited in the Nizami of 900/1494–5 (Or. 6810, British Library, London). Produced for ʿAli Farsi Barlas, the manuscript was probably a diplomatic gift from Husayn Bayqara. Thus a frontispiece attributable to Mirak, and showing the dedicatee cross-legged and wearing pink, is surely intended to show him as of lesser status than Bayqara.[33] The king Hurmuz is depicted as rather resembling Husayn, but he is somewhat older and in an older posture. Instead, it is to Iskandar that Husayn is assimilated, and in two profound pictures he is shown wearing turquoise-green and kneeling.[34] The posture is required for 'Iskandar visits the Hermit', but in 'Iskandar with his Seven Philosophers' the choice is probably deliberate (Plate 10).[35] Iskandar here inclines forward, combining royal dignity with an element of deference. He is to be understood as being *primus inter pares*, in the narrative a philosopher-king, or in the world of Herat almost a Sufi shaykh. By contrast, outside the wall, the gate-keeper sits in the formerly royal posture with pendant leg. The new iconography is also used to transform an illustration whose subject is not royal. Robed in tur-quoise-green, virtuous Bishr kneels as he fishes in the well for drowned Malika; in a very similar composition of the 1420s he had been shown standing.[36] It is not clear whether Bishr is intended to refer to directly to Husayn Bayqara, but the scene gains immea-surably in solemnity.

The conception of the kneeling ruler was adopted by the Safavids but it is not clear when this took place. The *Shahnama* for Shah Tahmasp suggests that it was not in the early sixteenth century, but a seventeenth- or eighteenth-century mural in the Chihil Sutun would have us believe that Tahmasp already kneeled.[37] Whether following the tradition of Tabriz or of Herat, Mughal painting from an early period showed kneeling figures on formal occasions, as demonstrated by 'Princes of the House of Timur' (1913.2–8.1, British Museum; Plate 11). In painting for Akbar, the emperor himself kneels occasionally but is more often cross-legged; by contrast, his grand-father Babur is usually portrayed kneeling.[38] Jahangir sits variously, including in a European manner, but as 'Lord of Time' he kneels to convey respect for dervishes.[39] Under Shah Jahan protocol is aptly used in the dynastic trios in which Timur and Akbar sit cross-legged, respectively between kneeling Humayun and Babur, and Jahangir and Shah Jahan.[40] Shah Jahan also kneels alone on the Peacock throne (651.1983, Arthur M. Sackler Museum, Harvard University Museums, Cambridge; Plate 12). Whether or not he is mindful of his ancestor Bayqara, he holds in his hand a flower.

Thus an innovation of the late fifteenth century long continued influential: at the dawn of the period of empires it must have suited a new conception of kingliness.

Notes

1. Laurence Binyon J. V. S. Wilkinson, and Basil Gray, *Persian Miniature Painting* (repr. New York, 1971), pls LXX A-B, no. 83; Thomas W. Lentz and Glenn D. Lowry, *Timur and the Princely Vision* (Los Angeles, 1989), 260–1, no. 146; *Persian Masters: Five Centuries of Painting*, ed.

Sheila R. Canby (Bombay, 1990), 48–9. See also *The Arts of Islam* (London, Hayward Gallery, 1976), no. 581.

2. Assadullah Souren Melikian-Chirvani, 'Kh^wāje Mīrak Naqqāsh' *Journal asiatique* 276 (1988), 97–146, esp. 110 and figs 2 and 3. (Sheila S. Blair and Jonathan M. Bloom, 'Signatures on Works of Islamic Art and Architecture', *Damaszener Mitteilungen* 11 (1999), 60–1, are rather hasty in disputing the presence of a signature, since the ambiguity of its form is surely a deliberate *jeu d'esprit*). Compare the broad faces with glum mouths, the use of inscriptions and architecture with jars in niches. Presumably the painter's name was removed from the frontispiece because it was not Bihzad.

3. It appears that the robe of the extreme left-hand figure has been overpainted, changing russet to blue; this may have been at the hand of the original painter (Plate 7).

4. Like many another ruler, Husayn Bayqara was associated with the sun: W. M. Thackston (tr. and ed.), *Khwandamir: Habibu's-Siyar: Tome Three* (Cambridge, MA, 1994), 2:412.

5. Creatures depicted on the awning are probably decorative rather than symbolic by this period.

6. In 1613 Jahangir ordered a wooden railing decorated with silver, Alexander Rogers (tr.) and Henry Beveridge (ed.), *Tuzuk-i-Jahangiri* (repr. New Delhi, 1978), 1:242.

7. *Khwandamir*, 2:457; Badi' al-Zaman was probably born in 1458, 2:413 (and 382).

8. Robert Skelton, 'Imperial Symbolism in Mughal Painting', in *Content and Context of Visual Arts in the Islamic World*, ed. Priscilla Soucek (Philadelphia and London, 1988), 177–91, figs 5 and 2.

9. Distilling was evidently an Indian speciality, Norah M. Titley, *Persian Miniature Painting* (London, 1983), fig. 66.

10. Sir Thomas Arnold, *Bihzād and his Paintings in the Zafar-nāmah MS.* (London, 1930), pls I-II, III-IV, VII-VIII; Lentz and Lowry, *Timur*, 264–7; Ebadollah Bahari, *Bihzad, Master of Persian Painting* (London and New York, 1996), 70–7; see also Eleanor G. Sims, *The Garrett Manuscript of the Zafar-name: a Study in Fifteenth-century Timurid Patronage*, (New York University, unpublished Ph.D. dissertation, 1973), 97. With regard to the dating, see Barbara Brend, *Perspectives on Persian Painting: Illustrations to Amīr Khusrau's Khamsah* (London, 2003), ch. VI.

11. Lentz and Lowry, *Timur*, 243, 250, 279, 283; Bahari, *Bihzad*, 166–7.

12. Below the carpet is inscribed the word ṣuffa, which usually implies a dais, but there is no structure here. Other seemingly otiose inscriptions identify other structures. It is hard to believe that they are instructions to the painter, but puzzling to imagine why they would be added later.

13. Babur provides a description, Annette Susannah Beveridge (tr.), *The Bābur-nāma in English* (London, 1922), 258.

14. BWG, pl. LXVII; Basil Gray and André Godard, *Iran: Persian Miniatures – Imperial Library* (New York, 1956), pls XVI-XVII; Bahari, *Bihzad*, 110–11.

15. Carel J. Du Ry, *Art of Islam* (Baden-Baden and New York, 1970), 186; Esin Aıl, 'Ottoman Miniature Painting under Sultan Mehmed II', *Ars Orientalis* 9 (1973), 103–20, esp. 111; Filiz Çağman 'Ottoman', tr. Esin Aıl, in *The Anatolian Civilisations* (Istanbul, 1983), 3: E. 9.

16. Lorne Campbell, *Renaissance Portraits* (New Haven, 1990), 69. I thank Professor Francis Ames-Lewis for guidance on this point.

17. 'Kneeling Dervish' attributed to Bihzad shows a knowledge of European shading, Bahari, *Bihzad*, 176; F. R. Martin, *The Miniature Paintings and Painters of Persia, India and Turkey* (London, repr. 1968), pl. 85, may be a copy.

18. *Khwandamir*, 2: 420; *Babur-nama*, 159.

19. Basil Gray (ed.), *The Arts of the Book in Central Asia* (Paris and London, 1979) (henceforth *ABCA*), pl. XLV; Norah M. Titley, 'A Khamsa of Niẓāmī dated Herat, 1421', *The British Library Journal*, 4/2 (1978), 161–86, figs 20–1.

20. Ivan Stchoukine, *Les peintures des manuscrits tîmûrides* (Paris, 1954), pl. XIX.

21. Ibid., pl. XX.

22. David Talbot Rice, *The Illustrations to the 'World History' of Rashīd al-Dīn*, ed. Basil Gray (Edinburgh, 1976), *passim*; Oleg Grabar and Sheila Blair, *Epic Images and Contemporary History* (Chicago and London, 1980), *passim*.

23. Stchoukine, *Manuscrits tîmûrides*, pl. VII.

24. Lentz and Lowry, *Timur*, 105; Eleanor Sims, 'Ibrāhīm-Sultān's Illustrated *Ẓafar-nāmeh* of 839/1436', *Islamic Art* 4 (1991), 185–94; fig. 27 is the exception.

25. *ABCA*, pl. L; Lentz and Lowry, *Timur*, 111, 124 (fig. 40), 125.

26. Gray and Godard, *Iran*, pl. XI; *ABCA*, fig. 135; Bahari, *Bihzad*, 172.

27. Lentz and Lowry, *Timur*, 243; Bahari, *Bihzad*, 173. There seems no good reason to doubt that the portrait is contemporary.

28. Abolala Soudavar, *Art of the Persian Courts* (New York, 1992), 86–8, no. 29.

29. *Kwandamir*, 2:420–8.

30. In making the claim for Mirak, I beg to differ from Mr Soudavar. Faces suggest the hand of Mirak, other factors are argued in Brend, *Perspectives*, ch. VI.

31. Melikian-Chirvani, 'Khʷāje Mīrak Naqqāsh''; Lentz and Lowry, *Timur*, 279.

32. *BWG*, pls LXVI, LXX-A and B; Bahari, *Bihzad*, 106–7, and 156–65, esp. 156.

33. Bahari, *Bihzad*, 130–1.

34. Lentz and Lowry, *Timur*, 250; Bahari, *Bihzad*, 152, 155.

35. Among British Library manuscripts, Iskandar probably kneels in Or. 2931, 466a, but does not in Or. 2834, 346a, nor I. O. Islamic 387, 422b.

36. Bahari, *Bihzad*, 150, Or. 6810; contrast Ernst J. Grube, *The Classical Style in Islamic Painting* (New York, 1968), no. 18.

37. Martin Bernard Dickson and Stuart Cary Welch, *The Houghton Shahnameh* (Cambridge, MA and London, 1981), *passim*; *The Arts of Persia*, ed. Robert Ferrier (New Haven and London, 1989), 215, pl. 32. It has been suggested that the latter dates from the early eighteenth century, after the fire that destroyed the hall in 1706: Stephen P. Blake, *Half the World: The Social Architecture of Safavid Isfahan, 1590–1722*, Islamic Art and Architecture 9 (Costa Mesa, 1999), 68; I would like to thank the editor for bringing this to my attention.

38. Geeti Sen, *Paintings from the Akbar Nama* (Calcutta, etc., 1984), *passim*; M. S. Randhawa, *Painting from the Bābur-nāmā* (sic) (New Delhi, 1983), *passim*.

39. Stuart Cary Welch, *Imperial Mughal Painting* (London, 1978), pl. 22.

40. Amina Okada, *Imperial Mughal Painters* (Paris, n.d.), 30, 32.

CHAPTER SIX

Musical Beasts: The Swan-Phoenix in the Ibn Bakhtīshūʿ Bestiaries

Anna Contadini

As Robert Hillenbrand has shown considerable interest over the years in the 'reading' of paintings, including those in bestiaries,[1] it seems appropriate to dedicate this paper to him especially as the topic to be discussed also ties in with his love of music.

In what have become known as the bestiaries of the Ibn Bakhtīshūʿ tradition the treatment of each animal is normally divided into two sections: a discussion of characteristics which derives from Aristotle's Zoology; and a listing of medicinal preparations utilising different parts of the animal which derives from Ibn Bakhtīshūʿ himself.[2] The last member of a renowned family of Nestorian physicians who ran the School of Medicine at Jundīshāpūr (south-west Iran), ʿUbayd Allāh Ibn Jibrāʾīl Ibn Bakhtīshūʿ (d. 1058), was a contemporary and friend of Ibn Butlān. Of his various works on medicine the most celebrated is the *Kitāb tabāʾiʿ al-ḥayawān wa khawāṣṣihā wa manāfiʿ aʿḍāʾihā* ('Book of the characteristics of animals and their properties and the usefulness of their organs'), which, however, only survives as incorporated into the composite text of the *Kitāb naʿt al-ḥayawān* (henceforth *Naʿt*) and the later bestiaries of the same tradition.

A text for the swan-phoenix is present in two of the illustrated Ibn Bakhtīshūʿ bestiaries: the *Naʿt*, where it is called *arghūn* (Plate 13) and the Escorial *Manāfiʿ*, where it is called *suryānās*[3] (Plate 14). It is also found in a fourteenth-century unillustrated version of Ibn Bakhtīshūʿ's bestiary, where it is called *sīrinās*.[4] This animal is absent from the somewhat reduced version of the Paris *Manāfiʿ*, and likewise from the Morgan *Manāfiʿ*.[5]

Similar versions to the *Naʿt* and the Escorial *Manāfiʿ* are found elsewhere in zoological literature. For example, we find the following account in the fourteenth century author al-Damīrī in his *Hayāt al-ḥayawān* (*A Zoological Lexicon*), where, on the authority of al-Qazwīnī, it is called Abū Sayrās. Jayakar translates the passage as follows:

Al-Kazwînî states in *al-Ashkâl* that it is a certain animal found in thickets and having in its nasal cavity twelve perfect holes. When it breathes, there is heard coming from its nose a sound like the sounds of flutes, and the other animals thereupon gather (round it) to hear that sound; if any of them happens to become confounded with the sound, it seizes that animal and eats it, but if it does not find it practicable to seize any of them, it gives a terrible scream, upon which the other animals separate and flee away from it.[6]

As for al-Qazwīnī himself (end of the thirteenth century), we find in his *ʿAjāʾib al-Makhluqāt* two 'musical' animals represented, in the illustrated copies of this text,[7] not as birds but as quadrupeds, although the text itself does not specify the type of animal. It is only for the second one that we may infer, from the text, that it is a quadruped, as it has a horn. The texts may be translated as follows:

The Sīrānas. It is said that the Sīrānas is a creature which can be found in the thickets of Kabul and Zabulistan. It has twelve holes in its beak. Whenever it breathes, one hears in its breath the sound of the *mizmār* [a woodwind instrument], and it is believed that the *mizmār* was created after this creature's beak. Birds, wild animals and other creatures always gather around the Sīrānas in order to listen to its sound. Sometimes they are overwhelmed by the ecstasy of listening. When the Sīrānas notices that they have swooned away it kills as many as it wants. If it does not want to eat any of them it may be annoyed at them gathering around and so it lets out a fearful screech, from which all the animals flee.

The Shādawār. This is a creature that can be found in the furthest regions of the Byzantine empire. It is also called *ars*. It has a horn, and this horn has forty-two hollow branches. When the wind blows, the air collects inside and one can hear a very sweet sound coming from it. The animals gather around the creature to listen to the sound. It is reported that a horn of one of those animals was given to a king as a gift. He placed it in front of him when the wind blew, whereupon it produced a sound such that those who heard it were almost overwhelmed by delight. From the horn came such a wonderful sound that the king's ears almost stopped out of sheer rapture. Then he put it upside down, and out of the horn came a sound so sad that from hearing it people were almost compelled to weep.[8]

The text in the three Ibn Bakhtīshūʿ manuscripts is peculiar, as it does not strictly conform to the bipartite characteristics plus usefulness structure: the second section is missing in the *Naʿt*, and it is only briefly represented in the Escorial and Princeton manuscripts.

The text in the *Naʿt* is briefer than the other two, but congruent with them:

[Fo. 55r:] (*Characteristics of the arghūn*). The authorities on animals and the interpretation of ancient sources say that this is a sea animal

94

[fo. 55v] with a large beak in which there are various holes producing a variety of sounds (*Representation of the Arghūn*, and miniature) and melodies so marvellous that they render those who listen unable to move. Some claim that from it the Phrygians derived the reed-pipe (*zamr*), with which they used to cure various illnesses. It is also said that it is a sea animal which produces entrancing sounds and that seafarers call it 'the one who plays the reed-pipe (*zāmir*)'.

A more substantial version is related in the Escorial *Manāfiʿ* (and virtually identical in the Princeton manuscript) as follows:

[Fo. 112r:] *The suryānās, which is the one that plays a wind instrument* (miniature of the *suryānās*). According to the authorities on animals and those of musical science and those who interpret ancient sources, this is a sea bird with a big beak [fo. 112v] in which there are various holes producing a variety of sounds and melodies so marvellous that they render those who listen unable to move. Some claim that from it the Phrygians derived the reed-pipe (*zamr*), with which they used to cure various illnesses. It is also said that it is a sea animal which produces entrancing sounds and that seafarers call it 'the one who plays the reed-pipe (*zāmir*)'. We were told by Yānis ibn Isṭīfan, the interpreter who brought a missive from the Byzantine emperor to the noble presence of al-Naṣr (may he reign for ever!), that people heard these sounds on certain islands, tried to find them and encountered walls constructed with holes such that when the wind blew through them one could hear these marvellous sounds. The inhabitants of these islands call this *sīrīnā*. It seems that these people built these walls as a trap so that when this animal heard sounds similar to its own it would go there and in this way it could be hunted. [fo. 113r] Authorities on medical science have spoken of the useful properties of this animal, among which is that its bile, when mixed with a little musk and diluted in water of fleawort in the weight of a *qirāt* then being given as a nasal injection to the insane, is marvellously beneficial.

To what extent might this story relate to a real animal as well as being a weaving together of various mythical strands; and might one also suspect contamination with knowledge of mechanical contrivances? The names given already suggest a conflation, indeed a confusion, of ideas of differing origins. In the *Naʿt* we have *arghūn*, suggesting an association with an instrument, the hydraulis, a water-powered organ that was less purely musical than a sonorous part of the world of automata familiar with, for example, al-Jazarī, and in this connection one could well imagine a parallel, in the holes of the beak and the imitative sound-producing wall, with mechanical 'musical' or 'noise-producing' animals, not just in Byzantine times but also in the Islamic period, as, probably, witnessed by the Pisa Griffin.[9] The possibility of such a connection is strengthened by the fact that the *arghūn*/hydraulis was never integrated into Arab musical practice, remaining a curiosity: it was, essentially, a cultural reference helping to display knowledge of the Byzantine and ancient Greek worlds. It was of interest as a cunning mechanical contrivance, and was either understood as an extremely loud instrument used on the battlefield or misunderstood, revealingly, as a string instrument.[10] The various forms *suryānās* or *sīrīnās* bring us back to wind instrument, suggesting an echo of the Greek siren overlaid on *suryānay* (itself a variant of the more usual *surnāy*), a reed-pipe.[11]

The siren element of the narrative is incontestible, however brief the reference to the seductive voice that enchants those who hear it. As for the instrument on to which the voice is projected, the *nāy* element of the name will later denote a rim-blown flute, but although it is by no means easy to relate the early vocabulary of wind instruments to particular types, it seems likely that *nāy* could also designate a reed instrument, and the probability that the *surnāy* was such an instrument is reinforced by the introduction of the term *zāmir*, both in the narrative and in the title of the Escorial miniature. In more recent times the related forms *mizmār* and *zummāra* have been used to designate single-reed instruments, while *zurna*, *sorna* (*surnāy*) are associated with double-reed instruments of the shawm type. But irrespective of whether a single or double reed was intended, the association is reinforced by the reference to the Phrygians, who are, indeed, reported in Greek sources as having had a particular relationship with the aulos.[12]

Classical authority is, in any case, explicitly invoked at the beginning, through the reference to 'those who interpret ancient sources', and indirectly claimed for the later part, by couching it as information supplied by a contemporary Byzantine visitor, and classical derivations may reasonably be proposed for other elements in the narrative. The siren theme, for example, generates both the identification with a sea bird or animal, mention of seafarers, and the location of the sound lures on islands. Also of ultimately classical origin are the medicinal properties attributed to the reed-pipe, although these could well have been mediated through earlier Islamic texts, as the doctrine of affect/ *ta'thīr*, including the notion of the power of music to influence the various humours and hence restore their equilibrium, is one that is discussed by both al-Kindī and the Ikhwān al-Safā' and will later be elaborated into a specific theory of musical therapeutics.[13]

What remains is the crucial conversion of the siren into a musical bird. According to the Physiologus and Isidoro di Siviglia, the siren was half-woman and half-bird, of a type similar to a goose. This is the way three sirens are represented in a Roman mosaic of the third century AD within the 'Ulysses and the Sirens' panel: half-woman and half-bird (although evidently not a goose), one holding two aulos, one singing and one holding a lyra.[14] It seems that the image of half-woman and half-fish is a later version that appears in the *Liber monstrorum*.[15]

Particularly instructive is the contemporary portrayal of the *qaqnus* in Farīd al-Dīn 'Aṭṭār's *Manṭiq al-Ṭair* ('The Speech of the Birds'):

There is the Qaqnus, a peerless bird, heart-enrapturing;
This bird's abode in Hindustan.
It has a strong beak of astonishing length,
Like a reed-pipe, in it many apertures;
There are about a hundred holes in its beak.
It has no mate: it functions entirely virginally.
There is in every stop a different note,
Beneath every note of its, a different mistery.
When on all the stops it moans its plaintive song,
On its account birds and fishes are filled with ecstasy.
All the birds fall mute; In rapture at its lament, senseless do they fall.
There was a philosopher, he took to its harmonies:
The art of music from its singing he took.
The years of its life were about a thousand.
It clearly knew the time of its death.
When, the time of dying, it divorced its heart from itself,
Round itself it collected ten or more loads of brushwood bundles.
In the midst of all this kindling it set up a great commotion;
It emitted a hundred notes, its own mornful dirge;
Then from each of those stops, for its pure soul
Another keening wail, filled with awful grief, it uttered.
While from every hole, like the paid mourner,
It made a different lament in another key,
In the middle of the dirge for the sorrow of death,
All the time it was seized with trembling like a leaf.
At its shrieking all the birds of the air,
And at its piping all the beasts of the field
Came towards it as the onlookers.
Their hearts all at once divorced from the world:
Because of its grieving that day in its agony,
A multitude of living creatures with it would die.
All at its laments into confusion fell.
Some through lack of strength did expire.
It was a most amazing day, that day of its;
Tears of blood dripped at its soul-searing wail.
Then, when its life reached the final breath,
Its wings and flight feathers would it flap backwards and forwards.
A fire sprang out from under its pinions.
Then this fire changed the phoenix's state:
The fire quickly falling into the kindling faggots,
So that it flares up, completely to set the firewood alight.
The bird and the wood both turn to embers.
After the embers come the ashes too.
When no live embers are left to be seen,
A phoenix rises from the ashes to be seen.
Once the fire reduces that kindling to cinders,
From the midst rises up a baby Qaqnus.[16]

The parallels with the text of the bestiaries are striking. But what we encounter here is an actual identification, and a conflation of the phoenix legend with that of the swan-song.

As the bestiary texts nowhere identify a particular species, we need to turn to the two miniatures to see if there is any reflex of ʿAṭṭār's identification with the swan or, more generally, whether there was agreement as to what sort of bird this was thought to be.[17]

The Miniatures

The miniature in the *Naʿt* is very impressive (Plate 13). It is of a light-blue bird with the characteristic gold roundels to mark the upper part of the wings. There is only a red line to mark the lower part of the miniature, but despite the absence of landscape elements which would have given scale, the bird depicted is clearly meant to be rather large, as indeed occupies a large part of the page. Considered in relation to the other birds, the features that may provide identificatory clues are body shape, beak and feet. With regard to the feet, it may be noted that text and miniature are discrepant: for what is described as a seabird one would expect webbed feet, but although webbed feet were certainly part of the painter's repertoire, being given on the duck (fo. 10r), the feet of the *arghūn* are the generalised claw type given for all other birds, predatory or not. As far as the shape of the body is concerned, it is to be connected not with birds of prey, but, rather, with the heron, crane, duck or hen.

The gold beak has numerous holes in it, represented by black dots, and its shape is curved, similar to most other birds depicted in the manuscript, and, unlike the body, is not connected with that of the duck, but rather with birds of prey such as the falcon or the eagle (fos 29v and 27r).

In the Escorial *Manāfiʿ*, as is usual, the miniature is framed by thin blue lines with decorative devices at the corners, and the bird is set against a gold background (Plate 14). It is again rather large, but this time orange in colour. The neck and body bear a resemblance to a goose, a duck or a swan, but again it has not got webbed feet, but feet with claws. The beak is particularly long here, similar to a goose and some types of duck, thickening towards the end. The holes in the beak are rendered as small, regular circles. In this manuscript too webbed feet are only given to the duck and the goose (fo. 16r).

Although much more could be said about the miniatures, their composition remains analogous to that of the text, differing only in the range of motifs available to the painter. The text is a complex combination of multiple themes, shaping into a new form of narrative elements derived from myths of the sea and the sky, of sound and enchantment, endlessly reprocessed since classical antiquity and, for all the gaps in documentation, leaving a trail of textual residues that allow for detailed scholarly investigation of connections and origins. In echoing this material the miniatures also call upon a repertoire of pictorial conventions for which analogies and antecedents can be located, but have the harder task of creating a depiction of the imaginary through a playful combination of a relatively limited stock of visual conventions. Moreover, the imaginary elements to which the miniature must respond are primarily narrative: to help visualise the creature the only clues the text offers are that it is a seabird and has a large beak. Although by no means ornithologically naive (herons are not portrayed like grouse nor hawks like geese), the various bird miniatures can be viewed as variations on a set of types, each characterised by the standardised shapes of its various body parts and by size. It is hardly surprising, therefore, that both painters should have settled for a bird of imposing size and with the substantial plump body-type associated with ducks and geese, and that as much in order to accommodate the depiction of numerous holes as to follow the statements about the size of the beak both painters emphasise this feature, even if differing in the type chosen. That the feet of this seabird are not webbed can then be read as a further clue: if all the morphological features (apart from the holes in the beak) occur in the depiction of real birds, it is the abnormal combination of them that signals the imaginary.

Notes

1. Robert Hillenbrand, 'Mamluk and Ilkhanid Bestiaries: Convention and Experiment', *Ars Orientalis* 20 (1991), 149–87.
2. For an account of the text and textual tradition of the so-called Ibn Bakhtīshūʿ bestiaries, see Anna Contadini, 'The *Kitāb Naʿt al-Hayawān* (Book on the Characteristics of Animals, BL, Or. 2784) and the "Ibn Bakhtīshūʿ" Illustrated Bestiaries', Ph.D. thesis, SOAS, University of London, 1992, and Contadini, 'The Ibn Buḫtīšūʿ Bestiary Tradition: The Text and its Sources', *Medicina nei Secoli. Arte e Scienza*, 6/2 (1994), 349–64.
3. For the *Naʿt (Kitāb naʿt al-hayawān)*, British Library, Or. 2782, datable to c. 1220, see Anna Contadini, 'The *Kitāb Naʿt al-Hayawān*' and Contadini, 'A Bestiary Tale: Text and Image of the Unicorn in the *Kitāb naʿt al-hayawān*' (British Library, Or. 2784), *Muqarnas* 20, 2003, pp. 17–33. For the *Kitāb manāfiʿ al-hayawān*, probably Damascus, dated 755/1354 in the Biblioteca Real of San Lorenzo del Escorial, Ms 898, see Contadini, 'The *Kitāb Manāfiʿ al-Hayawān* in the Escorial Library', *Islamic Art* 3 (1988–9), 33–57.
4. Princeton, University Library, Ar. Ms. Garrett 1065, fo. 175v.
5. Ibn Bakhtīshūʿ, *Kitāb manāfiʿ al-hayawān*, dated 700/1300, probably Egypt, now in the Bibliothèque Nationale in Paris, Ar. 2782: see Anna Contadini, 'The *Kitāb Naʿt al-Hayawān*', 166–70; also *A l'ombre d' Avicenne: la médicine au temps des califes*, exhibition at the Institut du Monde Arabe, Paris, 1996, no. 32 with col. pls at 125–6 and 232; *Kitāb manāfiʿ al-hayawān*, in Persian, dated between 1295 and 1299, produced in Maragha, now in New York, Pierpont Morgan Library, M. 500, fo. 54r: see Contadini, 'The *Kitāb Naʿt al-Hayawān*', 153–61; Barbara Schmitz, *Islamic and Indian Manuscripts and Paintings in the Pierpont Morgan Library*, (New York, 1997), cat. no. 1.

6. *Al-Damīrī's Hayāt al-Hayawān (A Zoological Lexicon),* tr. from the Arabic by A. Ṣ. G. Jayakar (London and Bombay, 1908), vol. 2, pt 1, 96.

7. See, for example, the Qazwīnī manuscript in the National Library in Munich, Cod. Arab. 464, fo. 181v, where miniatures of both the Sīrānas and the Shādawār are found. For this manuscript and its illustrations, see H. C. Graf von Bothmer, 'Die illustrationen des Münchner Qazwīnī von 1280 AD', Ph.D. dissertation, Universität München, 1971. For reproductions of the Shādawār, which is sometimes identified with the unicorn, from various Qazwīnī manuscripts, see Richard Ettinghausen, *The Unicorn,* Freer Gallery of Art Occasional Papers, vol. 1, no. 3, Washington, 1950, pls 42 and 43.

8. Ferdinand Wüstenfeld, *Zakarija Ben Muhammed Ben Mahmud el-Cazwini's Kosmographie,* Dieterische Buchhandling (Göttingen, 1849), 397 and 398 (Arabic text).

9. See Anna Contadini, Richard Camber and Peter Northover, 'Beasts that Roared: The Pisa Griffin and the New York Lion', in W. Ball and L. Harrow (ed), *Cairo to Kabul: Afghan and Islamic Studies Presented to Ralph Pinder-Wilson* London, 2002, 65–83.

10. Henry George Farmer, 'Ibn Khurdadhbih on Musical Instruments', *Journal of the Royal Asiatic Society* (1928) 509–18 (esp. 512 and 516).

11. Henry George Farmer, *Studies in Oriental Musical Instruments,* first series (London, 1931), 56–8, also mentions the name *suryānayi* and says that this form occurs in al-Masʿūdī and in the *Kitāb al-mūsīqī al-kabīr* of al-Fārābī (d. c. 950). Also, he says that 'As far back as 1840, Kosegarten suggested that it was intended for surnāyī' (57). He suggests that *suryānayi* would appear to have been the original form, and it was due to the fact that it was a Syrian instrument (*nāy rūmī*), the word being derived apparently from *Suryā* (Syria) and *nayi* or *nāy* (reed). The Syrians had long been noted for their 'wood-wind' instruments (58).

12. M. L. West, *Ancient Greek Music* (Oxford, 1992), 330–1: 'The aulos is first attested at the end of the eighth century [BC]. From at least the fifth century the Greeks believed that they owed the introduction of aulos music to a Phrygian or Mysian piper called Olympus ... Another Phrygian, Hyagnis or Agnis, was held to [331] have been the first aulete of all ... But certainly the Greeks felt the aulos to be especially appropriate to the Phrygian mode, and Phrygian slave auletes were not unfamiliar figures in Archaic Greek society.'

13. See Eckhard Neubauer, 'Arabische Anleitungen zur Musiktherapie', *Zeitschrift für Geschichte der Arabisch-Islamischen Wissenschaften* 6 (1990) [pub. 1991], 227–72.

14. M. Blanchard-Lemée et al., *Mosaics of Roman Africa: Floor Mosaics from Tunisia* (London, 1996) fig. 185.

15. 'De Sirenis. Sirenae sunt marinae puellae quae navigantes pulcherrima forma et cantus decipiunt dulcitudine. Et a capite usque ad umbelicum sunt corpore virginali, et humano generi simillimae: squamosas tamen piscium caudas habent, quibus in gurgite semper latent', as in *Liber monstrorum de diversis generibus* ed. C. Bologna (Milan, 1977), 42, no.6.

16. Farīdu'd-Dīn ʿAttār, *The Speech of the Birds. Concerning Migration to the Real. The Mantiqu't-Tair,* presented in English by P. W. Avery, The Islamic Texts Society, Cambridge 1998, 208–10. For the Persian text, see the edition by Goharin (Tehran, 1374), 129–31. About the name Qaqnus, Avery gives the following explanation: 'Qaqnus or Qaqnūs, for the Greek *kúknos,* Latin *cycnus,* or *cygnus,* the "swan", especially

famed in ancient legend for its dying song, but the word might also be translated "phoenix". For, in addition to its having the power to produce amazing music by letting the wind on a mountain-top blow through, some accounts say, as many as three-hundred and sixty holes in its powerful beak, it is a bird that, after living a thousand years, collects a mound of brushwood, and then by ecstatically flapping its wings, produces fire which lights the faggots so that the bird is burnt away, but it parthenogenetically produces an egg that is left in the ashes so that, in its offspring, this bird may rise again.' See also M. H. Ibn al-Khalaf al-Tabrizī, *Burhān-i Qāti'*, ed. M. Mo'īn, 4 vols (Tehran, 1951–6), 3:1535–6.

17. C. R. Bravo-Villasante, *Libro de las Utilidades de los Animales* (Madrid, 1980), 100, identifies the bird as a pelican, but there is no supporting evidence for this identification either lexicographical or textual. The story of the pelican as is found in the medieval bestiaries of the west and in their predecessor the *Physiologus* is totally different from the *suryanas/arghūn* story in our bestiaries. In the *Physiologus* we find the very famous story which will then be repeated almost unchanged in the medieval bestiaries of the west: that the Pelican greatly loves its young, but when these grow up they rebel or attack their parents, who, becoming very angry, kill them. But after three days the parents regret what they have done and so the mother picks at her right side so that blood flows all over the young and in this way they are revived. This, in the moralising *Physiologus* and bestiaries, is a metaphor for Christ, who shed his blood to save humanity and so forgave its mortal sins.

CHAPTER SEVEN

Cup, Branch, Bird and Fish: An Iconographical Study of the Figure Holding a Cup and a Branch Flanked by a Bird and a Fish

Abbas Daneshvari

Little is known about the iconography of the imagery that adorns the ceramic ware of the Islamic world in the ninth and the tenth centuries. The morphologies and the schemes of representation from this early and formative period are fascinating, for they have often proven to be harbingers of the stylistic and iconographical themes that define the art of Islam in the many centuries hence. In addition the iconography of these images, when understood, frequently illuminate the socio-cultural context of their production.

One of the most tantalising of images from the ninth and the tenth centuries is that of the seated ruler or dignitary holding a branch in one hand and a cup in the other. This appears on a number of vessels, among them an Abbasid lustre plate (Figure 7.1), a Samanid imitation lustre bowl (Figure 7.2), a Samanid buffware bowl (Figure 7.3), and a number of Fatimid lustre plates (Figures 7.4–5).[1] The Fatimid examples and a Saljuq metal plate (Figure 7.6) are but a few examples, from the eleventh and twelfth centuries, that confirm the continuity of this iconographical legacy into the later periods.[2] There are, of course, many variations on this theme and almost all appear in buffware. These variations include a figure holding on to two branches (Figure 7.7), or showing his two flanking attendants, each holding a branch (Figure 7.8). Other variations show the figure with a branch in one hand and perhaps a moon crescent in another (Figure 7.9). A plate at the Freer Gallery of Art depicts two figures holding on to a central tree (Figure 7.10) which finds its morphological parallels in plates showing figures holding a central branch (Figure 7.11) or a wreath, the latter preserved on a glazed pottery fragment (Figure 7.12).

Of equal significance is the presence of the bird and fish (*murgh-u-māhī*) motif flanking the image of the ruler as seen in the Abbasid luster plate (Figure 7.1). The fish and bird motif also appears as a

Fig. 7.1 *Abbasid lustre ware, 9th–10th centuries.*

(Photograph: after *Islamic Art* from the collection of Edwin Binney 3rd.)

Fig. 7.2 *Samanid imitation lustre ware, 9th–10th centuries.*

(Photograph: after Wilkinson.)

Fig. 7.3 *Samanid buffware,
9th–10th centuries.*

(Courtesy of Los Angeles County
Museum of Art.)

Fig. 7.4 *Fatimid lustre
ware, 11th–12th centuries.*

(Photograph: after Philon.)

Fig. 7.5 *Fatimid lustre ware, 11th–12th centuries.*

(Photograph: after Kühnel.)

Fig. 7.6 *Provincial Seljuq metal plate, 12th century.*

(Photograph: after Marshak.)

Fig. 7.7 *Samanid buffware, 9th–10th centuries.*

(Photograph: after Wilkinson.)

Fig. 7.8 *Samanid buffware, 9th–10th centuries.*

(Photograph: after Fehérvári.)

Fig. 7.9 *Samanid buffware, 9th–10th centuries.*

(Photograph: after Wilkinson.)

Fig. 7.10 *Samanid buffware, 9th–10th centuries.*

(Photograph: after Atil.)

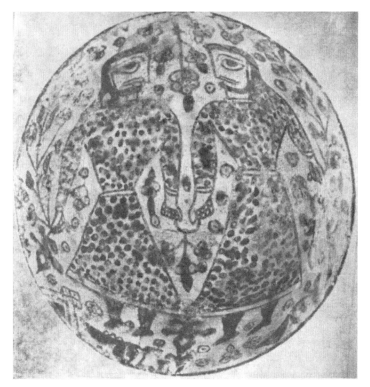

Fig. 7.11 Samanid
buffware, 9th–10th
centuries.

(Photograph: after Ettinghausen.)

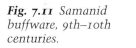

Fig. 7.12 Samanid
buffware, 9th–10th
centuries.

(Photograph: after Ettinghausen.)

theme in itself, as exemplified in a polychrome painted underglaze Amol bowl, now in the Gluck collection (Figure 7.13) and a Samanid imitation lustre bowl from north-eastern Iran (Figure 7.14). Other arrangements of this *murgh-u-māhī* ensemble is the reduction of the fish and bird to birds.[3] These birds, lacking their fish attachment, are almost always set in pairs and often in a circulatory course around the figure of the ruler or the dignitary (Figures 7.3, 7.6 and 7.10).

First, let us briefly examine the image of the cupbearer without the branch. This image is ubiquitous and should be considered universal or even a connate impulse that assumes specific configurations in particular contexts.[4] There are thus many extant images of the cupbearer in the immediate geographical territories of the Islamic world and may be considered as imagery derived from or related to it. In India the image stood for fertility and life everlasting, and the cup's content, *soma* (*haoma* in Iranian languages), was the nectar of the moon.[5] In China it signified the *yin* of the *yang* and was likewise a moon's attribute and symbolised a prosperous land and kingdom.[6] The history of the cupbearer and its significance has been discussed by Emil Esin and Katharina Otto-Dorn, who have also offered a summary of the cup's functions and meanings in the neighbouring cultures of Iran and, to a lesser extent, in the Islamic world.[7] Both authors, of course, have always favoured Turkish and Central Asiatic precursors for understanding Islamic images.[8] However, the image of the cupbearer also appears frequently on Sassanian silver (Figure 7.15)[9] and its extant Middle Eastern antecedents may be traced back to the proto-dynastic images of Mesopotamia. It should also be mentioned that in Sassanian Iran the cup symbolised the sun (Jamshid, sun-cup, is one attestation to this meaning) and the cupbearer appeared as the sun king. This meaning appears to have remained intact in the early Islamic periods.

Regarding the cupbearer, Otto-Dorn and Esin have amply indicated that the image is the codification of the rituals of investiture, ontological mutations (funerary, religious and blood-bonding rituals) and celebrations of victory in battle.[10] Likewise, both authors have quoted Ibn Bibi's account of the investitures of the Anatolian Muslim rulers Ghiyāth al-Din and Kayqubād, which clearly indicates a cultural continuum from the pre-Islamic into the Islamic cultures. For the sake of clarity it is useful to quote Ibn Bibi's narrative of Kayqubād's enthronement:

> 'When 'Alaeddin Kaiqobad was enthroned, he put on a royal mantle and was offered a cup of wine. While the king drank, the drums beat continually as in the Shamanist and Tabgac ceremonies . . . after the king drained his cup; dignitaries were also presented cups of a drink. Finally when the king was once more enthroned in the capital of Konya, a last drinking ceremony took place.'[11]

Ceremonial drinking is, however, abundantly mentioned in the historical and literary sources of early Islam. Baīhaqī's *Tārīkh-ī*

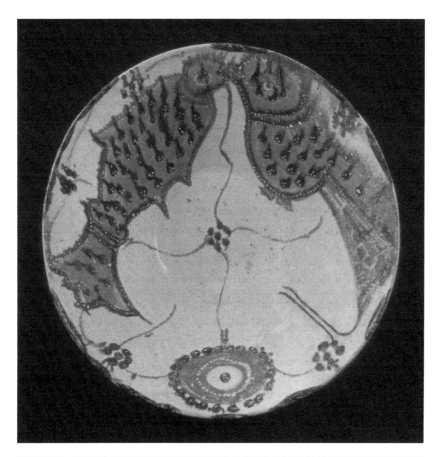

Fig. 7.13 *Amol polychrome ware, 9th–10th centuries.*

(Photograph: after Gluck.)

Fig. 7.14 *Samanid imitation lustre ware, 9th–10th centuries.*

(Photograph: after Atil.)

Fig. 7.15 *Sassanian silver plate, c. 6th–7th centuries.*

(Photograph: after Marshak.)

Baīhaqī and the *dīvān*s of Manūchihrī, Farrukhī, Salmān and almost all others often mention the ruler in the act of drinking wine, and the occasion is viewed, either explicitly or implicitly, as significant for the court and the king's subjects.[12]

This chapter, however, is not concerned with the symbolism of the cup rites, which have already been studied, but with the iconography of the cup and branch and its sometimes accompanying images of the bird and fish. The figure with the cup in one hand and a branch in the other has its roots in both pre-Islamic Central Asia and in Sassanian Iran. One of its most elegant depictions is in a Central Asian mural painting from a structure in Balayk-tepe, Uzbekistan (Figure 7.16). Here, a seated female of exquisite grace holds a branch in one hand and a golden cup in the other. There are similar representations on Sassanian silver plates where a branch or flower accompanies the cup-bearing king (Figures 7.17–18). What these images may have symbolised in Central Asia and pre-Islamic Iran is often a matter of conjecture, for the literary sources regarding their iconography are sadly lacking. However, in early Islamic Iran the sources are not silent on this subject and these references, in spite of their brevity, are, in my view, quite revealing. Moreover, given the continuum of traditions from the pre-Islamic into the Islamic period then it is reasonable to assume that readings of the Islamic period imagery are in many ways contiguous with those of the pre-Islamic times.

112

Plate 1 *Ceramic bowl from Nishapur, 10th century, with a bird in the frontal position. Its anatomical details have been stylised into vegetal ornament, and it is possible that there is a 'hidden' benedictory message in the way the croup and wings have been painted.*

(Private collection, photograph © S. Auld.)

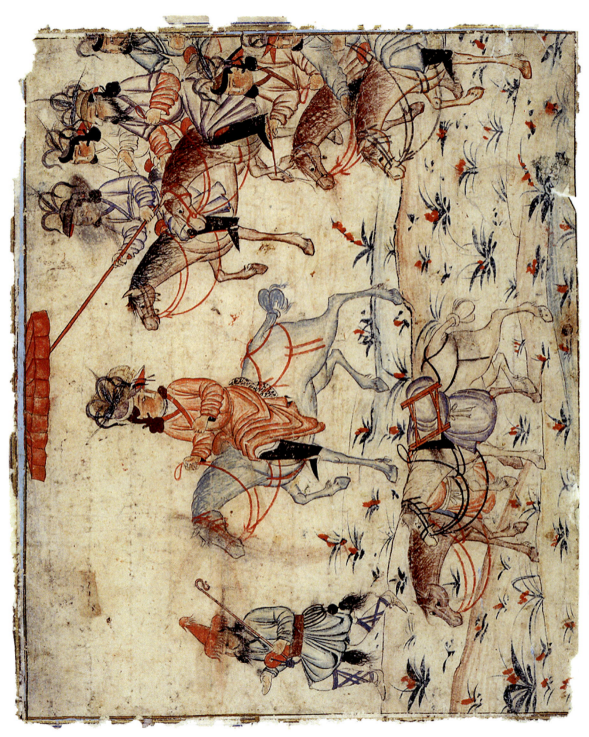

Plate 2 *'Princely Procession'.* 25.8 × 21 cm.

(Berlin, Staatsbibliothek, Preussischer Kulturbesitz, Orientabteilung, Diez A, fol. 71, S. 50.)

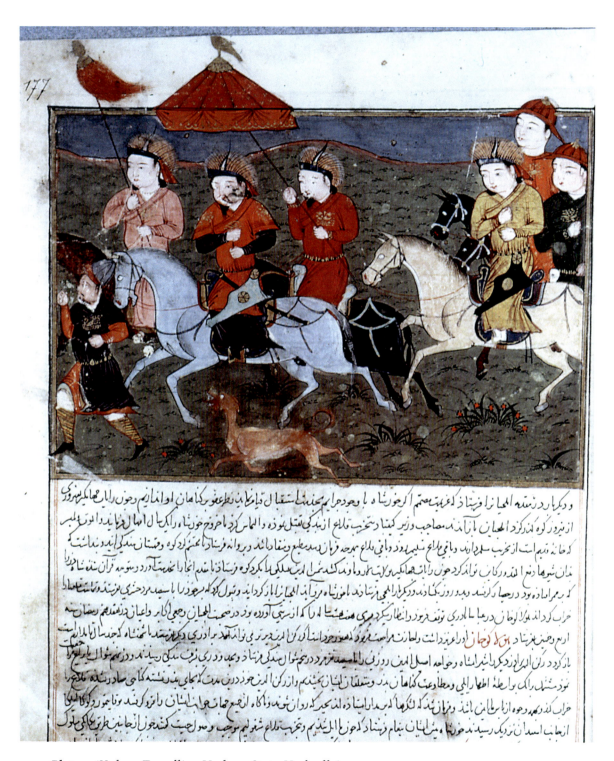

Plate 3 *'Hulegu Travelling Under a State Umbrella'.*

(Paris, Bibliothèque nationale, ms. suppl. pers. 1113, fol. 117a.)

Plate 4 *Palermo, Cappella Palatina, pavement in the aisle with curvilinear twist patterns.*

(Photograph: after Tronzo, pl. II.)

Plate 5 *Palermo, Cappella Palatina, pavement in the nave with angular interlace designs.*

(Photograph: after Gabrielli and Scerrato, fig. 30.)

Plate 6 *Monreale Cathedral, pavement.*

(Photograph: after Gabrielli and Scerrato, fig. 228.)

Plate 7 *Frontispiece (left-hand), f. 2a,* Bustan *of Saʿdi, adab fārsī 908, General Egyptian Book Organisation, Cairo.*

Plate 8 *Frontispiece (right-hand), f. 1b, Bustan of Saʿdi, adab fārsī 908, General Egyptian Book Organisation, Cairo.*

Plate 9 *Husayn Bayqara in mature age, 1958.59, Arthur M. Sackler Museum, Harvard University Art Museums.*

(Courtesy of the Arthur M. Sackler Museum, Harvard University Art Museums, Gift of John Goelet, former collection of Louis J. Cartier.)

(Photograph Peter Siegel. © President and Fellows of Harvard College.)

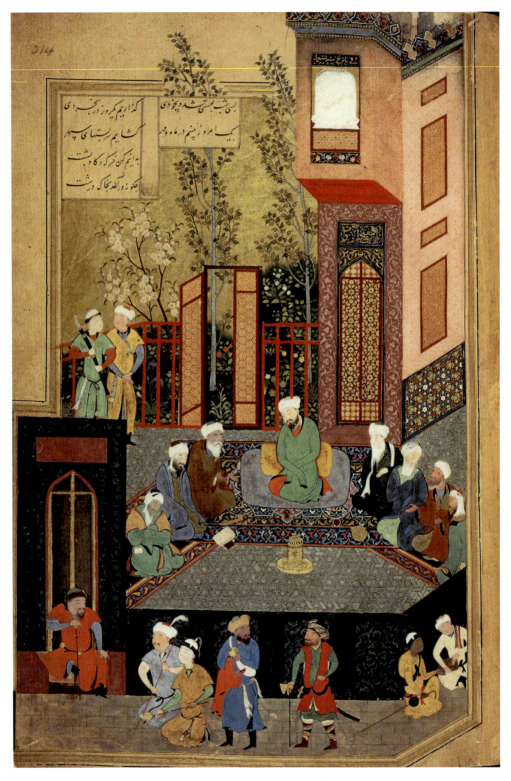

Plate 10 *'Iskandar with his Seven Philosophers', f. 214a,* Khamsa *of Nizami, Or. 6810,*
British Library, London.

(By permission of the British Library.)

Plate 11 *'Princes of the House of Timur' (detail), 1913.2-8.1, British Museum, London.*

(© Copyright The British Museum.)

Plate 12 *'Shah Jahan on the Peacock Throne', 1983.651, Arthur M. Sackler Museum, Harvard University Art Museums.*

(Courtesy of the Arthur M. Sackler Museum, Harvard University Art Museums, Private Collection.)

(Photographic Services. © President and Fellows of Harvard College.)

Plate 13 *The* arghūn *(or swan-phoenix), Ibn Bakhtīshū', Kitāb na't al-ḥawayān, probably North Jazira, c. 1220. Miniature 80 × 120mm.*

Plate 14 The suryānās *(or swan-phoenix), Ibn Bakhtīshū‛,* Kitāb manafi‛ al-ḥawayān, *probably Damascus, dated 755/1354. Miniature 72 × 120mm.*

(Biblioteca Real, San Lorenzo del Escorial, MS 898, fo. 112r.)

Plate 15 '*Anjar, Small Palace, fragment of frieze.*

(Photograph © B. Finster.)

Plate 16 '*Anjar, capital.*

(Photograph © B. Finster.)

Fig. 7.16 *Mural painting, Balayk-tepe, northern Turkistan, Uzbekistan, 6th–7th centuries.*

(Photograph: after Azarpay.)

As we shall see below, the branch and wine image was a popular and meaningful feature of the ruler's appearance during the new year and investiture ceremonies. We shall see that in fact the cup identified the ruler with the sun and the branch with wealth, prosperity and a paradise-like domain, and that the image in its totality manifested the different modalities of the sun in material form.

Let us begin with a poem by Farīd al-Dīn Aḥmad ibn Muhammad Izadyār al-Kāfī (fifth/eleventh century), written in praise of Sultan Ghīyāth al-Dīn and his two attributes, shadow and sunlight. Al-Kāfī's description of the festivities of the court is in the form of a *ghazal*

Fig. 7.17 *Sassanian silver plate, c. 6th–7th centuries.*

(Photograph: after Marshak.)

Fig. 7.18 *Sassanian silver plate, c. 6th–7th centuries.*

(Photograph: after Marshak.)

titled 'On Flower and Wine: A Panegyric for Sultan Ghiyāth al-Dīn and in Praise of [his attributes] Shadow and Sun-light.' The poem is as follows:

> You whose [ruby-red] lips and visage are the pride of flowers and
>   wine
> Now that the wine-red flowers have bloomed bring us the
>   flower-red wine
> The flower is in the shape of a [wine] cup and the colour of the
>   wine is the colour of flowers
> Both wine and flowers borrow their features from one another
> The flower receives its light from the wine and the wine finds
>   its splendour because of flowers
> Enjoy your wine and flowers free of thorns and drowsiness
>   after drinking
> Where would the flower be in this time of wealth if it were cold
>   and stormy?
> Where would the cup be without wine in this time of repose?
> Chiefly, [behold how] the great Sultan holding a cup of wine
>   and with flowers held [by the Sultan?] in front of him
> Called upon the musicians to play and granted his subjects
>   an audience.[13]

It is important to note that the shadow and the sun attributes of the king correlate to the cup (which stands for the sun) and the branch (which provides shade). In fact the solar symbolism of the cup is implicit in the third stanza: 'the flower receives its light from the wine'. A more direct reference to the symbolism of the cup as sun is offered by Manshūrī Samarqandī, a poet at the court of Maḥmūd of Ghaznavid, when he describes the arrival of his ruler at a ceremony: 'The universe has tonight transformed the sun into a cup/Here comes the king holding the brimful cup in his hand.'[14]

To return to al-Kāfī's poem, we can easily surmise that the shade is the king's attribute of generosity, protectiveness, benevolence and beneficence,[15] and the sun is his attribute of divine authority, fecundity and strength.[16] The sun and shade are simultaneously creative and destructive. They manifest the double modality of every power that the ruler embodies: the same force that brings death to his enemies bring life to his subjects and companions.

Moreover, Kāfī's poem creates a metonymic chain of signifiers when he equates the colours of wine, of flowers and the sultan's ruby-red lips and face, or when he describes the flower as the cup's analogy. The integration of these attributes points to the interrelated meanings of these elements where they, either individually or collectively, evoke fertility, fecundity and renewal through the branch (flowers) and divine rule, power and fecundity through the goblet and its content.

A panegyric by Mukhtārī Ghaznavī (fifth/eleventh century), written for a ruler whose name is effaced from the poem, is, above all, a graphic description of the ruler with wine in one hand and a branch in the other. Moreover, his wording is a limpid explanation that resolves without doubt the symbolism of the wine goblet as the sun and the branch, here referred to as Pleiades, as a symbol of the king's *primavera* (spring):[17] fecundity, wealth and paradise. He wrote:

'Pure wine and newly (blossomed) flowers are present,
[The king] holds the sun in one hand and the Pleiades in the other.'[18]

The Pleiades (*Parvīn, al-Thurayyā*), resembling a cluster of grapes or a vine, are one of the stations of the moon during the fall season and are an allegory of wealth, abundance and benignant showers.[19] Al-Biruni's description of the Pleiades further elucidates the symbolism of the branch in Islamic art:

Althurayya consists of six stars close to each other, very similar to a cluster of grapes. According to Arabs they form the *clunis* of Aries, but that is wrong because they stand on the hump of Taurus.
    The word is diminutive of *tharwa*, i.e., a collection and great number of something. Some people maintain that they were so called because the rain which is brought by their *nau'*, produces *tharwa*, i.e., abundance. They are also called *al-najm* . . .
    The forty days during which this station disappears under the rays of the sun are, according to the Arabs, the worst and most unhealthy of the whole year . . .[20]

So far we have seen that the branch is a symbol of spring, fertility and wealth (the Pleiades), benevolence, mercy and protection, and so on. Yet as a symbol of wealth and prosperity it was also associated with money (dīnārs). This is significant because an Abbasid lustre plate found in Iran (Figure 7.19) shows two men holding on to branches, each by one hand, and holding onto what appears to be sacks of money, in their other hands. This relationship between money and branches is found in Baīhaqī's account of 'the remainder of the year 424'. He describes how Ṭāhir at *nawrūz* placed dīnārs and *dirhams* inbetween flower petals and then distributed them among his guests. Ṭāhir himself wore a crown of flowers and drank wine from golden and silver cups.[21] Clearly the equation of flowers with dīnārs is a corollary of its meaning as wealth and prosperity. Manūchihrī, for example, likens the blossoms of a tree to dīnārs. He wrote:

'Like a coiner of money the branch of red blossoms
strikes new round dinars perpetually.'[22]

The symbolic similitude between money and flowers is obvious in a poem by Farrukhī-i Sīstānī, describing the majesty and the glory of the palace of Aḍad al-Dawla Yūsuf al-Sipasālār, the brother of Sultan Mas'ud the Ghaznavid. He wrote:

Fig. 7.19 *Abbasid lustre ware, 9th–10th centuries.*

(Photograph: after Grube.)

The subjects and the dependents of the king in that palace
Are engaged in festivities, exultant, happy and in full glory
Here is one who has in one hand wine and in the other dinars
And here is another one holding in one hand wild flowers and in
   the other a cup of wine.[23]

Now let us examine the image of the bird and fish placed counter-clockwise around the image of the seated ruler holding on to a branch and a cup of wine (Figure 7.1). The bird and the fish motif has its precursors in the Sassanian period. A silver plate found in the territory of Perm and most likely dating from the sixth century shows the figure of a lion (nursing two dog-like cubs) by a body of water and against a central tree flanked by two birds, each holding a fish in its mouth (Figure 7.20). The compositional scheme of this representation is somewhat similar to our Abbasid lustre bowl (Figure 7.1). The ruler with a branch and a cup is represented as a lion and a tree. Given that the cup, the lion and the ruler all symbolise the sun and are cosmological equivalents then this silver plate may serve as an iconographical antecedent for our Islamic examples.

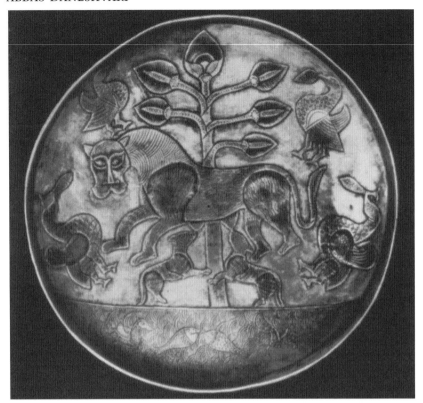

Fig. 7.20 *Sassanian silver plate, c. 6th–7th centuries.*

(Photograph: after Marshak.)

We know that in the Islamic *Zeitgeist*, as the textual sources reveal, the fish and the bird are cosmological symbols. Zick-Nissen has theorised that these images, especially when they appear in buffware, represent astro-cosmological elements.[24] However, without rejecting Zick-Nissen's ideas, it is easy to see that almost all the medieval sources refer to the macro-cosmos in the microcosmic terms of *murgh-u-māhī* or *murgh-u-māh* (fish and bird or fish and moon).

The fish, upon whose back stands the bull of the universe,[25] represents the lowest stratum[26] of the world's axis. The bird or the moon on the other hand represents its highest point. Together they stand for the axis of the universe, as does the *lat* column in Buddhism.[27] In fact the Islamic sources, whenever describing the cosmos, refer to the fish and bird (or the fish and moon) as its symbolic limits.

Nāṣir Khusraw sees the bird and fish as a cosmogonic sign of totality. He wrote, 'Those people who accept knowledge, have the bird and fish (*murgh-u-māhī*) around their necks.'[28] The image of the world as *murgh-u-māhī* (bird and fish) is abundant in the literary sources of early and medieval Islam. ʿAttar, for example, writes, 'that the day from the onset of dawn was burdened by his grief and at night his cry would not allow anything to sleep from *murgh to māhī*'.[29] Likewise Farrukhī, when separated from the ruler Amir Ayaz Uymaq

118

(a vassal of Sultan Mahmud the Ghaznavid), describes the throes of this separation as enormous enough to have reached *murgh-u-māhī*.[30] Or as ʿAṭṭār describes the effect of a spiritual calamity, 'This pain reaches as far as *murgh-u-māhī* and does not allow anyone to sleep at night.'[31] The poet Khāqānī, describing his heartache over the death of his son wrote: 'From a broken heart sodden in pain my eyes cried so much, that [the universe from] *murgh* to *māhī* each and everyone [in it] cried for me.'[32]

Thus the bird and fish or the moon and fish are metaphors of the universe.[33] As ʿAṭṭār writes, 'Whatever there is, from the back of the fish to the moon, are all evidences of His Essence.'[34] *Murgh u māhī* or *murgh-u-māh* represent the axis of the universe from its base to its apex. Muʿizzī Samarqandī in praise of Sultan Malikshah and his conquest of Samarqand described the ruler as a being 'whose feet reach the fish and his head is at the moon'.[35] It is therefore obvious that the appearance of the fish and the bird on each side of the ruler references the world in its entirety. Perhaps, and this is just a conjecture, the counterclockwise motion of the pair of *murgh-u-māhī* may be referring to the cycle of day and night.

It is reasonable to conclude that the image of the ruler with cup and branch identifies the ruler with the sun and earthly abundance and the bird and fish serve as a sign of the universality of this abundance, generosity, wealth, justice, comeliness and his paradisial domain.

However, a deeper meaning suggests itself and offers a genesis for the symbol of the ruler with the cup, branch and *murgh-u-māhī*, namely the three natures of the *senmurv* symbolising the lower heaven as fish (scales), the middle heaven as a dog and the upper heaven as a bird. The *senmurv* lived on a tree that was watered by the seas. The Islamic transformations of this image may have replaced the dog of the middle heaven with the image of the earthly ruler, the water with the cup and the tree with the branch. This transition and metamorphosis, if correct, may be the root of the cosmological structure of the ruler flanked by bird and fish.[36] Moreover, we cannot ignore the relationships of the imagery shown in Figure 7.20 with the *senmurv* and the image of the Muslim ruler. It is fascinating to note that these images equate on so many iconographical layers. The sun equates with the cup and the lion and also the ruler and the bird, while the fish symbolises the waters and the netherworld. The branch equates with the tree of life, wealth, fertility and fecundity.[37]

Variations on the theme of the ruler with branch and cup flanked by *murgh-u-māhī* are abundant and appear for the most part in buffware of the Samanids in north-eastern Iran.[38] Buffware is of course different from other ware of the Samanids because of its rich imagery that relates it on many levels to the art and iconography of the pre-Islamic Sasanids. Buffware also has been found in a wide range of terrain and its influences on the neighbouring ceramics of Amol (Zīyārīd?) are quite obvious. Variations on the theme of *murgh-u-māhī* appear as representations of birds without the fish (Figure 7.3) or of *murgh-u-māhī* without the ruler (Figures 7.13–14) or of the ruler without any references to either the fish or the bird.

Johanna Zick-Nissen has interpreted these birds as astrological symbols. Relying upon the writings of certain astronomers, chief among them ʿAbd al-Raḥmān ibn ʿUmar al-Ṣūfī, she has interpreted the figures on buffware bowls and their arrangements as signs of constellations marked upon the globes.[39] As to whether a collective iconographical scheme may have determined the shapes and the compositional arrangement of the images on buffware, this chapter is not the place for its discussion. However, regarding the images of the two birds it is more likely that these birds stand for a simplified version of the original *murgh-u-māhī* cosmogram.

Variations on the branch theme may appear as two figures holding on to a central tree (Figure 7.10) or two figures holding a branch between them (Figure 7.11) and or two figures holding on to a branch in the shape of a wreath (Figure 7.12). Ettinghausen interpreted the branch-holding figures in Samanid art as iconographical degenerations of earlier Sassanian scenes of investiture.[40] His argument, focused on a glazed pottery fragment displaying images holding a wreath (Figure 7.12), supports the notion of abbreviation and simplification of imagery either across time or across socio-economic stratas.

One buffware example (Figure 7.9) is quite interesting as it shows four figures seated around the wide rim of the bowl. Two of these figures, seated on stools, hold a branch in one hand and one of them has a flower in his other hand while the other holds in his other hand what appears to be a crescent moon. Likewise the other two figures, seated in a cross-legged position, hold respectively a crescent moon, and a crescent moon upon a globular object. As the branches are understood, the crescent moons may be survivals of either the Sassanians and/or Central Asiatic representations of figures with branches and the sun or the moon in their other hands. Such images are seen in Uighur art such as a fragmentary banner painting from Hisar depicting a six-armed deity holding a cup with two hands and planetary signs with the other two hands.[41] Likewise a number of silver plates from the provinces of the Sassanian empire show the images of four-armed rulers or deities holding on to a crescent moon in one hand and the sun in the other (Figure 7.21). Clearly this buffware may be a legacy of the Sassanian and Central Asiatic references to the cup as a luminous substance.

It is obvious that a great deal more research needs to be done in order to offer a clear and full view of these images in their artistic and literary contexts. However, I hope that this article will raise the interests of some to pursue the iconography of these images in early Islam.

Fig. 7.21 *Sassanian silver plate, c. 6th–7th centuries.*

(Photograph: after Marshak.)

Notes

1. For another example that I am unable to reproduce here, see, A. Yu. Yakubovsky and M. M. Diakonov, *Zhivopis Drevengo Piandzhikenta* (Moscow, 1957), pl. VII, illustrating a buffware with two figures holding drinking cups and flower sceptres at a fire altar.

2. For the many Anatolian Saljuq images on Kubādābād tiles depicting men that hold two branches, see Katharina Otto-Dorn, 'Die menschlichen Figurendarstellung auf den Fliesen von Kobadabad', in *Forschungen zur Kunst Asiens, In Memoriam Kurt Erdmann*, ed. Oktay Aslanapa and Rudolf Naumann (Istanbul, 1969), pls 1, 6–9.

3. Perhaps the abstract bird that accompanies the figure of the musician in an Abbasid lustre plate, now in the Freer Gallery, is one such act of reduction and simplification. See Esin Atil, *Ceramics from the World of Islam* (Washington, DC, 1973), pl. 3.

4. For a brief summary of sources and studies regarding the cup rites of the Scythians, Chinese, Inner-Asian Turks, Bulgars and others, see Emil Esin, ' "And," The Cup Rites in Inner-Asian Turkish Art', in *Forschungen zur kunst Asiens, In Memoriam Kurt Erdmann*, ed. Oktay Aslanapa and Rudolf Naumann (Istanbul, 1969), 224–5.

5. Esin, 'Cup Rites'. For the cup and the tree as a symbol of immortality in Indian art, see Odette Viennot, *Le culte de l'arbre dans l'Inde ancienne* (Paris, 1954), 28–34.

6. Esin, 'Cup Rites', 226. See also Marcel Granet, *Danses et légendes de la Chine ancienne* (Paris, 1957), 91–103.

7. Esin, 'Cup Rites', 224–61 and Katharina Otto-Dorn, 'Das Seldschukische Thronbild', *Persica* 10 (1982), 149–94.

8. See, for example, their discussion of the sarcophagus of the Kök Turk king Bilge Khan (d. 734) and its visual similarities to those in the Islamic world: Otto-Dorn, 'Thronbild', 149–78 and Esin, 'Cup Rites', 230–58.

9. For more examples, see *Sassanian Silver*, exh. cat., The University of Michigan Museum of Art (Ann Arbor, 1967), pls. 14–15.

10. See Esin, 'Cup Rites', 237; Otto-Dorn, 'Thronbild', 150–78. An example of the use of the cup is reported by Ibn Fadlan regarding the Bulgar king's conversion to Islam. The king drank a cup of some brewed concoction (due to the Islamic proscription of wine) with the ambassadors of the Abbasid caliph as a sign of his allegiance to Islam: Esin, 'Cup Rites', 237.

11. H. W. Duda, Die *Seltschukengeschichte des Ibn Bibi* (Copenhagen, 1959), 70; Otto-Dorn, 'Thornbild', 155, 158, 171, and Esin, 'Cup Rites', 242.

12. See, for example, Muhammad ibn Husain Baīhaqī, *Tārīkh-i Baīhaqī*, ed. 'A. A. Fīāz (Tehran, 1971), 54, 55, 374, 736, 808, for some of the wine-drinking ceremonies. The works of Farrukhī and Manūchihrī are cited throughout the text.

13. *Majma' al-Fuṣaḥā*, gathered by Riḍa Qulī Khān Hidāyat, ed. M. Muṣṣaffā (Tehran, 1957), 1:220–1.

ای گل و می را بر خسار و لب تو افخار   چون گل میگون بیار آمد می گلگون بیار

شکل گل چون‌شکل جام و رنگ می چون رنگ گل   هست گوئی هر دو را از هم صفتها مستعار

گل ز می جوید شعاع و می ز گل گیرد فروغ   با گل و می عیش کن بی زحمت و خار و خمار

با غرابی گل کجا باشد در این هنگام قدر   جام را بی می کجا باشد در این موسوم قرار

خاصه چون سلطان اعظم گل بپیش می بدست   مطربانا خواند پیش وبندگانرا داد بار

14. *Majma' al-Fusaḥā* (Tehran, 1961), 1176.

ز آفتاب یکی جام کرد چرخ امشب   بباد شاه بکف بر نهاد مالامال

On the significance of wine (wine-cup) as sun see also A. S. Melikian-Chirvani, 'From the Royal Boat to the Beggar's Bowl', *Islamic Art* 4 (1991), 3–112 and Melikian-Chirvani, 'The wine Bull and the Magian Master', in *Recurrent Patterns in Iranian Religions: From Mazdaism to Sufism*, ed. P. Gignoux, Studia Iranica Cahiers 11 (Paris, 1992), 101–34. Of significance is a quote from Abū Nuwās (c. 2 AH/8 AC): 'Of nectar someone seeing it said to me/The sun has been trapped for us in a wine bowl': 'From the Royal Boat', 13.

15. It is important to note that the commentary of Muhammad Awfī (d. thirteenth century AD) on this poem states that, 'the sultan like the sun is the shade of God's mercy'. See *Majma' al-Fuṣaḥā*, 1:220, n. 1, extracted from Awfi's *Lubāb al-bāb*, 110–11. For more information on the role and significance of shade, also see Abbas Daneshvari, *Medieval Tomb Towers of Iran: An Iconographical Study* (Lexington, KY, 1986), 9–17.

16. The remainder of the poem clearly indicates the symbolism of the sun as strength and divine justice. See *Majma' al-Fuṣaḥā*, 1:220–1.

17. The significance of the wine and of the flower or branch as life ever-lasting and perpetuity is evident in one of Manuchihri's poems describing the arrival of spring in terms of flowers and wine. Manuchihrī Dāmghānī, *Dīvān*, ed. M. Dabīr Sīyāqī (Tehran, 1977), 59. He wrote:
    'The Spring has arrived with red flowers
    Drink rose-coloured wine and arrange the roses.'

آمده نوروز ماه با گل سوری بهم   باده سوری بگیر بر گل سوری بچم

18. *Dīvān*, ed. R. Humāyūn Farrukh (Tehran, 1957), 318.

از باده ناب و سمن تازه فراز آر   یکدست بخورشید و دگر دست پیروین

19. It should be mentioned that the branch in the Abbasid lustre bowl (Fig 7.1) and, to a lesser extent, the branch in the imitation luster bowl (Fig. 7.2) resemble a cluster of grapes.

20. Abu Raīhan al-Bīrūnī, *Athār al-bāqīya* (390–1/1000), tr. E. Sachau as *The Chronology of Ancient Nations* (London, 1879), 343–4. See also Daneshvari, *Tomb Towers of Iran*, 61–4.

21. Baihaqi, *Tārīkh-i Baīhaqī*, 498.

میان برگ گل دینار و درم بود .....   فرمود تا مشربه های زرین و سیمین آوردند
......
وآنرا در علاقه ابریشمین کشیدند و بر میان چون کمری و تاجی از مورد بافته
و با گل سوری بیاراسته بر سر نهاد

22. *Majmaʿ al-Fusaḥā*, no vol. no., 1271.

ضراب وار شاخ گل سرخ هر شبی   دینارهای گرد مجدد کند همی

23. Farrukhī-i Sīstānī, *Dīvān*, ed. M. Dabīr Sīyāqī (Tehran, 1956), 130.

بندگان و رهیان ملك اندر آن كاخ   دست برده به نشاط و دل پر ناز و بطر
این بدستی در می کرده و دستی دینار   آن بدستی گل خود روی و بدستی ساغر

24. See n. 38 below.
25. Gurgānī for example, when describing the world and its reaches writes: '. . . as far as the back of the fish upon which the world stands': *Visramini*, tr. by O. Waldrop, London, 1966, p. 278). Farid al-Din ʿAttār, *Manṭiq al-Taīr*, ed. H. Hamīd (Tehran, n.d.), 4, writes of the world as a bull standing on the back of the fish.
    ʿAttār writes in *Muṣībat-nāmeh* (ed. N. Vaṣāl, Tehran, 1959, p. 234): 'The dark bull of the world is so because of you, Beneath the bull the fish too is so because of you.'

در زمین گاو سیاهی از شماست   زیر بار گاو ماهی از شماست

26. As the lowest stratum the fish is often identified with the lowest self. ʿAttār writes, 'If you are released from the fish that is your *nafs* (self) you will then become the companion of Yūsuf in the highest levels (of enlightenment):' *Manṭiq al-Taīr*, 41–2.

گر بود از ماهی نفست خلاص   مونس یونس شوی در صدر خاص

27. Niẓāmī evokes the image of an axis when he writes that 'God created the world so that the bird could view the fish': *Majma' al-Fuṣaḥā*, 1:1430.

زمین را مرغ بر ماهی نگارد

28. *Dīvān*, ed. M. Suhailī (Tehran, 1974), 449.

مردم چو پذیرای دانش آمد   گردنش نهادند مرغ و ماهی

29. *Khusrownāma*, ed. A. S. Khunsārī (Tehran, 2535/1976), 182.

نه روز آسود تا شب از پگاهی   نه شب خفت از خروشش مرغ و ماهی

30. *Dīvān*, 161.

ز گربانی که هستم مرغ و ماهی   همی گریند بر من همچو من زار

'My lamentation reaches from the bird to the fish They cry for me as I do for myself.'

31. *Dīvān*, 10.

چو مرغ و ماهی از این درد شب نمی خسبند

32. *Ātishkada-yi Āżar*, gathered and written by Bīgdilī Shāmlū, ed. H. S. Naṣīrī, 185.

گر بقدر شورش دل چشم من بگریستی   بر دل من مرغ و ماهی تن بتن بگریستی

33. I should point out that the usage of these two signs, *murgh-u-māh* (bird and moon) and *murgh-u-māhī* (bird and fish), are paradigmatically and syntagmatically identical. ʿAṭṭār writes: 'He could not sleep even if he closed his eyes, even the fish and the moon lamented his pain': *Khusrownāma*, 182.

نبودش خواب گر یکدم بخفتی   برو ماهی و مه ماغ گرفتی

Awḥidī Kirmānī in praise of the Prophet Muhammad writes: 'Like the moon this lamp took away the darkness from the fish to the moon': *Majma' al-Fuṣaḥā*, 1:246.

چون ماه چراغ با سیاهی   بگرفته ز ماه تا ماهی

34. *Manṭiq al-Ṭair*, 4.

هر چه هست از پشت ماهی تا ماه   جمله ذرات بر ذاتش گواه

35. *Majma' al-Fuṣaḥā*, n.v., 1307.

بنش رسیده ماهی سرش رسیده ماه

36. For the three heavens, see Camilla V. Trever, *The Dog-Bird, Senmurv-Paskudj* (Leningrad, 1938) and Hans-Peter Schmidt, 'Senmurv', *Persica* 9 (1980), 23–4. Schmidt rejects Trever's theory of the three heavens but accepts the idea of the three universal elements (air, earth and water) as a possibility.

37. The symbolism of the tree and the sun and the bird and sun have been studied by A. J. Wensinck and the relations of these ideas with the Islamic imagery need to be further explored. See A. J. Wensinck, *Tree and Bird as Cosmological Symbols in Western Asia* (Amsterdam, 1921), 1–47.

38. It is important to note that buffware is distinguished by a number of features that relate it strongly to the artistic traditions of pre-Islamic Sassanian Iran. Although there are also influences, such as the splashing technique, from Turkestan and China, animate and non-animate representations on buffware find their closest parallel in Sassanian art (for similarities between buffware and the Central Asian art, especially the cycle of paintings at Panjikent, see Yakubovsky and Diakonov, *Zhivopis* and Ernst J. Grube, *Islamic Pottery in the Keir Collection* (London, 1976), 84–5. Human representations on buffware, with their angular features and long straight nose lines, also seen in Mesopotamian lustre, are perhaps derived from Sassanian art. Grube may well be right (ibid., 84) in suggesting, after Yakubovsky and Diakonov, that the iconography of buffware is Zoroastrian-influenced. See also Yakubovsky and Diakonov, pl. VII, for a buffware showing figures holding drinking cups and flower sceptres at a fire altar.

39. For a discussion of her ideas on this subject see the following: 'Gabri Ware und Nishapur-Keramik', *Keramos* 64 (1974), 35–46; 'Figuren auf mittelalteriche orientalische Keramikschalen und die Sphaera Barbarica', *Archaelogische Mitteilungen aus Iran*, N.F., 8 (1975), 217–40 and 'Medieval Ceramic Bowl Decorations Interpreted as Constellations', *VI International Congress of Iranian Art and Archeology* (Tehran, 1976), 349–67.

40. Richard Ettinghausen, 'A Case of Traditionalism in Iranian Art', in *Forschungen zur Kunst Asiens, in Memoriam Kurt Erdmann*, ed. Oktay Aslanapa and Rudolf Naumann (Istanbul, 1969), 88–110.

41. Esin, 'Cup Rites', 249–51 and fig. 15B.

CHAPTER EIGHT

Islamic Incense-burners and the Influence of Buddhist Art

Géza Fehérvári

The influence of Buddhism and Buddhist art on the Iranian world has already been investigated by several scholars. The most exhaustive studies have been carried out and published by Melikian-Chirvani.[1] It was during the Kushan period that Buddhism spread over from India to the north, beyond the Hindukush and gained a strong foothold in Western-central Asia. Several Buddhist monuments have survived and were excavated in Turkestan and Uzbekistan,[2] nevertheless it was Afghanistan which became and remained the bulwark of this new religion until the advent of Islam. Traces of Buddhism were clearly visible in the country until quite recently. Perhaps one of the most important Buddhist sites in Afghanistan was Bamiyan. Apart from the hundreds of caves used by Buddhist monks, there were the remains of the two large Buddha statues which were carved into the side of the Hindukush, destroyed by the Taleban in early 2001. There were also the remains of three large stupas in the Kabul region at Guldarra, Shevaki and Top Darra, restored by French conservators in the early 1960s.[3] They also fell into ruins and were further damaged by the Taleban.

Apart from these architectural remains, the French and Afghan excavations at Begram and at Hadda near Jalalabad and the Italian excavations at Ghazni, all brought to light objects which clearly demonstrate the influence of Buddhist art on Muslim artists and craftsmen. Geometrical and vegetal patterns, lions and mythical creatures which decorate Buddhist ivory panels and stone carvings reappear later in Islamic art, either faithfully copied, or in somewhat modified forms. However, the impact of Buddhism is perhaps most strongly manifested in early Islamic metalwork. Surprisingly not only the decorative designs were borrowed from Buddhist art, but more explicitly, Islamic metalworkers copied the forms of Buddhist monuments, first of all the shape of stupas. The best examples to substantiate this claim are the early Islamic bronze incense-burners.

The striking similarity between stupas and bronze incense-burners was already recognised and well demonstrated by Melikian-Chirvani in 1972.[4] Later he published two incense-burners which, he claimed, were in the shape of stupas and, he proposed, perhaps are evidence that such a stupa or stupas may have existed in the Herat region. One of these two incense-burners was in the Museum of Kabul, while the other was in Herat. He dated them to the Samanid period, that is, eighth–tenth centuries.[5] The Tareq Rajab Museum in Kuwait possesses a number of bronze incense-burners, allegedly originating from Afghanistan and similarly demonstrate the strong Buddhist impact on Islamic art. Here five of the most interesting examples will be discussed, together with one more remarkable and related piece which is in the Freer Gallery in Washington.

Buddhist stupas are solid stone or brick-built structures. The earlier ones, like those of Sanchi, Barhut and Sevaki, were hemispherical, crowned by a *chatri*, a lotus parasol or umbrella. The *chatri* was a standard decorative symbol and an essential feature of Buddhist stupas. Some of these had multiple umbrellas, like the stupa at Sanchi, which has a triple *chatri*. On top of the dome, below the lotus parasol there is a rectangular feature, the *harmikā*, in which the relics were preserved. Furthermore, there are four gates providing access to the shrine to enable the pilgrims to circumambulate the stupa. Later on stupas became more complex, with a large and tall square base and a high drum capped by a hemispherical dome with a *chatri* finial. One of the earliest of these square stupas is the so-called Ali Masjid stupa in the Khyber Pass.[6] A second early square stupa is the above-mentioned one at Guldarra in the Kabul region (Figure 8.1).

Fig. 8.1 View of the Buddhist stupa of Guldarra in Afghanistan (c. 1st century BCE–2nd century CE).

(Photograph © Géza Fehérvári.)

These square stupas were imitated in early Islamic architecture. A look at the Samanid mausoleum at Bukhara, which was built at the beginning of the tenth century, is an early such example. It has a square base, a zone of transition hidden behind a series of arches, a hemispherical dome and is crowned by a small pavilion which is an Islamic substitute for the *chatri*. The arched recesses on the lower square base were replaced by doors (Figure 8.2). But Buddhist architectural traditions were present even much later. Sultan Sanjar's mausoleum at Merv (c. 1157–60) has a similar shape. When we compare these two mausolea to the stupa of Guldarra, we cannot fail to notice the close similarity. Both have tall square bases, zones of transitions and huge domes. We also notice that in Bukhara at the corners of the platform above the zone of transition there are small

Fig. 8.2 *View of the Samanid mausoleum of Isma'il at Bukhara (before 331/943).*

(Photograph © Gunther Mullack.)

solid domes. At Merv, the mausoleum, like most such buildings of the Saljuq period, had a double dome, which unfortunately has since nearly disappeared. Hence we cannot say whether the top of its outer dome was capped by a pavilion or any other structure. This close relationship between Buddhist stupas and Islamic mausolea is repeated in bronze incense-burners of Central Asia, made during the early Islamic period.

Like the stupas, the early Islamic incense-burners also reveal two major types: the hemispherical ones and the square-shaped type which are capped by hemispherical lids. Of the six examples to be discussed here both types are represented. First, we should look at the hemispherical type of which two specimens are included.

The first is a comparatively large object, measuring 22.5cm in height and 28cm in diameter (Figure 8.3).[7] It is made of cast bronze decorated with engraved and openwork designs and was constructed of three parts. The lower part is circular, consisting of a shallow dish holding the incense resting on three animal-shaped paws; it has a flat slightly everted rim on top and a narrow one at the base. The long cylindrical pipe-shaped handle has an openwork scroll design on top and terminates in the shape of a lotus. The sides of the dish are plain. The tall hemispherical lid is attached to the dish by a hinge and on top it has a smaller second hemispherical dome which is crowned by

Fig. 8.3 Incense-burner, circular type, bronze with openwork and incised decoration.

(Tareq Rajab Museum, Kuwait, inv. no. MET81TSR.)

what appears to be a 'double *chatri*'. The lower and taller part of the lid carries a wide decorative band which includes six circular medallions, alternately decorated with six-pointed stars and groups of dotted circles, partially in openwork. Above this band there are three small medallions with simple engraved patterns and tiny holes. Four small circular openings can be seen on the smaller upper dome.

This hemispherical incense-burner comes close to those which were studied by Melikian-Chirvani. It presents somewhat more opulent decoration, but its shape and decorative design bears all the hallmarks of the Khurasan school. Perhaps it is not as early as the examples noted by Melikian-Chirvani, but most likely falls within the Samanid period, probably of the late fourth/tenth century.

Two similar incense-burners which are in the Mayer Memorial Institute in Jerusalem were published by Eva Baer. While she does not offer us a date for these two vessels, she attributes them to eastern Iran or Central Asia and emphasises the Buddhist influence and their similarity to Buddhist stupas.[8] Their shapes and decorations, in the view of this author, suggest a similar date to the above examples.

The second round example is considerably larger and more complex: the round upward-tapering body is supported by the protomes of three lions. On one side of the body a long and heavy handle is attached, while on top there is a domical lid, crowned by a blossoming lotus (Figure 8.4).[9] The tapering body is decorated with a series of

Fig. 8.4 *Incense-burner, circular type, bronze with openwork and incised decoration.*

(Tareq Rajab Museum, Kuwait, inv. no. MET212TSR.)

vertical bands, alternately with rising zigzag lines, executed in openwork. Each one is decorated by two rising incised lines and plain
zones which also have incised lines and a series of chevron patterns in
between. The wide lid is attached to the body by a hinge. It has a
narrow flat rim, then has a sloping inner circle, which is decorated by
a continuous zigzag line, identical to those on the sides of the body. It
surrounds the central domical part, on top of which is the blossoming
lotus. The handle is square in section with openwork on the sides and
terminates in the shape of a lamp with a small lid on its top in the
form of a lion's head; next to this, the handle it ends in the shape of a
large widely opened disc.

The somewhat simple decoration of openwork zigzag lines on the
body, the lid and on the handle, the chevron patterns and the
blossoming lotus are all characteristic of Samanid metal vessels.
Nevertheless the application of lion protomes as supports points
to a slightly later date, possibly to the early Ghaznavid period, that
is, the second half of the eleventh century.

The examples of the second, or square-type of incense-burner are
perhaps even more interesting. They reveal even closer affinity to
Buddhist stupas. The first example of this square type, from the Tareq
Rajab Museum, is again a large vessel with an elaborate shape, but
rather reserved surface decoration (Figure 8.5).[10] It was cast in bronze
in several pieces, then soldered together. The low and square dish
rests on four duck-shaped feet. Narrow projecting rims frame the
main body above and below. On the upper body there is another
narrow openwork panel formed by two entwined geometrical scrolls.
The long and square handle is attached to one side of the lower part of
the dish. The handle is in two parts: a long horizontal part sharply
turned down at the end to form a vertical part, which gives it a firm

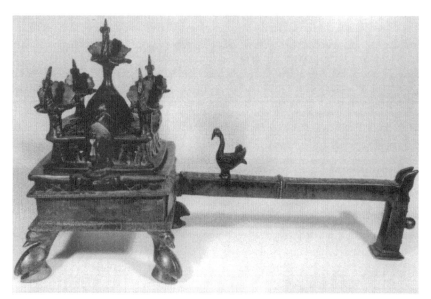

Fig. 8.5 Incense-burner,
square type with a domical
lid and square handle, cast
bronze with openwork and
incised decoration.

(Tareq Rajab Museum, Kuwait,
inv. no. METI284TSR.)

132

support. The upper part has a series of rosettes placed in small squares; they are executed in openwork with the details engraved; closer to the dish there is a small sitting bird, most likely a peacock. About halfway along a rounded rib embraces the handle on three sides. At the end, where it turns vertical, there are two simple horns and on its outer side a small circular hook. The opening lid is more complex: it is square with an openwork zigzag line running around. The opener is in the shape of a peacock. At the corners of the slightly rising top there are larger peacocks and the base has an openwork design, similar to that of the upper part of the dish. It surrounds the small domical and openwork decorated central part on which a further peacock is standing.

While this type of incense-burner is comparatively unusual and rare, it is not unknown. A few more modest examples exist. There is a square-shaped incense-burner with a pyramidal lid in the Mayer Memorial Institute in Jerusalem. It is supported by four columnar feet and similar tubular columns stand at the corners of the lid. In the centre there is a blossoming lotus. Eva Baer, who published this vessel, attributed it to Central Asia or eastern Iran and dated it to the Samanid or later period.[11] A somewhat closer type of incense-burner, with small peacocks standing at the corners of the pyramidal lid and decorated with several parallel zigzag lines, was sold at Sotheby's and dated ninth tenth century.[12] A further related incense-burner is in the *Dar al-Athar al-Islamiyyah* in Kuwait, but it was attributed to Spain and dated to the eleventh century.[13] While the dating may be correct, the attribution can be questioned. Neither the shape, nor the incised decoration, together with the so-called 'Solomon's seals' or 'Buddhist eternal knot' on the lower part of the lid indicate a western origin. Previously, however, as will be shown below, most examples of this type of incense-burners were considered to be Spanish, or from Coptic or Fatimid Egypt.

The lid of a similar square incense-burner is in the Tareq Rajab Museum (Figure 8.6).[14] The lower part has rounded corners, while the panels between are decorated with an elongated version of the 'Solomon's seal' or the 'Buddhist eternal knot'. The domical upper part has openwork geometrical interlace on its lower side and on top is capped by a blossoming lotus. This lid belongs to the same category and accordingly can be attributed to eastern Iran or Central Asia and dated ninth to early eleventh centuries.

An extremely large and impressive bronze incense-burner was acquired by the Tareq Rajab Museum in the early 1990s. This object is remarkable not only because of its size, but because of its beauty and the striking similarity it demonstrates to Buddhist stupas. It may be one of the largest Islamic incense-burners known today (Figures 8.7–8.9). It was cast in several pieces, which were then soldered together. It has an extensive openwork decoration, while the decorative details are chased. Its size and weight are remarkable: the total height with its dome is 38.5cm; the height of the body with the

Fig. 8.6 *Lid of a square incense-burner, cast bronze with openwork and incised decoration.*

(Tareq Rajab Museum, Kuwait, inv. no. MET199TSR.)

supporting legs, but without the dome is 19.8cm; the dome itself is 18.7cm high; the body measures 25 × 25cm; the handle is 14.8cm long, the hight of the handle support is 27.8cm and the lions on top of the corners measure 9cm in height. The total weight is 9.47kg.[15] Because of its form, size and the weight this object is exceptional, the only comparable piece, which will be discussed below, being in the Freer Gallery of Art.

When the object was acquired it was covered with dirt and corrosion inside and out. It was cleaned and restored by the Museum's conservator, Miss Renata Nalepa.[16] The incense-burner is made of six parts: the body, the dome, the handle, the front support of the handle, the four supporting legs and the four lions at the corners of the body.

The square body has a long handle attached to it on one side. It rests on four zoomorphic legs. On top there is a large dome capped by an umbrella-shaped finial, a *chatri*, while at each corner of the body's

Fig. 8.7 *Large square-type incense-burner, cast bronze with openwork and incised decoration.*

(Tareq Rajab Museum, Kuwait, inv. no. MET2375TSR.)

Fig. 8.8 *Panel B of the large incense-burner, inv. no. MET2375TSR.*

flat top there is a lion's head. The sides and the top of the vessel have extensive openwork decoration. Our examination starts with the side panels. Three sides have similar designs, namely three registers, the central one being much wider then the one on top and the one below. The upper register has a series of five-lobed palmettes, each emerging from a widely opened U-shaped design. The wide central band carries an inscription around on three sides, executed in openwork in cursive style over scrollwork. On all three

135

Fig. 8.9 *Top view of the large incense-burner, inv. no. MET2375TSR.*

sides the inscription is interrupted by a round medallion depicting a seated figure. The inscription reads:

1. *al-ʿizz wa'l-iqbāl wa* (glory and prosperity and . . .)
2. *al-dawla / wa'l-saʿād[a]* (good fortune and felicity)
3. *wa al-salā / ma wa'l-saʿā[da]* (and peace and felicity)

The inscription is written in a fully developed *thuluth*. The details of the letters, particularly the hastae of *lām*s and *alif*s are chased. The inscription at first apears to be an ordinary one of praise which is repeated so frequently on early and medieval metalwork. However, as has been pointed out by Melikian-Chirvani, it is not an ordinary saying, but a *duʿā*, a prayer, calling for God's blessing to the owner of the object.[17]

The seated figures in the round medallions are very much alike apart from some small details (Figures 8.7–8.8). All three figures are shown in cross-legged position and are flanked by what appear to be supports of a chair or a throne. They have haloes around their heads with a ray-like radiating line. However, these haloes are not single ones as they appear on later miniature paintings, metalwork or in ceramics, but doubles ones (cf. Figure 8.8). It is the inner ones which have a series of short ray-like chase lines. They continue below the head and neck of the figures and are then connected with the garments. Of course these could be neckpieces or shawls. Such ornaments are shown on Buddhist paintings, particularly on Tibetan Tankas. The figures are shown in frontal positions, but the faces of two are turned towards the right. They are holding different objects in their hands which could be cups, flowers, or even prayer-mills.

The third narrow register on all three panels is separated from the central one by narrow frames formed by a double band of geometric scrolls, which actually appears as series of triangles. These third

136

registers depict animals in the chase. On each panel there are two animals, a dog and a hare.

The fourth side or panel of the body is different, due to the attached handle (Figure 8.7). Above, in the top register we find the same type of five-lobed palmettes, but in the central one there is a large wing motif in relief flanking the handle. When one observes this panel together with the handle's support, which is in the shape of the protome of a lion, it becomes clear that the artist intended it to represent a winged lion. Below to the right and left are two hares running in opposite directions.

The handle is an irregular octagon in section (Figures 8.7, 8.9), since the corner panels are narrow. The sides once more depict two animals in the chase. The lower panels are plain, but on top there is an epigraphic band, written in Kufic:

> wa'l-birr wa'l-baraka wa'l-daula . . . wa'l-karāma . . . wa'l-birr (and loyalty and Divine blessing and power and . . . Divine favour and loyalty.

To make this support even stronger, the artist attached a quarter-circle loop, connecting the inner side of the leg to the lower part of the handle (Figure 8.7). The lion's head is attached to the lower part by a hinge, so that it can be opened. The lion's body is decorated with a fine floral scroll in openwork. Special attention was paid by the artist to decorate the lion's ears with chased designs, resembling a semi-palmette.

The flat top of the vessel's body around the dome reveals extensive openwork floral scroll decoration (Figure 8.9). On two sides, flanking the dome there are Kufic inscriptions turned inwards. They are identical and repeat the same phrase:

> al-yumn wa'l-yasirr (God's favour for him [the owner] and wealth).

This is also part of a du'ā; similar examples can be found on some early Khurasan bronze vessels.[18]

Before examining the large dome, the body's four legs and the four lion heads at the corners of the flat top should be described. The legs are all in zoomorphic forms in the shape of hares' protomes (Figures 8.7–8.8). The heads and the upper parts of the hares' bodies also form the corners of the vessel, while the solid parts are in the shape of paws. The breasts are decorated with openwork and in the centre they include a round medallion with a long-eared bird inside them. The comparatively large eyes are open and the long ears plain. The four lion heads on top at the corners are partially executed in openwork, while the ears have chased designs, showing a semi-palmette. The eyes, like those of the four hares, are open.

The dome has a well-proportioned hemispherical shape, crowned on top by a chatri-like finial, which clearly imitates a Buddhist stupa's umbrella, the lotus parasol. There is also a large openwork leaf which serves as a thumb-piece of the hinge (Figure 8.7). The dome's decoration is entirely in openwork and is divided into four equal zones. The lowest narrow one, just above the base, carries a series of five-lobed palmettes, identical to those which decorate the upper zone around the body. This is followed by a wide epigraphic band, written in the same cursive *thuluth* style like those around the body and it is a repetition of the same *du'ā*. The inscription is interrupted by two round medallions, each with seated figures similar to those already seen on three sides of the body.

This incense-burner with its three major parts, body, dome and *chatri*, recalls the stupa of Guldarra (Figure 8.1). The *chatri* in particular clarifies beyond any doubt that the artist or artists were deliberately imitating a shape that was familiar to them. As has already been mentioned above, Melikian-Chirvani believed that the circular incense-burners may have copied a stupa which must have existed near Herat. The decorative details of these vessels all bear the characteristics of the Khurasan school, particularly of the Samanid period. One of these characteristics was the application of the five-lobed palmettes.[19] Indeed, there are numerous early Islamic metal vessels which display such five-lobed banded palmettes. They also appear on several carved marble plaques which were discovered at Ghazni and until recently were preserved in the National Museum of Kabul. Several of these also reveal running animals.[20]

The seated figures which are shown in the centre on three sides of the body and on the dome also betray the impact of Buddhist art. They are remarkably similar to Buddhist statues and paintings. These seated figures are not 'enthroned monarchs', as they are shown on later metal and pottery vessels and miniature paintings, but Boddhisattvas. Such representation is not surprising since the artists of the period encountered such paintings and statues every day. This writer first discussed the possible connection between pre-Islamic art, that is, Buddhist paintings of Central Asia, and the decoration of early Islamic lustre-painted pottery nearly forty years ago.[21] The statures of the figures are quite unlike those of princes or monarchs. They are seated in the position called *padmasana*, with their right hand in *bhumisparsa*. It is not proposed here that the artists who created the incense-burner deliberately includes Boddhisattvas on this object, simply that they produced figures that they were familiar with.

Before we enter into the question of provenance and date of this last incense-burner we should examine another one, which in shape comes very close to this. In fact the Tareq Rajab Museum's vessel was probably modelled on this earlier example from the Freer Gallery of Art in Washington (Figure 8.10). It was attributed to Egypt and dated to the eighth–ninth centuries.[22] It has similarly a square body resting on four lion-head-decorated animal paws, a large dome on top in the centre and four smaller ones at the corners (Figure 8.10). The large and the small domes are surmounted by blossoming lotuses and

Fig. 8.10 *Large bronze square-type incense-burner, cast bronze with engraved and incised decoration.*

(Freer Gallery of Art, Washington, DC, purchase, F1952.1.)

were originally crowned by eagles, of which now only two survive. There is also a long handle terminating in the head of an ibex, but its lower body, which supported it, is now also missing. The vessel has a rich overall openwork decoration, on the side displaying geometrical interlace or, more precisely, basket-work.

Atil et al. stated that while this vessel seems to be modelled on a building, 'there are no extant buildings of the period which could have been used as the model for the Freer piece. Although the Byzantine plan of a square surmounted by five domes can be traced to the 9th century . . .' They add nevertheless that the only comparable building is the later tenth-century Samanid mausoleum of Is-ma'il at Bukhara.[23] Indeed, the earliest and closest example is the Samanid mausoleum at Bukhara (Figure 8.2), but, as we try to show here, it must have been modelled after the stupa at Guldarra. At the same time it is also evident that this incense-burner must have been also modelled on the same, or some other similar, Buddhist stupa in Afghanistan. It was Eva Baer who first questioned the Egyptian provenance of this incense-burner and suggested that its most likely provenance was Central Asia.[24] Perhaps we shall be able to narrow down the provenance of these two incense-burners.

While both seem to be the work of the Khurasan school, the question arises: in which centre were they made? It has already been proposed that this school had three major centres, Herat, Nishapur and Merv.[25] To these three we may be able add another: Ghazni. The Italian excavations at Ghazni brought to light several metal objects and some of these excavated pieces and other locally discovered metal vessels were acquired by different museums in Afghanistan.[26] However, there is no absolute evidence that Ghazni was a metal-working centre. Nevertheless the architectural form of these two vessels, which were modelled on the stupa of Guldarra, situated in the Kabul region, points to a more easterly workshop than Herat or Merv and one further east than Nishapur. They were most likely made in a place closer to the Buddhist centres, that place being Ghazni. In spite of earlier claims, mainly by M. Marchal,[27] Melikian-Chirvani was very sceptical about the possible existence of such a centre at Ghazni.[28] At the same time one may add that there is neither historical nor archaeological evidence to contradict this theory. James Allan has remarked that Ghazni could have been a metalworking centre until it was sacked by the Ghurids in 545AH/AD1150–1.[29]

As to the possible date of these two incense-burners, it is beyond doubt that the Freer piece is the earlier one, being most likely Samanid, perhaps ninth or tenth century. The Tareq Rajab Museum example, because of its fully developed cursive script, is considerably later, probably of the later Ghaznavid period, but certainly before the sacking of the town by the Ghurids in the middle of the twelfth century.

Notes

1. Cf. 'The Buddhist Heritage in the Art of Iran', *Mahayanist Art After AD900*, Percival David Foundation of Chinese Art Colloquies on Art and Archaeology 2, ed. William Watson (London, 1971), 56–73; idem., 'Le legs littéraire du bouddhisme iranien,' *Le Monde Iranien et l 'Islam* 2 (1974), 1–71; 3 (1975), 1–61.
2. Cf. G. Frumkin, *Archaeology in Soviet Central Asia* (Leyden, 1970).
3. A. Lézine, 'Trois stupa de la région Caboul,' *Artibus Asiae*, 17/1–2 (1964), 5–24; also A. S. Melikian-Chirvani, 'Recherches sur l'architecture de l'Iran bouddhique I. Essai sur les origines et le symbolisme du stūpa iranien,' *Le Monde Iranien et l'Islam*, 3 (1975), 1–61.
4. Melikian-Chirvani discussed for the first time this similarity in *Le Bronze iranien (VIIe-XIe s)* (Paris, 1972).
5. Melikian-Chirvani, 'Recherches sur l'architecture,' 55–8, pls. XII/a-b. One of these two, the Kabul Museum's piece, was also discussed and illustrated in his *Islamic Metalwork from the Iranian World., 8th–18th centuries* (London, 1982), 32, fig.7.
6. Benjamin Rowland, *The Art and Architecture of India* (London, 1953), pl. 41/A.
7. Inv. no. MET81TSR.
8. Eva Baer, *Metalwork in Medieval Islamic Art* (New York, 1983), 49–51, figs. 34–5.
9. Inv. no. MET212TSR. Height 14cm; diam. of body 18cm, length of handle 20cm.
10. Inv. no. MET1284TSR. Height 23cm; Length with handle 38.5cm; diam. of body 13.5cm.

11. Baer, *Metalwork*, 48–49, fig.33.
12. Sotheby's sale catalogue, 25th April, 1995, lot 216.
13. Inv. no. LNS41M. Cf. *Islamic Art in the Kuwait National Museum. The al-Sabah Collection,* ed Marilyn Jenkins (Kuwait, 1983), 40.
14. Inv. no. MET199TSR. Height 13cm; diam. 9.5cm.
15. Inv. no. MET2375TSR.
16. This object will be published in greater detail and our conservator's work will be fully described and the different layers she discovered will be illustrated in a forthcoming article.
17. Melikian-Chirvani, *Islamic Metalwork*, 29.
18. Melikian-Chirvani, *Islamic Metalwork*, 29.
19. Melikian-Chirvani, *Islamic Metalwork*, 34, fig. 9 and n. 64.
20. Frances Mortimer Rice and Benjamin Rowland, *Art in Afghanistan. Objects from the Kabul Museum* (London, 1971), pls. 169–70. For the decoration of the marble plaques cf. also Alessio Bombacci, 'Introduction to the Excavations at Ghazni,' *East and West,* N.S.10 (1959), 3–22.
21. Géza Fehérvári, 'Two 'Abbasid Lustre Bowls and the Influence of Central Asia', *Oriental Art,* N.S. 9 (1963), 79–88.
22. Inv. no. F.1952.1. It was first published and illustrated in colour by Esin Atil, *Art of the Arab World* (Washington, D.C., 1975), no.8; see also E. Atil, E.T. Chase and P. Jett, *Islamic Metalwork in the Freer Gallery of Art* (Washington, D.C.), 1985, 58–61, no.2.
23. Atil, Chase and Jett, *Islamic Metalwork*, 58.
24. Baer, *Metalwork*, 46–7, fig. 32.
25. James Allan, *Persian Metal Technology 700–1300AD* (Oxford, 1979); also idem., *Nishapur, Metalwork of the Early Islamic Period* (New York, 1982).
26. Melikian-Chirvani, *Islamic Metalwork*, 'Chapter II. The Later Khorasan School,' 55 ff.
27. M. Marchal, 'L'art du bronze islamique d'Afghanistan,' *Revue du Louvre* 1 (1974), 7–18.
28. Melikian-Chirvani, *Islamic Metalwork*, 76–7.
29. Allan, *Nishapur*, 20.

CHAPTER NINE

Vine Ornament and Pomegranates as Palace Decoration in ʿAnjar

Barbara Finster

The palatial city of ʿAnjar, situated on the slopes of Anti-Lebanon, has until now posed a challenge to research. As a ruin, this construction has its own history, which extends far into the twentieth century and has defined its character. The Great Palace, a bold construction by contemporary architects, possesses, as an adaption of Umayyad art, its own symbolic value that complicates an objective historical description.[1] ʿAnjar's ground plan is a square of 310 × 370m, whose longitudinal dimension stretches from south to north and is structured by terraces. Its characteristic features are the streets of *cardo* and *decumanus*, bordered by arcades and lined by rows of little shops, which define it as a commercial centre of this region. This, however, it never was, because ʿAnjar was not completed. The generous plan and the palaces that were finished reveal a caliphal commission: the buildings were most certainly ordered by the caliph al-Walid b. ʿAbd al-Malik (705–15) (Figure 9.1).[2]

The Great Palace, a quadrangle, comprises a courtyard with basilical audience halls at the south and north sides. The courtyard, equipped with a portico, is enclosed by bait groups. The Small Palace on the north side of the *decumanus* possesses only a large reception room, which, however, is given prominence by aediculae on the façade. Here again, the courtyard is enclosed by arcades; bait groups are adjoined on the east and west. The mosque, built like the two palaces at an earlier phase, is situated between both palaces.[3] The elevations of the buildings are largely unknown; it is doubtful whether they could be reconstructed at all.

Apart from the ground plan and the rows of arcades, the fragments of the building's ornamentation are testimony to the intention to construct a representative piece of architecture. Presumably the fragments, excluding the capitals of the arcades alongside the *cardo* and *decumanus*, have to be assigned to the three main buildings.

The layout of the ornamental parts is not clear. It can safely be assumed that the arcades were bordered by acanthus interlaces, and

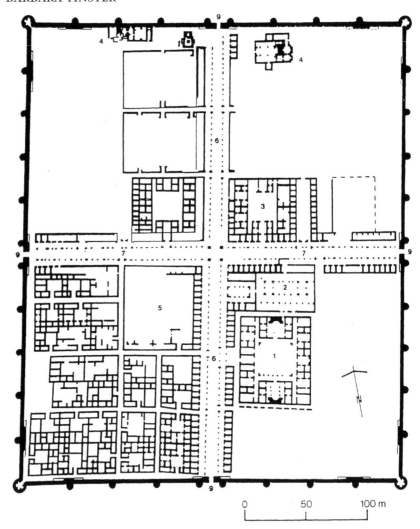

Fig. 9.1 *ʿAnjar, ground
plan.*

(Courtesy of Department of
Antiquities and Museums,
Beirut.)

that ornamental friezes – as reconstructed at the Great Palace – lined
the windows. The round multi-foil windows, their placement and
height, are, however, problematical (Figures 9.2–3). Moreover, there
is confusion in the multiplicity of ornaments and in the variants of
patterns that makes one suspect that the instructions contained only
approximate directions and that it was left to the artisans how to
implement them in each case.

As far as one can trust the extant findings, the ornamental groups of
the three main buildings differ in decor and elaboration.[4] The ornamentation of the Great Palace is flat; the patterns form part of the
background, as if cut out, and their surface is free of further carvings.
The ornaments of the Small Palace, however, cover the ground; the
individual structures are elaborated with a certain kind of plasticity,
and the ribs of the leaves are embedded. Parts of the workmanship are
of poor quality, unlike some capitals which were found in the Great

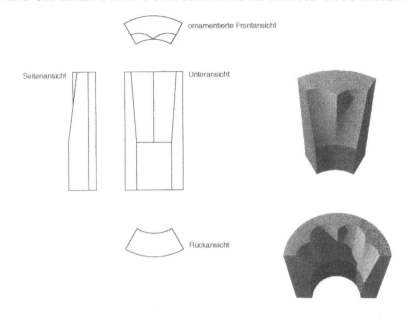

ornamentierte Frontansicht

Seitenansicht

Unteransicht

Rückansicht

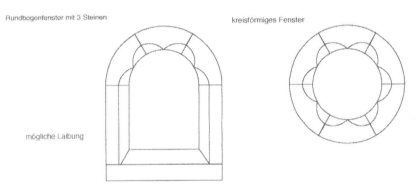

Rundbogenfenster mit 3 Steinen

kreisförmiges Fenster

mögliche Laibung

Fig. 9.2 ´Anjar, reconstruction of round-arched window.

(Drawing © A. Kreisel.)

Palace and which suggest that originally fine artists had been at work. The basic motif of the ornamental repertoire is acanthus tendrils with heavily stylised leaves, reminiscent of Coptic work (Figure 9.4). Various kinds of undulating tendrils together with acanthus leaves may show serrated leaves, or they can be enriched by rosettes in the form of disks. Meander bands with figural depictions belong to the adoption of antique models just as much as, among others, capitals with depictions of animals. Two other motifs dominate the decoration of the palace, the pomegranate and the bunch of grapes. Whereas pomegranates predominate in the Small Palace, vine ornaments with grapes seem to be important in the Great Palace, together with tendrils with outspread five-pointed leaves which can be interpreted as vine leaves. The mosque also possessed a rich decoration of vine scrolls with pendant grapes, acanthus tendrils with heavy balls at the tips of the leaves and elegant undulating tendrils with softly lobed acanthus leaves.

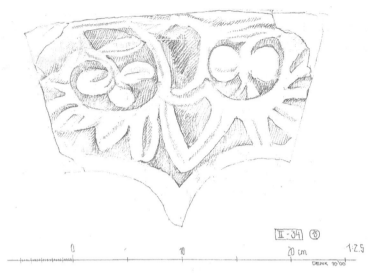

KLEINER PALAST- ANJAR- LIBANON
MEHRPASSFENSTER BOGENSTEIN

Fig. 9.3 ´Anjar, Small
Palace, window fragment.

(Drawing © M. Denk.)

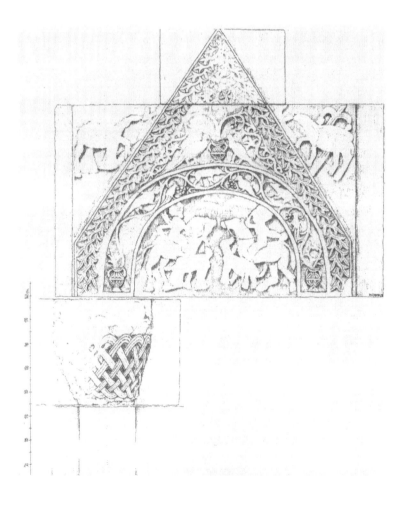

Fig. 9.4 ´Anjar, Great
Palace, capital and
tympanum.

(Drawing © M. Denk.)

The pomegranate ornamentation was apparently concentrated in the Small Palace.[5] The pomegranate is not depicted solely as a fruit; it is rather linked with acanthus tendrils (Figure 9.5), or forms, within undulating tendrils, the centre of a loop (Plate 15). In addition, small pomegranates grow out of the leaves of stylized interlace patterns (Figure 9.6) or alternate with grapes in the acanthus tendrils (Figure 9.7). There is a fragment on which loosely tied tendrils appear, all of whose branches end in a fruit and play around wreaths (Figure 9.6).

Typically, there are long branches of pomegranates with pointed leaves arranged in a row, out of which the fruit grows (Plate 16). This kind of depiction corresponds to the branches of pomegranates on the façades of Armenian churches, for example at Zwart'nots.[6] These branches are also combined with extended tendrils, which again show serrated pomegranate branches. Branches of pomegranates occur likewise at the centre of oval tendrils twined around them.

As a major motif, an acanthus branch with pomegranates covers the tympanum of an aedicula, which may have flanked the entrance to the courtyard of the Small Palace and thus formed the counterpart to the aediculae of the audience chamber (Plate 17). Tendrils with pomegranates enclose the edges of a tympanum of a second aedicula; at their tips they end in a depiction of an eagle with outspread wings (Figure 9.8).

The fruit itself is depicted either as a round apple with a crowning trefoil or, especially in the case of large fruits, with two almost circular bulbs, out of which grow the three small leaves of the former

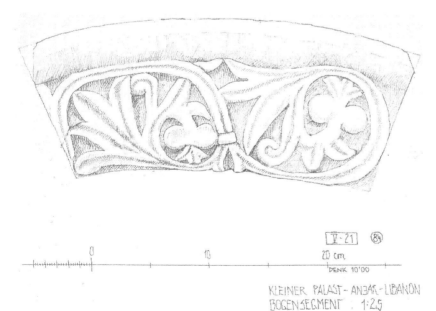

Fig. 9.5 'Anjar, Small Palace, fragment of arch.

(Drawing © M. Denk.)

Fig. 9.6 *'Anjar, Small Palace, fragment of frieze.*

(Drawing © M. Denk.)

KLEINER PALAST - ANJAR. LIBANON
FRAGMENT - FRIES   1:5

Fig. 9.7 *'Anjar, Small Palace, fragment of frieze.*

(Photograph © B. Finster.)

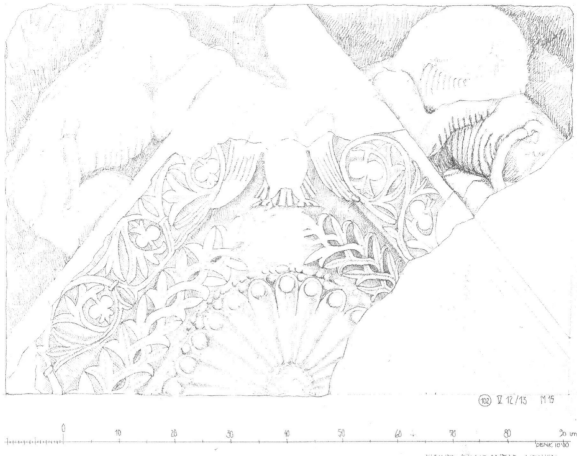

KLEINER PALAST·ANJAR - LIBANON
GIEBELSTEIN MIT KONCHE 1:5

blossom (Figures 9.9–10). The concentration of this motif in the decor of the Small Palace is striking, because it is a central theme and as such is not found in any other early Islamic palace.

Fig. 9.8 ʿAnjar, Small Palace, fragment of frieze.

(Drawing © M. Denk.)

Pomegranates in an elegant acanthus tendril together with trefoils[7] appear on the marble relief slabs at Khirbat al-Minya, a building which is also attributed to the Caliph al-Walid b. ʿAbd al-Malik; they can again be found in the palace of Qasr al-Hair al-Gharbi, which must be dated later. The inner entrance of the building is decorated by a delicate acanthus tendril with a cluster of three pomegranates. The bursting fruits show an abundance of pips, which are regarded as symbols of fertility.[8]

On the wooden tables of the al-Aqsa mosque, pomegranates are tied into acanthus tendrils or appear as elements of the rosettes after Sasanian models. The original marble decoration of the Great Mosque of Damascus also contained the depiction of a pomegranate, framed by winged palmettes.[9]

In the Orient, the pomegranate was, since earliest times, associated

149

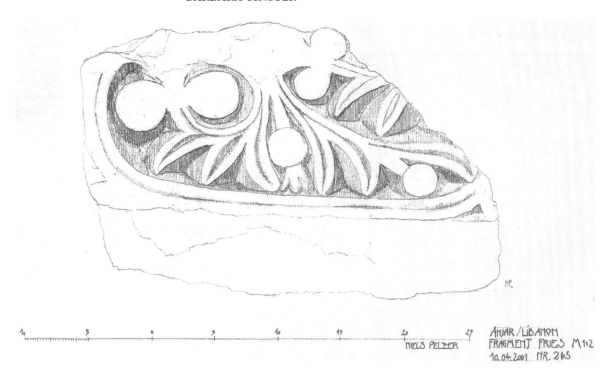

ANJAR / LIBANON
FRAGMENT FRIES M1-2
10.04.2001 NR. 265

NIELS PELZER

Fig. 9.9 ´Anjar, Small Palace, fragment of frieze.

(Drawing © N. Pelzer.)

with the tree of life, as Assyrian cylinder-seals demonstrate. It was considered the fruit of the Great Goddess, later of Aphrodite and also of Hera.[10] As the fruit of life it could also be given into the hands of the dead. It seems likely that occasional pomegranates on branches and trees in the churches of the near east were taken as symbols of the hope for a life after death or for eternal life. In combination with a kantharos and together with branches, the pomegranate was again, as in earliest times, associated with the motif of the tree of life.[11] The pomegranate could possibly also be understood as a symbol of 'happiness, abundance, and blessing', while the pomegranate tree itself signified peace or the Golden Age.[12]

It is in this admittedly rather loose sense that the depiction of pomegranates and bunches in the Qubbat al-Sakhra, the al-Aqsa mosque and in the Great Mosque of Damascus has to be understood. In the mosaics of the Qubbat al-Sakhra small fruits grow out of acanthus tendrils, are found on the leaves of the archivolts of the arcades, or protrude from a cornucopia.[13] The pomegranate does not, however, occupy a prominent position in the decor of the Qubbat al-Sakhra, remaining subordinate to the acanthus tendrils and vine-scrolls. The pomegranate can also be found in the ornamental borders of early Qur'an manuscripts, but, compared to other motifs, it is little more than a citation. Nevertheless, a pomegranate tree was added to the *ansa* of a ninth-century Qur'an; its branches end in fruits by which it is adorned, as was the earlier tree of life from Assur.[14] A sacral connotation can therefore be assumed.

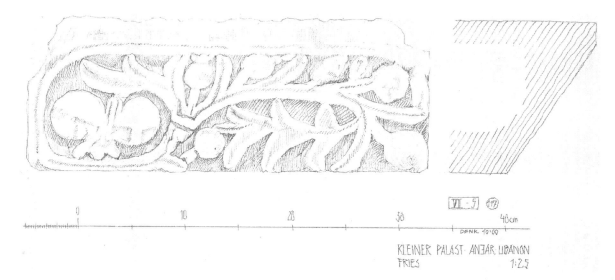

Fig. 9.10 ˊAnjar, Small Palace, fragment of frieze.

(Drawing © M. Denk.)

Thus it appears that the pomegranate was used in Islamic art as one motif among many others, to which, in contrast to grapevines, no great importance was attached.

The association of vine and pomegranate, established in late antiquity because of its inherent symbolic content, can also be observed in the ornaments of ˊAnjar.[15] Grapes and pomegranates appear in an undulating tendril on an archivolt of the Small Palace, alternately placed in the interior of a loop, and hence are to be regarded as of equal value (Figure 9.7). A similar tendril surrounds a multi-foil window, with the grape always constituting the centre of the ornament (Figure 9.13). Acanthus tendrils with grapes, or branching vine-scrolls with their grapes, also lined the court arcades of the Small Palace (Figure 9.12).

In the Great Palace, vine-scrolls were presumably the major decor of the audience chamber. Here again they extend around arcades,

Fig. 9.11 ˊAnjar, mosque, fragment of frieze.

(Drawing © M. Denk.)

Fig. 9.12 *'Anjar, Small Palace, fragment of frieze.*

(Photograph © B. Finster.)

either – as reconstructed today – around the window arches and/or around the arcades of the columns. As mentioned above, the vine-scrolls are laid on the even ground as broad flat ribbons. Vine leaves and grapes remain flat and, lacking interior patterns, have their effect only as forms in their contours. By way of compensation the movement of the tendrils is delicately sketched; the little branches and the grapes intertwine playfully (Fig. 9.11; Plate 18).

With their loops, manifold turns and knotted tendrils, the vine-scrolls offer a wide spectrum of artistic representation for which there are scarcely any models. They rather seem to have originated in a delight in invention which seems to surpass itself and gives life to the vine-scrolls by the moving contours (Plate 19). Various animals romp about in the animated vine-scroll which grows out of stylised kantharoi in the tympanum of the aediculae; there are peacocks in the tympanum, drinking out of a kantharos with overflowing tendrils (Figure 9.4).

In addition to the flat, unmodelled friezes of vine-scrolls there are variants which are likely to have belonged to the decoration of the mosque. There they also lined the arcades as ornamental friezes. Among them one finds generously drawn acanthus tendrils with double loops which surround standing and hanging grapes. The leaves are carved with ribs and furrows, showing thereby that a certain

I·14; II·52 ⑥
0   10   20 cm
DENK 10'00   1:2.5

KLEINER PALAST·ANJAR·LIBANON
MEHRPASSFENSTER BOGENSTEIN

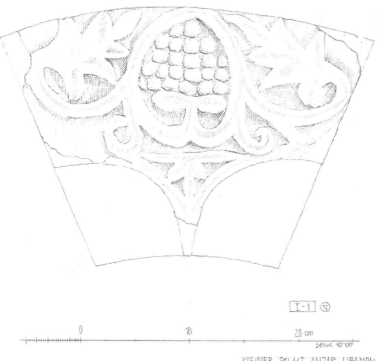

I·1 ⑫
0   10   20 cm
DENK 10'00

KLEINER PALAST·ANJAR·LIBANON
MEHRPASSFENSTER BOGENSTEIN 1:2.5

Fig. 9.13 ʿAnjar, Small Palace, window fragments.

(Drawings © M. Denk.)

plasticity was intended (Figure 9.12). In contrast, thin interlacing scrolls with ribbed vine leaves and delicate pearly grapes compose a finely meshed net on their flat surface.

Since earliest times, vine-scrolls with grapes belonged to the decoration of important mosques. Vine-scrolls with pendant grapes completely covered the round columns in front of the mihrab in the mosque of Hajjaj ibn Yusuf in Wasit. Glittering acanthus tendrils produce round pearl-like grapes at the Qubbat al-Sakhra. In the Great Mosque of Damascus the golden *karma*, the vine-scroll on the principal mihrab, is counted as one of its wonders.[16]

The sacral connotation of the vine becomes evident on the frontispiece of the early Qur'an from Sana'a. On its upper margin, vines together with their fruits grow between the cypresses and should be understood as part of the mosque which is represented on this page.[17] In later times, vines still remain the major decoration of the mihrab, as the vine on a golden ground in the niche of the mosque of Qairawan shows. In the same way vines as part of the tree of life are displayed in the centre of the mihrab of the Khassaki mosque in Bagdad. In the mihrab of the mosque of Na'in it seems to form a bower together with the columns of the mihrab bay.[18] The representation of a vine in the architecture of a mosque and in book illustration can be understood as the adoption of the then widely known symbol of the hope for a life after death.[19]

On the other hand, and since earliest times, the vine was just as much part of the secular world and as such associated with princely power. This is evident in the relief of Assurbanipal (669–627 BCE), which shows him at dinner in a vine arbour, celebrating a victory together with his wife.[20]

In the bath of Qusair 'Amra, whose frescoes follow an entirely different pictorial programme than that of 'Anjar, profuse vine-scrolls cover the vaults and turn the room into a vine arbour. Pomegranates and grapes appear hanging between the leaves. In the vestibule of the citadel of Amman, a construction probably dating from the time of Hajjaj ibn Yusuf, a stiffly upward-growing vine ornament with stylised grapes covers one of the large blind niches of the courtyard. A major decor of this important space, it appears next to a rosette and leaf candelabra, which may be associated with the tree of life.[21] It is more likely, however, that these vine-scrolls correspond to models from Mesopotamia and belong stylistically to the eastern Sasanian world.

Vine-scrolls and pomegranate branches are also part of the general decoration of the palaces of the later Umayyad period, namely at Qasr al-Hair al-Gharbi and Khirbat al-Mafjar, whose figural richness again comprises a different iconography of princely power.[22]

Of outstanding significance is the vine-scroll on the façade of the palace of Mashatta, where the vines can be understood as the tree of life, whose branches cover large areas of the façade like a web.[23] In Qasr al-Hair al-Sharqi one also finds the depiction of a vine-scroll with grapes, on the blind arcades above the portal.[24] The claim of sovereignty made by this kind of architecture thus receives an additional accentuation.

It has become apparent that, even in the Islamic era, the motif of the vine ornament acquires significance in the architecture of palaces. Because of its Dionysian implications, grapevines were in late antiquity part of the iconography of princely power, which also extended to Sassanian territory.[25] On the other hand, the vine stalk and the vine generally signified the tree of life, which was applicable equally to the princely thrones of the east and the west.[26] In the Islamic period, vine-scrolls could therefore be interpreted as symbols of claims to rulership.

In comparison, the pomegranate seems to have played a minor role in Islamic art; but as the example of Anjar shows, it was deliberately adopted. At Qusair Amra the pomegranate was also woven into the tendrils; on the marble panels at Khirbat al-Minya it occupies the centre of the acanthus tendrils. All three constructions were commissioned by the caliph al-Walid b. ʿAbd al-Malik. The significance, which was nevertheless given to the pomegranate, becomes apparent in Qurʾanic illumination.[27]

The connections between vine-scrolls and pomegranates can already be found in pre-Islamic times.[28] In Christianity, this connection between the two symbols suggests itself because of their possible allusions to the idea of an afterlife.

In pre-Islamic times, the vine stalk as well as pomegranates were understood to be elements of the tree of life. On the façades of the Church of the Holy Cross in Aghtamar (915–21) vine-scrolls and branches of a pomegranate tree are twisted into a whole which allows practically no separation. They belong to the upper zone which does not exhibit scenes from the Old and New Testaments but from hunting. Hence, they are scarcely part of the sacral programme, which is located in the lower zone, but of a secular programme which culminates in the depiction of a seated ruler.[29]

In the decoration at ʿAnjar, the depiction of pomegranate branches corresponds to the kind of representation found in Armenian churches, which may have acted as a model.

The directions given to the artisans were, however, part of a meaningful programme, as was the whole construction of ʿAnjar. These directions include the pilaster capitals of the Small Palace with their depiction of an eagle surrounded by lions' heads, as well as the aediculae, whose gables were framed by lions (Figure 9.8), and other figural representations, of which today only fragments remain.[30] In this context, one should also mention the portraits on the capitals of the arcades near the North Gate, which depict the Byzantine emperor and the Sassanian ruler[31] (Plates 16 and 20). Apparently, they were meant to show that the builder of ʿAnjar, that is, Walid b. ʿAbd al-Malik, was to be understood as the ruler over the east and the west. A similar interpretation may be assumed in the case of the two riders, a horseman and a rider on a dromedary, who are placed opposite each other in the tympanum of the aediculae in the courtyard of the Great Palace (Figure 9.4).

Accordingly, vine-scrolls and ornamental pomegranates were intended to serve as signs of caliphal rule, borrowed from models in the art of late antiquity. It remains an open question whether this should be seen in association with the motif of the tree of life or whether there is a wider context.[32]

In later times, though, for example in the tenth century, the walls of the Salon Rico in Medinat al-Zahra were covered with representations of the tree of life, in the same way in which they can be seen in the mihrab of the Great Mosque of Cordoba.

Altogether, the ruins of ʿAnjar testify to a precisely calculated plan, to the creative power of its builder who took his cue from works of art of the antique culture. One can rule out the assumption that arbitrary ornaments were chosen for palace decor. As in his other major commissions, the caliph al-Walid b. ʿAbd al-Malik revealed that antique art served as an inspiration, but that its forms were selected and utilised deliberately. In this way, he created the basis for an understanding of his own individuality and for an art which, time and again in the course of its development, had recourse to antique elements in order to express a certain political ideology.

Notes

I would like to express my gratitude to Professor K. P. Jochum, who kindly translated the original German text into English. Among the numerous studies written by Robert Hillenbrand there is also a discussion about the city of ʿAnjar and its plan, ' ʿAnjar and Early Islamic Urbanism', in *The Idea and the Ideal of the Town between Late Antiquity and the Early Middle Ages*, ed. G. P. Brogiolo and Bryan Ward-Perkins (Leyden, 1999), 59–98.

1. The ruins of ʿAnjar have been excavated since the year 1952 for more than twenty-five years by the Lebanese Department of Antiquities. There are two preliminary reports written by Maurice Chehab and cited by Hafez K. Chehab (see n. 2 below) and a guidebook: *Anjar, Baalbak, Guide Archéologique* (Beirut, n.d.). The excavation is mentioned by B. Condé, *See Lebanon* (Beirut, 1960), 420–4. With the support of the Fritz Thyssen Stiftung, the University of Bamberg is engaged in studying and publishing the architectural remains and the decoration of the ruin.
2. Hafez K. Chehab, 'On the Identification of ʿAnjar (ʿAyn al-Jarr) as an Umayyad Foundation', *Muqarnas* 10 (1993), 42–8.
3. Plan after M. Chehab (1975); by courtesy of Mr F. Husseini, the Director of the Department of Antiquities and Museums in Beirut, we got permission to study the ornaments in the ruins of ʿAnjar and to prepare a new ground plan which will be published in Baal.
4. A specific type of ornament was deposed in the Small Palace which seems to be part of the decoration there, whereas the ornamentation of the mosque was collected at a different place.
5. The importance of the Small Palace is underlined by the richly

decorated entrance and the aediculae in front of the throne-room. In the courtyard two antique female statues were found, one of which is now exhibited in the Museum of Ba'albak.

6. Palace church of Zwart'nots (seventh century), Sirarpie Der Nersessian, *L'art arménien* (Paris, 1989), fig. 27; Friedrich Muthmann, *Der Granatapfel: Symbol des Lebens in der Antiken Welt* (Bern, 1982), 167–72.

7. Markus Ritter, 'Die Baudekoration des umayyadischen Palastes Hirbat al-Minya am See Genezareth', unpublished MA thesis, University of Bamberg, 1993, fig. 48.

8. Daniel Schlumberger, 'Les fouilles des Qasr el-Heir el-Gharbi (1936–8)', *Syria* 20 (1939), fig. 18.

9. K. A. C. Creswell, *Early Muslim Architecture*, 2nd edn (Oxford, 1969) (henceforth *EMA*), 2: pls 26h, 27b, f, g, 27h; R. W. Hamilton, *The Structural History of the Aqsa- Mosque* (Jerusalem, 1949), pls LII–3W; LIV–6E (at the apex of the arch), LVII, LIX–11W, LX–13E ; LXI, LXIV–18E, LXV–19EL, XVIII–E; Finbarr Barry Flood, *The Great Mosque of Damascus: Studies in the Making of an Umayyad visual Culture* (Leyden, 2001), Fig. 29; Jens Kröger, *Sasanidischer Stuckdekor*, Baghdader Forschungen 5 (Mainz, 1982), 97–9.

10. Muthmann, *Granatapfel*, 39–40.

11. Ibid., 127–8.

12. Josef Engemann, *Granatapfel*, Reallexikon für Antike und Christentum, 12, ed. T. Klauser et al. (Stuttgart, 1983), 715–16; according to Kröger, *Sasanidischer Stuckdekor*, 43, the pomegranate motif had a special Christian meaning in a Christian house in Tell Dhahab near Ctesiphon.

13. *EMA*, 1.1: fig. 221m, pl. 4b; Said Nuseibeh and Oleg Grabar, *The Dome of the Rock* (New York, 1996), as part of a tree of life: 57, 84, 85, 92, 94, 100; as elements of a candelabra: 76; combined with a cornucopia: 191.

14. *EMA*, 1.1:187; Martin Lings, *The Quranic Art of Calligraphy and Illumination* (Westerham, 1976), pl. 5. Compare the Assyrian tree of life, Muthmann, *Granatapfel*, figs 8–10; the lotus-flower obviously has a special meaning.

15. *Lexikon der christlichen Ikonographie*, ed. Engelbert Kirschbaum et al. (Rome and Freiburg, 1972).

16. *EMA*, 1.1, pl. 39b; Barbara Finster, *Frühe Iranische Moscheen* (Berlin, 1994), pl. 47/2; grapevines and the tree of life with lotus-flowers as main motif in the Qubbat al-Sakhra: Nuseibeh and Grabar, *Dome of the Rock*; for the *karma* in the Umayyad Mosque in Damascus, see Flood, *Great Mosque*, 111–12.

17. Hans-Caspar Graf von Bothmer, 'Architekturbilder im Koran: Eine Prachthandschrift der Umayyadenzeit aus dem Yemen', *Pantheon* 45 (1987), fig. 1.

18. See Flood, *Great Mosque*, 111; Finster, *Iranische Moscheen*, 118, 214–18.

19. A. Thomas, 'Weintraube', in *Lexikon der christlichen Ikonographie*; according to Philo, the tree of life is a huge grapevine, see Z. Ameisenowa, 'The Tree of Life in Jewish Iconography', *Journal of the Warburg Institute* 2/4 (1939), 330f; Andreas Alföldli, 'Die Geschichte des Throntabernakels', *La Nouvelle Clio* 1–2 (1949–50), 552–3.

20. Der Alte Orient, *Geschichte und Kultur des alten Vorderasien*, ed. Barthel Hrouda (Munich, 1991), 354–5.

21. Martin Almagro et al., *Qusayr 'Amra* (Madrid, 1975), pls XXII–XXIII; Alistair Northedge et al., *Studies on Roman and Islamic 'Ammân*, vol. 1 (Oxford, 1992), pls 20, 27–8.

22. Not so frequent in Qasr al-Hair al-Gharbi; scrolls with grapes as a frame around Gaea, see *EMA*, 1,2: pl. 90; Daniel Schlumberger et al., *Qasr el-Heir el Gharbi*, Bibliothèque Archéologique et Historique 120 (Paris, 1986), pls 84a, 55d; R. W. Hamilton, *Khirbat al-Mafjar: An Arabian Mansion in the Jordan Valley* (Oxford, 1959), scrolls with pomegranates: figs 186, 222, 229; grapevines: figs 187–189, 193, 199, 205, 209, 215; as a frame or inside the vaulting of a niche: pls XXVII 17, 20, XXVIII 10, 12, 13; as part of a panel at the entrance: pl. XXXIV 1; inside the vaulting: pl. XXXVII; at the entrance of the bath-hall: pls XLI 3, XLIII 1, XLIV 5; inside the *diwan* as an ornament between the wall panels: pls LVII, XLIX 7, LII 2–3, LVII 2; at the baluster of the courtyard: pls LXVI 2–4, LXVII, LXVIII.

23. *EMA*, 1.2: figs 188, 189, 655, pls. 121–9, often as an inhabited scroll; Volkmar Enderlein and Michael Meinecke, 'Mschatta – Fassade', *Jahrbuch der Berliner Museen* 34 (1992), 152–8; compare Flood, *Great Mosque*, 113, n. 263.

24. *EMA*, 1.2: fig. 574; the so-called khan of Qasr al-Hair al-Sharqi has to be seen as the qasr at that place, which is demonstrated by the portal and its decoration and the quality of the masonry.

25. Victor F. Lenzen, *The Triumph of Dionysos on Textiles of Late Antique Egypt* (Berkeley and Los Angeles, 1960), 21–3, Richard Ettinghausen, *From Byzantium to Sasanian Iran and the Islamic World* (Leyden, 1972), 10, understands the 'reception' of Dionysiac scenes as a 'transfer'; compare Muthmann, *Granatapfel*, 149–58, 167–72.

26. See Flood, *Great Mosque*, 90–2, for a one-sided interpretation of the motif.

27. See n. 14 above.

28. *Lexikon der Christlichen Ikonographie*; compare the composition of vine-scrolls and pomegranates at the Ionian capitals at the façade in Pthni, Ayrarat (beginning of the seventh century): Jean-Michel Thiery, *Armenische Kunst* (Freiburg, 1988), fig. 28.

29. Muthmann, *Granatapfel*, pl. 147; Thiery, *Armenische Kunst*, fig. 42.

30. The lion is found as a sculpture at Mashatta, at the feet of the princely figure in Khirbat al-Mafjar, as a relief at the parapet in Qasr al-Hair al-Gharbi. The imposing eagle at Qasr al-Hair al-Gharbi resembles the eagle at the temple of Baʿal Shamin in Palmyra. The lion and the eagle continued to be used as symbols of royalty.

31. The two figures of emperors at Qasr al-Hair al-Gharbi are to be interpreted in a similar way, one wearing an eastern dress and one a western Roman one.

32. Christian Ewert, *Die Dekorelemente der Wandfelder im Reichen Saal von Madînat az-Zahrâ', Eine Studie zum westumaiyadischen Bauschmuck des hohen 10. Jahrhunderts* (Mainz, 1996); the tree of life used in the same way as decoration in the mosque and the palace leads to the assumption that the palace has to be seen in a sacral connotation, though there is no such association in the Umayyad literature of al-Andalus. The comparison of the palace with paradise used in medieval times seems to be a topos in east and west. But the identification of the palace with paradise was already found in tenth-century eastern Iran at the palace of the Saffarid Abu Jaʿfar Muhammad b. Ahmad in Sistan. In Qasr al-Hair al-Gharbi there is a beautiful tree of life on a tympanum, which can hardly be interpreted as pure decoration. There it seems that the seated ruler, the eagle and the tree of life belong to one iconographic conception: Schlumberger, *Qasr el-Heir*, pl. 75.

CHAPTER TEN

Persianate Trends in Sultanate Architecture: The Great Mosque of Bada'un[1]

Finbarr Barry Flood

In recent years much has been done to remedy the neglect of pre-Mughal Islamic architecture in South Asia, which Robert Hillenbrand noted in his analysis of the Ghurid Friday Mosque of Ajmir.[2] Somewhat paradoxically, this burgeoning of research has also served to highlight glaring lacunae in the architectural record, manifest both in the nature of the surviving monuments (mostly religious foundations such as mosques and madrasas), and in their chronological spread. Despite the survival of numerous foundation inscriptions, and additions to the Ghurid Friday Mosque of Delhi (the Qutbi mosque), no major north Indian congregational mosques survive from the period between the arrival of the Ghurids in the late twelfth century and the accession of the Tughluqid dynasty over one hundred and twenty years later.[3]

There is, however, a behemoth among pre-Mughal Indian mosques, which can help fill this gap in the architectural record while elucidating more general principles of Indo-Islamic religious architecture in the thirteenth and fourteenth centuries. Descriptions of the Great Mosque of Bada'un in Uttar Pradesh were published by the Archaeological Survey of India in the colonial period, and short notices or passing references (largely dependent on these earlier descriptions) have appeared subsequently, but the building has never been the subject of any detailed analysis.[4] The observations below, based as they are on a brief visit to the site, are somewhat tentative, but offer a preliminary assessment of the mosque's chronology and historical importance. The existing structure preserves fragments of a mosque built on the site by Iltutmish, but is largely a product of the early fourteenth century; the form and decoration of the mosque are strikingly Persianate in their affinities. Given the ability of the mosque to shed new light on both the architectural patronage of Iltutmish (itself an oddly neglected topic) and Persianate trends in fourteenth-century Indo-Islamic architecture, topics on which Robert has published,[5] it seemed appropriate to offer these preliminary remarks in a volume intended to honour the unusual breadth and depth of his scholarly interests.

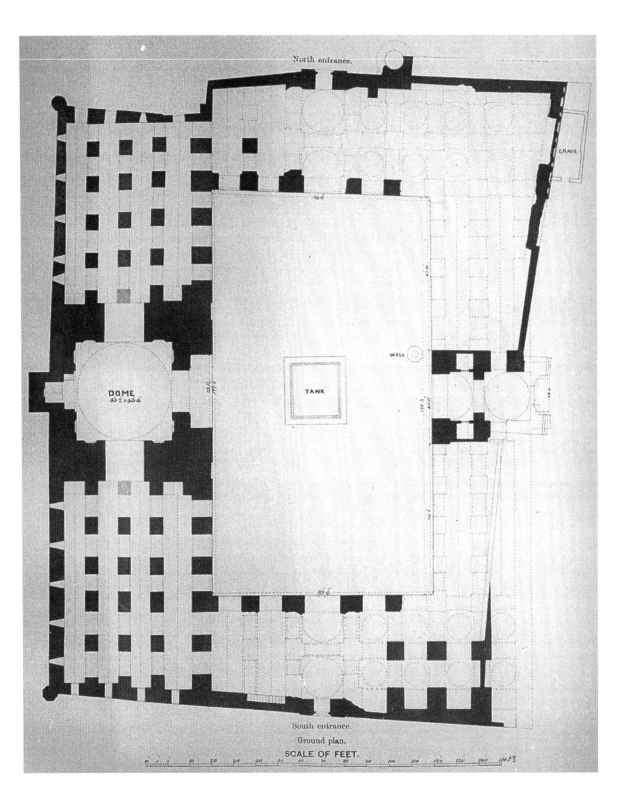

North entrance.

GRAVE

DOME
45·2 × 45·4

TANK

WELL

South entrance.

Ground plan.

SCALE OF FEET.

As it stands today, the mosque comprises an irregular trapezoid measuring approximately 60 × 85m, broader than it is long (Plate 21; Figure 10.1), with a baked brick superstructure supported on a course of good ashlar masonry, which stands to a height of roughly 3.6m (Figure 10.2). While half the size of the Adina Mosque at Pandua (1375), the largest mosque of pre-Mughal India, the Bada'un mosque encloses an area almost twice that of the original Qutbi mosque (1192–3 onwards), but comparable to that of Tughluqid congregational mosques such as the mosque at Jahanpanah (c. 1343).[6] The impression produced by the exterior is one of severe monumentality, the principal articulation being achieved by the use of window-openings, the rectangular projection of the mihrab, and narrow tapering corner bastions with horizontal bands of decorative brick-work (Figures 10.2–3).[7]

The interior, by contrast, is articulated by means of arcades framing a central courtyard, which measures approximately 30 × 53m. At the centre of each side of the court a shallow *iwan* is incorporated into a *pishtaq*, a monumental entrance that projects above the level of the surrounding roofs. The largest of these precedes the entrance to the prayer hall on the western side of the court (Figure 10.4). The façades of the *iwan*s and arcades were once richly decorated with floral, geometric and epigraphic ornament, executed in cut brick (and possibly terracotta), some of which was glazed (Figure 10.5). The glazing and most of the details of the ornament are now obscured

Fig. 10.1 (opposite) *Great Mosque of Bada'un, plan.*

(After Blakiston, *Jami Masjid*.)

Fig. 10.2 *Great Mosque of Bada'un, southern exterior elevation.*

(After Blakiston, *Jami Masjid*.)

South elevation.

SCALE OF FEET

Fig. 10.3 *Great Mosque of Bada'un, exterior bastion at south-eastern corner.*

(Photograph © F. B. Flood.)

beneath layers of whitewash, which have accumulated since it was first applied in the nineteenth century.[8]

The prayer hall consists of a rectangular space divided into four bays, which run parallel to the qibla, roofed with pointed barrel vaults supported on massive brick piers (Figure 10.6), and interrupted by a central monumental domed chamber. With an interior span of 12.5 × 12.5m, this is comparable in size to the domed chambers in the Saljuq mosques of Iran, but larger than any dome found in surviving thirteenth- and fourteenth-century Indian mosques with the sole exception of the recently published Tughluqid mosque at Warangal

Fig. 10.4 *Great Mosque of Bada'un, qibla* iwan *and southern side of courtyard.*

(Photograph © F. B. Flood.)

in the Deccan (c. 1322–3).[9] From what remained of the northern and southern bays of the court in the nineteenth and early twentieth centuries, it is clear that this arrangement of barrel-vaulted aisles carried on rectangular piers once continued two bays deep on the lateral sides of the court (Figure 10.1).[10] It seems likely that the same arrangement was followed on the eastern side of the court, although we cannot be certain, since most of what exists there now was rebuilt relatively recently.

The main entrance to the mosque is at the centre of its eastern side, facing the qibla, as was standard in Indian mosques even before the Ghurid conquest.[11] As we will see below, the monumental eastern entrance through which one enters the mosque today is a nineteenth-century replacement for an earlier gateway. In it has been reset the foundation text of the thirteenth-century mosque, two registers of Arabic carved in *naskhī* script on a sandstone plaque (Figure 10.7), which reads:

> Enter it in peace safely [Qur'an 15:46]. The magnificent sultan, the most exalted *shahinshāh*, the Lord of the necks of the people, the sun of the state and religion, the help of Islam and the Muslims, the most just of the kings and sultans, the victorious Iltutmish, the 'Royal Retainer' (*al-sulṭānī*), the helper of the Commander of the Faithful, may God perpetuate his kingdom. In the months of the year 620 [AD 1223].[12]

163

Detail of brick archway facing courtyard on north side of grand dome.

SCALE OF FEET

Fig. 10.5 *Great Mosque of Bada'un, detail of western courtyard arcade in 1888.*

(After Blakiston, *Jami Masjid.*)

Although it has generally been overlooked in discussions of sultanate architecture, Iltutmish's architectural patronage during his long reign (1211–36) was clearly extensive, and not confined to the imperial capital of Delhi. Even ignoring the many foundation inscriptions from structures erected during his reign that do not mention him as patron,[13] the number of north Indian civic and religious monuments ascribed to Iltutmish by epigraphic evidence or the historical sources testify to his role as a prolific patron of monumental architecture. Among the surviving monuments are the Qutb Minar (the second to fourth storeys of which Iltutmish completed), and the iron pillar in the courtyard of the Ghurid Friday Mosque of Delhi, which was set up in this position on his orders probably around 1229, when he also ordered the extension of the monumental screen that Qutb al-Din Aybak had added to the façade of the prayer hall.[14] The similar screen in the Ghurid Friday Mosque of Ajmir is datable to the same period (Figure 10.8).[15] To Iltutmish's patronage is also ascribed the tomb of his son, Nasir al-Din Mahmud in Delhi, which housed the Mu'izzi madrasa that he founded.[16] Before his death in 1235, the sultan is also presumed to have initiated work on the magnificent tomb adjacent to the Qutbi mosque that is believed to house his remains.[17] Elsewhere in Delhi, an inscription found in a fort at Sirsa records the fact that Iltutmish renovated the building in the 1230s. Whether contemporary with the renovation or later, the inscription attests Iltutmish's involvement in the construction of

164

Fig. 10.6 *Great Mosque of Bada'un, vaulting of prayer hall.*

(Photograph © F. B. Flood.)

civic monuments, which included the monumental water-tank in Delhi known as the Hauz-i Shamsi.[18]

Outside of Delhi, Iltutmish is reported to have founded another madrasa in Multan, while a mid-thirteenth-century stone inscription comparable in size to the Bada'un text records the earlier construction of a mosque at Gangarampur in West Bengal on Iltutmish's orders.[19] The Mughal emperor Babur (r. 932–7/1526–30) refers to

165

Fig. 10.7 *Great Mosque of Bada'un, detail of Iltutmish's foundation text above eastern entrance.*

(Photograph © F. B. Flood.)

Fig. 10.8 *Ajmir, Ghurid Mosque, detail of Iltutmish's screen.*

(Photograph © F. B. Flood.)

another congregational mosque founded by Iltutmish in the fort of Gwalior. Although no longer extant, the construction of a mosque within the fort follows Ghurid and early sultanate practice witnessed in Delhi, Bada'un and possibly Khatu in Rajasthan; a fragment of a stone *naskhī* inscription which looks to be of early thirteenth-century date in the Gwalior fort museum may have come from the vanished structure.[20] Babur also noted an inscription dated 630/1232–3 bearing the name of Iltutmish associated with a water-tank at Urwah, near Gwalior fort; given the sultan's reported involvement in the construction of the Hauz-i Shamsi in Delhi, his patronage of such a monument is by no means unlikely.[21] Finally, the style of a stray stone fragment carved with a geometric design, and now incorporated into the outer wall of Nagaur fort in Rajasthan (Figure 10.9) is sufficiently close to that of Iltutmish's screen in the Friday Mosque of Ajmir (Figure 10.8) to suggest that it may have come from a monument built by Iltutmish at Nagaur.[22]

In Bada'un itself, the congregational mosque may have been the centrepiece of an extensive building programme, for the massive baked brick *ʿīdgāh* of the city (over 90m in length) is traditionally ascribed to Iltutmish's activities while governor. Although to judge from its present appearance (Figure 10.10), the *ʿīdgāh* was remodelled in the Tughluqid period or later, the provision of such a monument would be consistent with Ghurid and early sultanate practice.[23] In addition, several fragmentary inscriptions preserved in later Bada'uni monuments appear to date from the reign of Iltutmish, among them one recording the erection of a city gate.[24]

Although Bada'un today is a relatively isolated provincial town, after its conquest in 594/1197 the city was of great strategic and political importance, functioning as an important nexus in the networks of military might, political influence and religious piety that bound together the various provincial capitals of the newly emergent Delhi sultanate.[25] The construction of a congregational mosque here by Iltutmish reflects both the importance of the city in its own right

Fig. 10.9 *Nagaur fort, fragmentary stone carving inserted into exterior walls.*

(Photograph © F. B. Flood.)

Fig. 10.10 Bada'un, Shamsī
'īdgāh.

(Photograph © F. B. Flood.)

and its role as a staging post in Iltutmish's political ascendancy. It was as governor of Bada'un that he acceded to the sultanate, and here that he later imprisoned his great rival, Taj al-Din Yildiz, after defeating him in 612/1215.[26] The value of the 'iqta of Bada'un as a potential power base for an ambitious governor is reflected later in the conferral of the governorship of the city on Rukn al-Din Firuz, Iltutmish's son and successor, during whose governorship the congregational mosque was constructed.[27] Evidence for the construction of mosques and other monuments in Gwalior and Baran (modern Bulandshahr), cities whose governorships he held prior to his Bada'un appointment, suggest that in exercising his celebrated piety, Iltutmish was also embellishing the cities with which he was most closely associated during his rise to power.[28]

As we will see shortly, however, in its present incarnation the Great Mosque of Bada'un seems to represent an early Tughluqid rebuilding of Iltutmish's mosque. Even the monumental entrance in which the foundation text of Iltutmish's mosque appears today is not the original entrance, but a nineteenth-century replacement for a fourteenth-century gate. Apart from the foundation text (Figure 10.7), and a fragment of an epigraphic frieze later reset in the courtyard façade (Figure 10.18), the best-preserved features of the thirteenth-

168

century mosque are to be found in the prayer hall, around the mihrab. The surviving fragments include two carved stone panels set high up on the qibla wall, on either side of the mihrab opening (Figure 10.11).[29] The cusping and lotus spandrel bosses on these panels mirrors the form of some of the minor arches on Iltutmish's extension to the Delhi screen, and recur on the decoration of the mihrab below (Figure 10.12), which may (like the flanking stone columns of standard Indic type) also survive from Iltutmish's mosque.[30] The framing epigraphic bands on the qibla panels are inscribed with Qur'anic quotations; the example illustrated here (Figure 10.11) contains the *kalima* and Qur'an 2:238:

> Be wakeful of your service of prayer, and the midmost service; and honour God by standing before Him in devotion.

The style of the *naskhī* and background ornament is sufficiently close to that of Iltutmish's foundation inscription above the eastern entrance to confirm that these are survivals from the thirteenth-century mosque; the obvious relevance of this *āya* to a prayer hall suggests that the panels have not moved far from their original context, if at all. It is perhaps fitting that the sole surviving fragments of the thirteenth-century mosque are epigraphic, since one of the

Fig. 10.11 *Great Mosque of Bada'un, stone panel above mihrab.*

(Photograph © F. B. Flood.)

Fig. 10.12 *Great Mosque of Bada'un, general view of mihrab.*

(After Blakiston, *Jami Masjid*.)

most striking characteristics of Iltutmish's monuments is their lavish use of monumental epigraphy.[31]

The importance of these fragments lies in the evidence that they offer for the combination of epigraphy and stylised vegetal ornament found in the Delhi and Ajmir screens, here in a mosque dated six years before the date traditionally ascribed to either. In this respect, the absence of the geometric ornament that characterises the later screens seems significant, suggesting that the decoration of the Bada'un mosque had more in common with the earlier screen of Qutb al-Din Aybak in Delhi (1199) than with the extension ordered by Iltutmish.[32] The lotus-flower bursts and spandrel bosses amid

170

loosely scrolling vegetal ornament are all very much in the Indic idiom of Aybak's screen, as is the stone medium. At Bada'un, however, both are used to produce a panel with strong structural affinities to the stucco decoration of Iranian mihrabs of the twelfth century.[33]

Although it has been assumed that many of the carved stones of the Bada'un mosque, as well its structural materials, are spolia taken from temples destroyed in the wake of the Ghurid conquest, spoliation is something of a topos in art historical writing on early Indian mosques, which often reveals more about modern assumptions regarding Islam than the cultural dynamics of medieval South Asia.[34] While the nature and likely source of any materials reused in the Bada'un mosque warrant further investigation, study of the Atala Masjid (c. 1360) at nearby Jaunpur has cast serious doubt upon the idea that the mosque was constructed from the remains of a despoiled temple.[35] Moreover, carved stone elements similar to those used around the Bada'un mihrab were carved *ex novo* for Ghurid mosques in Ajmir, and possibly Delhi, probably by masons trained in the north Indian temple tradition.[36] The decoration of the Bada'un mosque may similarly have been executed by masons who had previously worked for the Hindu rulers of the city, or by their descendants; the various orthographic peculiarities in the Qur'anic inscription (most obviously redundant *alif*s) suggest that those who executed it were not literate in Arabic.[37]

Despite the survival of these fragments of the thirteenth-century mosque, most of the present fabric seems to reflect a later rebuilding. This affected the monumental gateway on the eastern side of the mosque, into which Iltutmish's foundation text was set before its demolition in 1888.[38] An engraving made before the destruction of the gate shows that it was constructed from baked brick, with ashlar facing, in which broad and narrow courses alternated (Figure 10.13). The pointed arch at the summit of the structure was constructed using a distinctive form of corbelling, in which narrow rectangular stones are laid in sloping horizontal courses to form the arch profile. A similar technique was used in the Buland Darwaza, a monumental gateway at Nagaur in Rajasthan, which has traditionally been dated to the early thirteenth century, largely by comparison with the use of corbelling in Bada'un and in the Ghurid mosques at Delhi and Ajmir.[39] Recently, however, it has been convincingly argued that the gate should be re-dated to c. 1333, the date of an inscription that it bears.[40] This re-dating highlights the dangers that the persistence of regional idioms poses for any attempt to date sultanate monuments based on an implicit evolutionary scheme in which 'primitive' techniques are necessarily replaced by more sophisticated alternatives. It also offers a priori grounds for considering the former entrance to the Bada'un mosque as a fourteenth-century structure in which the earlier foundation text was reset, as it has now been in the modern gate. An Arabic inscription on a stone slab set above the

Fig. 10.13 *Great Mosque of Bada'un, eastern gate, now destroyed.*

(After Cunningham, *Report.*)

northern entrance to the mosque (Figure 10.14) confirms that there was a major campaign of renovation at this time:

> This building was ordered by his exalted majesty, the shadow of the merciful God, father of the *mujāhid*, Muhammad Shah the sultan, may God perpetuate his kingdom and reign, in the year 726 [1326]. Husayn b. Hasan, *kutwal* of the province of Bada'un, built it.[41]

Architecture was directly instrumental in Muhammad b. Tughluq's accession to power, which followed the death of his father by

Fig. 10.14 *Great Mosque of Bada'un, exterior of northern gate showing inscription of Muhammad b. Tughluq.*

(After Blakiston, *Jami Masjid.*)

the collapse of a newly built wooden *kushk*, an event that many believed the son to have contrived.[42] The new sultan (r. 725–52/1325–51) continued his father's patronage of monumental architecture (the apogee of which was the tomb of Rukn-i 'Alam at Multan, c. 720/1320), for he was responsible for the construction of several surviving monuments, including the tomb of Shaykh 'Ala' al-Din at Ajudhan (modern Pakpattan), in 737/1336 (Figure 10.15), and a congregational mosque at Jahanpanah (c. 1343) near Delhi.[43]

The Bada'un mosque pre-dates all these monuments by several years, providing an important insight into Muhammad b. Tughluq's early architectural patronage.[44] The epigraphic claim to have built the mosque is clearly exaggerated, for, as we have seen, fragments of a thirteenth-century mosque are preserved in the present structure. Moreover, the idea of a courtyard mosque with a prayer hall four bays deep, a central dome preceding the main mihrab and a *riwaq* two bays deep with lateral entrances is already found in the Ghurid Friday Mosque of Delhi. It is therefore possible (if far from certain) that the present plan was determined by that of the pre-existing mosque.[45] Nevertheless, there are many indications of extensive rebuilding and

Fig. 10.15 Pakpattan, Tomb
of Shaykh ʿAlaʾ al-Din.

(After Nabi Khan, ʿPākpatanʾ.)

remodelling in the early fourteenth century. In addition to the
monumental eastern entrance (now disappeared), it is likely that
the smaller domed entrances on the southern and northern sides of
the mosque (the latter containing Muhammad b. Tughluq's inscription) were built at this time, even if the same basic scheme existed in
the thirteenth-century mosque.[46] The squat ovoid profile and inverted lotus finials of the qibla dome and those over the northern and
southern entrances (Figures 10.2, 10.4) show sufficiently close affinities with the dome of Shaykh ʿAlaʾ al-Din's tomb at Ajudhan, built
by Muhammad b. Tughluq in 1336 (Figure 10.15), to suggest that they
preserve the form of the fourteenth-century domes,[47] even if two
inscriptions within the main domed chamber indicate that repairs
were undertaken in 1011/1602–3 and 1013/1604–5, perhaps as a
result of damage inflicted by the disastrous fire that swept through
Badaʾun in 979/1571–2.[48] Similarly, while the tapering corner

174

bastions with horizontal bands of brick ornament are quite dissimilar in form to those of Iltutmish's work at Sultan Ghari, they are comparable to those found in other early Tughluqid monuments such as the tomb of Rukn-i ʿAlam at Multan.[49] The slight batter of the exterior walls is also in keeping with early Tughlughid monuments at Multan, Tughluqabad and Warangal, but it is possible that the fortified appearance of the present mosque preserves the basic features of the original thirteenth-century scheme, reworked in the idiom of a century later. Like several Indian mosques built in newly conquered areas (at Hansi, Delhi and possibly Khatu), the Bada'un mosque stands within the ancient fort of the city.[50] This was a pragmatic move, for the reference to peace and safety in Iltutmish's foundation text expresses an optimism not borne out by the events of the century and a half that followed the mosque's construction, which saw local rebellions, Rajput raids and, on more than one occasion, Mongol incursions into the ʿiqta of Bada'un.[51] Whether the rebuilding of 1326 was the result of depredations suffered during one of these convulsions, the imposing austerity of the mosque may be less the product of an aesthetic choice than a reflection of the prevailing military and political instability during the thirteenth and fourteenth centuries.

Much of the interior arrangement of the mosque also appears to date from Muhammad b. Tughluq's rebuilding of 1326. The exteriors of the courtyard arcades were once richly decorated with vertical and horizontal friezes of ornamental brickwork and crowned by merlons, now best appreciated from nineteenth-century drawings (Figures 10.5, 10.16), since most of the detail has been obscured by cumulative layers of whitewash (Figure 10.17).[52] The bulk of the decoration is geometric and floral, with some fragments of horizontal epigraphic friezes and occasional occurrences of *Allāh*, *yā Allā'*, and *yā Muhammad*, similar to those found in earlier Indo-Islamic monuments.[53] Other elements, among them the miniature arcade (Figures 10.5, 10.17), feature in both early Sultanate and Tughluqid architectural decoration; comparison of the arcading and the vegetal motifs crowning the apices of the arcade arches with similar ornament on the Buland Darwaza in Nagaur would support a dating in the early Tughluqid period.[54] Merlons comparable to those of the Bada'un mosque are found in the tomb that Muhammad b. Tughluq built for Shaykh 'Ala' al-Din at Ajudhan, which makes use of similar floral, geometric and epigraphic brickwork (Figure 10.15).[55] Despite the indications of an early fourteenth-century date, it is possible that fragments from the earlier, thirteenth-century decorative scheme were preserved in the later rebuilding. A section of an epigraphic frieze that shows the same characteristic background ornament as the thirteenth-century foundation text has been incorporated into (or concealed by) the later decorative scheme (Figure 10.18), for example, and may have decorated an earlier arcaded entrance to the prayer hall, such as that found at Ajmir and Delhi.[56] Although it has been suggested that the qibla *iwan* is a creation of the early seventeenth

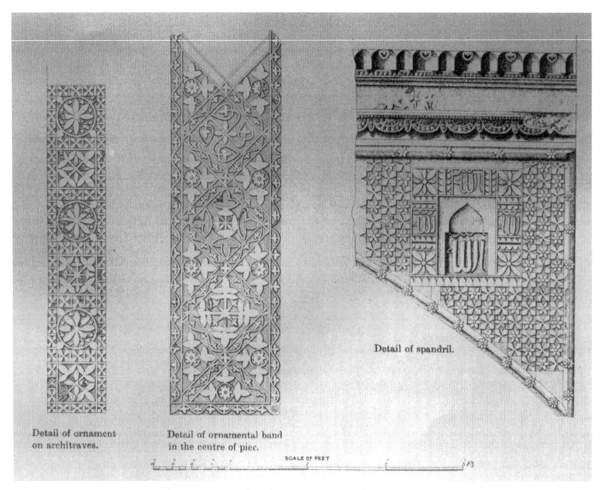

Detail of spandril.

Detail of ornament
on architraves.

Detail of ornamental band
in the centre of pier.

SCALE OF FEET

Fig. 10.16 Great Mosque of
Bada'un, detail of
ornament on courtyard
arcade.

(After Blakiston, *Jami Masjid.*)

century, a brief examination of its decoration casts doubt upon such a
late dating, although the two side bays and semi-domes (Figures 10.2,
10.4) may well have been attached in the renovations that followed
the fire of 979/1571–2.[57] The pronounced decorative banding upon
the engaged 'minarets' of the main *iwan* (Figure 10.19) is also found
on the external corner bastions of the mosque (Figure 10.3).[58] This
treatment of the towers recalls the 'brick and band' aesthetic of
monuments lying further to the west, a style that reaches its apogee
in the roughly contemporary tomb of Rukn-i 'Alam at Multan, but
that also asserts itself elsewhere in the medieval brick architecture of
the Indus Valley.[59]

It need hardly be pointed out that many of the features just
described have strong affinities with the architectural traditions of
regions to the west of the Gangetic Plain. In fact, it is remarkable how
little concession is made to either the standard media of north Indian
architecture (whether stone or rubble) or to the post-and-lintel idiom
that was employed in Ghurid mosques, and which continued to be
used for both small regional mosques and mosques built in recently

Fig. 10.17 Great Mosque of Bada'un, detail of western arcade today.

(Photograph © F. B. Flood.)

conquered areas into the fourteenth century and beyond.[60] With its four-*iwan* plan, arcuated forms and brick vaults, the mosque has much more in common with the medieval mosques of Iran than any extant thirteenth- or fourteenth-century mosque in north or south India. The most obviously Persianate features are the *iwan*s and *pishtaq*s, both forms long familiar from the Seljuq mosques of Iran.[61] Although the *iwan* concept is already present in the screens added to the Ghurid Friday Mosques of Delhi and Ajmir,[62] if (as all the indications are) the existing scheme at Bada'un reflects the work of 1326, then it post-dates the earliest recorded use of the four-*iwan* plan in Indian secular architecture (in Tughluqabad) by as little as a year.[63] Moreover, it represents the earliest surviving use of the four-*iwan* plan in an Indian mosque, pre-dating by almost two decades the previous claimant for this title, the Friday Mosque at Jahanpanah near Delhi, built around 1343, also by Muhammad b. Tughluq.[64] In fact, the Persianate details of the Jahanpanah mosque anticipated in Muhammad's earlier mosque at Bada'un extend well beyond the use of features such as domes, *iwan*s and *pishtaq*s, to the monumental eastern entrance (now destroyed), and the presence of non-functional 'minarets' on the qibla *iwan*, a feature first introduced to Indo-Islamic architecture in Iltutmish's screen in the Ajmir mosque.[65]

The brick medium, which stands in marked contrast to the post

Fig. 10.18 Great Mosque of Bada'un, fragment of 13th-century inscription integrated into later epigraphic frieze on courtyard arcade.

(Photograph © F. B. Flood.)

and lintel or rubble and mortar espoused in other early Tughluqid monuments outside the Indus Valley, also suggests an attempt to transplant a form of architecture associated with regions to the west of the Gangetic Plain, although it is conceivable that the use of brick was once more common in northern India than the surviving evidence indicates.[66] The use of ashlar masonry (or at least facing – this remains to be investigated) in conjunction with brick vaulting is admittedly unusual in an Iranian context (despite the frequent use of stone footings for brick monuments), but occasionally occurs earlier in Central Asian monuments and is found in some later Tughluqid monuments in India.[67] The Ghurid monuments of South Asia (brick in the Indus Valley, and stone in north India) demonstrate the willingness of early Muslim patrons to conform to regional practice, and it is possible that the combination of brick and stone seen at Bada'un represents the survival of pre-conquest building traditions.[68]

What is not in doubt is that the use of glazing on elements of the brick decoration, which would originally have heightened the lavish effect of the façades (Figure 10.5), is another significant indicator of an affinity with the architectural traditions of the Iranian world. These elements are now obscured by whitewash, but Cunningham reported the use of blue glaze for minor elements of the decoration, including epigraphic ornament; although the hue is not stated, it seems likely

178

Fig. 10.19 *Great Mosque of Bada'un, detail of 'minaret' on qibla iwan*

(Photograph © F. B. Flood.)

that this was light blue or turquoise, which is ubiquitous in the twelfth- and thirteenth-century monuments of Iran.[69] Cunningham conjectured that a similar use of glazed elements was made in the ʿīdgāh of Bada'un, a monument traditionally ascribed to the early patronage of Iltutmish, but there is little evidence to support this.[70]

That only one colour is mentioned in Bada'un points to a

conservative use of this expensive technique, which recalls the restricted use made on Iranian monuments of a century or two earlier.[71] Such ornament was evidently not a standard element of early Tughluqid architectural decoration, even in areas with a strong tradition of brick architecture, for despite the sophisticated use of a broad palette of glazed ornament in the tomb of Rukn-i 'Alam in Multan (c. 1325), glazing is absent from the tomb built by Muhammad b. Tughluq at Ajudhan (1336).[72] So far as we can tell, the nature and extent of glazed decoration in Muhammad b. Tughluq's Bada'un mosque was similar to that found over twenty years later in his Jahanpanah mosque (c. 1343), where 'small, inset blue-glazed tiles' were set into the façades of the courtyard.[73] Despite the conservative palette, the appearance of the technique in Bada'un provides a *terminus a quem* (if not a *terminus ante quem*) for the use of the technique almost twenty years before the Jahanpanah mosque, which has been claimed as the earliest use of the technique in Indo-Islamic architecture. Other monuments, such as the *ʿīdgāh* of Ripari at Hansi in the Panjab (dated 711/1311–12), which has a 'band of blue tiles' running across its multiple mihrabs, suggest that glazed elements were in vogue in north Indian architecture even earlier.[74]

Of the four characteristic decorative features of eastern Iranian architecture conspicuous by their absence from the earliest Indian monuments built after the Ghurid conquest – geometric ornament, glazed brick, terracotta and stucco – the first of these makes its first appearance by 1229, in the screens added to the Ghurid mosques at Ajmir (Figure 10.8) and Delhi.[75] Although the earliest surviving evidence for the use of decorative stucco is in the ruins of Tughluqabad (c. 1320–5), it seems likely that this inexpensive and highly effective decorative medium was used earlier, and that the Indian climate has conspired to efface the evidence.[76] The same may be true of glazed ornament, although the dominance of a stone medium in most areas of northern India may have inhibited the use of the technique, even if it was later adapted for restricted use in stone and rubble monuments like the Jahanpanah mosque. On the basis of the surviving evidence we suggest that glazed decoration was already used in Indian monuments by the Khalji period, but that its use was expanded in early Tughluqid monuments.[77]

Although many of the basic details of the Bada'un mosque anticipate the Persianate style of Muhammad b. Tughluq's Jahanpanah mosque, the plan and superstructure of the prayer hall in Bada'un differ dramatically from those of surviving Tughluqid monuments. The former consist of what is (for sultanate India, at least) a highly idiosyncratic arrangement, with four bays running parallel to the qibla, covered with pointed barrel vaults supported on massive rectangular piers (Figure 10.6); the same format was originally also used in the *riwaq*s of the courtyard (Figure 10.1).[78] The profile of the vaulted superstructure is similar to that of the pointed arches that open at intervals along the lateral walls of the long vaulted bays, to permit movement between them. While the arch profiles point towards a date in the fourteenth century, all the surviving Tughluqid mosques rely not on vaulting, but on the repetition of small domed units to span the prayer hall and *riwaq*s, as do the earliest mosques of Bengal.[79] The use of barrel vaults in the secular architecture of Tughluqabad points to other possibilities, but these were confined to relatively minor contexts and evidently not considered suitable for spanning large areas.[80] The adaptation of this type of vaulting for the prayer hall of the Bada'un mosque anticipates the more monumental (if more localised) use made of pointed brick barrel vaulting in the qibla *iwan* of the Adina Mosque at Pandua (1375), the largest mosque of pre-Mughal India.[81]

The unusual form of the prayer hall of the Bada'un mosque, like much else about the monument, suggests affinities not with any surviving Indian mosques, but with the architecture of the Indus Valley or regions further to the west.[82] A comparable use of vaulted brick corridors is made, for example, in a Ghurid monument at Kabirwala near Multan, datable to the late twelfth or early thirteenth centuries, and referred to as a mosque (*masjid*) in its foundation inscription, despite its current usage as a funerary monument.[83] The vaulting of the Panjabi monument has now collapsed, but the Great Mosque of Herat, begun in the early thirteenth century using some of the gold sent to the Ghurids from India, preserves areas of brick vaulting carried on massive brick piers, producing an effect comparable to that of the Bada'un *haram*.[84] Even closer parallels are offered by a number of thirteenth- and fourteenth-century Iranian mosques, in which barrel-vaulted aisles flank a central domed chamber.[85]

The striking contrast in conception and elevation between the Bada'un mosque and its Tughluqid predecessors and successors seem to reflect an exceptional openness towards Iranian architectural forms in fourteenth-century Bada'un. While we know too little about early Tughluqid architecture to place easily the apparent idiosyncrasies of the Bada'un mosque in any wider Indian context, it is clear that the Tughluqid period was one of innovative and inventive experimentation in the field of architecture.[86] A recent assessment of Tughluqabad, the city built by Muhammad b. Tughluq's father, notes how its architecture is 'closer in spirit to that of Central Asia and Iran, and indeed the rest of the Islamic world than to what is to be found elsewhere in the subcontinent'.[87] Even before the upheavals of the thirteenth century, there is epigraphic evidence for the involvement of individuals of Iranian origin in the construction of Indian mosques.[88] The human correlates of the Persianate trends witnessed in Tughluqabad, Bada'un and later in Jahanpanah are presumably to be sought in the waves of artisans, refugees and scholars who migrated eastwards in the wake of the Mongol invasion and the repeated incursions into north India that followed in its wake.

FINBARR BARRY FLOOD

Writing in the fourteenth century, 'Isami evokes the cosmopolitan atmosphere of Delhi during the sultanate of Iltutmish, when

'. . . many workmen (*kāsibān*) from the land of Khurasan, many painters from the country of China, many uluma of the Bukhara stock and many a devotee and men of piety came from different regions. Craftsmen of every kind and every country as well as beauties from every race and city; many assayers, jewellers and pearl-sellers, philosophers and physicians of the Greek school and learned men from every land – all gathered in the blessed city like moths that gather round the candle light. Delhi became the Ka'ba of the seven continents (*haft iqlīm*).'[89]

The impact of this influx of artisans upon the art and architecture of the sultanate is evident in the screens erected by Iltutmish at Ajmir and Delhi, in which geometric ornament, hitherto absent from the decorative repertoire of Indo-Islamic architecture, makes a sudden appearance.[90]

As the political and cultural crisis caused by the eruption of the Mongols into the *dār al-Islām* intensified during the thirteenth century, culminating in the sack of Baghdad and the effective end of the caliphate in 1258, the Delhi sultanate itself came under repeated attack from Mongol armies and their Chaghatai successors.[91] In 1305 a Mongol force raided as far as Bada'un and Awadh, a pattern repeated in 1327, during the Indian expedition of the Chaghatai ruler Tarmashirin. In the political chaos that followed the defeat of Tarmashirin, a new influx of refugees from Transoxiana sought refuge in India.[92] It is tempting to see the increasing size of Indian congregational mosques from the thirteenth to the fourteenth centuries as at least partly related to this influx of (mostly Muslim) refugees from eastern Iran and Central Asia.

The Indus Valley was particularly badly affected by these raids, as is clear from Ghiyath al-Din Tughluq's inscription in the congregational mosque of Multan, which recorded the sultan's victories over no less than twenty-nine Mongol (*tartar*) armies.[93] The Tughluqids had something of a special relationship with the Indus Valley, Ghiyath al-Din having risen to power as governor of Dipalpur, and both this sultan and his successor son were frequent visitors to the shrines at Ajudhan, one of which was built by Muhammad b. Tughluq.[94] The affinities between the 'brick and band' aesthetic that characterised the fourteenth-century rebuilding of the Bada'un mosque and the well-developed brick traditions of the Indus Valley have been noted above.[95] It is therefore possible that the strongly Persianate forms of the Bada'un mosque were not the result of an influx of Iranian artisans, but were mediated by craftsmen migrating eastwards from the Indus Valley in the late thirteenth and early fourteenth centuries, possibly with the blessing or sponsorship of the Tughluqid sultans.[96] Even in the absence of such an imprimatur, the continued instability in the Indus

182

Valley into the early fourteenth century created conditions ripe for the eastward migration of refugees, some of whom may have earlier come from Iran.[97] As a major political and religious centre, Bada'un would have made an attractive refuge, the occasional Mongol raid notwithstanding.[98] Equally, the abundance of craftsmen, diplomats, merchants, *mujāhid*s, soldiers and scholars from Khurasan, Transoxiana and regions further to the west in India during the first few decades of the fourteenth century is well attested.[99] Some of these immigrants were evidently engaged in architectural activity, even if their precise relationship with the Indian (largely Hindu) masons who built and subsequently repaired many thirteenth- and fourteenth-century Islamic monuments is far from clear.[100]

Whether the product of migrant Iranian craftsmen or a Persianate architectural tradition mediated via the Indus Valley, the Iranian affinities of the Bada'un mosque are many and pronounced, and point to the late Khalji or early Tughluqid periods as being pivotal in the dissemination of Persianate forms and decorative techniques in Indo-Islamic architecture. Some of these, such as the vaulted corridors, seem to hark back to an older tradition and were apparently not developed in subsequent monuments. Others, however, such as its *iwan*s, *pishtaqs*, ovoid domes, tapering bastions and glazed ornament, were to enjoy a longer history in the subcontinent, not least in the Sharqi monuments of Jaunpur.[101]

Given what Robert has characterised as Iltutmish's 'attempt to transplant the Saljuq architectural style to northern India',[102] Muhammad b. Tughluq's activities at Bada'un may have been intended to build upon Iltutmish's legacy, both literally and figuratively. The renovation of Iltutmish's Bada'un mosque demonstrates an interest in earlier Indo-Islamic monuments that may not have been confined to that city. The *Akhbār al-Jamāl*, an eighteenth-century history of Aligarh (medieval Kol), reports a chain of events that, although unverifiable, mirrors the scenario to which the epigraphic evidence from nearby Bada'un attests. According to this text, the congregational mosque built after the conquest of the city ' "having decayed,' Muhammad Tughluq constructed in its site a huge mosque with seven openings, in 733/1329', the date given in an inscription seen by the author of the text, but now lost.[103] The restoration of these early sultanate mosques may have been necessitated by damage inflicted during the regional political upheavals of the thirteenth and fourteenth centuries.[104] Equally, Muhammad b. Tughluq's interest in restoring early sultanate monuments anticipates the architectural activities of Firuz Shah Tughluq half a century later and may, like the latter, have been intended to associate the sultan with the perceived glories of the Ghurid and Shamsid past.[105] In either case, the architectural legacy of Muhammad b. Tughluq was the most enduring aspect of a reign that, through a combination of strategic miscalculation and military misadventure, resulted in the loss of Bengal and all of the territories of the Delhi sultanate south of the Vindhyas.[106]

Notes

1. Much ink has been spilled on the correct transliteration of this city's name. I have followed the *Encyclopedia of Islam*, but for the controversy see W. H. (Wolseley Haig), 'The Bābur-Nāma in English', *Journal of the Royal Asiatic Society* (1924), 272; Annette S. Beveridge, ' "Badaun" or "Badāyūn"?', *Journal of the Royal Asiatic Society* (1925), 517; Wolseley Haig, ' "Badaun" or "Badāyūn"?', *Journal of the Royal Asiatic Society* (1925), 715–16; C. A. Storey, 'Budāon, Badāūn, or Badāyūn?', *Journal of the Royal Asiatic Society* (1926), 103–4; T. Grahame Bailey, 'Badāyú and Badāú', *Journal of the Royal Asiatic Society* (1926), 104; E. Denison Ross, 'Badā'un or Badāyūn?', *Journal of the Royal Asiatic Society* (1926), 105.

2. Robert Hillenbrand, 'Political Symbolism in Early Indo-Islamic Mosque Architecture: The Case of Ajmīr', *Iran* 26 (1988), 105. The relevant publications are referred to in the notes below.

3. Although a number of small stone mosques of the thirteenth or early fourteenth centuries survive at Khatu, Ladnun and Nagaur in Rajasthan: Mehrdad Shokoohy and Natalie H. Shokoohy, *Nagaur*, Royal Asiatic Society Monographs, 28 (London, 1993), 29–30, 111–13, 116–17. The fragmentary congregational mosque at Tughluqabad (c. 1320–25), south of modern Delhi, is the earliest urban mosque of the Tughluqids so far known: Mehrdad Shokoohy and Natalie M. Shokoohy, 'Tughluqabad: The Earliest Surviving Town of the Delhi Sultanate', *Bulletin of the School of Oriental and African Studies* 57/3 (1994), 544–9. See also the Mosque of Zafar Khan Ghazi at Tribeni in West Bengal, dated 1298: Perween Hasan, 'Temple Niches and Miḥrābs in Bengal', in *Islam and Indian Regions*, ed. Anna Libera Dallapiccola and Stephanie Zingel-Avé Lallemant (Stuttgart, 1993), 90, drawing 1. There is apparently a small Khalji mosque at Deogir dated (or datable to?) 718/1318: Anthony Welch and Howard Crane, 'The Tughluqs: Master Builders of the Delhi Sultanate', *Muqarnas* 1 (1983), 128.

4. Alexander Cunningham, *Report of Tours in the Gangetic Provinces from Badaon to Bihar in 1875–76 and 1877–78*, Archaeological Survey of India Reports, Vol. 10 (Calcutta, 1888), 4–8; A. Führer, *The Monumental Antiquities and Inscriptions in the North-Western Provinces and Oudh* (Allahabad, 1891), 20–1; Muhammad Fadl-i Akram, *Āthār-i Badāyūn* (Bada'un, 1919), 74–80; Anon., 'The Shamsi Musjid of Badaun', *The Journal of the United Provinces Historical Society* 3 (1926), 132–38; Wolseley Haig, 'The Monuments of Muslim India', *Cambridge History of India*, vol. 3: Turks and Afghans, ed. Wolseley Haig (Cambridge, 1928), 624–5; J. F. Blakiston, *The Jami Masjid at Badaun and Other Buildings in the United Provinces*, Memoirs of the Archaeological Survey of India, no. 19 (Calcutta, 1926), 1–5; Percy Brown, *Indian Architecture: The Islamic Period* (Bombay, 1944), 14; Tsukinowa Tokifusa, 'The Influence of Seljuq Architecture on the Earliest Mosques of the Delhi Sultanate Period in India', *Acta Asiatica* 43 (1982), 51–4; K. V. Soundara Rajan, *Islam Builds in India* (Delhi, 1983), 20–1, pls 29–30.

5. Robert Hillenbrand, 'Ajmīr;' Hillenbrand, 'Turco-Iranian Elements in the Medieval Architecture of Pakistan: The Case of the Tomb of Rukn-i 'Alam at Multan', *Muqarnas* 9 (1992), 148–74. For other publications dealing with the architectural relationship between Iran and India, albeit at earlier and later periods than those with which I am concerned

here, see M. Abdullah Chaghtai, 'What India owes to Central Asia in Islamic Architecture', *Islamic Culture* 8 (1931), 55–65; Arthur Upham Pope, 'Some Interrelations between Persian and Indian Architecture', *Indian Art and Letters* 9 (1935), 101–25; M. Abdullah Chaghtai, 'Indian links with Central Asia in Architecture', *Indian Art and Letters* 11 (1937), 85–94; Klaus Fisher, 'Interrelations of Islamic Architecture in Afghanistan', *Marg* 24/1 (1970), 47–56.

6. The Qutbi mosque in Delhi measures 66 × 44m, the Jahanpanah mosque 90 × 94m, and the Adina Mosque at Pandua 155 × 87m: J. A. Page, *An Historical Memoir on the Qutb: Delhi*, Memoirs of the Archaeological Survey of India, no. 22 (Calcutta, 1926), 8; Welch and Crane, 'Tughluqs', 130, fig. 1; Y. Crowe, 'Reflections on the Adina Mosque at Pandua', in *The Islamic Heritage of Bengal*, ed. George Michell (Paris, 1984), 157.

7. Blakiston, *Jami Masjid*, pls II–III, X–XIb.

8. Anon., 'Shamsi Musjid', 135.

9. Phillip B. Wagoner and John Henry Rice, 'From Delhi to the Deccan: Newly Discovered Tughluq Monuments at Warangal-Sultanpur and the Beginnings of Indo-Islamic Architecture in Southern India', *Artibus Asiae* 61/1 (2001), 107.

10. The northern and southern *riwaq*s were ruined by the end of the nineteenth century, and restored in 1887–8: ibid.; Blakiston, *Jami Masjid*, 4.

11. See, for example, the twelfth-century mosques at Bhadreshvar in Gujarat: Mehrdad Shokoohy, *Bhadresvar: The Oldest Islamic Monuments in India* (Leyden, 1988), 21, 25, figs. 14, 26.

12. W. E. Begley, *Monumental Islamic Calligraphy from India* (Villa Park, 1985), 28–9, no. 3. see also J. Horovitz, 'Inscriptions of Muhammad Ibn Sam, Qutbuddin Aibeg, and Iltutmish', *Epigraphia Indo-Moslemica* (1911–12), 22; Blakiston, *Jami Masjid*: 2; Other published versions of this inscription include erroneous interpolations: H. Blochmann, 'Notes on Arabic and Persian Inscriptions', *Journal of the Asiatic Society of Bengal* (41, 1872), 112; Anon., 'Shamsi Musjid', 132. On the correct transliteration of this sultan's name, see Simon Digby, 'Iletmish or Iltutmish? A Reconsideration of the Name of the Delhi Sultan', *Iran* 8 (1970), 57–64.

13. Horovitz, 'Inscriptions', 21–3, 25; Maulvi Muhammad Shu'aib, 'Inscriptions from Palwal', *Epigraphia Indo-Moslemica* (1911–12), 3, pl. XXI; G. Yazdani, 'Inscriptions of the Turk Sultans of Delhi – Mu'izzu-d-dîn Bahrām, 'Alā'u-d-dîn Mas'ūd, Nāsiru-d-dîn Mahmūd, Ghiyāth-u-d-dîn Balban, and Mu'izzu-d-dîn Kaiqubad', *Epigraphia Indo-Moslemica* (1913–14), 14–15; Anon., *Catalogue of the Delhi Museum of Archaeology*, 2nd edn (Calcutta, 1926), 3; M. Abdulla Chaghtai, 'An Unpublished Inscription of the Time of Sultan Iltutmish – Showing the Construction of a Reservoir at Khatu (Marwar)', *Proceedings and Transactions of the Eighth All-India Oriental Conference, Mysore, December 1935* (Bangalore, 1937), 632–35; Z. A. Desai, 'The Mamluk Sultans of Delhi', *Epigraphia Indica, Arabic and Persian Supplement* (1966), 6–7, 16–17, pl. IVa.

14. Horovitz, 'Inscriptions', 26–8; Begley, *Islamic Calligraphy*, 30–1, no. 5; Shah Muhammad Shafiqullah, 'Calligraphic Ornamentation of the Quwwat al-Islam Mosque: An Observation on the Calligraphy of the Screens of Qutb al-Din and Iltutmish', *Journal of the Asiatic Society of Bangladesh* 39 (1994), 62–7. 'Afif's reference to Iltutmish erecting a

manāra buzurg in the Delhi mosque could refer to his completion of the Qutb Minar. However, since it occurs within a discussion of Firuz Shah's relocation of pre-Islamic pillars (also referred to as *manāra*s), it seems more likely to refer to the iron pillar that stands in the courtyard of the mosque: Shams Siraj ʿAfif, *Tarikh-i Firuz Shahi* (Calcutta, 1888), 316; Elliot and Dowson, *History of India*, vol. 3, 353; Finbarr B. Flood, 'Pillars and Palimpsests: Translating the Past in Sultanate Delhi', *RES* 43 (2003), 95–116.

15. Horovitz, 'Inscriptions', 29–30, 33; Tokifusa, 'Seljuq Architecture', 51; Mehrdad Shokoohy, *Corpus Inscriptionum Iranicarum. Part IV: Persian Inscriptions Down to the Early Safavid Period*, vol. XLIX, India: State of Rajasthan, Rajasthan I (London, 1986), 13–14; Hillenbrand, 'Ajmīr', 108, pls IIa, VIIb–IXa. Unfortunately the year of the date on the screen inscription is missing.

16. Horovitz, 'Inscriptions', 23–4; S. A. A. Naqvi, 'Sultān Ghārī, Delhi', *Ancient India* 3 (1947), 4–10; Anthony Welch, 'Qurʾān and Tomb: The Religious Epigraphy of Two Early Sultanate Tombs in Delhi', in *Indian Epigraphy: Its Bearing on the History of Art*, ed. Frederick M. Asher and G. S. Gai (New Delhi, 1985), 258–61; Anthony Welch, 'A Medieval Center of Learning in India: The Hauz Khas Madrasa in Delhi', *Muqarnas* 13 (1996), 175 and n. 32. The madrasa in the tomb of Nasir al-Din Mahmud should not be confused with the Nasiri Madrasa built later by Balban (r. 664–8/1266–87): Munibar Rahman, 'Madrasa', *EI* 2, vol. 5, 1135. An earlier Muʿizzi Madrasa in Badaʾun is ascribed to the activities of Qutb al-Din Aybak (r. 602–7/1206–10): H. R. Nevill, *Badaun a Gazetteer*, vol. XV of the District Gazetteers of the United Provinces, Agra, and Oudh (Allahabad, 1907), 133; Anon., 'Shamsi Musjid', 136.

17. Welch, 'Qurʾān and Tomb', 261–6.

18. J. G. Delmerick, 'Inscriptions from Abúhar and Sirsá', *Proceedings of the Asiatic Society of Bengal* 10 (1874), 72; K. A. Nizami, *Studies in Medieval Indian History* (Aligarh, 1956), 37–8; H. A. R. Gibb, *The Travels of Ibn Battuta A.D. 1325–1354*, vol. 3 (Cambridge, 1971), 624; N. B. Roy, 'The Victories of Sultān Fīrūz Shāh Tughluq', *Islamic Culture* 15 (1941), 459; Agha Mahdi Husain, *Futuhuʾs Salatin* (London, 1977), 2:227.

19. Yazdani, 'Turk Sultāns', 21–2, pl. VIIIa; Begley, *Islamic Calligraphy*, no. 8; K. A. Nizami, *Royalty in Medieval India* (New Delhi, 1997), 128.

20. Annette Susannah Beveridge, *The Bābūr-nāma in English* (London, 1922), 2:610; Michael D. Willis, 'An Eighth Century Miḥrāb in Gwalior', *Artibus Asiae* 46 (1985), 244, pl. 9. On stylistic grounds, I would date the inscription a decade or so later than Willis. For the construction of early Indian mosques within forts, see n. 50 below. The text of another inscription, commemorating Iltutmish's recapture of the Gwalior fort in 630/1232, has been preserved in the work of the poet Taj al-Din: John Briggs, *History of the Rise of the Mahomedan Power in India* (1829, reprinted, New Delhi, 1981), 1:119; Iqbal Husain, *The Early Persian Poets of India [A.H. 421–679]* (Patna, 1937), 154–5.

21. Beveridge, *Bābūr-Nāma*, 611. For royal patronage of hydraulic projects at a slightly later date, see Anthony Welch, 'Hydraulic Architecture in Medieval India: The Tughluqs', *Environmental Design* 2 (1985), 74–81.

22. The existence of this fragment and its stylistic relation to the Ajmir mosque has been noted by Willis, 'Gwalior', 245, n. 39.

23. Any inscriptions have now disappeared beneath accumulated layers of

whitewash, and the monument is attributed to Iltutmish largely on the grounds that it is referred to as the Shamsī ʿīdgāh: Cunningham, *Report*, 4; Mohammad Mokhlesur Rahman, 'A Note on Shamsī ʿIdgāh of Badāʾun (1202–9); some Observations on its Glazed Decoration', *Hamdard Islamicus* 10/3 (1987), 85–7. For a section and plan, see Rajan, *Islam Builds*, 68–9, fig. 32, pl. 20. For other early Indian ʿīdgāhs, see J. Burton-Page, 'Namāzgāh', *EI* 2, 947; Z. A. Desai, 'The Jalor Idgah Inscription of Qutb ud-Din Mubarak Shah Khalji', *Epigraphia Indica, Arabic and Persian Supplement* (1972), 12–19; Mehrdad Shokoohy and Natalie M. Shokoohy, 'The Architecture of Baha al-Din Tughrul in the Region of Bayana, Rajasthan', *Muqarnas* 4 (1987), 130–2, figs 36–7.

24. Desai, 'Mamluk Sultans', 14–15, 17–18, pls IIIc and IVb; Begley, *Islamic Calligraphy, No. 4*; André Wink, *Al-Hind, the Making of the Indo-Islamic World* (New Delhi, 1999), 2:221. A water–tank called the Hauz-i Shamsi may, like its Delhi counterpart, have come into being as part of Iltutmish's building activities in Badaʾun: Haig, 'Monuments', 624.

25. Wink, *Al-Hind*, 2:220–4. The Badaʾun gate of Delhi was the principal entrance to the city, and a key locus for royal ceremonial: Gibb, *Travels*, 3:621. For the many mosques and *dargah*s of Badaʾun, and its flourishing spiritual community in the thirteenth and fourteenth centuries, see Nizami, *Studies in Medieval Indian History*, 18, and Ziya-ul-Hasan Faruqi, *Fawaʾid al-Fuʾad: Spiritual and Literary Discourses of Shaikh Nizamuddin Awliya* (New Delhi, 1996), *passim*.

26. A. S. Bazmee Ansari, 'Iltutmish', *EI* 2, 1155. Even after his accession to the sultanate, Iltutmish had occasion to visit the city; a Sanskrit inscription mentions his presence in Badaʾun early in 1227: Pushpa Prasad, *Sanskrit Inscriptions of Delhi Sultanate, 1191–1526* (Delhi, 1990), 80.

27. Blakiston, *Jami Masjid*, 2; Peter Jackson, *The Delhi Sultanate: A Political and Military History* (Cambridge, 1999), 40.

28. For Iltutmish's political trajectory, see Jackson, *Delhi Sultanate*, 26; Ansari, 'Iltutmish', 1155. On the piety of Iltutmish see Ansari; Khaliq Ahmad Nizami, *Studies in Medieval Indian History and Culture* (Allahabad, 1966), 13–40; Rekha Joshi, *Sultan Iltutmish* (Delhi, 1979), *passim*. For the Gwalior mosque, see n. 20 above. The evidence for Iltutmish's role as architectural patron at Baran is more circumspect: in addition to a fragmentary inscription bearing the titles of Iltutmish, Barani refers to the existence of a *masjid-i jamiʿ* at Baran in the thirteenth century: Desai, 'Mamluk Sultans', 15–16, pl. IIIb; Kishori Saran Lal, *History of the Khaljis AD 1290–1320* (London, 1969), 59. On medieval Baran see F. S. Growse, 'Bulandshahr Antiquities', *Journal of the Royal Asiatic Society of Bengal* 48 (1879), 270–5; Führer, *Monumental Antiquities*, 4–6; Wink, *Al-Hind*, 2:224–5.

29. Although only one panel is shown here, the mihrab and its surrounding decoration is illustrated elsewhere: Blakiston, *Jami Masjid*, pls V and VIII; Rajan, *Islam Builds in India*, pl. 30d.

30. Page, *Historical Memoir*, pl. 3b.

31. Welch, 'Qurʾān and Tomb', esp. 261–7.

32. Page, *Historical Memoir*, 9–10, pls 2 and 3a.

33. At Mashhad-i Misriyan in Turkmenistan, or Ribat-i Sharaf in Khurasan, for example: Pope, 'Interrelations', 117; Ernst Cohn-Wiener, 'A Turanic Monument of the Twelfth Century AD', *Ars Islamica* 6/1 (1939), 90, fig. 10; André Godard, 'Khorāsān', *Āthār-é Īrān* 4 (1949), 45, fig. 36.

34. Cunningham, *Report*, 1, 4; Führer, *Monumental Antiquities*, 20; Bla-kiston, *Jami Masjid*, 4; Anon., 'Shamsi Musjid', 136–7. In addition to reporting a tradition that Hindu icons are buried beneath the *minbar* of the mosque, Cunningham even identifies the temple from which the material originated, on what grounds is far from obvious, although an inscription later reused in a gate of Bada'un fort mentions the con-struction of a Shiva temple at Vodamayuta (Bada'un) in the twelfth century: F. Kielhorn, 'Badâun Stone Inscription of Lakhanapala', *Indian Antiquary* 1 (1892), 61–6. Cunningham's *modus operandi* in this regard is, however, all too clear from his remarks on Iltutmish's vanished mosque at Gwalior: '. . . as the erection of a mosque by a Muhammadan conqueror always implies the destruction of a Hindu temple, I infer that the neighbouring temple of the sun must have been pulled down by Altamsh [sic], partly as an easy means of acquiring religious merit, and partly as a cheap means of obtaining ready-cut stones for the construction of his mosque': Alexander Cunningham, *Four Reports Made During the Years 1862–63–64–65*, ASI Reports, vol. 2 (repr. Varanasi, 1972), 354.

35. Fritz Lehmann, 'The Name and Origin of the Atāla Masjid, Jaunpur', *Islamic Culture* 52/1 (1978), 19–27. For a discussion of this problematic topic, see Alka Patel, 'Islamic Architecture of Western India (mid-12th–14th Century)', unpublished D.Phil. thesis, Harvard University, 2000, 229–37; Finbarr B. Flood, *Incorporating India: Culture, Conquest, and Colonialism in Islamicate South Asia* (forthcoming), ch. 4.

36. Michael Meister, 'The "Two-and-a-Half-Day" Mosque', *Oriental Art* 18/1 (1972), 57–63.

37. Nizami, *Royalty*, 158. For similar orthographic oddities in Arabic inscrip-tions on Ghurid monuments, see Finbarr B. Flood, 'Ghūrid Architecture in the Indus Valley: The Tomb of Shaykh Sādan Shahīd', *Ars Orientalis* 30 (2001), 141. Despite the picture of cultural rupture frequently conjured in writing on the Ghurid conquest of north India, it is noteworthy that the mint of Bada'un continued to operate without interruption after the conquest of 1197: John S. Deyell, *Living without Silver: The Monetary History of Early Medieval North India* (New Delhi, 1999), 198.

38. Cunningham, *Report of Tours*, 6, pl. 3; Führer, *Monumental Antiqui-ties*, 20.

39. Brown, *Indian Architecture*, 14; J. Burton-Page, 'Dihlī Sultanate, Art', *EI* 2, 274.

40. Shokoohy and Shokoohy, *Nagaur*, 34–6, figs 11–12, pls 7–8.

41. Blakiston, *Jami Masjid*, 2, pl. V. On Muhammad b. Tughluq's use of the *kunya Abū'l-mujāhid*, see Gibb, *Travels*, 3:657.

42. Gibb, *Travels*, 3:654–5.

43. Agha Mahdi Husain, *The Rise and Fall of Muḥammad bin Tughluq* (London, 1938), 118–19; Welch and Crane, 'Tughluqs', 130, fig.1.

44. An inscription from the *dargah* of Miranji at Bada'un, dated 728/1327–8, two years after the rebuilding of the congregational mosque, suggests that other monuments in the city (including perhaps the *'īdgāh*) were also built or rebuilt during the third decade of the fourteenth century: J. Horovitz, 'A List of Published Mohamedan Inscriptions of India', *Epigraphia Indo-Moslemica* (1909–10), 63, no. 356; Welch and Crane, 'Tughluqs', 124, n. 13.

45. For a good schematic plan of the Delhi mosque, see Catherine B. Asher, *Architecture of Mughal India*, The New Cambridge History of India I/4 (Cambridge, 1992), 3, pl. 1.

46. This is likely even if the southern entrance was later remodelled in the Mughal period, as Rajan suggests: *Islam Builds*, 71.

47. Ahmad Nabi Khan, 'The Mausoleum of Šaiḫ ʿAlā' al-Dīn at Pākpatan (Punjāb): A Significant Example of the Tuglug Style of Architecture', *East & West* N. S. 24 (1974), 318, figs. 2–3, 20–1. For the date of the monument, see Richard M. Eaton, 'The Political and Religious Authority of the Shrine of Bābā Farīd', in *Moral Conduct and Authority: The Place of* Adab *in South Asian Islam*, ed. Barbara Daly Metcalf (Berkeley, 1984), 339. In his publication on the tomb, Khan, 'Mausoleum', 313, gives the foundation date as 737/1330, referring to an inscription that is neither cited nor discussed in the article.

48. Blakiston, *Jami Masjid*, 3. On this I disagree with most previous discussions of the mosque from Cunningham onwards, which have attributed the dome in its entirety to the early seventeenth-century renovation. Rajan (*Islam Builds*, 70) dates the central dome to 'the late Khilji stage', on what grounds is unclear. It has been pointed out elsewhere that 'the dome is exactly of the same material as used in the lower portion of the walls': Anon., 'Shamsi Musjid', 134. For the fire of 979/1571–2, see ibid., 133, n. 2.

49. Hillenbrand, 'Turco-Iranian Elements', 156–7, figs 9–13. The heavy, cylindrical corner bastions in the Sultan Ghari tomb in Delhi, which is traditionally ascribed to the patronage of Iltutmish, are of quite different form. While these were affected by the renovations undertaken by Firuz Shah Tughluq, the original appearance of the thirteenth-century bastions was evidently preserved: Naqvi, 'Sulṭān Ghārī', 6. However, the presence of such bastions here, and in Ghurid monuments such as the *masjid* of ʿAli b. Karmakh in the Panjab (see n. 83 below), and the Ghurid Friday Mosque at Ajmir (Hillenbrand, 'Ajmīr', 114, pl. XIIb), leaves open the possibility that corner bastions were also used in Iltutmish's Bada'un mosque.

50. Page, *Historical Memoir*, 29; Mehrdad Shokoohy and Natalie H. Shokoohy, *Hisar-i Firuza, Sultanate and Early Mughal Architecture in the District of Hisar, India* (London, 1988), 87–90; Shokoohy and Shokoohy, *Nagaur*, 107.

51. Although conquered in 594/1197, like other north Indian fortified cities (Gwalior and Ranthambor for example), Bada'un periodically relapsed into Rajput hands after the Ghurid conquest. In fact, the surrounding area remained politically volatile until well into the fourteenth century. In 645/1247–8 Bada'un is said to have been back in the control of the local Katahriya Rajput chiefs, at whose hands the city suffered damage around 665/1266–7. The assassination of its governor by one of these chiefs, around 779/1377–8, led to a concerted effort on the part of the Delhi sultans to put an end to the disturbances in the area. In addition, the city was the site of a number of rebellions against the central authority of Delhi. In 691/1291, for example, ʿAla' al-Din Khalji came with a large force to quell a rebellion in the city: H. M. Elliot and John Dowson, *The History of India by its Own Historians* (Delhi, repr. 1990), 3:105–6; A. S. Bazmee Ansari, 'Badā'ūn', *EI* 2, 855; Mohibbul Hasan, 'Maḥmūd I', *EI* 2, 48; Wink, *Al-Hind*, 2:223–4; Jackson, *Delhi Sultanate*, 136–8. For Mongol incursions as far as Bada'un, see n. 92 below.

52. Blakiston, *Jami Masjid*, pls. VI–VII, IX. Although published in 1926, the drawings in Blakiston's report are dated 1888.

53. Flood, 'Ghūrid Architecture', 141.

54. Shokoohy and Shokoohy, *Nagaur*, 35, pl. 8a. Miniature arcades were also carved on the column erected later by Firuz Shah Tughluq at Hisar: Shokoohy and Shokoohy, *Hisar-i Firuza*, 33.

55. Nabi Khan, 'Pākpatan', 317–18, figs 8–11.

56. Some of the vertical geometric ornament on the main *iwan* is comparable to the decoration of Iltutmish's screen at Ajmir, but this may attest little more than a conservative repertoire among the fourteenth-century artisans.

57. Blakiston, *Jami Masjid*, 4–5. The potential reuse of earlier decorative brickwork may, however, complicate the question. The inscriptions and decoration of the main *iwan* await further investigation.

58. Ibid., pl. IX.

59. Holly Edwards, 'The Genesis of Islamic Architecture in the Indus Valley', unpublished D.Phil. thesis, New York University, 1990, 259–60.

60. See, for example, the Warangal mosque or the mosque of Makhdum Hussain at Nagaur: Wagoner and Rice, 'From Delhi to the Deccan'; Shokoohy and Shokoohy, *Nagaur*, 29, fig. 8.

61. For brick vaults and domes in Iranian mosque architecture from the twelfth century onwards, see Oleg Grabar, 'The Visual Arts', *Cambridge History of Iran*, vol. 5, The Saljuq and Mongol Periods, ed. J. A. Boyle (Cambridge, 1968), 629–36; Sheila S. Blair, 'Islamic Art, II, 5(i)(b). Architecture: Iran c. 1050–c. 1250', *The Dictionary of Art* (New York, 1996), 16:161–3. On the *iwan*, see Oleg Grabar, 'Īwān', *EI* 2, 287–9; Grabar, 'Ayvān', *Encyclopaedia Iranica*, 153–5. The Iranian or Central Asian affinities of the Bada'un mosque have been noted elsewhere: Anon., 'Shamsi Musjid', 130; Tokifusa, 'Seljuq Architecture', 54–60.

62. Tokifusa, 'Seljuq Architecture', 57, 59.

63. Shokoohy and Shokoohy, 'Tuqhluqabad', 534. It has been pointed out, quite correctly, that the *pishtaq* and *iwan* first seen in Delhi and Ajmir may have been a standard part of Indo-Islamic mosque architecture by the fourteenth century, and only genetically related to Iranian models: Patel, *Islamic Architecture of Western India*, 258–9. However, the cumulative weight of Persianate elements at Bada'un indicates a more immediate relationship.

64. Welch and Crane, 'The Tuqhluqs', 130, fig. 1. The original form of the earlier congregational mosque at Warangal (c. 1323) is not clear, since only the mihrab bay survives: Wagoner and Rice, 'From Delhi to the Deccan', 91–2, fig. 14. If the present scheme faithfully reflects the basic details of Iltutmish's mosque, as Tokifusa seems to believe, then this would clearly locate the beginnings of the four-*iwan* plan in India much earlier: 'Seljuq Architecture', 52–4. The issue requires further investigation.

65. Hillenbrand, 'Ajmīr', 111, 113, pl. VIb. Numerous examples may be found in the Ilkhanid architecture of Iran, at Abarquh, and Natanz, for example: Donald Wilber, *The Architecture of Islamic Iran: The Ilkhānid Period* (Princeton, 1955), 148, nos. 39, 73–4. However, the immediate inspiration for this non-functional feature should probably be sought in the Ghurid architecture of Afghanistan. See the suggestion that the remains of a diminutive minaret formerly found on one side of the entrance *iwan* of the Masjid-i Jami of Herat dated from the Ghurid period: Hillenbrand, 'Architecture of the Ghaznavids and Ghurids', 157.

66. See, for example, Mohammad Wahid Mirza, *The Nuh Sipihr of Amir Khusraw* (Oxford, 1950), xxi; Julia Gonnella, 'Indian Subcontinent VIII,

5(i) Pottery, (ii) Tiles', *The Dictionary of Art* (New York, 1996), 15:686. As Michael Willis notes, 'we must remember . . . that brick and stone traditions had points of contact' and were mutually influential: Michael D. Willis, 'A Brick Temple of the Ninth Century', *Artibus Asiae* 52 (1992), 30.

67. The eleventh-century Shaburgan-Ata mausoleum near Karakul in Uzbekistan has a brick superstructure borne on ashlar walls: Bernard O'Kane, 'The Gunbad-i Jabaliyya at Kirman and the Development of the Domed Octagon in Iran', in *Arabic and Islamic Studies in Honor of Marsden Jones*, ed. Thabit Abdullah et al. (Cairo, 1997), 4. For later Indian examples, see the Lātkī Masjid of Firuz Shah Tughluq at Hisar in the Panjab: Shokoohy and Shokoohy, *Hisar-i Firuza*, 33. While baked brick was the norm in Iran, occasionally monuments, such as the fourteenth-century shrine of Pir-i Bakran near Isfahan, were built from rubble masonry: Wilber, *Architecture of Islamic Iran*, 52.

68. For a similar combination of brick superstructure and stone substructure in earlier north Indian temple architecture, see R. C. Agrawala, 'Unpublished Temples of Rājasthān', *Arts Asiatiques* 11 (1965), 56, fig. 13. For regional trends in Tughluqid architecture, see Patel, *Architecture of Western India*, 255–9, 268–73.

69. 'The glaze has lost nearly all of its colour, but still preserves its lustre. It looks very like a piece of old blue silk cloth that has faded in colour, but still possesses its shiny surface': Cunningham, *Reports*, 7–8. A few traces of glazed ornament were still visible in the courtyard in the 1920s: Blakiston, *Jami Masjid*, 5. On the use of turquoise glaze, see Donald N. Wilber, 'The Development of Mosaic Faïence in Islamic Architecture in Iran', *Ars Islamica* (6, 1939), 28–9; Bernard O'Kane, 'Islamic Art II, 9(ii), Architectural Decoration: Tiles, (b) Eastern Islamic Lands', *The Dictionary of Art* (New York, 1996), 16:248.

70. Cunningham, *Reports*, 4. Although Rahman ('Shamsī 'Idgāh') takes Cunningham's conjecture as fact, it awaits confirmation by removal of the whitewash now obscuring the details of the monument.

71. A three-colour palette is first represented in the madrasa at Zuzan in Khurasan (1218), but was not standard at this period: Sheila S. Blair, 'The Madrasa at Zuzan: Islamic Architecture in Eastern Iran on the Eve of the Mongol Invasions', *Muqarnas* 3 (1985), 86–8. Of the five developmental steps in the use of glazed tilework in Iran noted by Robert Hillenbrand, the first two (its use for inscriptions and as tiny insets) are present in the decoration of the Bada'un mosque: Robert Hillenbrand, 'The Use of Glazed Tilework in Iranian Islamic Architecture', *Akten des VII. Internationalen Kongresses für Iranische Kunst und Archäologie, München 7–10 September 1976* (Berlin, 1979), 545. For surveys of the use of glazing in pre-Mongol Iranian architecture, see Wilber, 'Mosaic faïence', 30–8; Douglas Pickett, *Early Persian Tilework: The Medieval Flowering of Kāshī* (London, 1997), 21–33.

72. Hillenbrand, 'Turco-Iranian Elements', 166; Nabi Khan, 'Pākpatan', 320.

73. Welch and Crane, 'Tughluqids,' 130.

74. Mehrdad Shokoohy, 'Indian Subcontinent III, 6(ii)(b): 11th–16th-century Indo-Islamic Architecture: North', in *The Dictionary of Art* (New York, 1996), 15:340. This monument does not appear in the author's various publications on Hansi.

75. A full discussion of these screens will appear in Chapter 6 of my

forthcoming book, *Incorporating India*, but see Shafiqullah, 'Calligraphic Ornamentation'.

76. Shokoohy and Shokoohy, 'Tughluqabad', 535, pl. Xa. For the use of stucco in the Ghaznavid and Ghurid monuments of Afghanistan, see Hillenbrand, 'Architecture of the Ghaznavids and Ghurids', 199–201. The shift from carved stone to stucco and painting in the decoration of Indo-Islamic monuments between the thirteenth and fourteenth centuries is a phenomenon that merits further investigation.

77. The names and descriptions of some of the palaces of sultanate Delhi hint at colouristic effects possibly achieved through the use of glazed tiles: Rahman, 'Shamsī ʿIdgāh'; Shokoohy and Shokoohy, 'Tughluqabad', 518. For a discussion of the use of glazed elements in later Indo-Islamic monuments, see Tanvir Hasan, 'Ceramics of Sultanate India', *South Asian Studies* 11 (1995), 83–106.

78. Blakiston, *Jami Masjid*, pl. XId.

79. For thirteenth- and fourteenth-century mosques, see notes 3 and 6 above. The arch profiles are comparable to those of the Khirki mosque in Delhi, c. 1352–54: Welch and Crane, 'Tughluqs', pl. 8. The slight upturn of the arch apex is found in other monuments of the early fourteenth century, such as the Mosque of Makhdum Husain in Nagaur, dated 720/1320, although the arch profile here is quite different: Shokoohy and Shokoohy, *Nagaur*, pl. 6a. The likelihood that the vaulting dated from the 1326 rebuilding was first noted by Haig ('Monuments', 624), and later reiterated by Percy Brown (*Indian Architecture*, 14).

80. Shokoohy and Shokoohy, 'Tughluqabad', 527, 530, 532, pl. VIa-b.

81. Catherine B. Asher, 'Inventory of Monuments', in *The Islamic Heritage of Bengal*, ed. George Michell (Paris, 1984), 110.

82. Although brick vaulting is found at least one pre-conquest temple at Gwalior, this is datable to the ninth century, with no evidence for the continued use of such forms into the later medieval period: Michael Willis, 'Brick Temple', 30, pl. 10.

83. Holly Edwards, 'The Ribāṭ of ʿAlī b. Karmākh', *Iran* 29 (1991), 85, fig. 1, pl. VIIIc.

84. Derek Hill, *Islamic Architecture and its Decoration, AD 800–1500: A Photographic Survey* (London, 1964), pl. 130. A good plan of the mosque can be found in Rüdi Stuckert, 'Der Bauberstande der Masjid-al-Jami [sic] in Herat 1942/43', *Afghanistan Journal* 7 (1980), fig. A. For the suggestion that much of the vaulting dates from the Ghurid period, see Hillenbrand, 'Architecture of the Ghaznavids and Ghurids', 134; A. S. Melikian-Chirvani, 'Eastern Iranian Architecture: Apropos of the Ghūrid Parts of the Great Mosque of Herat', *Bulletin of the School of Oriental and African Studies* 33 (1970), 324.

85. See, for example, the Masjid-i Jami of Varamin, or a series of mosques (c. 1325) at Dashti, Eziran and Kaj near Isfahan that consist of a central domed chamber with flanking vaulted corridors: Wilber, *Islamic Architecture*, 56–9, nos 69–71; Grabar, 'Visual Arts', 629, fig. 1.

86. Anthony Welch notes of Tughluqid eclecticism: 'Under royal patronage so many building types were tried that any attempt at postulating a clear stylistic evolution is elusive': 'Architectural Patronage and the Past: The Tughluq Sultans of Delhi', *Muqarnas* 10 (1993), 315.

87. Shokoohy and Shokoohy, 'Tughluqabad', 539.

88. See, for example, Abū Bakr al-Haravī, whose involvement in the construction of the Ajmir mosque suggests a Herati connection:

Horovitz, 'Inscriptions', 15–16; Blair, 'Zuzan', 86. For an architect with a Kabuli *nisba* active in Bihar in 1265, see Yazdani, 'Turk Sultāns', 23–5. The architect of Muhammad b. Tughluq's mosque at Jahanpanah was another Iranian: Welch, 'Architectural Patronage and the Past', 315. Note, however, that *nisba*s were carried beyond the first generation, so that an Iranian *nisba* occurring in India in the fourteenth century is not necessarily indicative of an individual who had migrated from Iran: Patel, *Islamic Architecture*, 216, n. 88. See also the suggested links between the octagonal tomb of Nasir al-Din Mahmud, Iltutmish's son, and a number of similar burial mounds excavated at Kandahar: Maurizio Taddei, 'A Note on the Barrow Cemetery at Kandahar', *South Asian Archaeology* 1 (1977), 909–16.

89. Simon Digby, 'The Literary Evidence for Painting in the Delhi Sultanate', *Bulletin of the American Academy of Benares* 1 (1967), 52. See also Husain, *Futuhu's Salatin*, 2:227.

90. As Catherine Asher notes, 'the motifs on Iltutmish's screen relate closely to those seen on Ghurid structures, for example the Shah-i Mashhad in Ghargistan, north Afghanistan': *Mughal India*, 4. While agreeing with Willis ('Gwalior', 245) that the screen shows the impact of 'strongly Persian idioms', I disagree that it shows the rejection of 'the rich decorative repertoire of temple architecture'. See also n. 75 above.

91. For a detailed discussion of these raids, see Lal, *History of the Khaljis*, *passim*; Jackson, *Delhi Sultanate*, 105–22, 219–32, esp. 231–5 for the reign of Muhammad b. Tughluq.

92. Peter Jackson, 'The Mongols and the Delhi Sultanate in the Reign of Muḥammad Tughluq (1325–1351)', *Central Asiatic Journal* 19 (1975), esp. 127–9, 150–1.

93. C. Defrémery and B. R. Sanguinetti, *Voyages d'Ibn Batoutah* (Paris, 1919), 3:202.

94. Eaton, 'Political and Religious Authority', 338–9.

95. See n. 59 above.

96. Although none of the congregational mosques of the period have survived in the Indus Valley, they were undoubtedly of brick. Unfortunately, we know too little about how builders' guilds were organised in sultanate India to know if the same craftsmen were capable of translating their skills between brick and stone, even if some monuments of the period, such as the Buland Darwaza, seem to represent an attempt to replicate brick or stucco ornament in stone: Shokoohy and Shokoohy, *Nagaur*, 35, pl. 8a. See, however, the suggestion that those who worked on the Ajudhan tomb had earlier worked for Ghiyath al-Din Tughluq at Tughluqabad: Nabi Khan, 'Pākpatan', 318, and Mehrdad Shokoohy and Natalie M. Shokoohy, 'The Tomb of Ghiyāth al-Dīn at Tughluqabad – Pisé Architecture of Afghanistan Translated into Stone in Delhi', in *Cairo to Kabul: Afghan and Islamic Studies Presented to Ralph Pinder-Wilson*, ed. Warwick Ball and Leonard Harrow (London, 2002), 216.

97. Eaton, 'Political and religious authority', 335. The origins of the virtuosity seen in the glazed decoration of the Rukn-i ʿAlam at Multan remain to be satisfactorily explained, but Holly Edwards has pointed to the undated tombs at Lal Muhra Sharif near Dera Ismaʿil Khan as possible precursors, and made the interesting suggestion that the tombs represent a collaboration between local craftsmen trained in a brick medium that had been pushed to its limits, and craftsmen fleeing the Mongol invasions of the thirteenth century, who carried with them the

technological know-how to further embellish the local medium: Edwards, *Genesis of Islamic Art*, 250–4. Tanvir Hasan offered the complementary idea that experiments with the technique of glazing were used to supplement a highly developed indigenous brick tradition: 'Ceramics', 86, 97–8, 102–3. The migration of Iranian craftsmen is connected with the development of glazed decoration during the late twelfth to fourteenth centuries in several other parts of the Islamic world: Umberto Scerrato, 'Islamic Glazed Tiles with Moulded Decoration from Ghazna', *East & West* new series 13 (1962), 267; Michael Meinecke, *Fayencedekorationen Seldschukischer Sakralbauten in Kleinasien* (Tübingen, 1976), 78–88; Meinecke, 'Die mamlukischen Fayencemosaikdekorationen: Eine Werkstäte aus Tabrīz in Kairo (1330–1350)', *Kunst des Orients* 11 (1976–7), 85–144; Pickett, *Early Persian Tilework*, 37–8; Lisa Golombek, 'Timurid Potters Abroad', *Oriente Moderno* 76/2 (1996), 577–86.

98. Bada'un attracted a cosmopolitan array of refugees from many parts of Iran, and regions further west: Nizami, *Royalty*, 101. Although Ibn Battuta's ascription of the *nisba* al-Bada'uni to Ajudhan's Shaykh ʿAlaʾ al-Din might suggest a particular link between Bada'un and Ajudhan, both of which benefited from Muhammad b. Tughluq's architectural patronage, he appears to be confusing the Ajudhani shaykh with Delhi's celebrated saint, Nizam al-Din Awliyya al-Bada'uni: Gibb, *Travels*, 3:614, 653; Eaton, 'Political and Religious Authority', 340; K. A. Nizami, 'Niẓām al-Dīn Awliyā', *EI* 2, 68.

99. Iqtidar Husain Siddiqui, 'Sultan Muḥammad bin Tughluq's Foreign Policy: A Reappraisal', *Islamic Culture* 62/4 (1988), 18; Jackson, *Delhi Sultanate*, 233–4. Unique testimony to the migration of Iranian *mujāhid*s to India in the early fourteenth century is provided by a lustre plaque dated 711/1312 that records a dream in which Imam ʿAli gives his imprimatur to those setting out for India to fight *jihad* there: Oliver Watson, *Persian Lustre Ware* (London, 1985), 146, fig. 124.

100. The architect of Tughluqabad was apparently a nobleman of Anatolian (*rūmī*) origins: Shokoohy and Shokoohy, 'Tughluqabad', 518. See, however, n. 88 above.

101. Among the features that recur in the Jaunpur monuments are the fortified exterior appearance, the squat ovoid domes with inverted lotus finials, tapering corner bastions with horizontal bands of ornament and cusped arches: A. Führer, *The Sharqi Architecture of Jaunpur*, Archaeological Survey of India Reports, vol. 11 (Calcutta, 1889): pls XII–XIII, XLV, LIX.

102. Hillenbrand, 'Ajmīr', 115.

103. A. Halim, 'Kol Inscription of Sultān Altamash', *Journal of the Asiatic Society of Bengal Letters* 15/1 (1949), 3. Unfortunately, the *Akhbār al-Jamāl* has not been available to me, but the 'seven openings' recall the façade of the Bada'un mosque, or the screens added to the prayer halls of Ghurid mosques at Ajmir and Delhi. Although the text specifies that the earlier mosque was built by Qutb al-Din Aybak, epigraphic evidence suggests that it should instead be attributed to the patronage of Iltutmish: Desai, 'Mamluk Sultans', 8–11.

104. See n. 51 above. This was the case with Sultan Ghari, the tomb of Iltutmish's son in Delhi: Welch and Crane, 'Tughluqs', 154. The notion of decay in the lost Aligarh inscription may have cloaked destruction or damage by other means, as was sometimes the case in Roman rebuilding inscriptions: Edmund Thomas and Christian Witschel,

'Constructing Reconstruction: Claim and Reality of Roman Rebuilding Inscriptions from the Latin West', *Papers of the British School at Rome* 60 (1992), 140–9.

105. Welch and Crane, 'Tughluqs', 126–7, 154; Welch, 'Architectural Patronage and the Past', 316. See also the epigraphic similarities between the coins of Iltutmish and Muhammad b. Tughluq: Husain, *Rise and Fall*, 233–4; M. B. Roy, 'Transfer of Capital from Delhi to Daulatabad', *Journal of Indian History* 20 (1941), 167.

106. Husain, *Rise and Fall*, 141–91; Peter Jackson, 'Tughlukids', EI 2, 591; Jackson, *Delhi Sultanate*, 162–6.

CHAPTER ELEVEN

Silks, Pots and Jugs: Al-Jahiz and Objects of Common Use

Oleg Grabar

The study of the arts of traditional Islamic cultures is fraught with obstacles. Some of these difficulties are the result of the field's relative youth as a discipline of its own and of the paucity of its practitioners. Thus, large compendia of artefacts and catalogues of monuments, which are the basic staple of most artistic histories, do not exist and access to the basic material of study is difficult. Other obstacles derive from the importance taken in Islamic art by objects and techniques with practical functions, from textiles to glass, cups to candlesticks. The mass of available documents is impossible to master. This is so quantitatively if we consider the millions of fragments from archaeological expeditions or those lying in hundreds of local museums. It is also so qualitatively as the boundaries between outstanding works of art and routinely repeated types have not been established. Furthermore, a third obstacle is that, with a few exceptions, mostly of architectural remains, the historical, social, economic and personal context of most works of Islamic art is still unfortunately missing. For example, our knowledge of textiles is split into three separate spheres that do not always merge: remaining fragments analysed in many laboratories, texts about textiles gathered by R. B. Serjeant,[1] and clothes worn by generations of people or curtains and hangings put on walls of buildings. Or, to cite very recent examples, two superb books on Islamic glass have not only exhibited fascinating collections of objects, but also provided very successful technical analyses and a sense of the historical and regional development of glass-making.[2] What is missing in both books is a sense of why glass objects are made and how they were used.

This short article is an attempt to illustrate one possible way towards the definition of the context of medieval objects and it seemed to me a fitting tribute to a scholar who has often sought to elucidate, for his own contemporary audience of students, colleagues and amateurs, the setting of Islamic monuments. As I was reading a classic of early Islamic Arabic literature, I was struck by the many references to objects often incidental to the narrative of the story itself. And I wondered whether the systematic culling of the text for references to manufactured objects may not yield useful information about the place of these objects within the daily life of the culture.

The book is the *Kitab al-bukhala'* or *The Book of Misers* by al-Jahiz,[3] the celebrated litterateur who lived and wrote in Basra, Baghdad and Samarra between c. 776 and 868. The book was probably written late in his life, after his more polemical works supporting mu'tazilism and opposing sectarian movements of ideas. It is an anthology of stories and anecdotes around generosity and avarice, with interesting forays into cooking, which required verisimilitude of physical and human setting in order to be understood and appreciated. We may thus begin to create an inventory of household items plausible in a middle-class urban environment and, by collating it to lists provided by other texts or by the rich trove of information found in the Cairo Geniza fragments,[4] little by little we acquire a reasonably accurate sense of the objects which surrounded an individual. We may eventually connect such lists with actual objects and fit the collections assembled by museums and issued from excavations into the living establishments to which they belonged.[5] Let me add that the type of research I am proposing here is different from technologically directed investigations which also sought to relate a terminology known from texts to actual objects.[6] Both types of investigations use the same procedure of relating written sources to artefacts, but the questions they ask are not quite the same.

I was able to find thirty-eight references to objects used for a variety of purposes, but for the most part these involved in the preparation, presentation and consumption of food. The overwhelming technique is ceramics, to which I shall turn shortly. A few examples deal with glass. One (17–18/20–1) mentions a glass lamp, but the context, that is, saving oil by using a non-imbibing material, may indicate a fictional rather than an actual item. Then there is the rather curious story of a miser who picks up the trash in his street and sells some of what he finds to glass-makers and to ceramicists (123/142–3). A third reference to glass (36–7/46–7) is not to an object but to a technique of manufacturing associated with magic and thus, probably, outside my main frame of reference. There are two mentions of baskets (*tabaq*), but no indication of the materials used for them (105–6/123, 128/148).

There are several items of furniture: a bed (*sarīr*) (86/102), tables (*khuwān*), presumably low ones (20/23, 44–5/46–7, 172/195), one of which (44–5/46–7) belonging to one Yahya b. 'Abdallah was of onyx and covered with particularly fancy crockery. On the whole, however, the absence of references to items of furniture is striking and leads to the possible conclusion, a hypothetical one, of rather bare interiors in urban households. Wood, maybe even from as far as Siberia, was used for fancy bowls (45/54, 210/229), which is, however, a poetic image and may not have corresponded to anything real.

Metalwork is just about absent from the book, although the mention of a lamp set on a stand like a column (*'amūd*) (16/19) may well refer to an otherwise known type of tall lamp.

Textiles and items of clothing are mentioned more frequently. An Iraqi travelling to Merv has his own travelling clothes: a turban (*'imāma*), 'under cap' (*qalansuwa*) and a mantle (*kisā'*) (18–19/20). Food is carried to a picnic in a *mandīl* used then as a napkin. Footwear is slippers (*khufāf*) or sandals (*na'l*) (23–4/28). A woman who wants to show her daughter off for matrimonial purposes dresses her in silks of various colours (*al-wa'hi*), floss silk (*al-qizz*) and silks interwoven with wool (*al-khuzz*); draperies in the room are coloured with saffron for the occasion (25/30). The minimum worn by someone going to a market consists of trousers (*sarāwīl*), a robe (*thiāb*) and sandals (*hamūla*) (120/138). In an interesting story of creative recycling, old clothes and linings are transformed into smaller garments, cushions, or headgear and there is implied the existence of a trade in second-hand goods (182/205). But, just as with furniture, the relative paucity of references to textiles and even to clothing tells us something either about al-Jahiz's own lack of interest in clothes or about their secondary importance in the urban milieu he depicts. If the latter turns out to be true, its implication is considerable for the historian of the arts, because textiles in general and clothes in particular have played such a paramount role in the upper classes of medieval society.

Ceramics are mentioned at least twenty-five times. There are lamps (*misbah* or *misraja*) (15/18, 16/19, 18/21), cooking pots or cauldrons (*qidr*) (19/23, 204/224), frying pans (?*miqlāt*) (19/23), jars (*jarra* or *hubb*) (35/45, 42/51, 119/138, 175–6/199, 182/205), eating plates (*qas'a*, which could also be of wood, 45/54, 61/75), cups (*jām*) (105–6/123), shallow dishes (?*tubiq*) (132/153), large jars (*khabiyya*) (177/200) so difficult to carry that someone had to kick one and roll it to his house. The functions provided by these objects are personalised sources of light, storage of liquids, mostly water, and eating. Very little is said about drinking. A newly wed woman brings her own pots and pans (217/236). Al-Farazdaq wrote a poem on his cauldron (204/224), and a total miser seen once by a Bakrmakid prince is identified by his tattered clothes, a worn prayer rug, an often mended wooden bowl and some broken but still used ceramic items, a water jug, a pitcher and a bowl (182/205). I failed to find any significant evidence about glazing and glazed objects. One possible exception (35/45) occurs in a passage where a certain kind of ceramic is said to be sweating. Serjeant understood the image to reflect the green colour of commonly used green-glazed ceramics, which is a possible but not entirely convincing explanation. The point remains that those features and inventions which have created the fame of an art of Islamic ceramics find no presence in al-Jahiz's book, even though many of them are contemporary with his time.

This absence could simply be the result of its restricted subject matter: moralising and socially critical anecdotes about misers in and around the urban middle and lower classes of lower Iraq and Baghdad. Yet, even when compared with the evidence provided by the far more numerous and richer in content, but still socially restricted, fragments from the Geniza, the lists provided by al-Jahiz are quite small. Dialectal variations are also apparent in the different terms used for objects from Iraq or Egypt. Such comparisons must be pursued and should include both memoirs of contemporary life, like al-Tanukhi's stories of a judge, and fiction. For the investigation of a text from a single point of view is most similar to the search in an archaeological site for a layer of time or for evidence, even fragmentary, demonstrating the existence of a concrete activity. Each individual site, like a book, is restricted by any number of social, political, or economic factors, but all sites and all books share some information on the same subject. It is only when several sites are studied together that a picture can be drawn of the technology or the artefacts of a given time. The same goes with texts. Many more need to be studied from concrete limited perspectives in order to serve historians in relating written and material evidence to each other and in sketching out the arts and visual culture of a particular time.

Notes

1. R. B. Serjeant, *Islamic Textiles* (Beirut, 1972), bringing together in one volume his series of articles published in *Ars Islamica*.
2. Stefano Carboni, *Glass from Islamic Lands* (New York, 2000), Stefano Carboni and David Whitehouse, *Glass of the Sultans* (New York, 2001).
3. Al-Jahiz, *Kitab al-bukhala'*, ed. Taha al-Hajari (Cairo, 1958), is the edition I have used, which was also the one used by Serjeant in his translation, *The Book of Misers* (Reading, 1997). For a general introduction to the author, see Charles Pellat, 'al-Djāhiz', *Encyclopedia of Islam*, 2nd edn. References to the source are included in the body of the article, first the page number in the translation, then in the original text.
4. S. D. Goitein, *A Mediterranean Society* (Berkeley, 1967–93), esp. vol. 4, which deals with household items and vol. 6 with the invaluable index prepared by Paula Sanders.
5. Preliminary works in this direction were done by Joseph Sadan, *Le mobilier au Proche-Orient médiéval* (Leyden, 1976) and by the late Yedidad Stillman, as in her lengthy entry 'libas', in the *Encyclopedia of Islam*, 2nd edn. A related investigation is that of Muhammad Abdul Jabbar Beg, 'A Contribution to the Economic History of the Caliphate: A Study of the Cost of Living and the Economic Status of Artisans in Abbasid Iraq', *Islamic Quarterly* 16 (1972), 139–67. There may be others as well which have escaped my attention.
6. For example, J. Furon et M. Pinard, 'Céramique musulmane de Carthage', *Cahiers de Byrsa* 4 (1954), 51–2, and Jean Sauvaget's posthumous 'Introduction à l'étude de la céramique musulmane', *Revue des Études Islamiques* 33 (1965), 1–72.

CHAPTER TWELVE

Khusrau Parviz as Champion of Shi'ism? A Closer Look at an Early Safavid Miniature Painting in the Royal Museum of Edinburgh

Ulrike al-Khamis

For nearly a century the study of Persian miniature painting has focused largely on technical and stylistic issues, the identification of local schools or even individual masters. The historical, cultural and indeed religious context of the paintings has rarely been considered in depth, even though they would surely not have been created in a contextual vacuum, and are bound to reflect certain attitudes characteristic of their time. The analysis of an early Safavid miniature in the Royal Museum in Edinburgh may help to demonstrate the validity of such an assumption.

The painting in question (A.1896.70) (Plates 22–3) was purchased in 1896 as 'a battle scene illustrating a passage in the great epic poem of *Shahnama* by Ferdausi [*sic*]'. Since that time it has been published several times and its identity reassessed as 'The Battle between Khusrau Parviz and Bahram Chubina', an episode from the *Khusrau va Shirin* poem in Nizami's *Khamsa*. Executed around 1540, the painting is believed to have originally formed part of an exquisite *Khamsa* manuscript executed for Shah Tahmasp Safavi between 945/1539 and 949/1543 and now in the British Museum (Or 2265).[1]

The artist's visual adaptation of Nizami's literary model is remarkably accurate, both in terms of narrative and in terms of atmosphere.[2] Indeed, the immediate impression of vicious fighting and the skilful visual evocation of the noisy clamber of combat closely match Nizami's animated and detailed account of the battle, which takes up more than a third of the whole episode. The main characters, too, occur largely as Nizami describes them: Khursrau Parviz is enthroned on his royal elephant on the upper left of the miniature. His astrologer Buzurg Umid rides ahead of him, an astrolabe in his raised right hand to predict the favourable moment for the final assault. At their animals' feet, knocked off his imposing white horse, lies the main target of that assault, Bahram Chubina himself.[3]

However, there are iconographic deviations from the literary model, too. Some are minor but noteworthy nevertheless, such as the curious anthropomorphic sun which here illuminates Nizami's night battle, and the weapons utilised by Khusrau Parviz: a bow and arrow instead of the original sword and club. The most blatant discrepancy between the literary model and the miniature concerns the historical setting of the battle. Nizami's story has a Sassanian (and Zoroastrian) Khusrau Parviz tackle Bahram Chubina with the help of Byzantine-Christian forces. In the miniature, on the other hand, Shah Tahmasp had the event reinterpreted in an Islamic Safavid setting with faithfully rendered, contemporary arms and armour, textiles and costume: two individuals, Buzurg Umid and a young rider depicted beneath the royal elephant, wear the *tāj*, the characteristic headdress that identified adherents to the sectarian Shi'i cause of the Safavids.[4]

Most intriguing, however, is the standard which rises over Khusrau Parviz's head – carried, not as one might expect in the heat of battle, by a warrior or military standard bearer of strong physique, but by an old, not very belligerent-looking man with a long white beard. The standard combines a banner and finial with dragonheads projecting on both sides. The finial reads 'Allah, Muhammad, 'Ali', the flag '*naṣr min Allāh wa fatḥ qarīb*,' a Qur'anic quotation that translates as 'Help from God and imminent victory' (*sura* 61:13). Why would a pious Shi'i Muslim like Shah Tahmasp have a Shi'i Islamic banner introduced into a scene that depicts an event from Iran's pre-Islamic history, and furthermore, why use it to mark out a pre-Islamic ruler figure of Zoroastrian faith? After all, within the context of the story an ornamental banner like the Chinese-inspired one carried by one of Bahram's fleeing horsemen to the right of the miniature would have been perfectly appropriate. This is not an isolated incident, either. Banners with Shi'i and largely identical Qur'anic inscriptions feature repeatedly in early Safavid miniatures commissioned by Tahmasp and his father before him.[5]

Rarely, they occur in a truly Safavid context such as a miniature in the *Shahnama-yi Ismaʿil*, executed in Tabriz in 948/1541–2, where a large religious banner towers over the first Safavid Shah Ismaʿil in battle, its sentiments consolidated in Persian verse by an additional standard.[6] Most banners occur in scenes from Iran's ancient history, most notably in the remarkably numerous battle scenes of Tahmasp's spectacular *Shahnama*.[7] Of course, within the Safavid rendition of such scenes, the banners may simply represent yet another contemporary requisite without deeper significance. However, considering the attitude of the patron who commissioned them as well as the historical and religious context of these miniatures, this seems unlikely.

Shah Tahmasp was the most pious of the Safavid monarchs, even though Islamic art historians depict him primarily as a lively and

committed patron of exquisite art.[8] Born in 1514, he was the son of
Iran's first Safavid ruler Isma'il, a man of heart-felt religiosity and a
profound sense of mission.[9] His personal charisma had succeeded in
fusing his own, popular Shi'i convictions and his belief in being the
incarnation or at least representative of the hidden eighth Imam or
mahdi, with the extreme folk Islam of his mainly Turkoman or
Qizilbash devotees to forge a messianic fighting force that took Iran
by storm.[10] In 907/1501 he made Tabriz his capital and declared
Twelver Shi'ism as state religion. However, in his new role as Shah of
Iran Isma'il was emphatic in combining his religious, quasi-saintly
authority with his claim to legitimacy as the latest in a line of
glorious Iranian monarchs marked out by the ancient Iranian concept
of Divine Right, which in the Islamic context had been reinterpreted
as 'God's Shadow on Earth'.[11] With such a pedigree, he commanded
unquestioning obedience from his followers and subjects. Fighting
for him was worship, opposing him a deadly sin.

Even the devastating defeat at Chaldiran in 1514, the year of
Tahmasp's birth, did not change that situation as profoundly as is
often assumed. While Isma'il's air of invincibility was undoubtedly
destroyed and his self-esteem irrevocably scarred, his sanctity as Shi'i
Iman, representative of the *mahdī* and indeed as God-ordained Shah
of Iran, remained largely intact. Some even continued to worship him
as a god, despite Isma'il's ever increasing attempts to enforce the
orthodoxy of Twelver Shi'ism.[12]

Consequently, by the time Tahmasp was born, the charisma of the
Shah had come to rely on a complex array of religious and cultural
notions, and both Isma'il and Tahmasp's *Qizilbash* mentors would
have ensured that his education conformed to Safavid-Shi'i as well
as *Qizilbash* religious sensibilities.[13] Tahmasp's curriculum is unknown, but under the circumstances religious studies with specific
emphasis on the Safavid perspective would undoubtedly have been at
its heart, followed by other traditional subjects prescribed for Iranian
princes, such as statesmanship, the art of war, the sciences and art.
Given his father's sacred aura and his own position as heir to the
throne, Tahmasp would have been the subject of reverence and
allegiance from birth – the permanent internal power struggles
throughout his early years notwithstanding. He himself would gradually have developed a profound self-regard for his royal as well as
religious status and calling, based initially on the example set by his
father.

Indeed, we have indications that to start with he was groomed to
follow closely into Isma'il's footsteps. A Portuguese eye-witness at
Isma'il's court during the *Nauruz* festivities of 930/1524 was shocked
to see the ten-year-old Tahmasp drinking as heavily as his father and
subsequently conveyed reports that the boy had made a show of
killing with his own hands lions, bears and men.[14] When Tahmasp
found himself Shah shortly afterwards, the *status quo* in terms of
politics and the complex religious realities was maintained, first by

ULRIKE AL-KHAMIS

Tahmasp's trusted tutor, Div Sultan Rumlu, then a succession of
rival *Qizilbash* leaders. When Tahmasp finally took power himself in
940/1533, he fervently continued his father's efforts to promote
Twelver Shi'ism and personally adhered reverently to its teachings.
However, at the same time he continued to live with the some of the
unorthodox religious attentions of his – as yet indispensable –
Qizilbash followers.[15]

In the coming years religion remained central to Tahmasp despite
his hectic campaigning throughout Iran. According to his own testimony, he was convinced of being guided by a higher world with
dream apparitions of Shi'i saints advising him before important
decisions.[16] Viewing himself as the first servant of Shi'ism he assumed titles such as 'The dust of the threshold of His Holiness the
Best of Men ['Ali]', or 'propagator of the creed of the Twelve Imams',
or 'the own and faithful slave of His Holiness the Prince of the
faithful, Haidar, father of eternity'.[17] Safavid chronicles confirm
Tahmasp's characterisation as the aider of the 'Lord of the Age',
and emphasise his mission of preparing the world for the *mahdī's*
appearance at the end of time.[18] However, within this context
Tahmasp assumed personal sanctity, too. Referring to his court, he
boasts of the 'abode of angels, the court which resembles the heavenly throne, that refuge of the lote-tree of Paradise, the *qibla* of
those in need, the *Ka'aba* of those with prayers to ask'.[19]

His closest and most influential companions throughout were
theologians, spiritual figureheads in the Safavid Sufi hierarchy as
well as officials and intellectuals with considerable religious pedigree.[20] Among the Shah's own family, his pious sister Sultanim was
his closest confidante.[21] Even among Tahmasp's treasured and often
intimately befriended artists were numerous *sayyid*s known for their
piety, spiritual leadership or religious scholarship.[22] Beyond Tahmasp's court, popular expressions of religiosity were daily fare with
the devotion firmly focused on the Shah. His Turkman subjects
continued to venerate him as a god in all their public and social
rituals, despite the Shah's repeated attempts to suppress such ex-
tremism, and devotees made long and dangerous journeys to purchase
objects sanctified by contact with the Shah and believed to have
healing powers.[23]

In an environment of such profound personal and political religiosity, symbols like the *'alām*s in Tahmasp's miniatures must have
conveyed a specific message. In fact, *'alām*s had long been highly
symbolic in Iran. Alongside their military function as guiding devices
and rallying points during battle, they had long been important
requisites in Shi'i rituals. Within the Safavid context, with Shi'ism
as state religion, standards with Shi'i-Islamic quotations invoking
divinely induced victory were not only used in religious ceremonies,
but also identified Safavid forces and indeed the Shah himself.

Michele Membré, a Venetian envoy at Shah Tahmasp's court in
1540, reports that when the Shah rode out, banners went in front

'which they call *ʿalām* which are lances covered with red broadcloth, with two points and on top of the lance is a circle and inside the said circle certain letters of copper, cut out and gilded which say *ʿAli wali Allah la ilah illa Allah, ʿAli wali Allah wa Allahu akbar.*' They are carried in the hand on horseback . . .' The religious invocations were believed to exude *baraka* and have prophylactic efficiency.[24]

For Tahmasp himself, their symbolism went even further, as can be shown from several of his official communications with regional dignitaries and opponents. Whenever the Shah has reason to mention his army, he refers to his 'heaven-assisted armies' or, metaphorically, to his 'royal, victory-attended banners'.[25] Writing to the Venetian Doge, he states: '. . . soon, if the One Glorious God wills, by the help of the stainless Imams the victory-attended banners in glory, strength and power will bring destruction to the Turks'.[26] Noteworthy is also a poem by Tahmasp's court poet Mirza Qasimi which the Shah is said to have recited before the Battle of Jam in 1528: 'O you valiant, Rustam-like men, do not agonise over the war. Our numbers may be small and the enemy countless, but do not fear as the grace of God is with us and defeat of the enemy is our vocation. A formidable army does not perturb him who is assisted by the grace of God. God the Omnipotent is the source of victory; victory is God's and it is imminent.'[27] Here we have the very quotation that occurs on the Safavid banners in the Edinburgh miniature and the *Shahnama* battle scenes.

There can be little doubt that Tahmasp saw himself as the divinely ordained commander of a quasi-heavenly army that was guided and protected by God and the Imams, his vocation the dissemination of Shiʿi Islam in anticipation of the mahdi's return. Thus, in correspondence with his arch enemy, the Uzbek ʿUbayd Khan, Tahmasp points out how his victorious troops, guided by divine favour and the sanctity of the infallible Imams, overcame the enemy at 'the hand of the divinely ordained authority', that is, himself.[28] This image was also conveyed to his subjects. Thus, one of Mirza Qasimi's panegyric poems compared the young Tahmasp to the mahdi who is 'in command of the army of the End of Time'.[29]

Quite possibly, miniature painting as well as poetry may have served to disseminate such notions and it seems feasible that Tahmasp had the *ʿalāms* inserted into his paintings as symbolic markers of his vocation and mission. If this is so, the ancient heroes with whom the religious banners are associated in the *Khamsa* and *Shahnama* paintings may in turn take on a deeper significance. In the case of the Edinburgh miniature it is the last great Sassanian king, Khusraw Parviz, high priest of Zoroastrianism, who is depicted as an apparent champion of Safavid Shiʿism. An explanation for the seemingly contradictory combination of an ancient Iranian ruler figure with a potent Shiʿi can again be sought within the royal Iranian and Safavid context.

Throughout the history of Iranian royalty, rulers turned to the ancient heroes of the *Shahnama* for inspiration and consciously attempted to emulate their achievements. Court poets celebrated their efforts by likening the latter to events in the epic and compared their masters' character traits to those of legendary Iranian kings.[30] Literati in early Safavid times were no different. Thus, Qadi Ahmad calls Shah Tahmasp himself 'that Khusrau of the Four Climes' and refers to his grandson Shah Abbas I as 'a world-conquering Chosroes [sic], leading the army of the Lord of the Time.'[31]

For Tahmasp personally, his efforts could be likened to those of Khusrau Parviz on various levels. He was equal to Firdausi's legendary king in bravery, endurance and royal excellence. He might well have identified with the quest for virtue and the achievement of a higher self that characterised the Khusrau Parviz created by Nizami.[32] Finally, Tahmasp could identify himself with Khusrau in a religious, mystical sense. Contrary to popular belief, spiritual Sufism and mystic teaching continued to flourish under the early Safavids, particularly the illuminationist theosophy of Shaykh Shihab al-Din Yahya Suhrawardi (d. 587/1191), which entailed an Islamic synthesis of several ancient wisdom traditions including Zoroastrianism.[33]

According to Suhravardi, the ancient Persian priest-kings celebrated in the *Shahnama* – like Khusrau Parviz – were not only recipients but manifestations of Divine Wisdom and the Divine Light, both in turn prerequisites for being a just ruler in the Iranian context.[34] In Safavid times Shi'i figureheads were seen as continuing that tradition and it has been shown that Tahmasp certainly regarded himself as partaking of these qualities.[35] In view of such observations the figure of Khusrau Parviz may well have been meant to represent Tahmasp.[36]

If this is so, the secondary iconographic idiosyncrasies mentioned above may also be explained. As for Khusrau's bow and arrow, Membré reports that at audience Tahmasp was enthroned with his sword and a bow with four or five arrows.[37] That these items belonged to the royal insignia is proven by the fact that after the Battle of Jam in 1528 one of the Safavid fighters was honoured by the Shah with the position of bearer of the royal bow and arrow.[38] With regard to the anthropomorphic sun, early Safavid sources – leaning on conventions from the *Shahnama* – again refer to the battle of Jam thus: 'In the morning . . . the sun destroyed the legions of the stars and the universe was cleansed of darkness.' The metaphor of the sun destroying the black night was understood as analogous to the imminent battle between the Safavids representing the true religion and justice and the Uzbeks representing Sunni orthodoxy. The use of this metaphor also predicts the inevitability of the Safavid victory.[39]

It becomes obvious that the messages conveyed in the Edinburgh miniature may go beyond the mere visualisation of an ancient story. To Tahmasp himself, contemplating the image on his own, and indeed to the courtiers who may have viewed it with him in the context of a convivial *majlis*,[40] it offered confirmation of the Shah's supreme charisma as sacred propagator of Shiʿism and living manifestation of divinely ordained Iranian royalty. The event of which he as Khusrau Parviz is the protagonist may in turn mirror contemporary realities and echo his struggle to retain his empire in the face of rebellion by the Safavid governor of Herat and his younger brother, Sam Mirza, in 1535. If that is so, the old standard bearer may represent his long-time vizier Qadi-yi Jahan or the veteran *Qizilbash* commander of the Royal Guard, described by Membré as sporting a white beard,[41] and the young wearer of the *tāj* may be his loyal younger brother, Bahram Mirza.

This study suggests that Safavid miniatures like the Edinburgh painting were not merely illustrative, but may have conveyed messages of contemporary concern, including imperial propaganda. This in turn makes their creators artistic propagandists, whose task was to mirror the Shah's convictions, rather than pure artists that were merely employed – as Welch put it – because 'they brought delight and lustre to a court'.[42]

Notes

1. Laurence Binyon, J. V. S. Wilkinson and Basil Gray, *Persian Miniature Painting* (London, 1933), 133, 137, no. 166, pl. XCIV A; B. W. Robinson, *Persian Miniature Painting from Collections in the British Isles* (London, 1967), 55–6, no. 40, pl. 20; Robert Hillenbrand, *Imperial Images in Persian Painting* (Edinburgh, 1977), no. 148; Stuart Cary Welch, *A King's Book of Kings: The Shah-Nameh of Shah Tahmasp* (London and New York, 1972), 63–7; Stuart Cary Welch, *Wonders of the Age: Masterpieces of Early Safavid Painting, 1501–1576* (Cambridge, MA, 1979), 134–8, 177, pl. 66. I would like to express my gratitude to Dr Andrew Newman, Professor James Allan and Professor Robert Hillenbrand for help and advice regarding this article.
2. The general layout of the scene harks back to Timurid models. Cf. Karin Ådahl, *A Khamsa of Nizami of 1439* (Uppsala, 1981), 20, 26, pls. 4, 27.
3. J. Christoph Bürgel (tr.), *Nizami: Chosrou und Schirin* (Zurich, 1980), 110–14; Henri Massé (tr.), *Nizami – Le Roman de Chosroès et Chirin* (Paris, 1970), 84–7; Peter J. Chelkowski, Priscilla P. Soucek and Richard Ettinghausen, *Mirror of the Invisible World: Tales from the Khamseh of Nizami* (New York, 1975), 32–4.
4. Michele Membré, a Venetian envoy at Tahmasp's court in 1540, reports that only the Shah and his closest associates wore the *tāj*. No one else was allowed to sport it unless the Shah had given it as a token of allegiance. A. H. Morton (tr.), *Michele Membré: Mission to the Lord Sophy of Persia (1539–1542)* (London, 1993), xx, 41.
5. For ʿalāms with the Victory Verse in the earliest manuscript associated with Ismaʿil, see Welch, *Wonders of the Age*, 22.
6. British Library, Add. 7784, f. 107b, ill. in Hillenbrand, *Imperial Images*, 147, no. 147; my gratitude to Dr M. I. Waley, British Library, for reading the inscriptions in this painting.
7. The quotation of Qur'an 61:13 whole or in part is found on fourteen

banners in the Houghton *Shahnama*, invocations of holy Shiʿi personalities twelve times. The occasional occurrence of such banners on the
Turanian as well as the Iranian side remains to be explained. Martin
Bernard Dickson and Stuart Cary Welch, *The Houghton Shahnameh*, 2
vols (Cambridge, MA, and London, 1981), 2:539–42.

8. Said Amir Arjomand, *The Shadow of God and the Hidden Imam:
Religion, Political Order and Societal Change in Shiʿite Iran from the
Beginning to 1890* (Chicago and London, 1984), 188; Dickson and
Welch, *The Houghton Shahnameh*, 40.

9. For a historical summary of Ismaʿil's times, see H. R. Roemer, 'The
Safavid Period', in *The Cambridge History of Iran*, vol. 6: *The Timurid
and Safavid Periods* (Cambridge, 1986), ed. Peter Jackson, 189–350;
Roger Savory, *Iran under the Safavids* (Cambridge, 1980), 27–49.

10. There are indications that Ismaʿil's extremist claims were for the
public consumption of his Turkoman followers, while he personally
held more moderate views. Cf. Arjomand, *The Shadow of God*, 110;
Kathryn Babayan, 'Sufis, Dervishes and Mullas: The Controversy over
Spiritual and Temporal Dominion in Seventeenth-Century Iran', in
Safavid Persia: The History and Politics of an Islamic Society, ed.
Charles Melville, Pembroke Papers 4 (London and New York, 1996),
118; David Morgan, 'Rethinking "Safavid Shiʿism"', in *The Heritage of
Sufism*, vol. III: *Late Classical Persianate Sufism (1501–1750): The
Safavid and Mughal Period*, ed. L. Lewisohn and David Morgan (Ox-
ford, 1999), 26–7.

11. Arjomand, *Shadow of God*, 7, 95.

12. Roger M. Savory, 'Some Reflections on Totalitarian Tendencies in the
Safavid State', *Der Islam* 53 (1976), 239–40; David Morgan, *Medieval
Persia, 1040–1797* (London and New York, 1988), 117–18, Roemer 'The
Safavid Period', 225, 336; Arjomand, *Shadow of God*, 179.

13. Roger M. Savory, 'The Qizilbash, Education and the Arts', *Turcica* 6
(1975), 175.

14. Morton, *Michele Membré*, xvi.

15. Roemer 'The Safavid Period', 233, 246, 640, 642; Morton, *Michele
Membré*, xvii; Arjomand, *Shadow of God*, 179.

16. Morton, *Michele Membré*, xvii; Simin Abrahams, *A Historiographical
Study and Annotated Translation of Volume 2 of the Afzal al-Tavarikh
by Fazli Khuzani al-Isfahani*, unpublished Ph.D. thesis, Edinburgh
University, 1999, 95–6, 98.

17. Qazi Mir Ahmad Ibrahim Husayni Qummi, *Gulistan-i hunar*, tr. V.
Minorsky as *Calligraphers and Painters: A Treatise by Qadi Ahmad,
Son of Mir-Munshi (c. A.H. 1015/A.D. 1606)*, Freer Gallery of Art
Occasional Papers 3,2 (Washington DC, 1959), 55.

18. Arjomand, *Shadow of God*, 182.

19. Morton, *Michele Membré*, 64.

20. Abrahams, *Historiographical Study*, 104, 252; Morton, *Michele Membré*, xx, 19, 29, 74–6, 78–9, 83, 90.

21. Morton, *Michele Membré*, 80–1.

22. Qazi Mir Ahmad, *Gulistan-i hunar*, tr. Minorsky, 74–6, 79–81, 88, 91–
5, 101–3, 134–5, 138–9, 141–2, 144, 185; David J. Roxburgh, *Prefacing
the Image: The Writing of Art History in Sixteenth-Century Iran*,
Studies and Sources in Islamic Art and Architecture 9 (Leyden,
2001), 1, 34–5, 46, 50.

23. Arjomand, *Shadow of God*, 110; Morton, *Michele Membré*, xvii-xviii,
xxiii, 18, 41–2.

Plate 17 *'Anjar, Small Palace, fragment of aedicula.*

(Photograph © B. Finster.)

Plate 18 'Anjar, Great Palace, fragment of frieze.

(Photograph © B. Finster.)

Plate 19 ʿAnjar, Small Palace, fragment of frieze.

(Photograph © B. Finster.)

Plate 20 *ʿAnjar, arcade near north gate, capital.*

(Photograph © B. Finster.)

Plate 21 *Great Mosque of Bada'un, qibla iwan from the north-east.*

(Photograph © F. B. Flood.)

Plate 22 *'The Battle between Khusrau Parviz and Bahram Chubina', leaf from a* Khamsa *made for Shah Tahmasp, Iran, c. 1540.*

(Courtesy The Trustees of the National Museums of Scotland.)

Plate 23 *'The Battle between Khusrau Parviz and Bahram Chubina' (detail of Plate 22).*

Plate 24 *Umayyad marble veneer in the eastern vestibule, Great Mosque of Damascus.*

(Photograph © M. Milwright.)

Plate 25 *Umayyad marble veneer, Great Mosque of Damascus (detail).*

(Photograph © M. Milwright.)

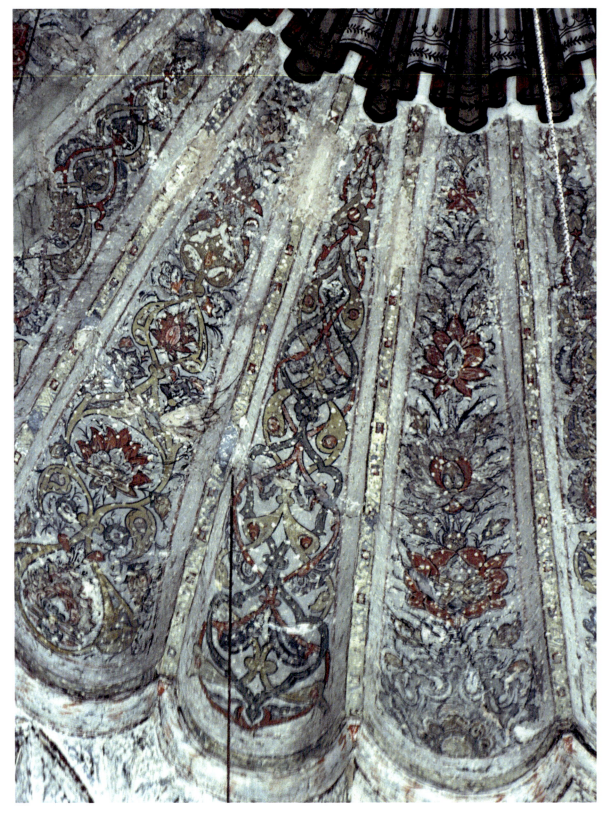

Plate 26 *Edirne, Uç Şerefeli mosque (1438–47), detail of painting in dome.*

(Photograph © B. O'Kane.)

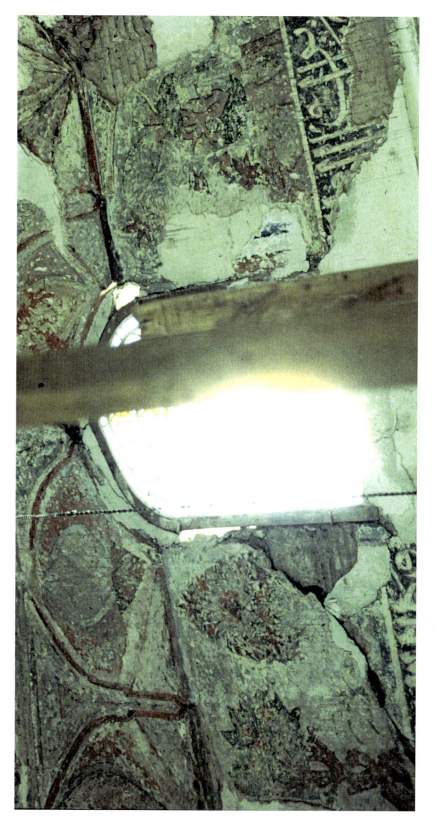

Plate 27 Edirne, Uç Şerefeli mosque (1438–47), detail of painting in zone of transition.

(Photograph © B. O'Kane.)

Plate 28 *'Rustam, Raksh and the Lion'*, Shahnama, *c. 1820.*

(Private collection.)

Plate 29 'Rustam and the White Demon', Shahnama, c. 1854–64.

(Present whereabouts unknown.)

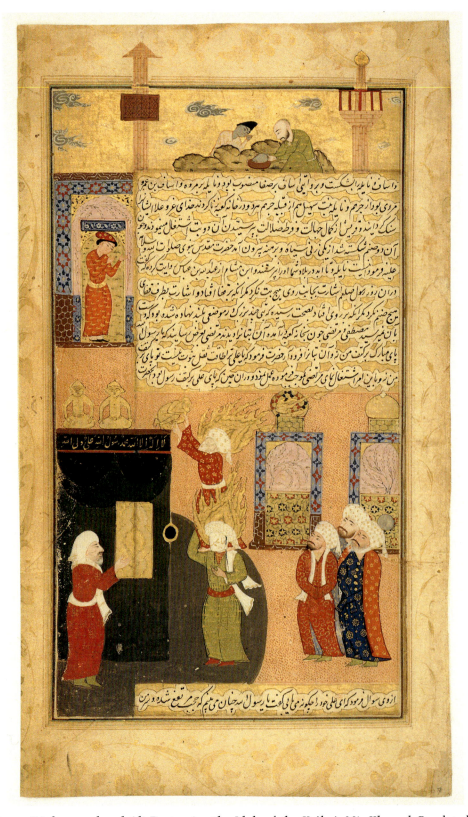

Plate 30 *'Muhammad and Ali Destroying the Idols of the Ka'ba', Mir Khvand, Raudat al-safa, Shiraz, c. 1585–95, The Islamic Museum in Berlin, I. 44/68.*

Plate 31 *Abu ʿAli Muhammad Balʿami*, Tarjuma-yi tarikh-i Tabari.

(Freer Gallery of Art, Washington DC, 57.16; f. 157a.)

Plate 32 *Basin made for al-Salih Ayyub.*

(Freer Gallery of Art, Washington, DC, 55.10.)

24. Morton, *Michele Membré*, 24, 85; J. W. Allan, '''Alām va 'Alāmāt', *Encyclopaedia Iranica* (Alp Arslan etc., 1985), 1:785–91; A. S. Melikian-Chirvani, 'Banners', *Encyclopaedia Iranica* (London and New York, 1988), 3:712–14. Melikian-Chirvani points out that banners with Shi'i inscriptions already occur in certain Timurid miniatures.

25. Morton, *Michele Membré*, 60–3; Abrahams, *Historiographical Study*, 197–8.

26. Morton, *Michele Membré*, 64–5.

27. Abrahams, *Historiographical Study*, 189.

28. Ibid., 207–8.

29. Ibid., 57.

30. A. S. Melikian-Chirvani, 'Le livre des rois, miroir du destin', *Studia Iranica* 17 (1988), 7–46; A. S. Melikian-Chirvani, 'Le *Shah-Name*, la gnose soufie et le pouvoir mongol', *Journal Asiatique* 272 (1984), 292–5, 300, 321–2.

31. Qazi Mir Ahmad, *Gulistan-i hunar*, tr. Minorsky, 44–5, 181.

32. Chelkowski et al. 1975, *Mirror of the Invisible World*, 4, 46, 47; Bürgel, *Nizami*, 331–64.

33. For a comprehensive study, see Mehdi Amin Razavi, *Suhravardi and the School of Illumination* (Richmond, 1997).

34. Ibid., 10, 15–16, 21, 84.

35. Ibid., 121–2.

36. There have been earlier attempts to interpret ancient heroes in Persian miniatures as contemporary rulers including Tahmasp, but always without detailed reasoning. Welch, *A King's Book of Kings*, 67; Dickson and Welch, *The Houghton Shahnameh*, 43, 102; Binyon et al., *Persian Miniature Painting*, 111, 114, 133, no. 142, 137 no. 163; Eleanor Sims, 'The Illustrated Manuscripts of Firdausi's *Shahnama* Commissioned by Princes of the House of Timur', *Ars Orientalis* 22 (1992), 54, 56.

37. Morton, *Michele Membré*, 21.

38. Abrahams, *Historiographical Study*, 190.

39. Ibid., 81.

40. Such literary gatherings at court are examined in Roxburgh, *Prefacing the Image*, 64–72.

41. Morton, *Michele Membré*, 21.

42. Stuart Cary Welch, *Persian Painting: The Royal Safavid Manuscripts of the 16th Century* (New York, 1976), 15.

CHAPTER THIRTEEN

'Waves of the Sea': Responses to Marble in Written Sources (Ninth–Fifteenth Centuries)[1]

Marcus Milwright

Marble[2] has played a key role in the monumental architecture of the Mediterranean Basin and the Near East since ancient times. Sources of marble in the ancient world were limited,[3] and activities such as quarrying, transporting, sawing veneer panels and paving stones, cutting opus sectile, carving architectural details and polishing stone all required teams of skilled craftsmen.[4] It is not surprising, therefore, that marble was seldom used as the principal material of construction. There is archaeological evidence for the facing of rubble masonry with decorative marble panels as early as the sixth century BCE in Greece,[5] and this ornamental use of marble remained popular in the architecture of the Roman, Byzantine and early Islamic periods. Whilst plain, monochrome stone was generally the preferred medium for freestanding sculpture or carved architectural details, heavily veined or polychromatic stones were deemed more suitable for veneer and opus sectile, and, to a lesser extent, paving and column drums. Importantly, it is the variable colouration and the patterning of veins within a given stone that form the basis of the decorative scheme. Skilled craftsmen learned to maximise the impact of such patterns through the careful selection and sawing of marble blocks, but other designs might come about by serendipity. Describing the activities of the sculptors of the island of Chios in the Archaic period, Pliny the Elder (d. 79CE) writes:

> All these artists, then, used only white marble from the island of Paros, a stone which they used to call *lychnites* because, as Varro reports, it was quarried in galleries by the light of lamps . . . A marvel is reported concerning the quarries at Paros; when a single block of stone was split with wedges, the stone-workers found that there was an image of Silenus inside.[6]

The event Pliny relates does not involve merely an act of observation. Rather, in surveying the peculiar arrangement of mineral staining, the quarrymen projected on to the surface of the stone the *idea* of how the figure of Silenus might look.[7] This process of imaginative projection is taken to much greater heights in the genre of rhetorical description of art and architecture (*ekphrasis*) developed during the late Antique and Byzantine periods. One of the most elaborate texts of this type is Paul the Silentiary's well-known account of the ambo of the St Sophia in Constantinople written in 563, in which the author constructs an involved simile of a 'sea-girt island' through the conflation of the variegated green Thessalian stone panelling on the pulpit itself ('whose abundant meadows delight the eye') and the setting of the structure, like a rocky promontory on a pavement of blue-veined Proconnesian marble ('an isthmus beaten by waves on either side'). He also notes, '. . . and in other places you may see natural markings of the stone that resemble in their changeful lines the moon and the stars'.[8] Whilst it may be asked to what extent such eulogies are truly representative of the experiences and perceptions of contemporary viewers, it is clear that Byzantine writers of the sixth century and later had become accustomed to 'seeing' landscapes, oceans, stars and flowers within stone slabs. Equally, craftsmen developed ever more complex designs in marble veneer to satisfy the demands of their educated audience. Patrons of the sixth century made specific reference to the ability of skilled marble workers to create pictures that imitated nature through the cutting and connection of patterned marble.[9] The accounts of medieval travellers to the St Sophia, St Vitale in Ravenna and St Mark's in Venice regularly claim to recognise representations of human figures in the marble panels adorning the walls.[10]

The practice of cladding the interiors of buildings with marble paving and veneer revetments also spread to the Middle East. Examples in Palestine known from written sources and archaeological evidence include the church of the Holy Sepulchre in Jerusalem, the cathedral of Tyre, the churches of St Stephen's and St Sergius in Gaza, and both the cathedral and the church of St Theodore in Jerash.[11] The techniques of sawing marble panels may have been exported beyond the confines of the Byzantine empire. Tabari (d. c. 923) claims that the 'Qaysar' (i.e. Justinian I) sent to Abraha, ruler of Yemen in the mid-sixth century, 'workmen and mosaics and marble (*al-ṣunnā' wa'l-fusayfasā' wa'l-rukhām*)' for the decoration of his church, called al-Qalis, in San'a'.[12] Whether this represents anything more than a literary *topos* – it bears obvious similarities to later accounts concerning the decoration of the Prophet's Mosque and Great Mosque in Damascus by al-Walid I (705–15)[13] – is not apparent, although other descriptions of the church make clear that marble, mosaic and other fine materials were employed.

The earliest references to the use of marble in Islamic architecture should perhaps be viewed with some caution. Writing in the sixteenth century Diyarbakri asserts that the caliph 'Uthman (644–55) made use of marble columns in his reconstruction of the Prophet's mosque in Medina.[14] This claim is not substantiated in other accounts. Mas'udi (d. c. 956) reports that in 684 Ibn al-Zubayr brought mosaics and three marble columns (*asātin min rukhām*) from the Yemeni church of al-Qalis for use in the rebuilding of the Ka'ba.[15] Whilst it is plausible that the fine materials were plundered for use in the Mekkan sanctuary, the fullest description of al-Qalis given by Azraqi (d. c. 865) states that the columns inside the church were of *sāj* (probably teak).[16] Much clearer evidence is available for the Umayyad period. Marble was employed extensively in the great building programmes of the caliphs 'Abd al-Malik (685–705) and al-Walid I in Mecca, Medina, Jerusalem and Damascus.[17] From the Dome of the Rock and the Great Mosque of Damascus there are examples of marble columns, capitals, veneer panels (Plates 24–5), and carved window grilles dating from the first phases of construction.[18] The use of marble was not confined to religious monuments; for instance, an account of an audience with Hisham (724–43) notes that the caliph's palace in Damascus was paved with marble and that the walls of the audience chamber were covered with marble panels held in place with gilded clamps.[19]

Descriptions of Marble

Marble is found in different forms in the structures of subsequent dynasties all over the Islamic world. This chapter focuses upon the range of responses to the appearance of marble (principally in the forms of veneer panels, opus sectile and columns) in Arabic and Persian texts of ninth to the fifteenth centuries. In particular, I am concerned with what the content and vocabulary of these descriptions can tell us about the meanings attached to marble in early Islamic architecture.

The descriptions of marble found in Arabic and Persian texts vary in form and detail. The terms *marmar*[20] and *rukhām* both appear in texts of the period under discussion, although the former is usually used to mean white stone without pattern or veining. *Rukhām* enjoys more varied usage from white stone (including alabaster[21]) to coloured and variegated marbles. In some cases the fact that the marble is coloured might be particularly emphasised; for instance, the thirteenth-century writer Abu Salih the Armenian describes the church of al-Qalis as being paved 'with coloured marble (*bi'l-rukhām al-mulawwan*)'.[22] Some descriptions merely note the colour of the stone, such as Ibn Rustah's (fl. ninth–tenth) description of the arrangement of red, white and green marble panelling on the interior of the Ka'ba.[23] Attempts are also made to identify other subsidiary colours or textures within types of coloured stone. Al-Biruni (d. 972) describes the black onyx (*jaza'*) stone of the Ka'ba as 'black striped (*mukhattat*) with white'.[24] The geographer al-Bakri (d. 1094) writes of the reuse of 'two red columns spotted/striped (*muwashshā*) with yellow, which are of matchless beauty' from an ancient church in the

construction of the Great Mosque of Qayrawan in 688–97.[25] The
Persian traveller Nasir-i Khusraw (d. c. 1088) saw on the platform of
the Haram al-Sharif in Jerusalem 'four piers of green marble that
resembles emerald (*zumurrud*), except that the marble has many
different coloured dots/flecks (s. *nuqta*) in it'.[26]

In *waqf* documents of the Mamluk period one encounters short
descriptive terms for coloured marble including *halībī* ('milk'), *sum-
māqī* ('sumac', i.e. porphyry), *zurzūrī* ('starling' or 'piebald'), *ghurābī*
('crow'), *marsīnī* ('myrtle'), *al-lahm wa'l-shahm* ('meat and fat'), and
muʿarraq ('veined').[27] It seems likely that these labels represent a
shorthand employed by architects, craftsmen and dealers in ornamental stone. Ibn Sasra (fl. late fourteenth century) indicates that this
may be the case in a description of the marble panelling of the Great
Mosque in Damascus:

> It is said that the two slabs of porphyry (*al-rukhām al-summāqī*) were
> from the throne of Bilqis [i.e. the Queen of Sheba] and there was no
> equal to them in this world. The walls were covered (*murakhkhama*)
> up to the edge of the mosaic with the same marble that is above the
> mihrab today, and there is nothing like it at this time. It is called the
> 'waves of the sea' (*mawj al-bahr*) by architects (s. *muhandis*), and
> when a man examines it, he sees it is one of the wonders and marvels of
> the world.[28]

The likening of the patterns within marble to water is a common
theme found in the works of Roman and Byzantine writers in the
centuries before the birth of Islam.[29] The same metaphor appears in
Jewish literature; the *Babylonian Amoraim* of the fourth century CE
describes the marble of the Herodian temple as being like the 'waves
of the sea'.[30] Even more elaborate comparisons between water and
marble are to be found in the talmudic story of the 'Four who entered
Paradise' in the mystical text the *Hekhaloth*. In one medieval version
of the story the shining surfaces of the marble in the sixth palace
create the impression that 'hundreds of thousands and millions of
waves of water stormed against him, and yet there was not a drop of
water'.[31] Other allusions to water appear in Arabic literature. The
poet Buhturi (d. c. 898) in his eulogy about the Samarran palace of al-
Kamil draws the following comparison:

> As if the glass walls of its interior
> were waves beating upon the seashore;
> As if its striped marble (*tafwīf al-rukhām*), where its pattern
> meets the opposite prospect,
> Were streaks of rainclouds arrayed between clouds, dark and
> light, and striped, coming together and mingling.[32]

The appearance of marble also provoked other comparisons. Nasir-i
Khusraw remarks that the flecked green marble of the balustrade

(dār-āfrīn) around the platform of the Haram in Jerusalem had the appearance of 'a meadow with flowers in bloom (marghazār-i gulhā-yi shukufta)'.[33] Hamdani (d. 945) in his book about the antiquities of southern Arabia mentions a stone slab (s. balāṭa) opposite the king's palace at Madr which he claims bears the 'image of the sun and the moon (ṣūrat al-shams wa'l-qamar)'.[34] Perhaps the most detailed account of marble panelling is given by Ibn Jubayr (d. 1217) in his description of the interior of the Ka'ba:

> In the wall facing the entrance, which is that running from the Yemen corner to the Syrian, are five marble panels set lengthways as if they were doors. They come down to a distance of five spans (s. shibr) from the ground, and each of them is about a man's stature in height. Three of them are red, and two green, and all have white tessellations (tajzī' bayāḍ) so that I have never seen a more beautiful sight. They are as if speckled (tanqīṭ). The red one adjoins the Yemen corner, and next to it at a distance of five spans is a green . . . They are all sited in this manner, there being between each panel and the other the distance we have stated. Between each pair is a marble [slab] of pure and unstained whiteness (rukhām abyad ṣāfi'l-lawn nāṣi' al-bayāḍ) on which Great and Glorious God had fashioned (aḥdatha), at its first creation, the remarkable designs (s. shakl), inclining to blue, of trees and branches (mā'ila ila'l-zurqa mushajjara mughaṣṣana), and another beside it with the same design exactly, as if they were parts [of the same stone]; and if one were placed over the other each design would correspond to its opposite. There is no doubt that each slab is the half of the other, and when the cut was made they divided to make these designs and each was placed beside its sister. The space between the green and the red panel is that of two slabs, their combined width being five spans, according to the number mentioned above. The designs on these slabs vary in shape, and each slab lies beside its sister. The sides of these marble slabs are braced by cornices two fingers wide (qadr iṣba' ayn), of marble tessellated with greens and speckled reds (al-rukhām al-mu-jazza' min al-akhḍar wa'l-aḥmār al-munaqqaṭayn), and whites, that are like wands turned on a lathe (anābīb mukhrūṭa), such as to stagger the imagination.[35]

The main focus of Ibn Jubayr's account is the pair of white panels carrying symmetrical designs. He is aware that this effect has been achieved through the splitting of a single block of veined stone. Interestingly, he asserts that the designs of trees and branches were 'fashioned, at its first creation' by God, thus implicitly denying the creative role of the viewer to project images on to the surface of the stone. Also noticeable is the avoidance of allusions to animate life; that is, things possessing a soul/spirit (rūḥ).[36] This restriction may be partially explained by the fact that most of the marble was located in religious buildings, but there remains the impression that the Arabic and Persian texts employ a more limited vocabulary than is seen in

Byzantine *ekphrasis*. In the following paragraphs I want to suggest two aspects of the discussion of marble that perhaps represent perspectives drawn from the culture of early Islam: first, the commemorative use of marble and other stones; and second, the association of the surface qualities of marble to patterned textiles.

Ibn Sasra's claim that the porphyry slabs in the Great Mosque in Damascus were part of the throne of Bilqis is found in earlier accounts.[37] This is one example of a widespread phenomenon of linking marble, and other stones, with locations, historical figures or pre-Islamic deities. It seems likely that this literary device was intended to set off chains of associations for readers of the texts (thus rendering less significant a description of the aesthetic qualities of the stone). For instance, the alabaster slabs in the roof, and perhaps also the red, white and green marble veneer, of the Ka'ba might evoke memories of the mythical splendours of the ancient palace of Ghumdan.[38] That, during the *jāhiliyya*, stone slabs or blocks were the focus of religious practices is recognised by Hamdani and Ibn al-Kalbi (d. 821).[39] In Jerusalem the black paving slab (*al-balāṭat al-sawdā'*) within the Dome of the Rock was believed to be a cover for one of the gateways of Paradise.[40] Other stones were associated with the life of the Prophet. A white (or red) marble paving slab in the Ka'ba was said to mark his praying place (*muṣallā*).[41] Tabari records that the mosque built in the time of Mu'awiya (661–80) upon the site of the house of Khadija contained a stone slab to the left of the doorway which the Prophet had used to shelter himself from stones thrown from neighbouring houses.[42] Recent research has suggested that the stone discs set into mihrabs (and possibly also the black stone of the Mekkan sanctuary) associated with the building programme of al-Walid were meant as a form of aniconic commemoration of the Prophet.[43]

The last point I want to make relates to the visual comparisons between patterned textiles (in particular, the *ikat* cloths of Yemen known as *washī* or *'aṣb*[44]) and marble. The central importance of textiles in the material culture and aesthetic sensibility of the Medieval Islamic world has been discussed by Lisa Golombek.[45] Decorative brickwork, stucco or tiles might function, like wall hangings as the 'clothing' for a building and in some cases the qualities of patterned textiles were imitated in architectural ornament.[46] In this context it is significant that the vertical bands ornamented with slightly blurred wavy lines (Fig. 13.1) found on *ikat* textiles bear striking similarities to variegated marble. The use of such textiles in architectural contexts has a long history in the Hijaz: *'aṣb al-yamanī* is specified as the material covering the Ka'ba before the time of the Prophet.[47] It is tempting to see the marble panelling used by al-Walid to cover the interior of the structure[48] as a means to echo, in a more lasting medium, the aesthetic qualities of varicoloured *ikat* hangings. Another aspect of this comparison can be seen in the vocabulary (terms based on the roots *w-sh-y*,[49] *f-w-f*[50] and *kh-ṭ-ṭ*[51]) used to describe both textiles and marble. Writing about

Fig. 13.1 Cotton ikat textile. Probably Yemen 10th century. Griffith Collection.

(Photograph © Ashmolean Museum, Oxford.)

Yemeni napkins (s. *mandil*), Ibn ʿAbd Rabbih (d.939) remarks that they are 'like the flowers of spring (*ka-annahā'l-nuwwār al-rabī*');[52] associations also employed by Byzantine writers and Nasir-i Khusraw when discussing marble. One type of Egyptian textile, known as *buqalamūn* or *abū qalamūn*, actually took its name from the semi-precious stone jasper because the use of different coloured threads for the warp and weft created an iridescent effect.[53]

This brief survey has encompassed descriptions ranging from the simple phrases found in *waqf* documents to more elaborate prose and poetry. Authors usually resort to a set of stock adjectives and metaphors in order to differentiate colours and textures of different types of stone.[54] Returning to the extant Umayyad marble panelling in the Great Mosque of Damascus, it is clear that the craftsmen who produced them were working within a late Antique idiom. Both the quarter-sawn veneer and the framed lozenge of coloured stone were designs that would have been familiar to a contemporary Byzantine viewer. Certainly, it is possible to detect in the texts discussed above parallels with Byzantine literary devices employed in the description of marble – although I am unaware of any example of the transmission from Greek to Arabic of a text of this nature[55] – but I believe that other concerns are also present in the works of Muslim authors. At one level, the visual qualities of the stone evoke comparisons to patterned textiles, and, at another, stones themselves become signifiers of other things, people or places. It is this allusive dimension that provides one of the challenges for those concerned with the interpretation of descriptions of material culture in written sources of the medieval Islamic period.

MARCUS MILWRIGHT

Notes

1. I would like to thank Mr Dominic Brookshaw, Dr Ruth Barnes and Dr Ruba Kana'an for their help in the preparation of this article.
2. The term 'marble' is used here to describe any hard stone that can be polished to a shine. This may include a wide range of stones including marbles, breccias, granites, porphyries, diorites, basalts and alabaster.
3. For the main marble quarries of the ancient world, see *Marble in Antiquity: Collected Papers of J. B. Ward-Perkins*, Archaeological Monographs of the British School in Rome 6, ed. Hazel Dodge and John Bryan Ward-Perkins (London, 1992), 15–16, fig. 3.
4. For a discussion of the labour involved in these activities, see Janet DeLaine, *The Baths of Caracalla: A Study in the Design, Construction, and Economics of Large-scale Building Projects in Imperial Rome*, Journal of Roman Archaeology. Supplementary Series 25 (Portsmouth, RI, 1997), 118–21.
5. Emerson Swift, *Roman Sources of Christian Art* (New York, 1951), 127, fig. 64.
6. Pliny the Elder, *Natural History* XXXVI.4.14.
7. I have borrowed the concept of 'projection' from Ernst Gombrich, *Art and Illusion: A Study in the Psychology of Pictorial Representation* (London, 1960).
8. The complete text is translated in Cyril Mango, tr. and ed., *The Art of the Byzantine Empire, 312–1453: Sources and Documents* (Englewood Cliffs, NJ, 1973), 91–96. See also comments in Gervase Mathew, *Byzantine Aesthetics* (London, 1963), 35–6, 76–7.
9. John Onians, 'Abstraction and Imagination in Late Antiquity', *Art History* 3 (1980), 10.
10. Onians, 'Abstraction', 9–10. Michael of Thessalonica draws an analogy between the veining of marble in St Sophia and human flesh: 'One of these stones even puts on the guise of living flesh, and, whitish in colour, displays all over itself what look like gaping veins of blood. A statue of such material would be a plausible counterfeit of a man'': tr. Cyril Mango and John Parker, 'A Twelfth-Century Description of St Sophia', *Dumbarton Oaks Papers* 14 (1960), 239.
11. Swift, *Roman Sources*, 131–3; John Crowfoot, *Early Churches in Palestine* (London, 1941), 7, 15, 58, 63; Mango, *Sources*, 60–72.
12. Tabari, Abu Ja'far Muhammad b. Jarir, *Ta'rikh al-rusul wa'l-muluk*, ed. Michael de Goeje (Leyden, 1879–1901), I.2: 935.
13. Hamilton A. R. Gibb, 'Arab–Byzantine Relations', *Dumbarton Oaks Papers* 12 (1958), 221–33.
14. Cited in K. A. C. Creswell, *Early Muslim Architecture*, 2nd edn (Oxford, 1969), 1.1:40.
15. Mas'udi, Abu'l-Hasan, *Les prairies d'or*, tr. and ed. Charles Barbier de Meynard (Paris, 1861–77), 5:192–3.
16. Al-Azraqi, Abu Walid Muhammad b. 'Abdallah, *Geschichte und Beschreibung der Stadt Mekka*, Die Chroniken der Stadt Mekka 1, ed. Ferdinand Wüstenfeld (Leipzig, 1858), 89–90. This interpretation relies upon the reading of *al-'umud al-sāj* (for *al-'amal bi'l-sāj*) proposed in *San'a': An Arabian Islamic City*, ed. Robert Serjeant and Raymond Lewcock (London, 1983), 45, n. 30.
17. The literary and archaeological evidence is reviewed in Creswell, *Early Muslim Architecture*, 1.1:65–196.
18. Very little of the marble veneer in either building dates to the Umayyad

period. See H. R. Allen, 'Observations on the Original Appearance of the Dome of the Rock', in B*ayt al-Maqdis: Jerusalem and Early Islam. Oxford Studies in Islamic Art* 9.2, ed. Jeremy Johns (Oxford, 1999), 206, 208–9. For photographs possibly showing original veneer panels, see Ernest Richmond, *The Dome of the Rock in Jerusalem: A Description of its Structure and Decoration* (Oxford, 1924), figs 4, 6–7, 59–60. The fire of 1893 destroyed most of the original marble veneer in the Great Mosque in Damascus.

19. Al-Isfahani, Abu al-Faraj, *Kitab al-Aghani* (Cairo, 1905), 5:157–8. The remnants of similar decorative programmes are reported from Khirbat al-Minya and Qusayr ʿAmra. See Creswell, *Early Muslim Architecture*, 1.2:385, 395, n. 10.

20. Derived from the Greek μάρμαρον.

21. Sometimes described as *rukhām malakī* or *rukhām malakī abyaḍ*. See Nikita Elisséeff, tr. and ed., *La Description de Damas d'Ibn ʿAsākir* (Damascus, 1959), 24 [16], n. 3.

22. Abu Salih, the Armenian, *The Churches and Monasteries of Egypt and Some Neighbouring Countries*, tr. and ed. Basil Evetts (Oxford, 1894–5), 139 (Arabic text).

23. Ibn Rustah, Abu ʿAli Ahmad b. ʿUmar, *Kitab al-Aʿlaq al-nafisa*, Bibliotheca Geographorum Arabicorum 7 (Leyden, 1892), 36.

24. Cited in Finbarr B. Flood, 'Light in Stone: The Commemoration of the Prophet in Umayyad Architecture', in Johns (ed.), *Bayt al-Maqdis*, 316.

25. Al-Bakri, ʿAbdallah b. Abu al-ʿAziz, *Description de l'Afrique septentrionale. Texte arabe*, ed. William M. de Slane (Paris, 1911), 22. See also Creswell, *Early Muslim Architecture*, 1.2: 518. The term *muwashshā* is also employed by al-Dimashqi in describing the marble quarries of Latakya. See *Cosmographie de Chems-ed-Din Abou Abdallah Mohammed ed-Dimachqui*, ed. Michael Mehren (St Petersburg, 1866), 209.

26. Nasir-i Khusraw, *Safar-nameh-i hakim*, ed. Muhammad Dabirsiyaqi (Tehran, 1977), 54; tr. W. Thackston as *Naser-e Khosraw's Book of Travels* (Albany, 1986), 33–4.

27. Examples are taken from the *waqf*s of sultans Faraj ibn Barquq and Qaytbay. See Salih Mostafa, 'The Cairene Sabil: Form and Meaning', *Muqarnas* 6 (1991), 40; *The Buildings of Qaytbay as described in his Endowment Deed*, ed. L. Mayer (London, 1938), 6, 12. See also comments in Jane Jakeman, 'Abstract Art and Communication in "Mamluk" Architecture', D.Phil. thesis (Oxford University, 1993), 100; J. Michael Rogers, 'The State and the Arts in Ottoman Turkey. Part 1. The Stones of Süleymaniye', *International Journal of Middle East Studies* 14 (1982), 73–4; Howard Crane, tr. and ed., *Risale-i Miʿmariyye: An Early-Seventeenth-Century Ottoman Treatise on Architecture*, Studies in Islamic Art and Architecture 1 (Leyden, 1987), 71–2.

28. Ibn Sasra, Muhammad b. Muhammad, *A Chronicle of Damascus, 1389–1397*, tr. and ed. William Brinner (Berkeley and Los Angeles, CA, 1963), f.120a.

29. Onians, 'Abstraction', 7–9.

30. Tziona Grossmark, '"Shayish" (Marble) in Rabbinic Literature', in Moshe Fischer, *Marble Studies: Roman Palestine and the Marble Trade*, Xenia 40 (Konstanz, 1998), 276–7.

31. Tr. in Gershom Scholem, *Major Trends in Jewish Mysticism* (New York, 1946), 52–3. See also Grossmark, 'Shayish', 277–8.

32. Buhturi, al-Walid ibn ʿUbayd, *Diwan al-Buhturi*, ed. H. al-Sirafi (Cairo,

1963), no. 641, tr. Julie Meisami, 'The Palace-Complex as Emblem: Some Samarran *Qaṣīda*s', in *A Medieval Islamic City Reconsidered: An Interdisciplinary Approach to Samarra*, Oxford Studies in Islamic Art 14, ed. Chase F. Robinson (Oxford, 2001), 73, verses 20–2.

33. Nasir-i Khusraw, *Safar-nameh*, 55; Thackston, *Travels*, 34.

34. Hamdani, Hasan ibn Ahmad, *Kitab al-iklil*, ed. A. al-Karmali (Baghdad, 1931), 8:116.

35. Ibn Jubayr, Muhammad ibn Ahmad, *Rihla*, E. J. W. Gibb Memorial Series 5, ed. William Wright, revised Michael de Goeje (Leyden, 1907), 93–4. Adapted from tr. in Ronald Broadhurst, *The Travels of Ibn Jubayr* (London, 1952), 89.

36. For a discussion of the legitimacy of figural representation based on the interpretation of *Qur'ān* and *ḥadīth*, see A. J. Wensinck and T. Fahd, 'ṣūra', *EI* 2; 9:889–92; Jakeman, *Abstract Art*, 64–5.

37. Elisséeff, *Description*, 51.

38. For instance, see Hamdani, *Iklil*, 16–26.

39. Hamdani, *Iklil*, 83: the author notes that the king would genuflect (*kaffara lihā*) when passing a stone slab embedded in a wall opposite the palace. Ibn al-Kalbi, Hisham, *Kitab al-asnam*, ed. and tr. Wahib Atallah (Paris, 1969), 11: al-Lāt is described as an 'idol block' (*ṣakhra murabba'a*) presumably indicating that it was not carved into a representative form. See also Gerald Hawting, *The Idea of Idolatry and the Emergence of Islam: From Polemic to History* (Cambridge, 1999).

40. Amikam Elad, *Medieval Jerusalem and Islamic Worship: Holy Places, Ceremonies, Pilgrimage*, Islamic History and Civilization. Studies and Texts 8 (Leyden, 1995), 78–81. See also Flood, 'Light', 327–9.

41. Azraqi, *Mekka*, 147; Thackston, *Travels*, 77; Ibn Jubayr, *Rihla*, 94. A green marble slab (*rukhām khiḍrā'*) in the *ḥijr* marked the tomb of Isma'il. See Ibn Battuta, Muhammad b. 'Abd Allah, *Voyages d'Ibn Battoutah*, tr. and ed. Charles Defrémery and B. Sanguinetti (Paris, 1853–8), 1:310.

42. Tabari, *ta'rīkh*, 1.3:1130.

43. Flood, 'Light', 353–7, although Muslim tradition places the black stone of Mecca in the lifetime of the Prophet. See Hawting, *Idolatry*, 85–6, 106.

44. These terms appear to be synonymous. '*Aṣb* refers to the practice of knotting the warp threads prior to dyeing them. This technique creates the variegated patterns when they are woven. See Carl Lamm, *Cotton in Mediaeval Textiles of the Near East* (Paris, 1937), 152–6, 236–7, pl. XVIII.d. See also Robert Serjeant, 'Material for a History of Islamic Textiles up to the Mongol Conquest (IV)', *Ars Islamica* 13 (1948), 75–88. For further examples of Yemeni *ikat*, see Georgette Cornu, *Tissus islamiques de la collection Pfister* (Rome, 1992), nos. 6744, 6751–3.

45. Lisa Golombek, 'The Draped Universe of Islam', in *Content and Context of the Visual Arts in the Islamic World*, ed. Priscilla Soucek (Pennsylvania, 1988), 25–50.

46. Golombek, 'Universe', 34, figs 13–16. The use of the term *hazār-bāf* ('a thousand weaves') to describe a style of brickwork suggests this relationship was recognised by Persian craftsmen.

47. Azraqi, *Mekka*, 173–4.

48. Ibid., 147.

49. E.g. Serjeant, 'Material (IV)', 79: a Yemeni cloak referred to as *ḥulla awfāf yamaniyya muwashshā*.

50. E.g. Edward Lane, *An Arabic-English Lexicon* (London, 1863–93), 2460: striped Yemeni cloth called *burdu afwāfin*.

51. E.g. Serjeant, 'Material for a History of Islamic Textiles up to the Mongol Conquest (I)', *Ars Islamica* 9 (1942), 80: Baghadi ʿAttābī cloth is described as *mukhaṭṭaṭ*. See also Lane, *Lexicon*, 499.

52. Ibn ʿAbd Rabbih, *Kitab al-ʿiqd al-farid* (Cairo, 1887), 1: 46.

53. Serjeant, 'Material (IV)', 95–6. Masʿudi makes the explicit link between the two. See *Prairies*, 2:437–8.

54. The author of the *Risale-i miʿmariyye* claims to be able to differentiate marbles according to the tone they make when struck. See Crane, *Treatise*, 68.

55. Cf. Franz Rosenthal, *The Classical Heritage in Islam* (London, 1975), 44–5, 265–6.

CHAPTER FOURTEEN

The Arboreal Aesthetic: Landscape, Painting and Architecture from Mongol Iran to Mamluk Egypt

Bernard O'Kane

Although three of the earliest Islamic monuments, the Dome of the Rock and the Great Mosques of Damascus and Madina, prominently figured naturalistic trees among their decoration, there is a long gap (with just one exception) in the surviving monuments until the frequent reappearance of trees in architectural decoration in the fourteenth and fifteenth centuries. In a recent study I showed how the late fourteenth-century landscape miniatures of a Muzaffarid-style manuscript, the Bihbihani *Anthology*, might have been related to landscapes with trees in two fourteenth-century monuments near Isfahan, the Ilkhanid shrine of Pir-i Bakran at Linjan (c. 1303) and the Muzaffarid Masjid-i Gunbad at Azadan (1365).[1]

The appearance of trees on paintings in Timurid monuments has previously been associated with funerary imagery. Recent discoveries in Uzbekistan have widened this corpus to include two mosques with similar examples, and trees have also been newly discovered, (and sadly, destroyed) during the restoration of the Üç Şerefeli Cami in Edirne. This chapter will question whether the widespread appearance of trees on this and other monuments in Turkey and Egypt in the thirteenth and fourteenth centuries should be credited to the Timurid International style, or whether they could be seen as being inspired by the prestige of the decoration of the main earlier monuments, the Dome of the Rock and the great mosques at Madina and Damascus. The relation of the decoration of those monuments to pre-Islamic arboreal lore is considered, although with the space at my disposal here, there is room only to tilt at this inexhaustible subject.[2]

Finally, I will address the reasons why the fourteenth and fifteenth centuries saw the reappearance of landscape in Iranian art and architecture, broaching a topic that has been largely ignored since it was promoted in the early twentieth century, namely the extent to which Iran's pre-Islamic heritage might have encouraged landscape

BERNARD O'KANE

depiction in the Islamic period. The importance of two catalysts that may have contributed to the timing of the new popularity of trees in Iranian art in the fourteenth century will be discussed: the reverential attitudes of the Mongols towards trees and the importation into Iran for the first time of landscape paintings from China.

Wall-paintings of Trees in Timurid Buildings

Examples of these survive in the following five mausoleums: at the Shah-i Zinda in Samarqand, Shirin Beg Agha (1385–6) and Tuman Agha (1404–5), at the mausoleum of Saray Malik Khanum in her madrasa at Samarqand (c. 1397), at the mausoleum of Tuman Agha in her madrasa at Kuhsan (1440–1) (Figure 14.1) and finally at the Gunbad-i Sayyidan at Shahr-i Sabz (1437). The treatment of the setting in these examples varies from depictions of trees bearing fruits in naturalistic landscapes in the first four examples to individual waving trees set within polylobed or star-shaped medallions, the latter appearing only at the Gunbad-i Sayyidan.[3]

Recent restorations have uncovered further examples of each of these kinds of painting, but in mosques. The first is in the mosque of the madrasa of Ulugh Beg at Samarqand (820–3/1417–21) (Figure 14.2).[4] Plaster removed from one point of the lower walls of the mosque, above dado level, revealed a series of small blind-arched niches that probably led to muqarnas at the base of transverse vaults.

Fig. 14.1 Kuhsan, complex of Tuman Agha (1440–1), detail of painting in mausoleum.

(Photograph © B. O'Kane.)

At the bottom of these arcades were tall rectangular niches that alternated geometric patterns with naturalistic fruit-laden waving trees, painted in blue, almost identical to those of the mausoleum of Saray Malik Khanum. It has been suggested that the 'Master of Landscape', on the basis of the resemblance of the paintings in the

Fig. 14.2 *Samarqand, madrasa of Ulugh Beg (820–3/1417–21), detail of painting in mosque.*

(Photograph © B. O'Kane.)

BERNARD O'KANE

Samarqand mausoleums to that at Kuhsan, accompanied Tuman Agha when she went to Khurasan,[5] but as this took place in 814/1411–2 before the decoration of the Ulugh Beg madrasa, it seems clear that, if indeed one person was responsible for this kind of decoration, he remained in Samarqand.[6]

The newly revealed painting on the interior of the masjid-i jami' of Ulugh Beg at Shahr-i Sabz (839/1435–6) in part shows a decorative scheme identical to that of the Gunbad-i Sayyidan opposite: waving palm trees with smaller vegetation at the base of their trunks, set within star medallions (Figure 14.3).

Fig. 14.3 Shahr-i Sabz, *masjid-i jami' of Ulugh Beg (839/1435–6), detail of painting.*

(Photograph © B. O'Kane.)

It is significant that whereas the previously known examples were all in mausoleums, these new discoveries are in mosques. The pervasiveness of this imagery under the Timurids can now be seen to be associated not only with its most obvious manifestation, paradisial imagery in a funerary context, but with their major religious buildings as well.

The popularity of the tree motif in architecture may have encouraged artists to adapt it later for use on objects. It appears for instance, on Turkman underglazed painted pottery;[7] inside a metal Safavid wine bowl,[8] and on Gujarati inlaid mother-of-pearl boxes (Figure 14.4).[9] Post-Timurid examples on architecture within or influenced by the Iranian world are relatively few.[10]

Ottoman landscapes

It is also in mosques that most examples of early Ottoman mural landscapes appear. The early Ottoman state was one in which Persian language and literature played a major role, as indeed it had in the earliest major Turkish state in the region, that of the Anatolian Seljuks. Evidence of Timurid taste is clearly present in early Ottoman architecture and architectural decoration, the most obvious example being the Yeşil complex in Bursa, where a Tabrizi workshop was involved and where the builder of the mosque, Hajji Ivaz, is known to have been a prisoner of Timur.

The earliest example of landscape painting may be at the Eski Cami in Bursa (805–16/1403–14), although I will first discuss the other Ottoman examples because of the problems interpreting the remaining evidence there. Better known are the wall paintings of the Muradiye mosque in Edirne (1436), although before its detailed publication in 1985 it was little known that its painted landscapes, revealed in restoration work between 1953 and 1960, were part of the original decoration of the building.[11] These include an impressive variety of trees and vegetation (Figure 14.5) that filled most of the three walls of the qibla *ayvān* above dado level, showing cypresses wound with creepers, fruit trees and a version of the floral sprays that emerge from vases in Timurid tilework, and for which preparatory drawings have been preserved in the Topkapi albums.[12]

The next major royal mosque in Edirne, the Uç Şerefeli (1438–47), was restored in the 1990s. I was fortunate to visit it in 1994 when the restoration was in progress, and the plaster was newly stripped away from most of the walls, revealing extensive wall painting. In addition to the central dome the mosque has four smaller domes at the corners. I was able to photograph two of these, those at the south-east and north-east corners. Each of the domes' facets or flutes are decorated with arabesques similar to those that have been revealed on the domes of the Yeşil Cami at Bursa, although at Edirne there is greater use of sinicising flowers (Plate 26). The greatest surprise was in the zone of transition of the south-east dome, where the area

Fig. 14.4 *Inlaid mother-of-pearl box, Gujarati, 16th century, Haghia Sophia treasury.*

(Photograph © B. O'Kane.)

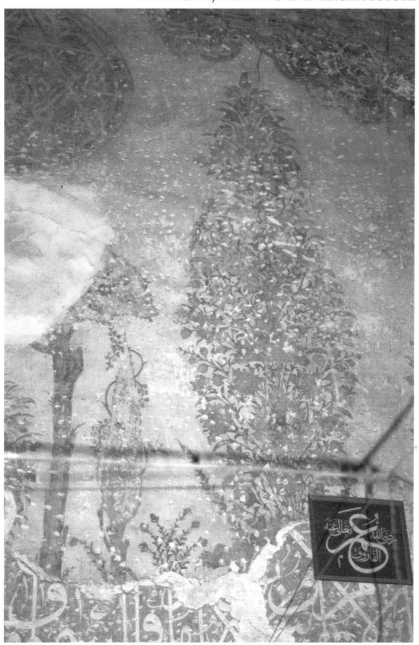

Fig. 14.5 Edirne, Muradiye mosque (1436), detail of painting.

(Photograph © B. O'Kane.)

between the muqarnas elements was shown to have had painted trees, some with twisted trunks, in the tallest portions nearest to the windows, and smaller shrubs and vegetal elements in the smaller areas next to the lowest tier of muqarnas (Plate 27). There is no reason to doubt that these formed part of the original decoration of the mosque. On my subsequent visit to this mosque in 2001, I was appalled to find that the landscape elements had been whitewashed over, and the original arabesques restored in garish fashion.

229

I was not able to visit the earlier Eski Cami at Edirne at the period during its restoration after 1994 when plaster was removed to reveal the original painting. In its present restored form trees are to be seen on several of the pendentives of the domes, and also around the bases of some domes (Figure 14.6). They were not visible before the restoration of the 1990s, and although they have been completely restored or at least heavily repainted, I assume that enough traces of them were found in the original to permit restoration in this way. They are not nearly as naturalistic as those of the Muradiye or Üç Şerefeli at Edirne, but this could be due to the heavy-handedness of the restorers. Perhaps some other lucky visitor, if not the restorers who were able to witness the paintings after they had been first revealed, may be able to shed more light on this matter.

The next surviving example of this arboreal series is the Yeşil Imaret Cami (also known as the Yahşi Bey Cami) (845/1441) at Tire in western Anatolia. This is also based on a **T**-plan, where the qibla area is in the form of a semi-dome. The four recesses at the base of this semi-dome are each decorated with a large arabesque medallion surrounded with cypresses or naturalistic floral forms.[13] The final example, from the Tiled Kiosk in the Topkapi Palace, is no longer

Fig. 14.6 *Edirne, Eski Cami (805–16/1403–14), detail of painting.*

(Photograph © B. O'Kane.)

extant and thus it is impossible to say whether or not it was related to the others in style. The Ottoman poet and vizir Ahmad Pasha wrote '(as for) that cypress which the illuminator has painted on its wall, the Tuba tree [in paradise] could serve as a simile for it', showing that he equated the symbolism of the painting with that of the foundation inscription which compares the palace as a whole to a heavenly mansion.[14] The architecture and decoration of the Tiled Kiosk are quintessentially Iranian,[15] and the trees presumably carried on the traditions we have seen in the earlier examples in Ottoman territory.

The tilework atelier that was responsible for the decoration at the Yeşil Cami in Bursa has been also credited with work at the Muradiye and Üç Şerefeli mosques in Edirne. The question of whether there are similar links between the painted programmes of these mosques has yet to be addressed. This is not the place for a full discussion of this matter, but from these preliminary observations the possibility arises that an allied team of artists could also have been responsible for designing the painted decoration at all three buildings.[16] If the Edirne Eski Cami murals are based on original designs, then these would represent the earliest surviving decoration of trees on Ottoman buildings, perhaps showing that the Timurid International style had penetrated far to the west of the Islamic world even in advance of its further diffusion by a Timurid atelier working on Ottoman territory.

Evidence for continuing Ottoman interest in this type of decoration may be shown by some paper-cuts with landscapes of trees, one including birds, in the album H. 2153 of the Topkapi Saray Library. Their similarity to the Bihbihani miniatures has already been re-marked on by Michael Rogers.[17] An Aqquyunlu provenance has been suggested for them, but there is little like them in surviving Aqquyun-lu painting. Their more delicate and intricate branches are perhaps closer to the landscapes of the Edirne Muradiye mosque, and could just as well be elaborations of them, painted by Ottoman artists.

The receptivity to this type of decoration in Ottoman territory may have been enhanced by the reports of a dream that the founder of the dynasty 'Uthman had, in which a moon arose from the breast of his host and sank in 'Uthman's breast, whereupon a tree sprouted from his navel whose shade encompassed the world, including mountains and streams from which people drank and gardens were watered. The dream was interpreted as a sign of 'Uthman's forthcoming imperial success, and was retold in many sources.[18]

Mamluk Landscapes

At about the same time as the Ilkhanid images emerge, we also find trees appearing on several Mamluk buildings and objects. The Qub-bat al-Zahiriyya in Damascus (1277–81) contains mosaic decoration in a frieze running around the walls above dado height. In addition to

BERNARD O'KANE

stylised vegetal motifs, some buildings and large naturalistic trees feature prominently in it (Figure 14.7). The mausoleum itself is situated not far from the Great Mosque of Damascus, which, like the Great Mosque of Madina, was renovated by the Umayyad ruler al-Walid in the early eighth century. Part of the original decoration in glass mosaic of trees and buildings which covered most of the upper walls of the building is still present in the mosque in Damascus.[19] Regarding the mosque of Madina, we have descriptions which tell us that equally extensive mosaics of fruit-laden trees and buildings survived at least until the twelfth century.[20]

Excavations in 1985 in the citadel in Cairo uncovered the remains of a reception hall (qā'a) that has mosaic decoration on its upper walls representing architecture and trees. The latter use both mother of pearl and golden balls outlined in black to indicate the copious fruits on their branches.[21] In the latest study of the citadel by Nasser Rabbat this has been identified as the Qa'at al-Ashrafiyya, built in 1292.[22] The author relates it to a description of another building in the citadel built by the father of Ashraf, Sultan Qala'un. Qala'un had built at the citadel the Qubbat al-Mansuriyya, which, according Ibn 'Abd al-Zahir, had walls on which were depicted the likeness of Qala'un's castles and citadels surrounded by mountains, valleys, rivers and seas.[23] The perhaps similar depictions on the Qa'at al-Ashrafiyya may also have been a celebration of al-Ashraf's conquests and the extent of the lands under his dominion. At the end of the eighteenth century, murals were still to be seen on the walls of parts of the citadel: in what he calls the women's apartments of the Palace of Joseph, Niebuhr recounts that they were decorated with representations of trees and houses, etc., in fine mosaic and mother of pearl.[24]

Trees are also found in two other Mamluk buildings. The first is the Taybarsiyya madrasa (1309–10), attached to the mosque of al-Azhar. On its mihrab, also in mosaic, the winding branches of a pomegranate tree in fruit elegantly fill up each spandrel (Figure 14.8). In the mosque of al-Maridani (1340) trees in stucco decorate the qibla

Fig. 14.7 Damascus, Qubbat al-Zahiriyya (1277–81), detail of mosaic.

(Photograph © B. O'Kane.)

232

Fig. 14.8 *Cairo,*
Taybarsiyya madrasa
(1309–10), mihrab, detail of
mosaic.

(Photograph © B. O'Kane.)

dome chamber, two being found beside each corner at the base of the
pendentives in the zone of transition, with another four appearing on
the qibla wall below, two on either side of the window above the
mihrab. Some of these are also depicted with pomegranate-like fruits,
while their naturalism is increased by showing smaller adjacent
shrubs springing from their horizon line (Figures 14.9–10). Judging
from the account of a fourteenth-century physician from Damascus,
trees in a naturalistic garden setting with flowers may also have been
common in public baths, although he mentions the trees as one of
three categories (the others being warriors and lovers) that were
designed to restore animal, spiritual and natural power.[25]

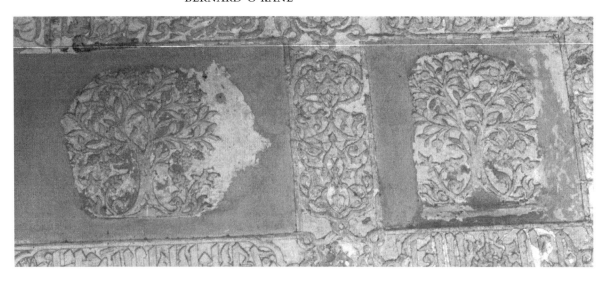

At almost the same time trees very similar to those on the walls of the al-Maridani mosque also become popular in the decoration of Mamluk metalwork. They appear on a ewer made for al-Malik al-Nasir Ahmad (d. 1342), now in the Islamic Museum in Cairo (Figure 14.11), and later on a box (datable to 1371) for Aydamir al-Ashrafi, the governor of Tripoli and Aleppo (d. 1374).[26] On the neck and base of the ewer of al-Malik al-Nasir Ahmad the swaying trunks and branches of the trees are depicted with unusual freedom of movement. On Aydamir's box two trees appear amid a chinoiserie vegetal background; flying birds and a lion chasing a quadruped also appear on each side of the trees.[27]

Six fifteenth-century examples of Mamluk metalwork also display trees, mostly, however, in a much more stylised manner rather similar in fact to the painted examples that now adorn the Eski Cami in Edirne.[28] A seventh example, on a bowl in the Museo Nazionale in Florence, is unique in incorporating, like the earlier mosaics, trees with pavilions. Three two-storey pavilions appear between a wide variety of fruit-laden trees, including pomegranate, orange, palm and cypress trees.[29]

Before investigating further what are the links, if any, between the reappearance of trees as decoration in Mamluk, Timurid and Ottoman architecture it is first necessary to revisit the Umayyad examples and their precedents.

Earlier Arboreal Lore

Tree cults were common in many pre-Islamic religions in the Middle East. An initial stage consisted of worship of individual trees, followed by those planted as an act of consecration in holy ground. In both cases the sacred tree could symbolise the divine spirit and the knowledge of good and evil. In a third stage sacred groves where

Fig. 14.11 Cairo, Islamic Museum, ewer made for al-Malik al-Nasir Ahmad (d. 1342), detail of decoration.

(Photograph © B. O'Kane.)

religious rites were performed supplemented the sacred space of temple enclosures.[30] Throughout the Greco-Roman world that preceded Islam, the paradisial iconography of the tree-filled garden was a message that was readily understood, and need not be laboured here.[31] In Iran a similar message was implicit, derived from the Zoroastrian principle that all plants are sacred and possess the gifts of health and immortality, and that they are therefore venerable.

Even before the coming of Zoroaster the Elamites, the principal dynasty in Iran before the arrival of the Achaemenids, situated their temples most frequently within sacred groves, where the holy precinct was fenced in and an altar formed the cult centre.[32]

In the *Shahnama* is a Zoroastrian tradition that Gushtasp commemorated his conversion to Zoroastrianism by planting a cypress sapling which soon attained a height and diameter of forty cubits.[33] Hamd Allah Mustaufi, the Ilkhanid historian writing in fourteenth-century Iran, identified this as a cypress then growing in Kashmar.[34]

236

He also mentions a cypress, which, incidentally, is still standing and still celebrated, at Abarquh in southern Iran.[35]

Concomitant with tree worship is a belief in tree oracles. Also in the *Shahnama* is the account of Alexander's conversation with the tree of male and female heads which prophesised his imminent death.

The several references to trees in the Qur'an connote a variety of desirable attributes. Various kinds are mentioned in the context of paradise, where they provide shade and fruit (56:28–30), specifically palm and pomegranate trees (55:68), and where one in particular, the *sidra al-muntahā* (the lote-tree) is situated near the Throne of God (53:14–16). A Qur'anic parable also compares the goodly word (probably to be interpreted as the Word of God) to a fruit-laden tree with firm roots whose branches reach to the heavens (14:24–5).[36]

Given these connotations of shade, fertility, nourishment and paradise,[37] it is not surprising that trees should figure prominently in the decoration of several of the earliest Islamic monuments. When the Prophet entered the Ka'ba in 629–30 he found on the wall, besides figural representations of angels and prophets, those of trees.[38] The Ka'ba was rebuilt under the Umayyads in 693, and again by al-Walid I, who sent columns, marbles and mosaic.[39] We have no indication of what the mosaic decoration was like, but, ironically, it was in the marble slabs that images of trees and branches were seen by Ibn Jubayr and which were, according to him, 'fashioned by God'.[40]

In the Dome of the Rock, we may speak of two types of trees in the mosaic decoration; those on the outer arcade, which have been interpreted as a 'ring of non-terrestrial trees surrounding a shrine';[41] and those on the inner face, usually more realistic, although sometimes with trunks studded with jewels. The naturalistic examples recall al-Tabari's account of the building of the temple by Solomon, who each morning found trees growing spontaneously on the site. In another version the trees were artificial ones made of gold, but which miraculously produced fruit; these may be equated with the bejewelled examples.[42]

The extensive mosaics of trees at the great mosques of Madina and Damascus in al-Walid's rebuilding have been mentioned above. Most recent commentators have suggested that their connotations are primarily paradisial in accordance with the eschatological nature of the Qur'anic verses that were to be found within the Damascus mosque, although this has been recently been questioned by Nasser Rabbat.[43] He points out that the themes of the Qur'anic verses are related as much to the Day of Judgement as to Paradise, that they were on the qibla wall and thus the culmination of a visit to the mosque, coming after rather than being identified with the mosaics on the courtyard, and that most medieval commentators saw the mosaics as representing worldly scenes, whether of Damsacus, Syria, or the Islamic world. Specifically, he quotes verses that had formerly been unnoticed of the court poet of al-Walid, al-Naghiba, as follows:

On every approach, (as if) decorated by God,
   Its interior was surrounded with Syrian marble (or: its interior was of
marble, surrounded by al-Sham)
   at the centre of the earth bounded by its quarters
      surrounced by rivers and the countryside.
   In it is the beginning of the Qur'an (al-mathānī) and (other) excellent
verses
      Here (in the verses) are Our Lord and (His) promises and threats.[44]

Rabbat intreprets the first distich as a possible reference to the depiction of Syria (or Damascus, al-Sham) in the mosaics, although it is at
least as likely that al-Shām is an adjective here referring to Syrian
marble.[45] The second verse, as he points out, could refer to the literal
rivers and countryside surrounding the mosque, or could be a metaphor for the mosaic scenes. However, if it is referring to the mosaic, it
is surprising that the trees or the buildings are not mentioned; the later
commentators, regarding whom Rabbat gives a comprehensive overview, refer to at least one or the other.[46] In any case, Rabbat is surely
right, as Flood has done before him,[47] in calling for a multi-layered
approach to the mosaic's iconography rather than pre-supposing that
only a single explanation is correct. But one need not lose sight of
paradisial explanations in the process. The twelfth-century writer Ibn
al-Najjar wrote of the (evidently very similar) mosaics on the mosque
of Madina (also restored by al-Walid) that images of trees and the
palaces of paradise were to be found there.[48] Flood's analysis of the
building types in the Damascus mosaics has shown how indebted they
were to Byzantine representations of heavenly cities; and elsewhere in
the mosque its celebrated vinescroll, the karma, underlines this
association.[49] If al-Nabigha interpreted the mosaics as worldly scenes,
and as we have seen, it is far from certain that he is referring to them at
all, his juxtaposition of them with the description of the Qur'anic
verses on the walls leaves open the possibility that in others' minds a
connection may indeed have been made between the verses and the
mosaics. Lastly, there is a fine distinction between the emphasis of the
suras on the Day of Judgement as opposed to Paradise. Whether or not
the deliberate absence of figures ruled out representation of the the the
Day of Judgement, Paradise, one of the 'promises' of God in the
Qur'anic verses mentioned in al-Nabigha's poetry, could well have
been connected with the mosaics by many viewers.
   A more conventional representation of trees from close to the same
period (late seventh century?)[50] may be in the images of mosques
from the trove of Qur'an pages from the Great Mosque of San'a.[51]
Two folios depict mosques with mihrabs flanked by naturalistic trees
of various kinds on a grassy verge. Although these trees have been
interpreted as representations of a garden that was situated at the
back of the mosque,[52] it is unlikely that the artist would have
considered a feature that was outside the walls of the mosque as
being worthy of illustration. Just as the doors are shown in elevation

at the bottom of the paintings, it is probable that at the top we are shown the qibla wall in elevation with a representation of its decoration to either side. Whether this decoration of trees was in mosaic or another medium is of course unknowable. The pages have been associated before with al-Walid's work at Madina and Damascus, but whether or not they date from his reign or from slightly before, we can agree with Barry Flood, that 'the design of the frontispiece and the decoration of al-Walid's mosques at Damascus and Medina belong, at least conceptually, to the same tradition'.[53]

The representation of trees may also reflect the actual practice of planting them in mosque courtyards, a not surprising way of providing shade for the faithful. The Great Mosque of Cordoba was provided with trees in the ninth century,[54] and an eleventh-century foundation inscription of a no longer extant mosque in Cairo contained the following: 'These palm trees that are within the mosque are all for the Muslims and they should neither be sold nor bought.'[55]

Although their stylisation places them at some remove from the naturalism of the majority of examples that are discussed in this chapter, the paintings in the Kharraqan I tomb tower (460/1067–8) of pomegranate trees should be remembered. The paradisial resonances of these and other aspects of its painting have been explored at length by Abbas Daneshvari, and need not be repeated here.[56] It should also be mentioned that the birds on the branches of the trees are paralleled in some of the later Timurid architectural examples.

The portrayal of realistic trees, often in a landscape setting, thus occurs over a wide chronological and geographical range. With the partial exception only of the Kharraqan tomb tower,[57] there is a large gap in the surviving works of art between the Umayyad monuments and the second half of the thirteenth century, when they appear simultaneously in Iran and Syria. The trajectory in the two areas is rather different, with the architectural examples found in the Mamluk dominions only until the middle of the fourteenth century, while they appear increasingly in Iran, and in related examples in Anatolia, from the fifteenth century onwards.

The sequence of landscapes or trees on Mamluk buildings starts with the mausoleum in close proximity to the Great Mosque of Damascus. It and most of the later Mamluk examples are in mosaic, a medium rarely employed in Fatimid and Ayyubid times.[58] This makes it more likely that the revival in Mamluk monuments and artefacts should be associated first and foremost with the attempts to revive the glories of the Umayyad monuments through this technique. As Nasser Rabbat has pointed out, both Baybars and Qala'un (who completed Baybars's mausoleum) spent considerable time in Damascus in proximity to the Umayyad mosque. By then, the eschatological associations of the mosaics seem to have been submerged by interpretations of them as worldy scenes, leaving the way open to the reuse of the medium as a vehicle for expressing the vastness of the sultan's dominions.[59]

Iran: the catalysts

As we have seen above, perhaps the most pervasive use of naturalistic landscapes with trees in Islamic architecture began in Iran in the Ilkhanid period. Why should it have happened at this time, and why particularly in Iran?

We noted earlier how the Ilkhanid historian Hamd Allah Mustaufi was aware of the reverence paid to trees in pre-Islamic Iran in his account of the cypress tree by which Gushtasp commemorated his conversion to Zoroastrianism. This reverence continued in the Islamic period, as revealed in his account of a tree which stood above the grave at the town of Bastam, on the road from Tehran to Mashhad, in the north of Iran:

> At Bastam is the shrine of the Shaykh of Shaykhs Abu 'Abd Allah Dastani and on his tomb stands a withered tree. Now when any one of the descendants of the Shaykh comes to be on the point of death, a branch of this tree breaks off. In certain documents it is stated that this tree was originally the staff of our prophet . . . and generation after generation it was inherited by his descendants, till it came to the Imam Ja'far al-Sadiq. The Imam Ja'far gave it to Bayazid of Bistam, and Bayazid stated in his testament that 200 years after his day a certain darvish would come out of Dastan and the staff would be his. Therefore when the Shaykh of Shaykhs Dastani made his appearance this staff became his, and after his death, by the provisions of his will, it was planted in the earth of his grave, above his breast. The same forthwith became a tree, and put forth branches. During the incursion of the Ghuzz one of its branches was cut off, and the tree withered; but of those who had thus cut off its branches most of them perished that same day, and from that time onwards the tree has always had the terrible property aforesaid inherent in it (of killing all who cut it).[60]

The echoes with the dream of 'Uthman, recounted above, may be noted.[61] Mongol Shamanistic rituals surely also played a part in maintaining or resurrecting reverence for trees. Genghis Khan himself so liked the shape of one tree that he dismounted and spent some time in its shade, experiencing an 'inner joy'. He selected it as his burial site, and it was reported that innumerable trees grew there after his burial.[62] Ögedei Khan, his son, is reported to have planted thickets there for the repose of the Genghis's soul; severe punishment was prescribed for anyone cutting branches from them.[63] Another fascinating episode is related by Rashid al-Din: in 1302, near Bisitun, Ghazan Khan remembered that on a previous journey at the same spot a revelation had come to him beside a tree and given him relief from his worries concerning rebels. On this he occasion he performed two *rak'ats* of prayer (i.e. in the Islamic manner) by the tree and then 'all those present tied tokens to the tree, and it became like a shrine.'[64] An amir related that Qutula Khan, one of Chengiz

Khan's ancestors, had once in Mongolia similarly tied pieces of coloured cloth to a tree in thanks to God for a victory that he had been granted, and had danced with his soldiers beneath the tree 'so hard that the area around the tree sank a yard into the earth'. Ghazan himself then danced beneath the tree at Bisitun.[65] The syncretistic nature of Ilkhanid beliefs, even after their conversion to Islam, could hardly be clearer.

The links of landscape painting to the Ilkhanids can be strengthened when we note that the first independent landscapes to occur in Islamic book painting were produced under Ilkhanid patronage. The earliest of these is in an Arabic *Kalila and Dimna* from the Royal Library in Rabat, which on stylistic grounds has been convincingly attributed to Baghdad in the third quarter of the thirteenth century, shortly after it was captured by the Mongols. One of its illustrations is to a story in which a bee enjoys the perfume of the water-lily so much that it forgets to fly away and is trapped when the flower closes at night. The painting in the manuscript is of a pool in which the flowers are growing (in the available reproductions there is no sign of the bee).[66] Would such a subject have been countenanced before the importation of Chinese landscape-dominated painting by the Mongols? Clear evidence for the importance of the latter occurs in two paintings in the *Jami' al-tavarikh* of Rashid al-Din (714/1314–15). These are pure landscapes, one depicting the mountains of India, the other the Jevatana, the grove of trees where Buddha achieved enlightenment.[67] Both show a clear debt to the style of contemporary Chinese painting.[68]

The importance of poetry, both secular and mystical, in Iranian society is well known, as is the centrality of the garden to Persian poetry. A detailed consideration of the garden would clearly be out of place here, even if there were space for it, but the connotations of the garden and the arbor cannot be entirely divorced. Trees may be explicitly part of garden imagery, as in Fakhr al-Din Gurgani's *Vis u Ramin*:

> I saw a tree atop a hill, all green,
>> that clears the heart from rust of grief and pain;
> A tree that lifts its head to Saturn's sphere;
>> whose shadow falls on all the world; so fair,
> Its beauty gives it likeness to the sun;
>> the whole world hoping in its fruit, its bloom.
> Beneath it, a bright wellspring gushes forth,
>> its pebbles lustrous pearls, its waters sweet.
> Upon its banks, tulips and roses bloom,
>> and violets, gilly-flower and hyacinth.
> A grazing bull of Gilan, by its verge,
>> now drinks its water, now eats of its flowers.
> May it endure, that shadow-spreading tree;
>> and may that shade more sweet than heaven be!

May ever flow the water of that spring.
and Gilan's bull there find his pasturing.[69]

The metaphor of the 'family tree' is a recurring one in Persian literature. The Saljuq historian Ravandi praises the sultan Kaikhus-rau as 'the fruit of the tree of Saljuq: a tree whose root is the strengthening and propogation of the faith, and whose fruit is the building of charitable foundations . . .' Ravandi then quotes from the *Shahnama*:

A tree in greenest Paradise I've sown
   its like not planted e'en by Faridun
In autumn when the cypress sends froth shoots,
   those branches green will reach palatial height.
A tree rejoices in its lofty height,
   observed by men of fortune and clear sight.[70]

This use of the image of the tree as a symbol of fertility and lineage echoes those recounted above in the accounts of the dream of 'Uthman and the staff of Bayazid. It is also used by Nizami in his description of Majnun's father:

. . . Anxious that his fortune's hand might make
from his dry tree spring forth a supple branch;
That should his noble cypress be cut short,
another tree might from its root sprout forth.[71]

Nizami in particular is celebrated for his use of imagery interweaving humankind and nature.[72] It has been argued that Nizami 'based the quest for poetic imagery and vocabulary partly on scientific knowledge of the geographical spread, agricultural needs and pharmaceutical properties of the trees', and that his use of trees in poetic imagery is exceptional, being 'building elements of the story itself, rather than mere pretty exercises of poetic imagination'.[73] Given this, it may be no surprise that the tree-filled landscape paintings in the Bihbihani *Anthology* appear between the chapters of Nizami's *Khamsa*. While they thus do not explicitly illustrate the text, it may be no accident that they appear within this text rather than the others within the anthology, and thus afforded an opportunity for the painter to mirror the concerns of the poet.

It has been suggested by Hushang A'lam that the animistic attitude towards venerable trees has continued in Iran with the transfer of devotion to Muslim saints, particularly Shi'i ones. Distinguished trees have often generated belief in their sacred origin and association with saints, who grant wishes or work miracles through the intermediary of their trees.[74] Manuchihr Sutuda saw this process at work in Gilan, where old trees are generally venerated by candles and lamps lit before them and by wishes for intercession tied to their

branches. He noted that in Gilan in the space of fifty years ten remark-able trees which were recorded by Rabino, British consul at Rasht, as standing alone, had been each flanked by constructions named the Imamzada Hasan, Imamzada Ibrahim, and so on.[75] Even today in many parts of Khurasan trees of great antiquity can be seen to be associated with the graves of many saints, such as the shrines at Taybad, Turbat-i Jam (Figures 14.12–13) and at Gazurgah near Herat. An indication of the importance of trees in the historical consciousness of even contem-porary Iranians is provided by the noted historian Iraj Afshar, who in his gazetteer of monuments in the Yazd region ranks eleven ancient trees as worthy of inclusion with the built examples.[76]

Fig. 14.12 *Taybad, grave of Shaykh Zayn al-Din with pistachio tree.*

(Photograph © B. O'Kane.)

Conclusions

The syncretism that characterises Iranian Islam in general, or Ilkha-nid Islam as practised by Ghazan in particular, is by no means unique.

243

Fig. 14.13 Turbat-i Jam,
grave of Shaykh Ahmad
with pistachio tree.

(Photograph © B. O'Kane.)

The holding of picnics by the burial site of one's family was long a custom in pre-Islamic Egypt and is still popular today. Another obvious manifestation of this is the boats which were associated with many tombs in Cairo – clearly a reference to the Pharaonic past.[77] In general, it has been suggested that 'Islam was adopted by ethnic groups in their own milieu, while maintaining their own cultural identity. There was hardly a break with past traditions, and pre-Islamic customs and beliefs survived.'[78]

244

One can believe, as Henri Corbin did, that the landscapes of the Bihbihani *Anthology* are infused with the spirit of the reverence for nature in the Zoroastrian *Bundahishn* without necessarily subscribing to his view that the painter was Zoroastrian.[79] It can be suggested, however, that it is likely that the celebrations of nature we have seen on fourteenth- and fifteenth-century Iranian art and architecture, whether or not they were coupled with Islamic ideas of paradise or were sparked by Mongol Shamanistic notions, are to be found in greater numbers in Iran and Iranian-influenced areas such as early Ottoman Turkey, because of these transformations of pervasive and long-lasting pre-Islamic beliefs.

Finally, although we have seen that the Arab and Perseo-Ottoman landscape representations are examples of divergent stylistic strains, the Umayyad mosques of Damascus and Madina may nevertheless be key to the development of each. They showed that eschatological images were appropriate not only in a funerary context but also for mosques, such as those of Ulugh Beg at Shahr-i Sabz and in his madrasa at Samarqand, and of course in numerous later examples, including the Ottoman landscapes at the Madina mosque.[80] We thus finally come full circle, not just at Madina, but with a reversal of the 'migration of paradisial symbol from mosque to mausoleum' that has been elucidated previously by Barry Flood.[81]

Notes

1. Bernard O'Kane, 'The Bihbihani *Anthology* and its Antecedents', *Oriental Art* 44/4 (1999–2000), 9–18. Another Timurid manuscript with landscapes has recently come to my attention. The *Divan* of Salman Saviji, Cairo, Dar al-Kutub, adab fārisī *mīm* 156, dated 841/1437–8, has one miniature (f. 245a) of two figures in a garden, but also two paintings (ff. 196a, 202b) in gold on a plain ground, each with two sinuous chinoiserie trees and other vegetation, one with a deer and a stag, on rocks in Shiraz style, the other with a deer and a single bird above the horizon. The latter is illustrated in Sayyid Mohammad Bagher Najafi, *Iranische Kunstschätze in Äegypten* (Cologne, 1989), fig. 199.

2. 'I have been frequently induced to make it [the reverence paid to trees] the object of personal inquiry among Asiaticks, and of literary research at home. The result now before me, would constitute a volume of no inconsiderable size. For the subject may be traced from the present day to the earliest ages of which written records furnish an account; through every country of the old, and even of the new world. The sacred Hebrew scriptures, allude to it in many places; we find it mentioned by Greek and Roman authors; various anecdotes respecting it occur in Eastern manuscripts, and it has been noticed by several European travellers and antiquaries': William Ouseley, *Travels in Various Countries of the East; More Particularly Persia*, 3 vols (London, 1819–23), 1:314. In general, see A. J. Wensinck, *Tree and Bird as Cosmological Symbols in Western Asia* (Amsterdam, 1921); for China, see Silvia Freiin Ebner von Eschenbach, 'Trees of Life and Trees of

Death in China', *Zeitschrift der Deutschen Morgenländischen Gesellschaft* 152 (2002), 371–94.

3. Lisa Golombek, 'The *Paysage* as Funerary Imagery in the Timurid Period', *Muqarnas* 10 (1993), 242–52.

4. I am most grateful to Galina Asanova for showing me the drawings of the restoration. She has published a preliminary account of the paintings, 'Zhivopis' mecheti medrese Ulugbeka v Samarkande', *Obshchestvennie Nauki v Uzbekistane* 5 (1994), 45–7.

5. Golombek, 'The *Paysage*', 250.

6. Hafiz Abru, *Zubdat al-tavarikh* ed. Sayyid Kamal Hajj Sayyid Javadi, 2 vols (Tehran, 1372/1993), 1:435–6. Other examples of mural landscapes may yet be discovered; a tentative removal of outer layers of plaster in a small part of the interior of the mausoleum of Qazi Zada Rumi at the Shah-i Zinda, for example, shows traces of painting in blue.

7. Best illustrated in a painting from the 'Big-Head' *Shahnama* of 899/1493–4: Glenn Lowry, *A Jeweler's Eye: Islamic Arts of the Book from the Vever Collection* (Washington, DC, 1988), pl. 22; Lisa Golombek, Robert B. Mason and Gauvin Bailey, *Tamerlane's Tableware* (Costa Mesa, 1966), 136.

8. Assadullah Souren Melikian-Chirvani, *Islamic Metalwork form the Iranian World: 8th–18th Centuries* (London, 1982), no. 117, Fig. 117A.

9. I am indebted to Julian Raby for the provenance and dating of this piece, which according to him is one of several with trees. He informs me that Simon Digby is preparing a catalogue raisonné of the complete corpus.

10. A remarkable example containing buildings resembling kiosks amid trees is the painting of the *dārskhāna* of the madrasa of ʿAbd al-ʿAziz Khan at Bukhara (1062/1651–2): Yves Porter, 'le *kitâb-khâna* de ʿAbd al-ʿAzîz Khân (1645–80) et le mécénat de la peinture à Boukhara', *Cahiers d'Asie Centrale* 7 (1999), pls 8–9. By the nineteenth century the copying of photographs and their landscapes had become common in Qajar tiles: Jennifer M. Scarce, 'Function and Decoration in Qajar Tilework', in *Islam in the Balkans: Persian Art and Culture of the 18th and 19th Centuries*, ed. Jennifer M. Scarce (Edinburgh, 1979), 77, figs 3–4. The Aba Khwaja mosque (eighteenth century or later) at the shrine complex near Kashgar has many painted landscapes in a 'chocolate-box' style that suggests they may be nineteenth century at the earliest: Bernard O'Kane, 'Iran and Central Asia', in *The Mosque*, ed. Martin Frishman and Hasan-Uddin Khan (London, 1994), 136. One stunning example in India should also be noted: the carved window grilles of the Sidi Said mosque (1572) at Ahmedabad, best illustrated in Alfieri, Bianca Maria Alfieri and Federico Borrromeo, *Islamic Architecture of the Indian Subcontinent* (London, 2000), 104. The contemporary city of Fatehpur Sikri has one pavilion with dadoes of carved sandstone displaying trees and vegetation in a naturalistic setting: Michael Brand and Glenn Lowry, *Akbar's India: Art from the Mughal City of Victory* (New York, 1985), 106. The tilework panels in the Wazir Khan mosque at Lahore are also unusual not only in the number of naturalistic trees that they display but also in that they are all portrayed as emerging from a horizon provided with plants that intertwine with the trunks of the trees: J. Burton-Page, 'Wazir Khan's Mosque', in *Splendours of the East*, ed. Mortimer Wheeler (London, 1970), 99.

11. Elisabetta Gasparini, *Le pitture murali della muradiye di Edirne*, Quaderni del Seminario di Iranistica, Uralo-Altaistica e Caucasiologia dell'Università degli Studi di Venezia 18 (Padua, 1985).

12. The drawings are illustrated in Bernard O'Kane, 'Poetry, Geometry and the Arabesque: Notes on Timurid Aesthetics', *Annales Islamologiques* 26 (1992), pl. 14b–c.

13. Gasparini, *Le pitture*, figs. 72–5; Ekrem Hakki Ayverdi, *Osmanli Mi'marisinde*, 4 vols (Istanbul, 1989); Ekrem Hakki Ayverdi, *Çelebi ve Sultan Murad Devri 806–855 (1403–1451)* 2: figs 948–9.

14. I am most grateful to Walter Andrews for this reference and for the translation.

15. Bernard O'Kane, 'From Tents to Pavilions: Royal Mobility and Persian Palace Design', *Ars Orientalis* 23 (1993), 252.

16. For Persian-Ottoman links in illumination in the early fifteenth century, see Zeren Tanındı, 'An Illuminated Manuscript of the Wandering Scholar Ibn al-Jazari and the Wandering Illuminators between Tabriz, Shiraz, Herat, Bursa, Edirne, Istanbul in the 15th Century', in *Art Turc/ Turkish Art, 10th International Congress of Turkish Art, Geneva, 17– 23 September 1995, Proceedings*, ed. François Déroche et al. (Geneva, 1999), 647–51.

17. J. M. Rogers, 'Ornament Prints, Patterns and Designs East and West', in *Islam and the Italian Renaissance*, Warburg Institute Colloquia 5, ed. Charles Burnett and Anna Contadini, 135–6, figs 8–9.

18. Cemal Kafadar, *Between Two Worlds: The Construction of the Ottoman State* (Berkeley, 1995), 8–9. Wensinck has discussed the links between navel, mountains and the provision of water in Jewish and Arabic literature: *The Ideas of the Western Semites Concerning the Navel of the Earth*, Verhandelingen der Koninklijke Akademie van Wetenschappen 17 (Amsterdam, 1917). As in Iran, the nineteenth century saw the use of landscapes based on European prototypes. Among the most impressive is a small mosque enlarged in 1810 with very realistic forest scenes: Evin Doğu, 'A Hidden Gem in Bademli: Kılcı Mehmet Ağa Camii', *Skylife* 207 (October, 2000), 168–77. The Mevlevi *sam'akhāna* in Cairo, redecorated in 1857, is another example. Bodo Rasch, the designer of the retractable umbrellas recently installed in the Madina mosque, has also informed me that naturalistic landscapes from the Ottoman period are still to be seen in parts of it.

19. For a twelfth-century description of the mosaics which marvels at their emerald trees with incorruptible fruit, see Ibn 'Asakir, *Tarikh madinat Dimishq*, tr. Nikita Elisséeff as *La description de Damas d'Ibn 'Asakir* (Damascus, 1959), 58.

20. Jean Sauvaget, *La mosquée omeyyade de Médine* (Paris, 1947), 80–1.

21. Nasser O. Rabbat, *The Citadel of Cairo: A New Interpretation of Royal Mamluk Architecture*, Islamic History and Civilization, Studies and Texts 14 (Leyden, 1995), 163, fig. 23.

22. Ibid., 156. Mosaic depictions of trees, including palms and hieratic animals survive at the Capella Palatina: Kenneth Clark, *Landscape into Art*, 2nd edn (New York, 1976), 7, fig. 5. Elsewhere in this volume Jonathan Bloom has argued that the mosaic pavements could be related to now lost Cordoban examples. Whether this should also apply to these figural examples, or whether they should be related to Fatimid prototypes, as had been assumed for the paintings of the muqarnas ceiling, remains a moot point.

23. Ibid., 166; Ibn 'Abd al-Zahir, Muhyi al-Din, *Tashrif al-ayyam al-'usur fi sirat al-Malik al-Mansur*, ed. Murad Kamil and Muhammad 'Ali al-Najjar (Cairo, 1961), 139.

24. Carsten Niebuhr, *Voyage en Arabie* (Amsterdam, 1776), 1:94, quoted in

K. A. C. Creswell, *The Muslim Architecture of Egypt*, 2 vols (Oxford, 1952–9), 2:261.

25. 'Ali Al-Ghuzuli, *Matali' al-budur*, quoted in Thomas W. Arnold, *Painting in Islam* (New York, 1965), 88.

26. D. S. Rice, 'Studies in Islamic Metal Work-IV', *Bulletin of the School of Oriental and African Studies* 15 (1953), 489–99; pls I–V.

27. Ibid., Fig. 6.

28. Ibid., 500–1; pls VI–VII.

29. Ibid., pl. X and fig. 11.

30. Thomas Barns 'Trees and Plants', in *Encyclopaedia of Religions and Ethics*, ed. J. Hastings, (Edinburgh, 1980), 448–57.

31. Annemarie Stauffer, *Textiles d'Egypte de la collection Bouvier* (Bern, 1991), 49; George Lechler, 'The Tree of Life in Indo-European and Islamic Cultures', *Ars Islamica* 4 (1937), 368–420; Vicenzo Strika, 'The Turbah of Zumurrud Khatun in Baghdad: Some Aspects of the Funerary Ideology in Islamic Art', *Annali, Istituto Orientale di Napoli* 38 (N.S. 28) (1978), 286–94.

32. Heidemarie Koch, 'Theory and Worship in Elam and Achaemenid Iran', in *Civilizations of the Ancient Near East*, ed. Jack M. Sassoon, 4 vols (New York, 1995), 3:1959–69. I am grateful to David Stronach for this reference.

33. Hushang A'lam, 'Derakht', *Encyclopaedia of Iran*, 7:317.

34. *The Geographical Part of the Nuzhat-al-qulub Composed by Hamd-Allah Mustawfi of Qazwin in 740 (1340)*, E. J. W. Gibb memorial series 23/2, tr. G. Le Strange (Leyden and London, 1919), 142.

35. Ibid, 120; Iraj Afshar, *Yadgarha-yi Yazd*, vol. 1 (Tehran 1348/1969), 356, fig. 213.

36. For a further elaboration of this parable, comparing the soul to the seed of a tree that the 'Gardener of Paradise' has planted, see Shihab al-Din Yahya Suhrawardi, *The Philosophical Allegories and Mystical Treatises: A Parallel Persian-English Text*, ed. and tr. Wheeler M. Thackston (Cost Mesa, 1999), 73.

37. For the ways in which later commentators expounded on these themes (and their relationship to the themes of earlier religions), see A. J. Wensinck, *Tree and Bird as Cosmological Symbol in Western Asia* (Amsterdam, 1921); John McDonald, 'Islamic Eschatology. VI. Paradise', *Islamic Studies* 5/4 (December 1966), 349–52, and al-Ghazali, *Kitab dhikr al-mawt wa ma ba'dahu*, tr. T. J. Winter as *The Remembrance of Death and the Afterlife* (Cambridge, 1989), 239–40. For an overview of the parallels between earthly and heavenly gardens, see Annemarie Schimmel, 'The Celestial Garden in Islam', in *The Islamic Garden*, Dumbarton Oaks Colloquium on the History of Landscape Architecture 4, ed. Elisabeth B. MacDougall and Richard Ettinghausen (Washington, DC, 1976), 11–40.

38. Avinoam Shalem, 'Made for the Show: The Medieval Treasury of the Ka'ba in Mecca', in this book, 274, (quoting al-Azraqi, *Akhbar Makka*, 1:110–11).

39. Barbara Finster, 'Die Mosaiken der Umayyadenmoschee von Damaskus', *Kunst des Orients* 7/2 (1970–1), 129–30.

40. See, in this book, Marcus Milwright, ' "Waves of the Sea": Responses to Marble in Written Sources (ninth–fifteenth Centuries)', 215.

41. Oleg Grabar, *The Shape of the Holy: Early Islamic Jerusalem* (Princeton and New Jersey, 1996), 88.

42. The latter account is by al-Muhallabi; both accounts are discussed in

Priscilla Soucek, 'The Temple of Solomon in Islamic Legend and Art', in *The Temple of Solomon*, ed. Joseph Gutmann (Missoula, 1976), 87, 97. Myriam Rosen-Ayalon, *The Early Islamic Monuments of al-Haram al-Sharif: An Iconographic Study*, Qedem: Monographs of the Institute of Archaeology, the Hebrew University of Jerusalem 28 (Jerusalem, 1989), 52, shows that in the fifteenth-century *Mi'rajnama* the illustration of the Emerald Tree in Paradise also displays a bejewelled trunk. However, given the Muslim associations we have pursued in the text above, her contention (ibid., 60) that the 'tree motif appears in place of the Cross' would appear to be redundant.

43. Nasser Rabbat, 'The Dialogic Dimension of Umayyad Art', *Res* 43 (2003), 79–94.

44. My translation, from *Diwan Nabighat Shaiban*, 2nd edn (Cairo, 1995), 53.

45. Rabbat, 'Dialogic Dimension', 90. For what it is worth, the editor of the published text vowels it as: *mubaṭṭan^{un} bi-rukhām^i al-shām^i maḥfūf^{u},* i.e. reading Syrian marble.

46. Rabbat, 'Dialogic Dimension', 91–2; expanding on his previous remarks in 'The Mosaics of the Qubba al-Zahiriyya in Damascus: A Classical Syrian Medium Acquires a Mamluk Signature', *Aram* 9–10 (1997–8), 237–9.

47. Finbarr Barry Flood, *The Great Mosque of Damascus: Studies in the Makings of an Umayyad Visual Culture* (Leyden, 2001), 33.

48. Jean Sauvaget, *La mosquée omeyyade de Médine: étude sur les origines architecturales de la mosquée et de la basilique* (Paris, 1937), 81.

49. Flood, *Great Mosque*, chs 2–3.

50. I am grateful to Robert Hillenbrand for the information that carbon testing has substantiated this date.

51. Hans-Caspar Graf von Bothmer, 'Architekturbilder im Koran – eine Prachthandschrift der Umayyadenzeit aus dem Yemen', *Pantheon* 45 (1987), 4–20; Oleg Grabar, *The Mediation of Ornament* (Princeton, 1992), pls 16–17.

52. Grabar, *Mediation*, 157.

53. Flood, *Great Mosque*, 64 (although there he was commenting on the vegetal frieze). One other Umayyad representation may be mentioned here, although its secular context gives it a different symbolic charge from the other examples. This is the diwan of Khirbat al-Mafjar, where the most important mosaic is dominated by a large fruit-bearing tree. The tree has been seen as encompassing the world, both the Dar al-Islam and the Dar al-Harb, or alternatively as an erotic embrace and a representation of the verse 'Salma, you were a paradise and its fruits in all their kinds near ripe for harvesting': Doris Behrens Abouseif, 'The Lion-Gazelle Mosaic at Khirbat al-Mafjar', *Muqarnas* 14 (1997), 16 and fig. 3.

54. D. Fairchild Ruggles, *Gardens, Landscape and Vision in the Palaces of Islamic Spain* (University Park, 2000), 216, although she also notes that jurists argued against their permissibility.

55. Gaston Wiet, *Catalogue général du Musée de l'Art Islamique du Caire: Inscription historiques sur pierre* (Cairo, 1971), 36, with references to other sources that mention trees in mosque courtyards. I will add just one later reference, that of Ibn Battuta to the mosque of 'Alishah at Tabriz, who states that its courtyard was filled with trees, vines and jasmines: *The Travels of Ibn Battuta A.D. 1325–1354*, tr. H. A. R. Gibb, 3 vols (Cambridge, 1958–71), 2:345. As Ibn Battuta visited it not long

after its foundation (1318–22), the plantings must have been an integral part of the design for the courtyard.

56. Abbas Daneshvari, *Medieval Tomb Towers of Iran*, Islamic Art and Architecture, 2 (Costa Mesa, 1986), 41–64. One may also mention here that trees were considered suitable decoration for tombstones, e.g. two from Egypt dated 248/862 and 250/864, each of which has an arch with a tree in each spandrel: Gaston Wiet, *Stèles funéraires*, vol. 2 (Cairo, 1936), nos 9129, 1274. Of course not every foliage in Islamic art can be related to paradise; for the dangers inherent in such an approach, see Terry Allen, *Imagining Paradise in Islamic Art* (Sebastopol, 1993), updated version at http://www.sonic.net/~tallen/palmtree/ip.html.

57. Partial in that they are more stylised than naturalistic.

58. The obvious exception of the Fatimid mosaics at the Mosque of al-Aqsa reinforces the links with the Umayyad examples.

59. Rabbat, 'The Mosaics of the Qubba al-Zahiriyya'.

60. *Nuzhat-al-qulub*, tr. le Strange, 272–3.

61. See n. 12 above. A'lam notes that Herodotus recounted another dream of prophetic import: 'Xerxes, contemplating an invasion of Greece, saw himself in a dream crowned with an olive branch from which other branches spread over the earth, a vision that the Magi interpreted as portending not only victory over Greece but also conquest over the world', 'Derakht', 318.

62. Rashid al-Din Fadl Allah, *Jami' al-tavarikh*, tr. W. M. Thackston as *Rashiduddin Fazlullah's* Jami'u't-tawarikh: Compendium of Chronicles, Sources of Oriental Languages and Literatures, 45, 3 vols (Cambridge, MA, 1999), 2:264.

63. V. V. Barthold, tr. J. M. Rogers, 'The Burial Rites of the Turks and Mongols', *Central Asiatic Journal* 14 (1970), 210.

64. Rashid al-Din Fadl Allah, *Jami' al-tavarikh*, 3:653.

65. Ibid., 3:654; see also Reuven Amitai-Preiss, 'Ghazan, Islam and Mongol Tradition: A View from the Mamluk Sultanate', *Bulletin of the School of Oriental and African Studies* 59/1 (1996), 1–10.

66. Marianne Barrucand, 'Le *Kalila wa Dimna* de la Bibliothèque Royale de Rabat', *Revue des Études Islamiques* 55 (1986), fig. 7.

67. Sheila S. Blair, *A Compendium of Chronicles*, The Nasser D. Khalili Collection of Islamic Art 27 (London, 1995), figs 42, 44.

68. Rashid al-Din's use of Byzantine models for his illustrations has been noted (ibid., 50–3), and it is interesting that an *Octateuch* for Isaac Comnenus (twelfth century), now in the Topkapi Saray Library, depicts a scene of the Earthly Paradise in the form of a landscape with a river flowing beneath trees populated by a variety of birds: Filiz Çağman, 'The Topkapi Collection', *Aramco World Magazine* 38/2 (1987), 16. However, its Byzantine style is markedly different from the Chinese style of the landscape paintings in the *Jami' al-tavarikh*. In the second half of the thirteenth century we also have evidence for mural landscape painting in sultanate Delhi, where Firuzshah Tughluq ordered his palace rooms decorated with various kinds of *bustān*, i.e. flowering orchards, rather than with the figural scenes which had previously been the norm there: B. N. Goswamy, 'In the Sultan's Shadow: Pre-Mughal Painting in and around Delhi', in *Delhi through the Ages: Essays in Urban History, Culture and Society*, ed. R. E. Frykenberg (Delhi, 1986), 133.

69. Julie Scott Meisami, 'The *Šâh-Nâme* as Mirror for Princes: A Study in Reception', in *Pand-o Sokhan: Mélanges offerts à Charles-Henri de*

Fouchécour, Bibliothèque Iranienne 44, ed. Christophe Balaÿ, Claire Kappler and Zhiva Vesel (Tehran, 1995), 260–1.

70. Ibid., 268.

71. Tr. Meisami in 'The Body as Garden', 265. Trees, like gardens, have been used for an enormous variety of metaphorical meanings: Just as the Qur'an compares the Word to a good tree (see n. 36 above), Nasir-i Khusrau adapts the simile to men, comparing them to good and bad trees: Annemarie Schimmel, 'Some Notes on Naser-e Xosrow as a Poet', in *Pand-o Sokhan: Mélanges offerts à Charles-Henri de Fouché-cour*, Bibliothèque Iranienne 44, ed. Christophe Balaÿ, Claire Kappler and Zhiva Vesel (Tehran, 1995), 263.

72. Hellmut Ritter, *Über die Bildersprache Nizamis* (Berlin and Leipzig, 1927), esp. section 3, 'der Mensch und die Natur', 41–66.

73. Christine van Ruymbeke, 'Nizāmī's Trees: An Arboricultural Investigation of the Miniatures of Shāh Ṭāhmāsp's *Khamsa* (British Library OR 2265)', *Edebiyāt* 11 (2000), 215–16.

74. Ouseley noted, on his journies in Iran, the trees covered with votive offerings of rags and termed *dirakht-i fāẓl* (excellent or beneficial tree): *Travels*, 1:313. I have seen many of these on my own travels in Iran and Afghanistan.

75. A'lam, 'Derakht', 316–19; Manuchihr Sutuda, *Az Astara ta Astarabad* (Tehran, 1347/1970, repr. 1374/1995), 6 (introduction).

76. *Yadgarha-yi Yazd*, figs 100, 137/1, 145, 155, 213, 229 (mistakenly captioned 239), 232, 239, 252, 255/1, 266.

77. See J. van Reeth, 'La barque de l'Imām aš-Šāfi'ī,' in *Egypt and Syria in the Fatimid, Ayyubid and Mamluk Eras II*, ed. U. Vermullen and D. de Smet (Orientalia Lovaniensia Analecta, 83) (Leuven, 1998), 249–64. In addition, in Cairene monuments, the minaret of the mosque of Ibn Tulun had a boat-shaped finial, and a model of a boat hung until recently in the mausoleum attached to the mosque of Sulayman Pasha on the citadel in Cairo; one still hangs in the symbolic tomb within the Ribat al-Athar.

78. Nehemia Levtzion, *Conversion to Islam* (New York and London, 1979), 19, *apud* Amitai-Preiss, 'Ghazan', 9.

79. Henri Corbin, tr. Nancy Pearson, *Spiritual Body and Celestial Earth: From Mazdean Iran to Shī'ite Iran* (Princeton, 1977), 31, 281. For earlier interpretations of the same paintings, see the list of previous publications in O'Kane, 'The Bihbihani *Anthology*', n. 52; and Ernst Diez, 'Die Elemente der persisichen Landschaftmalerei und ihre Gestaltung', in *Kunde, Wesen, Entwicklung*, ed. Joseph Strzygowski (Vienna, 1922), 116–36.

80. See n. 18 above.

81. Flood, *Great Mosque*, 243; Flood, 'Umayyad Architecture and Mamluk Revivals: Qalawunid Architecture and the Great Mosque of Damascus', *Muqarnas* 14 (1997), 57–79.

CHAPTER FIFTEEN

The Vicissitudes of Rustam

B. W. Robinson

The convincing depiction of a national hero demands enthusiasm, originality and a strong sense of tradition; he must be instantly recognisable and manifestly superior to surrounding figures. The poet Firdawsi describes Rustam in various terms, such as 'elephant-bodied', but the only distinguishing feature of the hero's costume that he mentions is the surcoat of tiger-skin (*babr-i bayānī*), and accordingly this feature is almost invariable in representations of Rustam in *Shahnama* manuscripts of all periods. The only notable exceptions are to be found in the earliest (early fourteenth century) examples., which occur in the *Jami' al-tavarikh* of Rashid al-Din dated to 1307[1] and in the Demotte *Shahnama* (or, in the now politically correct appellation, the 'Great Mongol *Shahnama*') of c. 1335 (Figure 15.1).[2] In these manuscripts Rustam is shown with features of Mongol type and wearing Mongol clothes. They are thus quite alien to Iranian tradition, and are soon superseded by types more suited to the spirit of the national epic, so we may pass them by. The 'small' *Shahnama*s (also probably of early fourteenth century date) are similarly outside our survey. Rustam appears in them dressed as a Mongol when in civilian clothes, but wears his tiger-skin when in armour.[3] But these miniatures are un-Persian in many respects, and I have long regarded them as Indian in origin for what appears to me to be a valid, if not decisive reason, in that they depict *tigers* in illustrating incidents where Firdawsi himself and unanimous Persian pictorial tradition demand *lions*. This opinion has so far met with neither acceptance nor refutation, though it was first voiced some twenty-five years ago.[4]

During the second quarter of the fourteenth century the Ilkhanid empire was gradually breaking up, with local chieftains and families achieving virtual independence. One of these was the Inju family at Shiraz. They were patrons of the arts, the poet Hafiz adorned their court, and they presided over a very original, and in some respects primitive, school of painting. Examples of this are to be found in several *Shahnama* manuscripts dating between 1331 and 1352.[5] In their miniatures Rustam always wears his tiger-skin, with the stripes indicated by rough brushstrokes, but otherwise his armour, including the helmet, corresponds to that of the other warriors depicted. The faces are not Mongol, but Persian (Figure 15.2).

Fig. 15.1 *'Death of Rustam', Demotte* Shahnama, *Tabriz, c. 1335.* (British Museum 1948-12-11-025.)

Fig. 15.2 *'Rustam and Ashkabus'*, Shahnama, *Inju, Shiraz, c. 1340.*
(British Museum 1933-9-29-02.)

B. W. ROBINSON

The same is true of paintings produced under the Muzaffarids, who drove the Inju from Shiraz in 1353. Two Muzaffarid copies of the *Shahnama* have survived, dated to 1370 and 1393 respectively;[6] illustrated in a style much refined after the folkish quality of the Inju school; it is indeed fundamentally different, and begins to resemble the classical style of the ensuing Timurid period. Here, in fact, we have one of the great mysteries of Persian painting; how and why did the Inju style at Shiraz completely disappear and the Muzaffarid style become firmly established in its place within a period of less than twenty years? No 'missing link' has so far appeared.

It has been suggested that the Muzaffarid style of painting represents a provincial form of the evolving classical style of the Jalayirids at Tabriz and Baghdad. The Topkapi Saray Library at Istanbul, as is well known, contains a series of albums in some of which a number of fourteenth-century miniatures, extracted from manuscripts, are included. Some of these come from copies of the *Shahnama*, and are of large size and high quality; they date in all probability from the latter half of the fourteenth century. Naturally enough, Rustam appears in a number of them, and his panoply corresponds with that in the paintings we have been considering.[7] These large detached miniatures must come from royal or near-royal volumes, and their scale and high standard of execution show up the Inju and Muzaffarid paintings of Shiraz for the provincial works they are.

Anybody who has seen a few *Shahnama* illustrations will have missed a prominent feature of Rustam's panoply in the miniatures so far described: the leopard's head mask covering the hero's helmet. Its introduction in the iconography of Rustam can, fortunately, be dated and placed quite accurately: Shiraz 1411. But the problem remains to determine why and by whom it was introduced.

In 1397 a pair of manuscripts[8] was completed at Shiraz; one contains the *Shahnama*, and the other four later epics celebrating, among other heroes, Rustam's great-great-grandfather Garshasp. The Shiraz origin of these two volumes is evident from the style of the illuminations – the minute unoutlined gold scrolls on a blue background – which goes back to the Muzaffarids and is still found in Shiraz Turkman work near the end of the fifteenth century.[9] I have suggested elsewhere that the excellent miniatures illustrating this pair of volumes may well be the work of Pir Ahmad Baghshimali.[10] Two of the miniatures in the *Garshaspnama* represent Garshasp wearing a leopard-skin coat with its head or mask on the hero's head (ff.18a, 29b) (Figure 15.3). Thus the idea of a leopard's mask on the head of a hero is introduced, but the hero is not yet Rustam. The latter does appear in the companion volume (the *Shahnama* in the Chester Beatty Library), but wearing an ordinary gilded helmet and the usual tiger-skin surcoat.

The resident governor of Shiraz till 1393 was 'Umar Shaikh, son of Timur, but after that he was absent from the city, leaving his son

256

Fig. 15.3 *'Garshasp and the Demons of Hadkir',* Anthology *of epics, Shiraz, 1397.*

(British Library Or. 2780, f. 18a.)

Iskandar Sultan, then aged nine, in charge.[11] In view of Iskandar's later pronounced taste for fine illustrated manuscripts it seems not unlikely that this pair of volumes was executed for him. Admittedly he was still very young (thirteen in 1397), but Timurid princes began their education early; the Berlin Library has a fine historical manuscript dated to 1412 with a dedication to Baysunghur, who was also no more than thirteen at that time.[12]

In 1410 Iskandar Sultan was again in Shiraz, this time as governor in his own right. He had already, it seems, begun to show his flair for fine manuscripts, and in 1410 he commissioned a remarkable *Miscellany*,[13] copiously illustrated (quite possibly by Pir Ahmad Baghshimali) containing selections from the works of Firdawsi, Nizami and others, as well as scientific and astrological material. The *Shahnama* extract comprises the romantic tale of the young Persian warrior Bizhan, and Manizha, the beautiful daughter of the arch-enemy Afrasiyab, King of Turan. The passage is illustrated by a very fine miniature (Figure 15.4), of the rescue of Bizhan by Rustam from the pit in which he had been confined, and here the latter's helmet is for the first time covered neatly by a leopard's mask secured to the helmet by little blue ties.

So now at last Rustam has achieved his full panoply, and the result may well appear to echo classical representations – as, for example, on the vases of Exekias or on the Olympia pediment – of the Greek hero Herakles wearing the skin of the Nemean lion with its mask on his head.[14] Is this a coincidence, or is there some closer connection? Iskandar Sultan accompanied Timur's campaign against the Ottoman Sultan Bayazid, in the course of which the great conqueror overran the whole of Asia Minor and Syria. The rich remains of classical and Hellenistic architecture and art still to be seen in those regions must have been even more plentiful in 1402. Might not the young prince have noted, or even sketched, some sculptured Herakles along the way? And, on his return, might not his notes have been communicated to his library staff? On the other hand, Iskandar certainly had a lively mind, and would have been quite capable of thinking of the idea himself. Or, perhaps, the painter Pir Ahmad Baghshimali had the idea, and 'sold' it to his patron. Such speculations cannot, of course, be proved one way or the other, but they are entertaining and stimulating as possibilities.

But the 'compleat Rustam' did not gain immediate and universal acceptance, and for the next fifty years or so the leopard's mask is only found in paintings of Shiraz origin. It nowhere occurs in Baysunghur's 'Great Book,' and only once in the *Shahnama* of Muhammad Juki, in the miniature of Rustam and Ashkabus (f. 145b),[15] which seems to belong to a small group contributed to the manuscript by a painter who had recently left Shiraz for Herat. No copies of the *Shahnama* are known to have been produced at Herat during the second half of the fifteenth century.

The *locus classicus* of the Shiraz-Timurid style is, of course, the *Shahnama* of Baysunghur's brother, Ibrahim Sultan, who governed Shiraz from 1414 till his death in 1435. In this splendid manuscript the leopard's mask has not yet completely ousted the plain gilded helmet on Rustam's head, but it is well on the way to doing so (the proportion of the leopard's mask to the plain helmet is almost three to one). The manuscript was dated to c. 1420 when it first appeared in public at Burlington House, but as it contains the Baysunghuri preface it must be later than 1426, and is probably best dated just after Baysunghur's Great Book of 1430. The *Shahnama* of Ibrahim Sultan contains the most truly epic portrayals of Rustam so far achieved.[16]

Fig. 15.4 (opposite) *'Rescue of Bizhan by Rustam'*, Miscellany, *Shiraz, 1411.*

(British Library Add. 27261, f. 298b.)

Between this fine (but sadly misused) copy and 1457 a considerable number of *Shahnama* manuscripts was produced, presumably at Shiraz, illustrated in the same style, and in them the leopard's mask is virtually invariable (Figure 15.5).[17] Under Turkman rule in the middle years of the fifteenth century this Shiraz style continued at first, but it had died out by about 1460, bequeathing many of its conventions, including Rustam's panoply, to the various styles then current. The most popular of these was what is known now as the

Fig. 15.5 '*Suhrab Slain by his Father, Rustam*', Shahnama, *Shiraz, c. 1440.*

(British Museum 1949-10-9-051.)

Turkman Commercial style, in constant use at Shiraz for the adornment of manuscripts intended for commerce or export (the Shiraz specialty) during the second half of the fifteenth century. It thus helped to spread the conventional idea of Rustam wherever the *Shahnama* was read (Figure 15.6).[18] As noted above, Herat artists seem to have avoided the *Shahnama* during Bihzad's career, but two or three *Shahnama* manuscripts of the later fifteenth century may be located in Transoxiana.[19] In general they follow the Herat Tradition: Rustam does not wear the leopard's mask.

Early Safavid court painting was a blend of the rather academic Bihzad-derived style of Herat and the bolder, freer manner of the Turkman court as practised at Tabriz under Ya'qub Beg (1478–90), the latter at first strongly dominating.[20] Two exceptional examples of this style which can be dated to c. 1505–10 were contributed to an unfinished *Shahnama*, probably commissioned by Shah Isma'il. They are the celebrated 'Sleeping Rustam' in the British Museum, and 'Rustam Lassoing the King of Sham' in the Museum für Kunsthandwerk, Leipzig. The portrayal of Rustam in these two superb miniatures, especially the latter, marks the culmination of the patriotic vision of a hundred years.[21] The panoply has been perfected, and even enhanced; the seven-fold plume above the leopard's mask in 'Lassoing the King of Sham' is an extremely effective adjunct, and the artist has also added a tinge of red to Rustam's moustache and beard. This latter feature is found in a number of later manuscripts; it is, of course, very rare in Persia, and is regarded as a sign of great strength. Later Safavid paintings may occasionally give the hero a single simple plume in the point of his helmet, but this seven-fold one appears to be unique. There is, in fact, every reason to accept Cary Welch's inspired attribution of the 'Sleeping Rustam' to the early years of the great master Sultan Muhammad,[22] and I would urge that the same attribution applies with at least equal force to its companion piece.

The showpiece of early Safavid painting is, of course, the Shah Tahmasp ('Houghton') *Shahnama*, but its miniatures follow the current trend in their portrayal of Rustam, and so call for no special comment in this context. Throughout the sixteenth century the main source of *Shahnama* manuscripts is Shiraz. The Shiraz artists were basically conservative, and in their work the established conventions for the portrayal of Rustam were invariably followed, but in a few cases attempts are made to indicate the hero's age (he was about 600 years old when he met his death) by giving him a rather stocky ungainly figure and, occasionally, touches of grey in his beard. No doubt this was well meant, in the interests of realism, but far preferable is the practice of the Timurid painters who treated Rustam, quite properly, as a timeless hero once he was grown up. Naturally in representations of him killing the white elephant he appears, correctly, as a young boy, often wearing his pyjama trousers and nightshirt (he had just been woken from sleep), though in the

Fig. 15.6 *'Death of Rustam'*, Shahnama, Turkman, Shiraz, 1486.

(British Library Add. 18188, f. 298a.)

Shahnama of Isma'il II (1576–7) he seems to have had time to grow a moustache and beard and to don his complete panoply before encountering the elephant.[23] In a few Safavid manuscripts he is depicted as a clean-shaven youth in his early exploits, such as the capture of the horse Rakhsh. Shiraz painters of the later sixteenth century occasionally exaggerated the size of the leopard's mask and expanded its ears horizontally; and the painters of Astarabad have left us half a dozen manuscripts, all dating between 1560 and 1630, illustrated in bold style with strong colours running riot, in which the mask on Rustam's helmet is often that of a tiger, but is sometimes omitted.

The Isfahan style, pioneered by Riza ('Abbasi) from the late sixteenth century, is smooth, languid, slightly decadent, and basically unsuited to epic illustration. Nevertheless some impressive *Shahnama* manuscripts were produced during the first half of the seventeenth century.[24] The general standard of execution of their miniatures is very high, and the depiction of Rustam remains the same, apart from the accommodation of treatment to the new style. Yet in battle scenes the hero seems to have lost some of his dominating quality, and often it is only his traditional panoply that distinguishes him from other warriors. Continued efforts to match his appearance to his reputed age also detract from his stature and dignity.

The second half of the seventeenth century begins with a group of *Shahnama* manuscripts illustrated by Riza's long-lived and prolific pupil Mu'in, which follow the trend of the time (Figure 15.7),[25] and at the end of the century we find the last great *Shahnama* of the classical period, dated to 1663–93, in the Metropolitan Museum of Art, New York. The miniatures in this large and presumably royal manuscript illustrate the confused state of Persian painting at this time. They are of three very different types: (1) 15 miniatures in a very mannered archaic style; the artist's name (which occurs, ill-written, only once) is probably readable as Pir Beg, but is otherwise unrecorded; (2) 21 miniatures by Mu'in and his assistant (?) Fazl 'Ali; these are all in typical Mu'in style, and both signatures appear on most of them; Fazl 'Ali is unrecorded elsewhere; (3) six miniatures in the then fashionable Europeanising style are by 'Ali Naqi b. Shaikh 'Abbasi and Muhammad Zaman (with his usual punning signature *yā ṣāḥib al-zamān*) (Figure 15.8). In all three types Rustam is depicted traditionally, except that in his combat with the White Demon (f. 64b, by Pir Beg) he wears a helmet surrounded by a golden crown.[26]

So we enter the barren period of the eighteenth century, from which no illustrated *Shahnama* is recorded. But at the end of it the reign of Fath 'Ali Shah (1797–1834) brought a revival of the arts generally, and particularly in the production of fine illustrated manuscripts. Several good copies of the *Shahnama* from his time are known, both complete and dispersed, and in all of them Rustam has been suddenly transformed into the wasp-waisted and amply

Fig. 15.7 *'Rustam Mourning the Death of Suhrab', by Mu'in. Shahnama, Isfahan, 1649.*

(British Museum 1922-7-11-02.)

Fig. 15.8 *'Rustam Leading the Persian Army', by Muhammad Zaman, Shahnama, Isfahan, 1696.*

(Metropolitan Museum of Art, New York, MS Cochran 4, f. 151b.)

black-bearded figure of the monarch himself. Whether this development was due to the excessive loyalty and patriotism of the painters, or the express wishes of Fath 'Ali Shah himself (his notorious vanity makes such a suggestion quite possible) we shall probably never know, but the effect is not unsatisfactory, though not, strictly speaking, in the tradition of epic illustration (Plate 28).

One more *Shahnama* manuscript, of the later Qajar period, demands mention. This remarkable volume, formerly an heirloom in the family of the Shiraz poet Visal (himself a noted calligrapher), and later acquired by Empress Farah, is, one hopes, preserved in a Tehran museum. Most of the miniatures, dated between 1854 and 1864, are by the Shiraz painter Lutf 'Ali Khan, best known for his exquisite flower studies, but one or two of them, highly original and much westernised, are by Visal's sons Dāvarī and Farhang. Lutf 'Ali depicts Rustam with a forked black beard, but otherwise in traditional style; at least he does not attempt to give him the likeness of Nasr al-Din Shah (Plate 28).[27]

To sum up: the earliest (early fourteenth-century) portrayals of Rustam are of completely Mongol appearance, and thus bear no relationship to the Iranian tradition of epic illustration. But in *Shahnama* manuscripts produced under the Inju dynasty at Shiraz (c. 1330–50) the hero appears in his tiger-skin surcoat with a normal helmet. This type is followed under the Muzaffarids, also at Shiraz (c. 1370–93), in the early Timurid *Shahnama* of 1397, and in subsequent copies of fifteenth-century date from Herat and Transoxiana. The leopard's mask is added to Rustam's helmet first at Shiraz in 1411, becomes prominent in the style patronized by Ibrahim Sultan, and gradually spreads throughout Iran, encouraged by the wide dissemination of the Turkman Commercial style, centred at Shiraz, during the later fifteenth century. The culmination of Rustam's traditional portrayal comes in two detached miniatures of c. 1505–10, known as the 'Sleeping Rustam' and 'Rustam Lassoing the King of Sham'; these are probably early works of the master Sultan Muhammad. Most sixteenth-century copies of the *Shahnama* are illustrated in the conservative style of Shiraz, maintaining the tradition unchanged except for occasional attempts to make Rustam 'look his age', and the same is true of seventeenth-century examples till the infiltration of European styles towards the end of the century. The eighteenth century is a blank, but there is an artistic revival under Fath 'Ali Shah, who actually appears as Rustam in manuscripts of his period.

Notes

1. Edinburgh University Library, Arab. and Pers. MSS 20, f. 15b (David Talbot Rice, *The Illustrations to the 'World History' of Rashīd al-Dīn* (Edinburgh, 1976), pl. 19). Rustam also appears on f. 6b of the same

manuscript, wearing his tiger-skin at the court of Minūchihr: Rice, *Rashīd al-Dīn*, pl. 18.

2. Oleg Grabar and Sheila Blair, *Epic Images and Contemporary History* (Chicago, 1980), 103, no. 23. Rustam also appears in the same manuscript wearing his tiger-skin (ibid., no. 20), and wearing ordinary armour and helmet (ibid., no. 21).

3. Marianna Shreve Simpson, *The Illustrations of an Epic: The Earliest* Shahnama *Miniatures* (New York, 1979); see, for example, pl. 27 (in armour) and pl. 30 (in civilian clothes).

4. See B. W. Robinson, 'Persian Painting and the National Epic', in *Proceedings of the British Academy 1982* (London, 1983), pl. II, fig. 3. Another instance of tiger for lion in the 'small' *Shahnama*s occurs in Pers. MS 104 (56) in the Chester Beatty Library, Dublin; see *The Chester Beatty Library: A Catalogue of the Persian Manuscripts and Miniatures*, ed. J. V. S. Wilkinson (Dublin, 1959), 1:15, and Simpson, *Epic*, pl. 73.

5. See Simpson, *Epic*, 346, nos 13, 14, 16, 19.

6. Topkapi Saray Library, Istanbul, H. 1511 (Basil Gray, *Persian Painting* (Lausanne, 1961), 63, and Cairo, Dar al-Kutub, Adab farisi 6 (L. Binyon, J. V. S. Wilkinson and B. Gray, *Persian Miniature Painting* (London, 1933), pls XXIX, XXX) respectively.

7. See, for example, Gray, *Persian Painting*, 41, 43, and M. S. Ipṣiroğlu, *Siyah Qalam* (Graz, 1976), pl. 32.

8. British Library, Or. 2780, ff. 18a, 29b: see Norah M. Titley, *Miniatures from Persian Manuscripts* (London, 1977), 39, MS 99 [2], [3] and Chester Beatty Library Pers. MS 114: Chester Beatty *Catalogue*, 1:30–2.

9. From the Bibliothèque Nationale, Paris, *Kalila wa Dimna*, Pers. 377 (Muzaffarid, c. 1390) to the *Shahnama* Pers. 228 of 1490. See B. W. Robinson, *A Descriptive Catalogue of the Persian Painting in the Bodleian Library* (Oxford, 1958), 10 and 60 respectively.

10. B. W. Robinson, 'Zenith of his Time: The Painter Pīr Aḥmad Bāghshimālī', in *Persian Masters*, ed. Sheila Canby (Bombay, 1990), 1–20.

11. A good summary of Iskandar Sultan's career is in Eric Schreoder, *Persian Miniatures in the Fogg Museum of Art* (Cambridge, MA, 1942), 57–60.

12. Staatsbibliothek, Berlin, Petermann I. 388 (*Pertsch 367*). See Ivan Stchoukine et al., *Illuminierte islamische Handschriften* (Wiesbaden, 1971), 17 and taf. 13.

13. British Library, Add. 27261: Titley, *Persian Manuscripts*, 39, MS 98. Some good reproductions from this manuscript are to be found in Robinson, 'Zenith'.

14. See B. W. Robinson, *The Persian Book of Kings* (London, 2001), n. 1.

15. Royal Asiatic Society, MS 239. See B. W. Robinson, 'The *Shāhnāma* of Muḥammad Jūkī', in *The Royal Asiatic Society: Its History and Treasures*, ed. Stuart Simmonds and Simon Digby (London, 1979), 83–102, esp. pl. III, fig. 1.

16. Bodleian Library, Ouseley Add. 176: see Robinson, *Bodleian*, 16–22; also B. W. Robinson, *Fifteenth Century Persian Painting: Problems and Issues* (New York, 1991) 14, col. pl. 1; Gray, *Persian Painting*, 98; and Eleanor Sims, 'The Hundred and One Paintings of Ibrahim-Sultan', in *Persian Painting from the Mongols to the Qajars: Studies in Honour of Basil W. Robinson*, ed. Robert Hillenbrand (London, 2000), 119–28, and references therein.

17. Notably Bibliothèque Nationale, Paris, Sup. pers. 494: see Robinson,

Bodleian, 23–5, where ten other Shiraz *Shahnama* manuscripts of this period are noted; and the Dufferin and Ava *Shahnama* of 1436–7: B. W. Robinson, 'Persian Epic Illustrations: A Book of Kings of 1436–37', *Apollo* (September 1982), 170–3.

18. A good example is the British Library *Shahnama* of 1486 (Add. 18188); see for others Robinson, *Bodleian*, 59–61; also 'A Magnificent MS: The British Library *Shāhnāma* of 1486', in B. W. Robinson, *Studies in Persian Art* (London, 1993), 2:246–58.

19. See Robinson, *Fifteenth Century*, 45–51.

20. See Martin Bernard Dickson and Stuart Cary Welch, *The Houghton Shahnamah*, 2 vols (Cambridge, MA, 1981), 1:15–27.

21. These two miniatures, especially the 'Sleeping Rustam', have been reproduced many times; the best versions (both in colour) are probably Basil Gray, *Persian Painting* (London, 1948), pl. 7, and P. W. Schulz, *Die persische-islamische Miniaturmalerei*, 2 vols (Leipzig, 1914), 2: taf. 47. See also B. W. Robinson, 'Origin and Date of Three Famous *Shāh-Nāmeh* Illustrations', *Ars Orientalis* 1 (1954), 105–12 and Robinson, 'Rustam in Battle: A Persian Masterpiece', Robinson, *Studies* (n. 18), 2:274–5.

22. See Dickson and Welch, *Shahnamah*, 1:51–87.

23. Reproduced (b/w) in Sotheby's Catalogues of 13 July 1971, lot 355 and 7 December 1971, lot 190A.

24. One thinks especially of British Library Add. 27257 (probably Khurasan, c. 1600), the Khalili Collection copy (perhaps also Khurasan: Sotheby's Catalogue of 3 April 1978, lot 162) of 1602, the Berlin copy (MS or. fol. 4251) of 1605; the Royal Library, Windsor copy (Holmes 152) of 1648, and the enormous copy in the Russian National Library, St Petersburg (Dorn 333) of 1648–51.

25. Dated between 1649 and 1682. See, for example, Sotheby's Catalogue (Phillips MSS) of 25 November 1968 (coloured frontispiece), British Library Add. 16761, and Schroeder, *Fogg*, pls xxvii–xxviii.

26. See B. W. Robinson, 'The *Shahnameh* Manuscript Cochran 4 in the Metropolitan Museum of Art', in *Islamic Art in the Metropolitan Museum of Art*, ed. Richard Ettinghausen (New York, 1972), 73–86.

27. For Visal (Wiṣāl) and his family, see E. G. Browne, *A Literary History of Persia*, vol. 5 (London, 1953), 300, 316ff. This *Shahnama* has so far not been published. I saw it at the house of Dr Vesal, the poet's descendant, at Shiraz in 1963.

CHAPTER SIXTEEN

Made for the Show: The Medieval Treasury of the Ka'ba in Mecca

Avinoam Shalem

Throughout history, precious gifts were sent to the Ka'ba in Mecca. Among the best known are the embroidered veil – (the *kiswa*) – , which was and is sent each year for the covering of the Ka'ba, as well as the keys and locks for securing its door.[1] Medieval literary sources, however, provide us with information concerning numerous presents, especially votive offerings, sent for different reasons by different rulers to be displayed in the Ka'ba.

In this study an attempt is made to elucidate the Ka'ba, and especially its treasury – (the *khizānat al-bayt*) – , as taking a new aim already in the pre-Islamic period (i.e. on the eve of the birth of Muhammad in 570). Generally speaking, as early as the first decades of the sixth century, the entire raison d'être of the treasury went through a crucial transformation, namely the shift from a storage place to a space of display. Moreover, the varied sources gathered here on the history of the treasury between the mid-sixth century and early eighth century suggest that the different types of artefacts accumulated, stored and exhibited there fulfilled varied purposes, which, in some cases, seem to have served rather political than purely cultic aims.

The Ka'ba, which is situated in the centre of the great mosque in Mecca, is a nearly cubic building, built of grey-blue Meccan stones (Figure 16.1).[2] Its roof is flat, although slightly sloping to the north-west corner, in which the *mī'zāb* (waterspout) is located. The façade of the house contains a door, and the famous black stone is set into the eastern corner of the building, on the left side of the entrance door. Six wooden pillars, arranged in rows of three, support the roof. It is likely that, despite the several rebuildings and renovations the House of the Ka'ba underwent through the centuries, it always kept its cubic form. And it seems likely that the present building still retains the shape of that erected by the Umayyads in 693.[3]

According to early Arabic sources, votive offerings were kept in the treasury of the Ka'ba already in the pre-Islamic period. Al-Azraqi, a

Fig. 16.1 *The Holy Sanctuary of the Ka'ba in Mecca.*

(After Snouck Hurgronje, *Bilderatlas zu Mekka* (Leyden, 1889), pl. 2.)

native of Mecca who completed his monumental book on the history of Mecca (*Kitab akhbar Makka*) around the mid-ninth century,[4] tells us that Muhammad's grandfather, 'Abd al-Muttalib, rediscovered the well of the sanctuary and found several objects in it. These objects were once buried by the last chief of the Meccan Arab tribe called Jurhum.[5] According to al-Mas'udi, the digging of 'Abd al-Muttalib took place during the reign of the Sassanian king Kisra Qubadh (488–531).[6] The treasure consisted of swords of a type called *qala'ī*, armour, two golden gazelles and, according to several traditions, a specific stone called *hajar al-rukn*.[7] Tabari (839–923) explains that in pre-Islamic times there existed the practice of putting precious objects donated to the sanctuary in the well of the Ka'ba.[8] According to the medieval Arab sources, the well was located within the Ka'ba or perhaps in a specific enclosure called *hatīm*, which was once part of the building.[9] This well was most probably dry and therefore served as an ideal pit for hiding treasures. It is likely that the objects were cast into the well to prevent their theft. The existence of a pit or dry well within the Ka'ba in pre-Islamic times, into which precious objects were cast, is highly important for our discussion, for the literary sources concerning this well or pit shed some light on the nature and importance of the pre-Islamic Meccan treasure house.

It is worth looking at the specific terms used for this specific large hole or pit. In the medieval sources it is usually mentioned as either *jubb* (cistern or pit) or *biʾr* (well). This suggests that, apart from the famous well of the Zamzam, there existed in the sanctuary area a further cistern, which, as Hawting has lately argued, is sometimes referred to as the well of the Kaʿba.[10] Al-Azraqi describes it as being located in a hollowed cavity in the Kaʿba (*fī jawf al-Kaʿba*), at the right-hand side of the entrance, and adds that its depth was three cubits (*wa kāna ʿamquhā thalāthah adhruʿ*).[11] It is worth mentioning that *jawf* might also suggests that the pit was located in the centre of the Kaʿba. In another incident it is said to be in the depth (*baṭn*, literary meaning belly) of the Kaʿba.[12] Thus, according to both references, it might be suggested that the treasury was a hollowed pit deeply dug in the ground of the Kaʿba building, and that treasures were stored within. However, it should be noticed that there is a faint possibility that this pit was located at the very centre of the Kaʿba.

Another interesting term given by al-Azraqi as referring to this pre-Islamic storage pit or cistern is *al-akhsaf*.[13] Dozy suggested that this name derived from Aramaic, namely *ḥ(a)sap* meaning vessel or pot.[14] Thus, this term might hint at the vessels hidden within the pit. But it must be emphasised that this Aramaic term usually refers to inexpensive vessels, especially those having no value at all.[15] It is more likely then that the term *akhsaf* derived from the Arabic verb *khasafa*, which means to sink (into the ground) or disappear. Thus, the name *akhsaf* given to this cistern in the Kaʿba is probably related to the tradition concerning the disappearance of the precious vessels and their rediscovery by Muhammad's grandfather later. In fact, the use of a term as such for a treasure also refers to the act of concealing valuable objects and recalls the specific Hebrew terms *matmon* and *geniza* (or *ganzakh*) for buried treasures and valuable objects. The word *matmon* derives from the verb *taman*, which means to put something into a hole in the ground and cover it up with earth. The *geniza* (or *ganzakh*) derived from the word *ganaz*, which also means to hide or bury.[16] It must be added that Tabari used the Arabic word *kanz* for the treasury of the Kaʿba; the word derived from the verb *kanaza*, which means to hide.[17]

Whether the *jubb* or *biʾr* indeed existed in the sanctuary of the Kaʿba cannot be answered. However, the custom of burying valuable objects in a pit located within the area of a holy shrine, usually under the altar, has a long tradition and was practised by varied ancient cultures in the Orient.[18] Moreover, Rubin has also suggested that, as far as the sanctuary of the Kaʿba is concerned, this custom might be also connected with rituals concerning the veneration of the dead.[19] Votive objects were usually buried near or even in tombs of noble or saintly figures. And, indeed, according to Muslim traditions, various prophets are buried in this specific area of the sanctuary.

In any case, the rediscovery of the pit with its treasures by Muhammad's grandfather ʿAbd al-Muttalib might be associated with common traditions and folktales concerning the recovery of objects that were hidden or had disappeared. In this specific genre of tradition, the objects' recovery was immediately understood as a sign indicating the beginning of a new era, as if objects are waiting like souls for their 'Resurrection Day' – the proper time to be reused by humankind. As far as the character of the treasury of the Ka'ba is concerned, the rediscovery of the pit with its treasures marks also the (perhaps fictitious) moment in which the treasury was transformed from concealed storage place to forum of display.

Detailed accounts of the rediscovery of the precious artefacts in the pit and their display in the Ka'ba are given by different Arabic authors. For example, al-Mas'udi (d. 956), in his *Muruj al-Dhahab* (*Meadows of Gold*) written around the mid of the tenth century, says that 'Abd al-Muttalib found in the pit several pieces of jewellery made of gold and inset with precious stone, seven swords and seven coats of mail (probably shields). The swords were placed on the door of the Ka'ba. One golden gazelle was set at the door and the other inside the house.[20] It is worth mentioning that these objects might have been Sassanian; according to al-Mas'udi, it is related that Sasan b. Babak on visiting the sanctuary cast (*dafana*) into the well of the Ka'ba two golden gazelles, jewellery and swords.[21]

Al-Biruni in his famous book on precious stones (*Kitab al-jamahir fi ma'rifat al-jawahir*) written in the eleventh century provides us with a slightly different version; al-Biruni confused, as did several other authors,[22] the pit of the sanctuary with the Zamzam well. He says: 'When 'Abd al-Muttalib had the well of Zam Zam dug out (after it had become plugged), two bright swords were discovered. These were placed at the gate of the Ka'aba. Two golden deer with patterns etched on them were also excavated. One was set at the door for decorative purposes, the other inside.'[23]

Furthermore, since the traditions concerning Muhammad's conquest of Mecca mention that an idol stood over the pit in the enclosure of the Ka'ba, it is likely that it was placed there by 'Abd al-Muttalib – probably as a guarding idol – sometimes after the pit was discovered. However, some traditions tell us that this was the idol of Hubal and that it was placed there by the custodian of the Sacred House 'Amr ibn Luhayy.[24] Al-Biruni provides us with a description of this idol: 'It is said that the idol, Hubal, which was in the Ka'aba during the Jahiliyah period was made of chalcedony. Its right hand was broken, and the Arabs had a gold hand fixed on it.'[25] But the exact site on which the idol of Hubal stood is difficult to ascertain.[26] This idol and 360, or at least 36, others are said to have been removed by Muhammad on entering Mecca in 629–30.[27]

An excellent piece of visual evidence for this transmission is to be found in a late sixteenth-century miniature from Shiraz (Plate 30) depicting both Muhammad and Ali. Ali stands on the shoulders of Muhammad in front of the house. He stretches out his hands to grab one of the idols, which is placed on top of the Ka'ba. Two other idols are exhibited also on the roof of the Ka'ba. The black covering of the

Kaʿba (kiswa) with its golden embroidered band of inscription is pulled up, and the golden door and the black stone set in the corner are revealed.[28]

It is likely, then, that – at least according to traditions – during the time span between the rediscovery of the pit and its concealed treasures by ʿAbd al-Muttalib, which was most probably in the first quarter of the sixth century, and the conquest of Mecca by Muhammad in 629–30, the sacred area and the Kaʿba were richly decorated.

Unfortunately the literary sources on this specific timescale cannot be attested. But, if we accept that these traditions retain an element of truth and have some validity, the literary sources concerning the rebuilding of the Kaʿba during this period, namely in the year 608, are quite interesting. It is related that a fire broke out in the sacred area and that the Kaʿba was severely damaged. Therefore a few members of the Quraysh tribe in Mecca took the decision to rebuild it. According to several Arabic sources they asked a Byzantine (rūmī) architect (bannāʾ) or carpenter (najjār) named Bāqūm (most probably Pachomius) to help them to rebuild the sacred house.[29] Moreover, they expressed their wish to build it on the model of churches (ʿalā bunyan al-kanāʾis), in a Syrian style (bunyan al-Shām).[30]

Very little is said about its shape or decoration. Several Arab writers inform us that the height of the walls of the Kaʿba was doubled, a roof was added, and the entrance door was located above the ground level, so that a ladder was needed in order to enter the building. Perhaps the sole account concerning the Kaʿba's decoration in 608 is the one telling of the setting of the black stone into the outer wall. The placing of the stone has of course a highly important religious function of marking the proper position of prayer. But one cannot ignore the aesthetic value of adding to the outer wall of the Kaʿba a relatively huge black stone. According to tradition, this was done by Muhammad. It is related that he put the stone within a cloak, which was held on each end by the heads of the tribes, then took it out and placed it in its proper position. Ibn Ishaq (704–67) tells us of this affair: '. . . he [Muhammad] said, "Give me a cloak", and when they brought it to him, he took the Black Stone and put it inside it and said that each tribe should take hold of an end of the cloak and they should lift it together. They did this so that when they got it into position he placed it with his own hand, and then building went on above it'.[31]

This specific scene is depicted in one of the copies of the *World History* of Rashid al-Din.[32] In this miniature (Figure 16.2), Muhammad is depicted as a young man holding the black stone with both hands. Members of the Meccan tribes hold the cloak on both ends. Two of them raise the *kiswa*, thus revealing the stone walls of the Kaʿba house to enable Muhammad to place the stone in its proper place.

Hence, if we take the following account at its face value, it might be also suggested that, at some point during the rebuilding of the

Fig. 16.2 *'Muhammad Lifting the Black Stone into Position in the Ka'ba'*, *Rashid al-Din*, World History, *Tabriz, 1314, Edinburgh University Library, M. Arab 20, f. 45a.*

(Courtesy, Edinburgh University Library.)

Ka'ba in 608, the walls of the Ka'ba were decorated with representations of biblical figures. It is related that, around twenty years after its rebuilding by Baqum, when the Prophet entered the sanctuary of Mecca in 629–30, he found on the walls of the sacred house representations of Christ, Mary, angels, Abraham (as an old man performing a divination rite with arrows?), the prophets and trees.[33] Muhammad, so the tradition goes, laid his hands on the depictions of Mary and said 'wash out all except what is below my hands' (*fawaḍa' yadahu 'alayhā waqāla imḥū mā fīhā min al-ṣuwar ilā ṣūrat maryam*).[34] This account suggests that the wish of the tribe of Quraysh to built the Ka'ba in 608 'on a Syrian model' might then refer to the inner decoration of the Ka'ba, namely the depiction of biblical figures on the walls.

Moreover, according to Ibn Ishaq, when Muhammad entered Mecca, 'he summoned Uthman ibn Talha [the custodian of the Ka'ba House] and took the keys of the Ka'ba from him, and when the door was opened for him, he went in. There he found a dove made of wood. He broke it in his hands and threw it away . . .'[35] It is tempting to suggest that the wooden dove in the Ka'ba might be the symbol of the Holy Spirit. Thus, the inner decoration of the House with its biblical figures, angels, trees and the wooden dove indeed recalled typical 'Syrian churches'.

Perhaps one of the most celebrated objects in the house of the Ka'ba, which is reported to be there at least from the time of the Prophet, is a pair of ram's horns (*qarnī al-kabsh*). The horns were traditionally associated with the stories about Abraham's sacrifice of his son, most probably Ishmael.[36] Rabbat, who has lately discussed the 'biography' of these horns,[37] stresses that it is not clear whether

274

the horns were originally associated with Abraham. However, his discussion of the account concerning the Prophet's order to veil them so that the worshipers would not be distracted[38] clearly suggests that they were displayed in a prominent place and also raises the question of their size.[39] According to al-Azraqi, the horns existed till the days of ʿAbdallah ibn al-Zubayr, who discovered them inside the Kaʿba when the house was rebuilt by him around 684.[40] The horns are reported to have crumbled in his hands. Rabbat has convincingly shown that the account concerning their crumbling away in the hands of ʿAbdallah ibn al-Zubayr was probably invented. The horns were probably sent towards the end of the seventh century by the order of ʿAbd al-Malik for display in the Dome of the Rock. They were exhibited there with two other famous objects: a Sassanian crown and the famous pearl called *al-yatīma* (the orphan). The horns and the *yatīma* reached the treasury of the Kaʿba later on, most probably in the tenth century. It is worth mentioning that, according to one of the visitors to the Kaʿba in 1191, they are reported to have been seen in the past hung on one of the columns inside the Kaʿba together with another object, described as the 'pendant of Mary'.[41]

With the rise of Islam and especially with the Arab conquests of the seventh century, many objects reached the treasury of the Kaʿba in Mecca. These were in the first place trophies of war. But some of them were sent as tokens of friendship or emblems manifesting recognition of Islam.

Al-Biruni mentions different kinds of presents sent to the Kaʿba during these early centuries of Islam. He also adds that the prototype for the habit of sending precious objects for display in the Kaʿba was ʿAbd al-Muttalib. Although his account goes slightly beyond the timescale discussed here – he also refers to presents sent by the first Abbasid caliphs – I cite the whole account. He says:

> Muslim kings held the Kaʿaba in great reverence and, following the practice of ʿAbd al-Muttalib, used to send precious objects there . . . The Holy Prophet also did the same thing. He had the *Golden Book* of the Zoroastrians, sent to him by Badhan the Persian after having embraced Islam in Yemen, suspended in the Kaʿaba. Badhan had sent the book of the Zoroastrians to the Prophet to convince him that he had abjured the faith of his forbears.
>
> Caliph ʿUmar bin Khattab also followed the *Sunna* of the Holy Prophet. Two crescents, together with a milking pan and two precious cups made from extremely costly stones, were sent to him after the conquest of Mada'in. They were deposited by him in the Kaʿaba. All of them were engraved with precious stones.
>
> Yazid bin Muʿawiyah had two crescents which were previously in one of the churches in Damascus, sent to the Kaʿaba. These were decorated with the *Kibrit-i-ahmar*, that is, the *rummānian* ruby. Each crescent was worth a hundred thousand dinars. Accompanying the crescents were two cups, one made of agate, the other crystalline, and

two bottles, made of agate and ruby. ʿAbd Allah bin Zubayr had the gate of the Kaʿaba gilded with gold.

ʿAbd al-Malik bin Marwan had two parasols and two crystal cups installed in the Kaʿaba. The middle column was gilded with pure gold. Walid bin ʿAbd al-Malik sent two cups, but authorities have not mentioned what these were made of. Saffah had a green plate which he had purchased for four thousand dinars sent, while Abu Jaʿfar Mansur sent a Pharaonic bottle along with a silver tablet, presented to him by the Byzantine emperor. Mamun sent the gold and silver idols surrendered by the commander-in-chief of Kabul after he had embraced Islam, together with the ruby which used to be suspended on the front of Kaʿaba during the month of pilgrimage. Mutawwakil sent a golden parasol studded with pearls, rubies and chrysolite. It was suspended each year during Hajj.[42]

This account suggests that during the Umayyad and the early Abbasid periods the habit of sending valuable objects to the Kaʿba continued. Some of the objects were sent to the Kaʿba simply because they were rare and extremely expensive. Objects made out of precious metals or stones were usually preferable to others. They were either hung inside the Kaʿba or kept in the treasury for use only on specific occasions. The presence of these objects in the Kaʿba probably emphasised the sanctity of the place or at least expressed the wish for splendour. Of course the decoration of the Kaʿba with rare and unusual objects hints at the desire for determining the Kaʿba as unique and unrivalled. Apart from the extraordinary black stone of the Kaʿba, the huge ruby which was sent by the Abbasid caliph al-Maʾmun, and used to decorate the façade of the Kaʿba during the month of pilgrimage, illustrates this aspiration for uniqueness. It is worth mentioning that a relatively big black onyx stone, called al-jazaʿ, was also sent to the Kaʿba during the Umayyad period. It was probably sent by al-Walid, to mark the muṣallā of the Prophet, namely the place where the Prophet was believed to have prayed.[43] The stone was set into the interior of the southern-western wall of the Kaʿba rebuilt by ʿAbd al-Malik in 693.

Votive or homage objects were also sent to the Kaʿba. These usually manifest the piety of their donors or, in some cases, their acceptance of Islam. This is clearly the case of the above-mentioned account about the suspended Golden Book of the Zoroastrians in the Kaʿba. But it should be emphasised that initially the best examples of caliphal devotion were the kiswas and the locks and keys which were regularly sent to the Kaʿba. In fact, any object sent by the caliphs to serve in a religious context was regarded as an act of piety.[44] It is quite obvious that this type of present established the caliph's authority as the amīr al-muʾminīn (the head [and guardian] of the believers). But it also supported his political concerns of the moment.

The sole surviving example known to me of a lock datable to this early Islamic period is the wooden one kept in the Topkapi Museum in

Istanbul (inv. no. 2/2294),[45] datable eighth-ninth centuries (Figure 16.3). The Kufic inscription carved on its surface reads: *la ilah illa Allah Muhammad rasul Allah sala Allah ʿalayhi wa salam.*[46]

The horns of the ram associated with Abraham and the sacrifice of his son belong to a particular group of objects kept in the Kaʿba. These objects were associated with specific religious figures and therefore served as references of religious history; to some extent – and I refer to their function as aide mémoire – they might be compared with the role of relics in medieval Christianity.[47]

The majority of presents in the Kaʿba in these centuries, however, were trophies of war. Indeed with the fall of al-Madaʾin in 637, many treasures fell into the hands of the Arabs and were later on sent to the Kaʿba and other Islamic treasuries.[48] Like any trophies of war, the looted precious objects exhibited in the Kaʿba proclaim, in the first place, the victory of Islam. It is almost impossible to tell whether the trophies manifested the political or religious supremacy of Islam, if a distinction as such is valid at all in this period. But it is quite clear that the display of the trophies in public places immediately after the victorious battle in al-Madaʾin answered informational needs, as if the looted objects told the spectators the story of the battle. It is related that the swords of the Sassanian king and the last Lakhmid king al-Nuʾman, and the king's finery, crown and garments looted also in al-Madaʾin were sent to the caliph ʿUmar 'for the Muslims to see and for the nomadic tribesmen to hear about'.[49]

Nonetheless, it is important to note that, as far as trophies of war are concerned, the decision over which objects should be sent to the Kaʿba and which should not and which should be stored and which should be displayed are interesting questions. For example, it is related that the famous Sassanian carpet, the *qitf* (*bahār-i Kisrā*), which was looted after the fall of al-Madaʾin in 637, was also sent to the caliph ʿUmar in Medina. This was done in order to prevent the soldiers from dividing it. However, instead of sending it to the Kaʿba in Mecca, ʿUmar took the decision to cut it into equal pieces and distribute the pieces among the warriors.[50] It is also related that, during the reign of the Abbasid caliph al-Maʾmun (813–33), a marvellous Sassanian brazier (*kānūn*) was sent to the Kaʿba in Mecca. The caliph al-Maʾmun thought that this brazier might be a proper present to the sanctuary of the Kaʿba and could be used 'to burn aloeswood and *nadd* in it night and day'. But the brazier was destroyed out of fear that the Kaʿba might be turned into a fire temple.[51]

But usually artefacts associated with the defeated kings, like their armour, royal vestments and crowns, were chosen to be sent to the Kaʿba. The display of this type of trophies was the best evidence for the downfall of the rulers' kingdoms. At any case, their permanent display in public places turns them into commemorative objects. They could have told not only the story of the fall of al-Madaʾin but also the names of their donors. The acceptance of this type of artefact

Fig. 16.3 *Wooden lock. Datable 8th–9th centuries* CE, *Topkapı Museum, Istanbul, 2/2294.*

(After Yilmaz *Locks and Keys* (Istanbul, 1993), cat. no. 1.)

into the treasury of the Ka'ba hints at new aims in exhibiting treasures in the Ka'ba. Whereas the former objects were mainly votive objects, donated by pious persons to demonstrate their devotion to this place, or specific objects associated with the *sacred* history of the site (like the horns of Abraham)[52], the Sassanian trophies in the Ka'ba acted as triggers of Muslim collective memory, calling to mind the heroic events of the Muslim past. These treasures in the Ka'ba functioned then as memorabilia and the House of the Ka'ba also became a history-revealing locale.

In sum, with the rediscovery of the buried valuable objects in the Ka'ba by Muhammad's grandfather 'Abd al-Muttalib, the treasury went through major changes which later formed its medieval character. The exposure of the artefacts, which were till then cast into the pit and concealed, marked an entirely new concept of the role of precious objects in a sacred context, at least by the polytheistic Arabs in Mecca. The concealed votive offering gathered in the pit probably served magical purposes. The offering and concealing of these objects in the Ka'ba were probably regarded as an act protecting the donor and perhaps the Ka'ba from bad omens. This suggests that valuable artefacts were less to be appreciated for their aesthetic merits, and their ability in transmitting message or evoking specific memories was also ignored. They were out of sight. It was rather their concealed or secret presence in the Ka'ba which was so important. Thus, the ancient treasury of the Ka'ba was not the result of collecting or an indication for the existence of aesthetic recognition of preciousness and beauty.[53] As far as the ancient treasures of the Ka'ba are concerned, the focus was put on the act, or perhaps the ritual, of donating them rather than on the objects as objects. It was probably the donor's ability to part with these valuables, which was regarded as obligatory of pious believers, or his wish to embellish the House of God with the best that he possessed and he thus revealed his veneration.[54] In fact the valuables presented to the treasury were not even once used. It is related, for example, that, when Muhammad entered Mecca in 629–30, 'he found in the well, which was in the Ka'ba, seventy thousand [*sic*] *ūqiyya* of gold from what was formerly offered to the House [of God], worth one million nine hundred ninety thousand dinars'.[55] This amount of gold is said to have remained in the treasury until 814.[56]

Of course, it might be argued that the traditions relating to the hidden treasury of the Ka'ba concern popular beliefs, which claim that with the reappearance of valuable objects a new era usually starts. But, despite the possibility that some of the traditions concerning the pre-Islamic history of the Ka'ba are told from a specific Islamic point of view, it seems that the different accounts reflect the atmosphere of the pre-Islamic period that shaped this site.[57] The decision of 'Abd al-Muttalib to decorate the Ka'ba with votive offerings is therefore revolutionary. The hidden treasuries, or at least part of them, were then exhibited.[58] The display of artefacts in the Ka'ba hints at a new approach towards objects. It demonstrates that there was an awareness of the object as a vessel through which information can be transmitted. This suggests a change in the perception of artefacts. It also indicates a transfer in the use and meaning of objects. Objects were not hidden but rather seen, and it was through seeing that the historical event associated with them was evoked. As far as the objects in the treasury are concerned, the main focus once put on their meaning involved their existence in the treasury was replaced by the historical context associated with each of them. Objects which once did not need any explanation now required it.

The second major alteration of the treasury took place in 629–30, when Muhammad gave it its new Islamic character. It is true that with the Islamisation of the sanctuary by Muhammad, the Haram of the Kaʿba was 'reshaped' and many ornaments from its pagan past were destroyed. But, at the same time, we do hear of Muhammad's decision to keep specific ornaments. More importantly, it is related that a new type of devotional offerings was displayed – and I refer to the royal gifts expressing the acceptance of the newly born religion, namely the account of the *Golden Book* of the Zoroastrians. The display of objects as such in the Kaʿba probably served a new function. Apart from the obvious message that they carried, namely the recognition of Islam, the fact that they were sent from different and distant geographical regions manifested the broad borders of the new Islamic empire. Concomitantly, their display in the Kaʿba emphasised Mecca as the centre of the new religion.

The inclusion of trophies of war in the Kaʿba treasury, which mainly began to reach the treasury in the early Umayyad period, marks an additional step in the changing nature of the Kaʿba's medieval treasury. For, while the treasures in the Kaʿba till then had primarily religious connotations, the trophies were mainly evidence of the heroic moments, regardless of sacred or secular, in Muslim history.

Notes

1. For the *kiswa*, see mainly, M. Gaudefroy-Demombynes, 'Le voile de la Kaʿba', *Studia Islamica* 2 (1954), 5–21; Richard T. Mortel, 'The Kiswa: Its Origins and Development from Pre-Islamic Times until the End of the Mamluk Period', *Ages: A Semi-annual Journal of Historical, Archaeological and Civilizational Studies* (Riyadh) 3,2 (1988), 38–43; Abdelaziz Gouda, 'Die Kiswa der Kaʿba in Makka', unpublished Ph.D. thesis, Frei Universität Berlin, 1989; Gouda, 'Die Tiraz-Werkstätten der Kiswa für die Kaʿba in Makka', *Der Islam* 71 (1994), 289–301; William C. Young, 'The Kaʿba, Gender, and the Rites of Pilgrimage', *International Journal of Middle East Studies* 25 (1993), 285–300; Hiilya Tezcan, *Curtains of the Holy Kaʿba* (Istanbul, 1996, in Arabic). For the locks and keys of the Kaʿba, see mainly Janine Sourdel-Thomine, 'Clefs et serrures de la Kaʿba', *Revue des Études Islamiques* 39 (1971), 29–86; Tercan Yilmaz, *The Holy Kaʿba: A study of the*

Collection of Locks and Keys Kept at Topkapi Museum in Istanbul (Istanbul, 1993, in Arabic).

2. It measures 12m in length, 10m in width and its height is c. 15m.

3. For the history of the building see mainly K. A. C. Creswell, *Early Muslim Architecture*, 2nd rev. edn of vol. 1 in two parts (Oxford, 1969), 1.1: 62–4 and 653–4. See also Uri Rubin, 'The Kaʿba: Aspects of its Ritual Functions and Position in Pre-Islamic and Early Islamic Times', *Jerusalem Studies in Arabic and Islam* 8 (1986), 98–104; see also A. J. Wensinck and J. Jomier, 'Kaʿba', *Encyclopaedia of Islam*, 2nd edn (henceforth *EI* 2); F. E. Peters, *Mecca: A Literary History of the Muslim Holy Land* (Princeton, 1994). For a specific approach in which the Christian character of the pre-Islamic building of the Kaʿba is discussed, see Günter Lüling, *Der christliche Kult an der vorislamischen Kaaba als Problem der Islamwissenschaft und christlichen Theologie* (Erlangen, 1992), esp. 43–52.

4. Al-Azraqi, *Akhbar Makka*, ed. F. Wüstenfeld as *Geschichte der Stadt Mekka*, 3 vols (Leipzig, 1858, repr. Beirut, n.d.). See also Oleg Grabar, 'Upon Reading al-Azraqi', *Muqarnas* 3 (1985), 1–7.

5. Azraqi, *Akhbar Makka*, 1:286. See also W. Montgomery Watt, 'Djurhum', *EI* 2.

6. Masʿudi, *Muruj al-dhahab wa maʿadin al-jawhar* (Beirut, n. d.), 2:127. See also Rubin, 'The Kaʿba', 115.

7. The naming of the stone as *ḥajar al-rukn* (the cornerstone) immediately raises the question as to whether this stone was the famous black stone of the Kaʿba. For a discussion on the *ḥajar al-rukn*, see G. R. Hawting, 'The Origins of the Muslim Sanctuary at Mecca', in *Studies on the First Century of Islamic Society* ed. G. H. A. Juynboll (Carbondale and Edwardsville, Ill., 1982), 38–40 (esp. 40 and n. 66, in which the tradition concerning the finding of this stone is also discussed).

8. Tabari, *Taʾrikh al-rusul waʾl-muluk*, ed. M. J. de Goeje, *Annales* (Leyden, 1879–1901), 1:1130.

9. Rubin, 'The Kaʿba', 116; see also Hawting, 'The Origins of the Muslim Sanctuary', 33–6.

10. G. R. Hawting, 'The Disappearance and Rediscovery of Zamzam and the "Well of the Kaʿba"', *Bulletin of the School of Oriental and African and Studies* 43 (1980), 44.

11. Al-Azraqi, *Akhbar Makka*, 1:73.

12. Ibid., 1:73.

13. Ibid., 1:170 (and the name of this [well] the well of *akhasf*: 'fa-summiyat tilka al-bīʾr al-akhsaf').

14. R. Dozy, *Die Israeliten zu Mekka* (Leipzig, 1864), 176–7.

15. See, for example, the Aramaic expression *haspa beʿalma* as referring to anything which is worth nothing or which is not important. See s.v. 'hasap', 'haspa' in Yehuda Gur, *Hebrew Dictionary* (Tel Aviv, 1947).

16. The word treasury is derived from the Latin thesaurus, which in turn is derived from the Greek, and means to hoard or store. Thus, this word hints at the treasury as a repository magazine, namely a collection. The Latin word thesaurus is similar to the biblical Hebrew term *ozar*, which also means to hoard and store.

17. Tabari, *Annales*, 1:1130.

18. For the custom of depositing votive offering in temples and tombs in pre-Muslim Arabia, see Joan B. Connelly, 'Votive Offerings from Hellenistic Failaka: Evidence for Herakles Cult', in *L'Arabie préislamique et son environnement historique et culturel, Actes du Colloque*

de Strasbourg, 24–27 juin 1987, ed T. Fahd (Leyden, 1989), 145–58. Another example is the legend about the sacred vessels of the Temple of the Jews, which are traditionally believed to be buried in the Samaritan sanctuary in Mount Grizim. See the discussion of Hawting, 'The Disappearance and Rediscovery', esp. 47–50; see also Marilyn F. Collins, 'The Hidden Vessels in Samaritan Tradition', *Journal for the Study of Judaism* 3 (1972), 97–116; Alexander Zeron, 'Einige Bemerkungen zu M. F. Collins "The Hidden Vessels in Samaritan Tradition"', *Journal for the Study of Judaism* 4 (1973), 165–8.

19. Rubin, 'The Ka'ba', 117.

20. Mas'udi, *Muruj*, (Beirut, n. d.), 2:127.

21. Ibid., 1:242.

22. See Hawting, 'The Disappearance and Rediscovery'.

23. Al-Biruni, *Kitab al-jamahir fi ma'rifat al-jawahir*, ed. F. Krenkow (Hyderabad, 1936), 66; for the English translation, see al-Beruni, *Book Most Comprehensive in Knowledge on Precious Stones*, tr. Hakim Mohammad Said (Islamabad, 1989), 56; see also al-Azraqi, *Akhbar Makka*, 1:287. It is tempting to suggest that the Umayyad bronze stag, which probably functioned as a fountain-head in one of the courts of the caliphate of Cordova, was made as a copy of the famous gazelles of the Ka'ba in Mecca. For this stage (Cordova, Archaeological Museum no. 500) see mainly *The Arts of Islam*, Hayward Gallery, exh. cat., ed. by D. Jones and G. Michell (London, 1976), no. 172; *Al-Andalus: The Arts of Islamic Spain*, exh. cat., The Metropolitan Museum of Art (New York, 1992), 210, no. 10; see also *Les Andalousies: de Damas à Cordoue*, exh. cat., Institut du Monde Arabe (Paris, 2000), 114, nos 90–1.

24. See for example, al-Azraqi, *Akhbar Makka*, 1:73. For the account of the erection of several idols in the sacred area of the Ka'ba by 'Amr ibn Rabi'a ibn Luhayy, see Hisham ibn al-Kalbi, *Kitab al-asnam*, tr. Nabih A. Faris as *The Book of Idols* (Princeton, NJ, 1952), 6–7.

25. Al-Beruni, *Book Most Comprehensive*, 151. See also Faris, *The Book of Idols*, 23: 'It [Hubal] was, as I was told, of red agate, in the form of a man with the right hand broken off. It came into the possession of the Quraysh in this condition, and they, therefore, made for it a hand of gold.'

26. Different accounts gathered by Rubin inform us that Hubal was located in front of the door of the Ka'ba; the idol of Manaf opposite the black stone; Isaf and Na'ila near the Zamzam. See Rubin, 'The Ka'ba', 104. For a discussion concerning the existence of the idol Hubal within the Ka'ba and other idols in the Ka'ba area, see J. Wellhausen, *Reste arabischen Heidentums* (Berlin, 1897), 73–9.

27. For the account concerning the destruction of the idols during the conquest of Mecca, see Tabari, *The History of al-Tabari, Ta'rikh al-rusul wa'l-muluk*, tr. and annotated Michael Fishbein (Albany, NY, 1997), 8:160–92, esp. 187–92. See also F. V. Winnett, 'The Daughters of Allah', *The Moslem World* 30 (1940), 113–30. I am also indebted to Professor Barbara Finster for providing me with the unpublished article of Thomas Weber, 'Griechische Götterbilder in Mekka? Die vorislamische Idolatrie Arabiens im Licht der paganen Heilkulte des Ostjordanlandes', which was read in the IV Erlanger Colloqium, *Die arabische Halbinsel zur Zeit Muhammads* (July, 1998); Geoffrey R. D. King, 'The Sculptures of the Pre-Islamic *Haram* at Makka', in *Cairo to Kabul: Afghan and Islamic Studies Presented to Ralph Pinder-Wilson*, ed. Warwick Ball and Leonard Harrow (London, 2002), 144–50.

28. For a similar depiction (dated 1595) taken from a *Rawdat al-safa* once in the possession of Messrs. Luzac and Co. (fol. 83 b), see Thomas W. Arnold, *Painting in Islam* (repr. New York, 1965), pl. XXIa. See also the miniature 'Ali destroys the Idols' (dated 1573), Russian National Library, St Petersburg (Dorn 456, f. 124a), depicted in Karin Rührdanz, 'The Illustrated Manuscripts of Athar al-Muzaffar: A History of the Prophet', in *Persian Painting from the Mongols to the Qajars: Studies in Honour of Basil W. Robinson*, ed. Robert Hillenbrand (London and New York, 2000), 213, fig. 9. Muhammad is depicted with a mace in his right hand in the miniature from St Petersburg. This suggests that the tradition here derived from Ibn Ishaq: 'The messenger was standing by them [the idols] with a stick in his hand saying, 'The truth has come and falsehood has passed away' (Quran 17:81). Then he pointed at them with his stick and they collapsed on their backs one after another.' Cited by Peters, *Mecca*, 82.

29. Al-Azraqi, *Akhbar Makka*, 1:114; some other traditions claim that he was a Coptic Christian, see for example *The Life of Muhammad*, a translation of Ishaq's *Sirat Rasul Allah*, with introduction and notes by A. Guillaume (Oxford, 1955), 84 (paragraph 122).

30. Al-Azraqi, *Akhbar Makka*, 1:114 (on a Syrian model).

31. *The Life of Muhammad*, 86 (paragraph 125).

32. Edinburgh, University Library MS Arab 20, f, 45a. See Robert Hillenbrand, 'Images of Muhammad in al-Biruni's Chronology of Ancient Nations', in *Persian Painting from the Mongols to the Qajars: Studies in Honour of Basil W. Robinson*, ed. Robert Hillenbrand (London and New York, 2000), 129–46.

33. Al-Azraqi, *Akhbar Makka*, 1:110–11.

34. Ibid., 1:113

35. *The Life of Muhammad*, 552 (paragraph 821), cited in Peters, *Mecca*, 82.

36. Al-Azraqi, *Akhbar Makka*, 1:156. See also Tabari, *Annales*, 2:87, 90.

37. Nasser Rabbat, 'The Dome of the Rock Revisited: Some Remarks on al-Wasiti's Accounts', *Muqarnas* 10 (1993), esp. 72–3.

38. Ibid., 73.

39. See also al-Azraqi, *Akhbar Makka*, 1:156.

40. Al-Biruni told us that ʿAbd Allah ibn al-Zubayr covered the door of the Kaʿba with gold. See the account of Al-Biruni given in the text.

41. Rabbat, 'The Dome of the Rock Revisited', 72. Tabari also mentions that the horns were seen in the Kaʿba in the past, see Tabari, *Annales*, 2:90: 'Some also say that the ram's horn was seen hanging in the Kaʿbah (which could suggest that the sacrifice took place near Mecca and must therefore have involved Ishmael, since Isaac was in Syria). This is not a sensible argument either, because the horn could possibly have been brought from Syria to the Kaʿbah and hung there.' For the history of the *yatima*, see Avinoam Shalem, 'Jewels and Journeys: The Case of the Medieval Gemstone Called al-Yatima', *Muqarnas* 14 (1997), 42–56.

42. Beruni, *Book Most Comprehensive*, 56–7. See also al-Azraqi, *Akhbar Makka*, 1:156–8.

43. This stone was lately discussed by Finbarr B. Flood, 'Light in Stone: The Commemoration of the Prophet in Umayyad Architecture', in *Bayt al-Maqdis, Jerusalem and Early Islam*, Oxford Studies in Islamic Art, 9/2, ed. Jeremy Johns (Oxford, 1999), esp. 316–21.

44. Donations of lamps to the House of the Kaʿba are also mentioned, mainly in later accounts, which are beyond timescale discussed here.

45. Length, 23cm, width 7cm, thickness 6.5cm.

46. Yilmaz, *Locks and Keys*, 27, cat. no. 1.

47. This specific group consists of famous articles like the Qur'an, written by the third caliph 'Uthman (644–65), and many other items traditionally associated with the Prophet and his family. Several relics as such are kept at present in the Topkapi Museum in Istanbul.

48. See Avinoam Shalem, 'The Fall of Al-Mada'in: Some Literary References Concerning Sassanian Spoils of War in Medieval Islamic Treasuries', *Iran* 32 (1994), 77–81.

49. Tabari, *Ta'rikh al-rusul wa'l-muluk* , tr. and annotated Gautier H. A. Juynboll as *The History of al-Tabari* (Albany, 1989),vol. 13 (tr.), 27 (2447); Ibn al-Athir, *al-Kamil fi'l-ta'rikh*, ed. C. J. Tornberg (Leyden, 1851–76), 2:402.

50. Tabari, *Ta'rikh al-rusul*, 13:34 (2454); Ibn al-Athir, *al-Kamil fi'l-ta'rikh*, 2:404.

51. Al-Qadi al-Rashid ibn al-Zubayr, *Kitab al dhakha'ir wa'l-tuhaf*, ed. Muhammad Hamidullah (Beirut, 1959), 183–4 (paragraph 236), tr. Ghada al-Hijjawi al-Qaddumi as *Book of Gifts and Rarities* (Cambridge, MA, 1996), 186–7.

52. The specific stone located in *Maqam Ibrahim* was also associated with the history of the Ka'ba and especially with the figure of Abraham; see M. J. Kister, 'Maqam Ibrahim: A Stone with an Inscription,' *Le Muséon* 84 (1971), 477–91.

53. For collecting pagan artefacts in the early Christian era, see Dericksen M. Brinkerhoff, *A Collection of Sculpture in Classical and Early Christian Antioch* (New York, 1970), esp. 43–62. For a discussion of this topic in Byzantium, see Anthony Cutler, 'Reuse or Use? Theoretical and Practical Attitudes towards Objects in the Early Middle Ages', *Settimane di Studio del Centro Italiano di Studi sull'Alto Medioevo, Ideologie e Pratiche del Reimpiego nell'Alto Medioevo, 16–21 April 1998* (Spoleto, 1999), 1056–83. See also Cyril Mango, 'Antique Statuary and the Byzantine Beholder', *Dumbarton Oaks Papers* 17 (1963), 53–75.

54. The latter was extensively researched by anthropologists and social historians. The idea of replacing the ritual of sacrifice, and even human sacrifice, with donations of valuable presents and money was recently discussed by Maurice Godellier, *L'énigme du don* (Paris, 1996).

55. Ibn al-Zubayr, *Kitab al-dhaka'ir*, 155 (paragraph 175); for the English translation cited here see, Qaddumi, *Book of Gifts*, 166.

56. Ibid.

57. For critical aspects concerning early Islamic sources, see A. A. al-Duri, *The Rise of Historical Writing among the Arabs*, tr. L. Conrad (Princeton, 1983).

58. I do refer in this article to the treasures of the Ka'ba. But, as far as the Ka'ba as a whole is concerned, the notion of exhibiting was always evident. In the first place these are the different valuable wall-hangings which were to cover the outer walls of the Ka'ba. But also decorating the door and sending precious locks and keys, which were also exhibited on the main door of the Ka'ba, suggest a notion for exhibiting. One may even argue this is evident, for the setting of the black stone on the outer wall of the Ka'ba was most probably done at the very beginning of the history of this building.

CHAPTER SEVENTEEN

A Pictorial Representation of the *Ḥadīth al-thaqalayn* in an Ilkhanid Copy of Balʿami's *Tarjuma-yi tarikh-i Tabari* in the Freer Gallery

Raya Y. Shani

Ḥadīth al-thaqalayn

And the Prophet said: 'I leave behind me among you two weighty things (*thaqalayn*) which, if you cleave to them, you will never go astray – that is the Book of God and my Family (*ʿitra*), the people of my House (*ahl bayt al-nabī*).'[1]

The subject of this paper is a single painting in the Freer manuscript of Abu ʿAli Muhammad Balʿami's *Tarjuma-yi tarikh-i Tabari*. It appears on f. 157a of vol. 57.16, one of three volumes constituting this copy.[2] The painting (Plate 31) was first published in 1988 by Priscilla Soucek in a study of several illustrations depicting events from the life of the Prophet Muhammad, some in the Freer copy and some in other manuscripts, all produced during the early Ilkhanid period.[3] Soucek titles the painting 'The Prophet's Genealogy Considered'.[4]

The painting, placed at the beginning of an illustrative cycle describing Islamic history under Muhammad, is indeed located in a passage of text containing the Prophet's genealogy, and is framed by Muhammad's genealogical chart, inscribed along a rectangular frame surrounding the image.

The chart surrounding the image lists Muhammad's progenitors (*nasab*), starting with his primogenitor, Adam, whose seed was transmitted through a chain of noble ancestors, such as the biblical figures of Sheth, Noah, Ibrahim and, most notably, Ismaʿil. Through the latter it reached his Arab posterity – that is, all of the Quraysh tribe, forefathers of the Prophet.[5]

However, it seems to me that the subject matter of the painting is

RAYA Y. SHANI

more concerned with the future, namely the legacy the Prophet wished to leave the young community of the faithful after his death. In particular, I believe, it represents the *hadīth al-thaqalayn* delivered by the Prophet during his farewell pilgrimage to Mecca, referred to in Muslim historiography as *khutbat hajjat al-wadāʿ*, that is, the sermon which, according to the Shiʿi version, he delivered to his people on their way back from the *hajj al-wadāʿ*, at Ghadir Khumm.

The first clue is given by an additional list of names inscribed in rows running downwards on a rectangular panel inserted into the frame of the painting, on the left.[6] Unlike the chart of Muhammad's *nasab*, the names included in this list are of those who led the Muslim community after the death of Muhammad. This list includes those descended from four main households, whose heads figure in the genealogical chart: the descendants of

1. ʿAbd al-Muttalib: Hamza, ʿAbbas, ʿAli b. Abi Talib, and ʿAli's two sons, Hasan and Husayn;
2. ʿAbd al-Manaf: ʿUthman b. ʿAffan, Muʿawiya b. Abi Sufyan, Marwan b. al-Hakam and Marwan's two sons, ʿAbd al-Malik and ʿAbd al-ʿAziz;
3. Qusayy: Zubayr b. ʿAwam and his two sons, ʿAbd Allah and Musʿab b. Zubayr;
4. Murra: Abu Bakr b. ʿUthman and ʿUmar b. al-Khattab.

In all, the list contains fifteen names. Five of these are followed by a list of their own genealogies, inscribed along the rows dividing the panel (Zubayr, third row; Marwan, fourth row; Muʿawiya, fifth row; Abu Bakr, sixth row, upside down; ʿUmar and ʿUthman, seventh row). The remaining names are written in diagonal lines over the top rows, arranged according to descent. Among these, the names of ʿAli and his two sons, Hasan and Husayn, are physically close to that of their ancestor, ʿAbd al-Muttalib, itself inscribed along the top of the rectangular frame as second in the Prophet's genealogy (as his grandfather). Their names, together with those of Hamza and ʿAbhas who precede them, are emphasised by an extra density of ink; together they create a kind of genealogical tree which stems directly from ʿAbd al-Muttalib. The names of Zubayr's and Marwan's sons, on the other hand, are lightly drawn and are linked to their own respective fathers, whose names, as recalled, appear on the third and fourth rows of the rectangular panel. Finally, the names of the first four caliphs as well as those of Hasan and Husayn are accompanied by the title *amīr al-muʾminīn*,[7] whereas those of the Umayyad caliphs, Muʿawiya, Marwan, and ʿAbd al-Malik, do not carry this title.

Whatever was the initiative behind the list of names written inside the rectangular panel, the scribe certainly seems to have accepted the caliphate of the four *khulafāʾ rāshidūn*, while ignoring that of the Umayyads. He also gave the title *amīr al-muʾminīn* to Hasan and Husayn,[8] suggesting that anti-Umayyad feelings were accompanied

286

by a pro-ʿAlid inclination; namely, that after the death of ʿAli, the fourth of the *khulafāʾ rāshidūn*, those entitled to succeed him in the caliphate were his two sons and not the Umayyads.

The pro-ʿAlid inclination is also apparent from the fact that, of the four *rāshidūn*, ʿAli is the only one whose name, as recalled, is affiliated to the genealogical chart of the Prophet himself, that is, to the name of ʿAbd al-Muttalib, their common grandfather.

The above listing, with its evident preference for ʿAli and his two sons, seems to reflect the well-known Sunni-Shiʿi dispute concerning the interpretation that should be given to the Qurʾanic idiom *ahl al-bayt*. An instance of the dispute between the two parties refers to Qurʾan 26:214, 'And warn thy nearest kindred': in the Sunni *Sahih Muslim*, the 'nearest kindred' mean the Quraysh on whom the Messenger of God called when this verse was revealed. Then, according to *Sahih Muslim*, Muhammad made a particular reference to certain tribes among the Quraysh which he considered the 'nearest kindred' – the sons of Kaʿb b. Luwayy, of Murra b. Kaʿb, of ʿAbd al-Shams, of ʿAbd al-Manaf, of Hashim and of ʿAbd al-Muttalib – warning them to rescue themselves from the fire, for 'I have no power (to protect you) from Allah in anything except this that I would sustain relationship with you.'[9] According to the Shiʿi faith, however, this verse descended as God's revelation concerning the *ahl al-bayt* in its restricted form, that is, ʿAli, Fatima, al-Hasan and al-Husayn.[10] Thus, according to a common *ḥadīth* told by Shiʿi authors in connection with this verse, following its revelation, Muhammad gathered together the Banu ʿAbd al-Muttalib, in the house of Abu Talib, and announced his mission to them. Then, the Prophet said that whoever accepted his mission and followed him will become his brother (*akh*), his assistant (*wazīr*), the executor of his testament (*waṣī*), his inheritor (*wārith*) and, after his (the Prophet's) death, his delegate (*khalīfa*). Among the members, the story continues, ʿAli was the only one to accept Muhammad's mission, to which the Prophet responded by designating him as his *akh*, *wazīr*, *waṣī*, *wārith* and *khalīfa*.[11]

This verse (26:214) indeed occurs in Balʿami's copy, on f. 165a, third line. Thus quoted by the author a few pages after the illustrated page on f. 157a, it is also accompanied by the same above-mentioned Shiʿi-oriented *ḥadīth* about the whereabouts of the Banu ʿAbd al-Muttalib meeting called by the Messenger of God after the verse had been revealed to him.[12]

Moreover, the whole episode is followed in Balʿami's Freer version with another Qurʾanic verse (5:67), appearing on f. 165b, fifth line, which is taken by Shiʿi authors as significant evidence of the explicit designation (*naṣṣ*) of ʿAli as Muhammad's *walī*. Thus according to Shiʿi writings, this verse, which reads 'O Apostle, make known what has been revealed to you from our Lord. If you do not do it, you will not have made known His message,'[13] was taken as revealing to the Prophet the explicit designation of ʿAli's imamate at Ghadir Khumm.[14]

Notably, both these Qur'anic quotations are lacking in the extant manuscripts of al-Tabari's *Tarikh*, one of the many discrepancies between al-Tabari and Bal'ami, a question which is beyond the scope of this study.[15] In the context of the Freer Bal'ami, however, the inclusion of verses crucial to the Shi'i faith may have been intentional; it might indicate something about the copyist's or patron's acquaintance with the Shi'ite interpretations, which he may have intentionally used in order to express his own tendencies.

Presuming the manuscript was made for a patron at the Ilkhanid court, a matter discussed below, one may point out the close contacts which prominent members of the early Ilkhanid courts had with Nasir al-Din al-Tusi (d. 672/1274), and Hasan B. Yusuf b. 'Ali b. al-Mutahhar al-Hilli, known as al-'Allama al-Hilli (648/1250–726/1326); indeed, these were two of the most distinguished Shi'i scholars of the late thirteenth and early fourteenth centuries,[16] the period in which the Freer manuscipt was presumably produced.[17]

The first, al-Tusi, worked for the Ilkhans in Maragha, where he constructed an observatory, and the second, al-Hilli, studied under him, presumably at Maragha.[18] Al-Hilli, the younger of the two, was born in Hilla, a Shi'i centre between Kufa and Baghdad, which, according to contemporary sources, was visited quite frequently by Ghazan,[19] the first Ilkhan to successfully make Islam the official Ilkhanid religion (in 694/1295).[20] According to Hafiz-i Abru, al-Hilli was one of those who influenced Ghazan's intention to exclude the names of the first three caliphs from the Friday prayers.[21] After the death of al-Tusi in 627/1274, al-Hilli left Maragha and during the following twenty years he taught partly in Hilla and partly in nearby Baghdad,[22] a city which served Ghazan and his brother and successor Uljaytu as their winter capital.[23] Finally, many historical sources attribute to al-Hilli a decisive role in Uljaytu's conversion to Shi'ism in 709/1310.[24] In fact, among the works of al-Hilli some are dedicated to Uljaytu, thus introducing the latter to Shi'ite theological dogma.[25]

Al-Hilli's theological works, better preserved than those of his teacher, deal with the principal tenets of Twelver Shi'ism, elaborating, in particular, on the proofs of 'Ali's imamate. They also contain references to the Shi'i interpretations given to the two verses appearing in the Freer copy (see notes 11–14 above).

Thus we may conclude that the epigraphic evidence on f. 157a and the related pages of text suggest that the copyist or patron had a special sympathy for the members of *ahl al-bayt* as viewed by the Shi'is, and that he could have been acquainted with the doctrine through contacts with contemporary Shi'i scholars, in particular al-Hilli.

As I intend to show next, the same applies to the painting. It evidently has to do with the issue of the continuation and preservation of the Islamic legacy after the Prophet's death; that is, by which of Muhammad's successors (named in the rectangular panel) and in what way his religious legacy was to be transmitted and preserved by future generations of Muslim believers. As such, I believe, it represents the idea standing behind the *ḥadīth al-thaqalayn* as viewed by the Shi'a.

A. The Event in Theological Literature

In both the Shi'i and Sunni sources one often reads that during his last sermon, the Prophet presented his community with the 'two weighty things' (*thaqalayn*) to which they should remain attached.[26] This saying by Muhammad, since then known as the *ḥadīth al-thaqalayn*, is recorded for example in the Sunni composition of *Mishkhat al-masabih*, where it is cited as transmitted by al-Tirmidhi.[27] Among the Shi'i compositions it appears in al-Mufid's *Kitab al-irshad* [28] and in al-Hilli's *Minhaj al-karama*, dedicated by the latter to Uljaytu.[29] In both works, the event is said to have occurred at Ghadir Khumm, the place where, according to the Shi'a, 'Ali was designated by the Prophet to become his successor.[30]

Shi'i scholars in fact made use of the *ḥadīth al-thaqalayn* to adapt their own theological approach to the general principles of Muslim jurisprudence (*uṣūl al-fiqh*). Accordingly, the 'two weighty things' were regarded by the Shi'a as proof of the authority of the imams as the sole interpreters of the Qur'an after Muhammad for the purpose of religious law.[31] Basing themselves on the famous *ḥadīth al-thaqalayn* and on a number of other traditions, Shi'i commentators like Abu Ja'far al-Tusi (d. 460/1067) and al-Tabrisi (d. c. 1155) persistently adhered to the view that the imams, expert in deducing the hidden secrets from the Qur'an, were the only authority for its interpretation.[32] As al-Hilli claims, the imams are the *afḍāl*s and the only ones qualified by God to lead the Islamic community; for they truly correspond to the Qur'anic verse 'He who leads to the Truth deserves that he should be followed' (10:35).[33]

The works by al-Hilli also contain extensive references to the role of 'Ali, Hasan and Husayn as the depositors of religious law (*ḥāfiẓ al-sharī'a*), and as 'the best judges (*qāḍī*)'[34] to the extent that the companions consulted 'Ali about their problems,[35] and all doctors of Law (*fuqahā'*) used to turn to his sons and their descendants for advice.[36] The author further declares that their role as *ḥāfiẓ al-sharī'a* came upon them because of their supreme knowledge ('*ilm*) after Muhammad,[37] and because they were, like the latter, impeccable and infallible (*ma'ṣūmūn*).[38]

Most relevant for our further discussion is the fact that, according to the Shi'i interpretation of the *ḥadīth al-thaqalayn*, the Book of God and the infallible *ahl al-bayt* as its sole interpreters 'will never be divided'.[39]

B. The *ḥadīth al-thaqalayn* in the Painting

The 'two weighty things' indeed appear to be similarly intertwined in our painting, as follows.

The first element to note is the diagonal link between the two large seated figures, on the upper right and the lower left respectively, and the pair of small boys seated between them. This compositional structure is produced by the green of their robes and by the locks of dark hair falling over their shoulders.[40] These, according to my interpretation, are Muhammad and the male members of the *ahl al-bayt*, 'Ali and his two sons Hasan and Husayn. The similar appearance of the four,[41] emphasised by the green diagonal leading the eye from Muhammad, through the two boys, to 'Ali, is complemented by the green curtain which follows the line of the inscribed units containing the names of the Prophet, 'Abd al-Muttalib and the latter's descendants.

The Prophet, on the upper right, is seated on a prayer-rug with a trilobed niche in which the word *Allah* is inscribed. He is pointing with his left hand to an open book which he holds in his right. This probably represents the Qur'an, the first of the 'two weighty things' referred to in Muhammad's last sermon. Its revelation through the archangel Jibril is perhaps indicated by the angel depicted behind the Prophet. The second 'weighty thing', that is, the *ahl al-bayt*, is represented by 'Ali, the large figure seated at the lower left corner, and by Hasan and Husayn, the two boys placed in the middle of the diagonal between Muhammad and 'Ali.

The latter holds in his right hand a golden pen and another object which can be interpreted in two different ways: one is that it is a club, naturally signifying 'Ali's supreme power and courageous exploits during the early battles of Islam. Clubs of this sort are commonly used in the *zūrkhāna*'s ceremonies by men of physical strength, called *pahlavān*s. Their performances, basically meant to manifest physical strength, are inherently connected with the cult of 'Ali, the heroic model of any *pahlavān*. Provided the object held by 'Ali was meant to represent a club, its combined presence with a pen would thus be a perfect means to signify two major aspects in the latter's personality; one being his physical power, the other being his more literary or spiritual side, for which Muhammad chose him as his personal secretary.[42] A second possibility is to interpret the object as a writing pad of some sort. In fact, there are traditions affirming that 'Ali had his own copy of the Qur'an, traditionally described as *al-ṣaḥīfa al-ṣafrā*,[43] the yellow scroll, which was a special copy in which the text dictated to him by Muhammad also contained additional writings which he had annotated according to conversations he had held with the Prophet. The yellowish colour at the edges of the supposedly brown scroll in our painting may thus be a reference to the yellow scroll (*al-ṣaḥīfa al-ṣafrā'*); namely, to 'Ali's special copy of the Qur'an, which is the original one, with esoteric interpretations dictated to him by the Prophet himself. The oblong shape given in our painting to the supposedly 'yellow scroll' may be associated with some organic material, like palm-tree bark or camel skin on bone, used by Muhammad's companions in noting his words.[44]

The pen and the ṣaḥīfa, if the second identification is correct, are both unusual attributes in the case of ʿAli, whose regular companion is the *dhu'l-fiqār*.[45] They may thus refer to his role as the secretary of the Prophet, who dictated to him the Qur'anic verses as he received them. This might then be a representation of the process by which the Qur'an was brought down to humanity; a process starting with the revelation through the angel, continuing with the Prophet receiving the message and concluded by the one who wrote it down during the event – ʿAli.

At the same time, the depiction of ʿAli with a writing pad can be understood beyond his secretarial position during Muhammad's lifetime. It may be associated with the spiritual task entrusted to him by the Prophet during his last sermon, according to the *ḥadīth al-thaqalayn*: to safeguard the Qur'anic message in its initial, purest, form for generations to come, that is, for the time when the Prophet was no longer there, and prophecy no longer existed. Thus appointed by the Prophet to carry out the role of the depositor of the divinely revealed law (*ḥāfiẓ al-sharīʿa*), ʿAli was to consult the Qur'an and its interpretation as transmitted to him by the Prophet himself.

The scroll in ʿAli's hand may be taken, then, as symbolising his common denomination as the 'Keeper of the Book' (*qayyim al-Qur'ān*),[46] and the depositor of the divinely revealed law (*ḥāfiẓ al-sharīʿa*).[47]

The colour green worn by Muhammad and the three male members of the *ahl bayt al-nabī*, beyond its part in giving pictorial shape to the whole group, may also be associated with the sacred significance assigned to this colour in the Islamic world. Thus in Sufi writings green is associated mostly with individuals of the highest spiritual level.[48] A contemporary example in the Sufi context is connected to Shaykh Safi al-Din Ishaq (1252–1334),[49] whose contacts with the early Ilkhanid courts are well recorded.[50] Similarly, in the contemporary Shiʿi context we find evidence of the preference given to green as a symbol of sanctity. Thus in al-Hilli's *Minhaj al-karama*, the author quotes a *ḥadīth* according to which Muhammad said: 'Gabriel appeared to me by God's order with a green page on which was written in white the obligation to love (*maḥabba*) ʿAli, and to thus transmit this obligation (*farḍ*) to his people.'[51] A portion of our painted page, now missing, seems to have contained an inscription written on a green ground,[52] which may have been used to convey the same notion of sanctity.

In this context, the significance assigned in mystical writings to green in connection with *ahl bayt al-nabī* may derive from the common belief that Muhammad's robe – the *khirqa* – which was green, was transmitted by him to ʿAli and his descendants.[53] An interesting anecdote in this context is given in al-Biruni's *Athar al-Baqiya*, in a passage on the twenty-eighth of the month Safar. On this date, says al-Biruni, the Muslims commemorate the day that the ʿAbbasid caliph al-Ma'mun gave up the green dress which he had worn during five and a half months, and adopted instead the black colours of the ʿAbbasid party.[54] The five and a half months evidently refer to the period during which al-Maʾmun accepted the Imamate of the eleventh Imam, ʿAli Reza, because of which, according to al-Biruni, his party became restless, so that he was obliged to reverse his decision. In particular, the green robes may be associated with the so-called hadīth al-kisāʾ, often connected in Shiʿi writings with the Qurʾan 33:33, which reads: 'Allah's wish is but to remove uncleanness far from you, O Folk of the Household (ahl al-bayt), and cleanse you with a thorough cleansing.'[55] What the hadīth al-kisāʾ actually says is that, when this verse was revealed, the Prophet took his robe (al-kisāʾ) and wrapped it around his son-in-law, his daughter and his two grandchildren, saying: 'O Allah, these are my family whom I have chosen, take the pollution from them and purify them thoroughly.' The ahl al-bayt, says al-Hilli, is the divinely selected Pure Family (al-ʿitrah al-ṭāhira/al-dhuriyya al-ṭāhira) referred to in 33:33, which descended as God's revelation concerning ʿAli, Fatima, al-Hasan and al-Husayn, confirming their quality as imams.[56] The green robes, common to Muhammad and the three members of his ahl al-bayt, may thus refer to their inherent immunity from sin (ʿisma).[57] Unlike the Sunni theologians, who attribute inherent immunity from sin only to Muhammad, in Shiʿi thinking, ʿisma is an innate quality not only of Muhammad but also of the imams.

The underlying reason behind asserting the sacred linkage between the four protagonists by giving them identical robes can at the same time be explained by the Sufi custom of transferring the 'mystic robe' (khirqa) from a shaykh to his follower, as a sign of acceptance into the mystic community. In the Sufi approach, the colour green indeed signifies initiation.[58] Regarding the Ilkhanid period we are discussing, we may refer to contemporary historical accounts regarding Ghazan and his contacts with the Sufi Shaykh Sadr al-Din Ibrahim Hammuya (born in 644/1246 in Amul), whose father, Shaykh Saʿd al-Din Hammuya (d. 650/1252), was a celebrated mystic and a disciple of Najm al-Din Kubra.[59] As recorded by the contemporary historian Banakati, Sadr al-Din sent a woollen cloak (ṣūf) inherited from his father for the ceremony of Ghazan's initiation (to Islam). In another text, that of Daulatshah, the woollen cloak is specifically named khirqa.[60] This episode, which may suggest that Ghazan himself was actually initiated as a Sufi, provides evidence of the significance assigned at the Ilkhanid court to the khirqa, which in Sufi tradition was brought green from heaven and was first worn by Muhammad. Then, according to the Sufi and Shiʿi tradition, it was transmitted to ʿAli and his descendants.

Needless to say, Sufis in general, whether Sunni or Shiʿi, regard ʿAli as the ancestor of all the mystic fraternities and they also manifest warm sympathy towards the ahl al-bayt.[61] The outcome of such tendencies was naturally a gradual infiltration of moderate Twelver Shiʿism features into the Sufi orders, whose leaders, although Sunni, nevertheless exalted the role of the *ahl al-bayt* and especially that of ʿAli.[62] An instance is found in al-Hilli's comment on the *khirqa* worn by the Sufis, which, they claim, originated with ʿAli himself.[63]

The specific quality of the green robes might therefore be associated with influences reaching the IlKhanid court from two parallel directions: first, from the Sufi orders prevalent in those days, that is, through the influence of the shaykhs of Ardabil, who became regular visitors at Uljaytu's court or, even earlier, through Sadr al-Din, who installed Ghazan with the *khirqa* of his father, whose connections with the *ṭarīqa* of Kubra were well known; or second, from the writings of the Shiʿi scholars at court.

Either way, the green robes in our painting could finally be explained by the wish to represent the simultaneous initiation of the *ahl al-bayt* performed by the Prophet at Ghadin Khumm. The ceremony of their designation is indeed a crucial principle of the Shiʿi *imāma* doctrine, inherently connected with that of *ʿiṣma*;[64] only an explicit designation (*naṣṣ*) can qualify a person to become the imam of his community after Muhammad. This view is repeatedly stressed in the writings of al-Hilli in referring to the providential designation of the infallible ʿAli and his two sons as the succeeding imams, as the protectors of the Sacred Law (*ḥāfiẓ al-sharīʿa*).[65]

In fact, the providential designation of ʿAli at Ghadir Khumm was followed by that of his sons, Hasan and Husayn. This is inferred, according to al-Hilli, from the so-called 'authority-verse', 4:62, which reads as follows: 'O ye who believe! Obey Allah and obey the Messenger and those among you invested with authority.' Al-Hilli's interpretation of this verse is: 'When he (Muhammad) had finished establishing the Imamate of ʿAli, he began to establish the Imamate of the Imams who were steadfast in authority after him.'[66] According to al-Hilli, the ceremony at Ghadir Khumm was indeed preceded by Muhammad's sermon about the two 'weighty things'[67] – the two components of the *ḥadīth al-thaqalayn* underlying the intention of our painting.

I shall now go on to discuss three further points directly related to the Shiʿi aspect of our painting as it is expressed in the compositional structure. These are the following: first, the connection of the *ahl bayt al-nabī* with the figure in the lower right corner and with the angel behind the Prophet; second, the identity of the two men seated in front of Muhammad; and third, the meaning of the middle group in the lower part of the painting.

First, the figure depicted in the lower right corner of the painting, whose gesture of blessing is directed to the two boys in the middle, namely the imams Hasan and Husayn. In his gesture and appearance, with scarf-like headgear, not usually part of Arabic costume, this personage could represent a biblical prophet. His head-covering, associated with contemporary conventions used for depicting biblical prophets, or important personalities in the religious and clerical sectors of society,[68] supports this interpretation.

Also notable is the fact that the very concept of biblical predictions regarding the advent of the Prophet of Islam is in fact known to us from yet another painting created during the early Ilkhanid period. It appears on f. 10b of the Edinburgh copy of al-Biruni's *Athar al-baqiya*, dated 1307, in the Edinburgh University Library.[69] Based on Isaiah's statement from the Bible, chapter 21, the original biblical prophecy is illustrated here from the Islamic viewpoint, prophesying the advent of Jesus and Muhammad, both depicted on the left riding an ass and a camel respectively. They are viewed by a watchman looking through a window of a tower, on the right, his head covered by a scarf, signifying his state of 'prophecy.'

The same scheme, thus repeated in our painting through the depiction of the figure under discussion, may indicate a similar interpretation: namely, that this supposedly biblical prophet represents, perhaps, the prediction of the providential coming of Muhammad, the prophet of Islam. This, according to Islam, was already foretold in pre-Islamic sacred writings. In the genealogical context, moreover, this prophetic figure could be identified as Muhammad's primogenitor, Adam, whose name comes first in the list of ancestors inscribed around the painting.

As mentioned, the gesture of blessing by this figure appears to be directed to the two boys in the middle, namely to Hasan and Husayn. This could mean that, apart from his prophesying the coming of Islam, this biblical prophet also relates to the way in which the revelation of Muhammad will be kept and guarded after his death. In other words, this supposedly biblical prophet might just as well represent the prediction of the providential coming of the *ahl al-bayt*, the second of 'the two weighty things', a matter to which I will return in due course.

According to the Shi'a, moreover, the prediction of the providential coming of the *ahl al-bayt* was already foretold to Adam right after his creation, in fact referring to the primordial existence of the *ahl al-bayt* prior to the creation of humankind. This concept, essential to Shi'i doctrine, is expressed for example in al-Hilli's interpretation of Qur'an 2:37: 'Then Adam received from his Lord words [of revelation], and He relented toward him.'[70] The words spoken to Adam by God refer, according to al-Hilli, to Muhammad, 'Ali, Fatima, Hasan and Husayn.[71] Their providential role after Muhammad's death, that is, as continuation of his genealogical tree stemming from Adam (which encloses the painting), is thus pictorially expressed by the reference to ancient authority.

The angel depicted flying forwards behind the Prophet belongs to the same context. Apart from his above-noted role of revealing the Qur'anic verses to the Prophet, he may also be a reference to the divine inspiration that descended to the Imams themselves: their position as *hāfiz al-sharī'a* required, according to Shi'i doctrine, that in case 'something came which was new and without precedent in the Book or Sunna [i.e., the Qur'an and its interpretation as transmitted to ʿAli by the Prophet], God would inspire them [through His messenger, the archangel Jibril].'[72]

ʿAli himself is distinguished by a withdrawn pose. The hand supporting his chin, as well as the pondering look in his eyes, clearly exclude him from his immediate surroundings, crowded with people who in gesture and look seem to be involved in some intensive action. One may conjecture, therefore, that the detached attitude assigned to ʿAli was deliberately designed in order to communicate the Twelver Shiʿi view that the imam is the recipient of inspiration (*mulḥamūn*), transmitted to him by an angel. ʿAli, in other words, is here depicted in a state of deep inspiration descending on him from the angel. The latter, appearing behind the Prophet, is also detached in bearing; his eyes gaze in abstract contemplation while his hands seem to be blessing an unidentified object. The abstract contact created between the two can be explained by yet another concept related to the inspired imam: that of *muḥaddath*, which means that while receiving his inspiration the imam can only hear the angel's voice but not see him.[73]

My second point is related to the identity of the two men seated in front of Muhammad. The elderly man opposite the Prophet is probably Abu Bakr, identified by his white beard. The second figure, just below him, is armed with a double-edged sword, the famous *dhu'l-fiqār*, which, as we know, was a convention used in representing ʿAli.

However, I would like to suggest that the armed man seated below Abu Bakr is not necessarily ʿAli. He might just as well represent ʿUmar, whose association with a sword is easily explained by the role this caliph played in defending the Islamic faith: the significant conquests made under his rule.[74] The *dhu'l-fiqār* may thus be taken as a symbol, used to express the power by which the Islamic faith was disseminated and defended from its enemies.[75]

Following the same line of thought, the person seated below the presumed figure of ʿUmar could be ʿUthman, with the book on a stand on his right representing the Qur'an, which he edited. Thus, together with the figure seated at the lower left corner, whom I have identified as ʿAli, the four could represent the four *khulafā' rāshidūn*, each designated by an attribute related to the role he played in significant matters pertaining to the Islamic faith: expansion and preservation of the Islamic mission after its founder's death. This would also provide a correlation between their appearance in the painting and the title *amīr al-mu'minīn* in the list of names inscribed within the rectangular panel.

Having said that, the fact that the presumed figure of ʿUmar holds a double-edged sword, the *dhu'l-fiqār*, which by tradition is associated only with ʿAli, makes one hesitate over the actual identity of the figure. Considering, moreover, that in other respects, discussed earlier, the painting fully conforms with Shiʿi doctrine, which regards the first three *khulafā' rāshidūn* as usurpers,[76] the representation of ʿUmar would be rather enigmatic.

How then can one explain the apparent presence of the three first caliphs? In fact, the same question may be raised regarding the epigraphic section, where the names of Abu Bakr, 'Umar and 'Uthman are preceded with the title *amīr al-mu'minīn*. A possible solution would be that the painting, like the epigraphic section, reflects the co-existence of opposite trends in the more moderate religious atmosphere prevalent under the early Ilkhanid rulers.[77]

As remarked by Bausani: 'The Mongol period is important for a number of reasons: First, it saw a strengthening of Shi'ism as a consequence of the fall of the 'Abbasid caliphate, and this was accompanied by a proportionate mitigation of the Shi'i-Sunni dispute, the appearance within Sufism of trends towards Shi'ism, and a leaning towards a certain *tashayyu' hasan* (moderate Shi'ism), in Sunni circles.'[78]

In this context, I would like to refer to the presence within the Ilkhanate territories of both Mu'tazilite and Zaydi scholars who, while backing the caliphate of 'Ali's predecessors, at least that of Abu Bakr and 'Umar, ranked 'Ali above them in excellence, regarding him as *afḍal al-nās* (the most excellent of men).[79] Most illuminating is the Mu'tazili view of Ibn Abi al-Hadid (d. 656/1258) expressed in his commentary (*Sharḥ*) on the *Nahj al-balagha*, a famous collection made by the Shi'i scholar al-Sharif al-Radi. These views, also accepted by Zaydism, reappear in an abridged version of Ibn Abi al-Hadid's *Sharḥ* written by the Zaydi Fakhr al-Din 'Abd Allah b. al-Hadi, also translated into Persian.[80]

It is against this background, then, that one could regard the depiction of the three *khulafā' rāshidūn* as a compromise that the painter or patron was ready to make in order to allow different viewers to 'read' the painting according to their own inclination.

In fact, of the three *khulafā' rāshidūn* preceding 'Ali, the first two, Abu Bakr and 'Umar, were comparatively positive in their attitude to 'Ali. This applies in particular to Abu Bakr, who, according to al-Hilli, was the only one among the three usurpers who truly regretted his initial denial of 'Ali's right to the caliphate, and even declared in public that 'Ali was the best of them all.[81] A similar attitude is attributed to 'Umar; for after Muhammad's speech at Ghadir Khumm, as described in the *Kitab al-irshad*, which also involves the *ḥadīth al-thaqalayn* episode, 'Umar was actually 'among those who were profuse in their congratulations on his ('Ali's) position', thus acknowledging his command over the faithful.[82]

More to our concern, the Zaydi concept that 'Ali, Hasan and Husayn had been invested as imams by the Prophet, but that their designation had not been clear, might also be of interest. This would minimise the offence of the Companions and the early Muslim community in ignoring it and backing the caliphate of 'Ali's predecessors.[83] Of particular relevance is the Zaydi claim that the imamate of the first two caliphs could not have been a mistake since they were otherwise decent and honourable men and their imamate was agreed to by 'Ali himself.[84]

All this could mean that at least the depiction of Abu Bakr and ʿUmar was here intended also to refer to the role they played in two significant matters pertaining to the Islamic faith: expansion and preservation of the Islamic mission after its founder's death. This would provide a correlation between their appearance in the painting and the title *amīr al-muʾminīn* in the list of names inscribed inside the rectangular panel.

I tend to think, however, that the depiction of these two *khulafāʾ rāshidūn* should rather be viewed as yet another means used by the artist to illustrate the *ḥadīth al-thaqalayn* episode at Ghadin Khumm. This could mean that the two figures in the upper part of the painting simply represent the community as such in the persons of Abu Bakr and ʿUmar. In this context, moreover, the 'down-to-earth' depiction of the two relative to the spiritual appearance designated to ʿAli, could be interpreted as yet another means used by the artist to emphasise the contrast between them and ʿAli, who, as mentioned, is the only *afḍal*. A certain anecdote may throw light on the inferior position of Abu Bakr and ʿUmar vis-à-vis the *ahl al-bayt* in our painting. This tale is included in a tradition, also cited in Sunni sources, which reads: 'the Prophet's pronouncement that 'There is one among you who will fight for the [correct] interpretation of the Qurʾan just as I myself fought for its revelation' was delivered by him in the presence of Abu Bakr and ʿUmar. When each asked whether these words refer to him, the Prophet answered in the negative and stressed that his words referred to ʿAli b. Abi Talib.[85]

As for the *dhuʾl-fiqār* attributed to the presumed figure of ʿUmar, it could be considered as yet another kind of a compromise intentionally created to enable the viewer to 'read' the painting optionally. For any anti-Umayyad, let alone a Shiʿi-inclined viewer, the fact that the sword's edges are pointed towards Marwan and his two descendants was certainly most agreeable.[86]

My third point refers to the middle group in the lower part of the painting, consisting of two men bending towards a book on a stand and a third person seated on their left, the possible figure of ʿUthman noted above.

As I see it, the whole group, including the supposedly ʿUthman figure, may also be viewed as directly connected with the *ḥadīth al-thaqalayn*. It may represent the Shiʿi ʿulumāʾ and their practice during the imam's absence; under the so-called 'Great Occultation' (*al-ghayba al-kubrā*), which will last until the reappearance of the imam as *mahdī*.

Thus, in the absence of the infallible authority of the divinely guided imams, which offered humankind certainty (*yaqīn*) in religious questions, the Islamic community is to be guided by the *ʿulamāʾ*. According to the early Shiʿa, the duty of the latter is limited to preserving traditions in the imams' name and making them available to the believer.[87] This approach changed dramatically, however, during the historical period under discussion, and in fact was instigated by al-Hilli. Unlike the early Shiʿi scholars, who denied the validity of the very principle of personal effort to derive the law (ijtihād),[88] al-Hilli argued that, in the absence of explicit textual evidence in the Qur'an or the imami Sunna, the ʿulamāʾ were permitted to elaborate in personal efforts (ijtihād) provided they were unable to establish proof for matters pertaining to the rules of the sacred law.[89] The criterion for being a mujtahīd, according to al-Hilli, is that he should know the biographies of the transmitters of Traditions (aḥwāl al-rijāl) so that he could distinguish the sound reports from the defective. To that end, ʿAllama al-Hilli elaborated the methods of imami ijtihād by the production of a copious literature on ḥadīth criticism and legal methodology (uṣūl al-fiqh). In John Cooper's words: 'As the first explicit endorsement of ijtihād, the statement (by al-Hilli) is a hallmark in the evolution of clerical authority in Shiʿism.'[90]

Accordingly, the figure seated on the left of the central group may represent a mujtahīd, rather than ʿUthman. This conclusion may be supported by the fact that ʿUthman had a very bad image in the eyes of many Muslim historians, including Tabari and Balʿami.[91] In fact, the same attitude is implied in two other paintings in our manuscript.[92] Further, the shawl over the personage's head may indicate the high spiritual status assigned to the mujtahīds in contemporary Shiʿi society.[93] The two readers bending towards the book on the stand are perhaps his assistants who are trying to find an answer to a question about fiqh in books on imami traditions and biographies of their transmitters.

A final word regarding the pictorial contrasts still established in the painting between the main protagonists of the Shiʿa, ʿAli, Hasan and Husayn, and the aforementioned group of mujtahīds. It may reflect the Shiʿi concept that unlike the spiritual, rather passive, existence of the imams, that of the second group is characterised by action; they simply need to consult the books to verify the legality of previous pronouncements.

To conclude, let me quote from the tafsīr of Abu Jaʿfar al-Tusi regarding the ḥadīth al-thaqalayn, which may express the Shiʿi concept articulated in the painting: 'And this tradition proves that it [the Qur'an] exists in every generation, since it is unlikely that he [Muhammad] would decree that we keep something which we cannot keep, just as the family of the Prophet, and those we are ordered to follow [i.e. the ʿulamāʾ who were later endowed by al-Hilli with the role of mujtahīds] are present at all times.'[94] In other words, the open Qur'an in Muhammad's hands in the painting would remain meaningless after his and the imams' disappearance unless it had beside it the book of imāmī ḥadīth on uṣul al-fiqh which is placed below on a stand, whereby mujtahīds were enabled to follow the imams, and thus invest the Qur'an with life.

Conclusion

This painting, it would thus appear, was meant to deliver a dogmatic message about the Islamic faith established by Muhammad: primordial origins, revelation and the way in which the Prophet planned to preserve the faith after his death.

The seemingly prosaic subject matter of genealogy, as I have suggested, was transformed into a painting based on a profound meditation about the providential programme of the universe under the Islamic faith.

In this context, the eternity of the Qur'an, the first and foremost component in Muhammad's mission, is expressed most prominently by the book in Muhammad's hand. Another means is perhaps the figure in the lower right corner of the painting, identified above as a biblical prophet, perhaps Adam himself. Apart from his role of predicting the providential existence of the *ahl al-bayt*, this prophet might simultaneously symbolise the providential coming of Islam. The figure thus accords with the conception that the Islamic faith is the climax of a universal programme established from eternity by God. The painting would indeed be a remarkable pictorial expression of the idea behind the genealogical chart leading to Muhammad, the seal of all prophets.

Then, the preservation of the Islamic legacy is signified by the farewell sermon of the Prophet, announcing the 'two weighty things' that are to safeguard his legacy for eternity. The pictorial expression of this notion, which appears to favour the Shi'i rather than the Sunni point of view, is emphasised by the power accorded to the *ahl bayt al-nabī*, on whom the Prophet bestowed the role of safeguarding the Qur'an – the essence of his mission. In this respect, the exclusive status of the *ahl al-bayt* is thoroughly established in our painting, which thus acquires a strongly religious tone.

Whatever the religio-ideological sources were, it seems clear from the above discussion that the patron or painter was not only inspired by the general veneration of the *ahl al-bayt* prevalent in those days among the Sufis but that he was also explicitly directed by the established Twelver Shi'i doctrine of imamism with which he must have been well aquainted, presumably through the writings of contemporary Shi'i scholars, al-Hilli in particular.

The decision to illustrate the *ḥadīth al-thaqalayn*, a subject used by prominent imami scholars to emphasise the divinely sanctioned rights reserved for 'Ali and his descendants as leaders of the Islamic community, may suggest a patron who was deeply interested in the issue of authority in the Islamic context.

As such, any of the early Ilkhanid rulers could be considered as a possible patron for the manuscript, especially one looking for a document concerning legitimate authority, suitable for reinforcing Ilkhanid rule after the fall of the 'Abbasid caliphate.

Since the Shi'i concept of Authority makes it possible to maintain a closer association between rulership, religion and the sacred law, one may assume that a newly converted ruler would be more inclined to turn to Shiʿi sources. The latter, as we have seen, were in fact readily available, in view of the close contacts between prominent Twelver Shiʿi thinkers and the Ilkhanid court.

In particular, I tend to believe that the manuscript was made under the royal sponsorship of Ghazan Khan, who, as a newcomer to Islam, surely felt the need to integrate fully the Ilkhanid dynasty into the scheme of Islamic historiography. In this respect, the Shiʿi notion of divinely sanctioned legitimisation of rulership through direct descent from the *ahl al-bayt* could be used by the Ilkhanid ruler for propagating his own legitimacy derived from his Chingizid descent. Considering his contacts with al-Hilli,[95] one could also refer to the latter's argument on the caliphate, in which he compares the descent-based legitimacy claimed by the *shīʿat ʿAlī* to that claimed by the Ilkhans, whose own Chingizid descent is likewise considered as a prerequisite for their supreme rulership as khans.[96]

In this context, it would be no wonder that among the figures participating in the scene described in our painting, only Muhammad and his *ahl al-bayt* are depicted with Central Asian facial features.[97] Another is the supposedly *mujtahīd*, which may apply to a similar code of preferences.

The physical location of the painting in the manuscript, where the genealogical chart follows that of the kings of Persia, may refer to the *raison d'être* of our painting as a document testifying to the divinely granted change in power and providing an argument for the legitimate authority of a newly formed *dawla*. The Persian language used in the manuscript certainly constitutes a further aspect of the effort to propagate a state-sanctioned, official ideology of Islamic history and dogma, presumably in defence of the new regime, headed by newcomers to Islam. It also thus emphasises the historical continuity of the Ilkhanid rulers within the context of the periods preceding Islam in their own area of domination, Iran and Iraq.[98]

Assuming the manuscript was made for Ghazan, either in the north-western Iranian cities of Tabriz and Maragha, or in Baghdad, the city which served him as his winter capital,[99] one may keep in mind the two factors mentioned above: first, the close contacts which Ghazan Khan had with the prominent Shiʿi scholar al-Hilli and his quite frequent visits to the latter's city, a significant Shiʿi centre located between Kufa and Baghdad.[100] Second, Ghazan's close relationship with the Sufi Shaykh Sadr al-Din Ibrahim Hammuya, who, according to contemporary historians, conducted his ceremony of initiation to Islam for which occasion he also transmitted to Ghazan the 'mystic robe' (*khirqa*) he had inherited from his father, a celebrated mystic and disciple of Najm al-Din Kubra.[101] Thus through his contacts with al-Hilli, this Ilkhanid ruler could have learned about the divinely ordained authority transmitted by the Prophet to the *ahl al-bayt*, and about the role of the latter in safeguarding Muhammad's legacy for generations to come. From Hammuya, Ghazan could have gained, among other elements, his deep awareness of the significant role played by the 'mystic robe' during any ceremony of initiation, let alone in the one depicted in our painting: the initiation of the *ahl al-bayt* by the Prophet.

That the manuscript was made during the early years of the Ilkhanid period, presumably under the rule of Ghazan, can be supported from the stylistic point of view as well, a matter that requires separate study, in particular regarding time and place of production.[102] Considering the range of formal modes current in the art of the book under the early Ilkhans, and the disparate artistic influences that prevailed simultaneously, one can only note at present that the miniatures of the Freer manuscript are probably to be connected with a group of paintings produced in Iran and Mesopotamia during the late thirteenth century and the early years of the fourteenth century: where the stylistic concepts strongly indicate that the artists were still attached to earlier traditions typical of Mesopotamia, to the so-called school of Arab painting in Baghdad and Mosul. These traditions are apparent, among other elements, in the solid red background; in the depiction of the subject matter on one page organised in several registers, as in the painting under discussion but also in other cases where the figures, behind and above each other, suggest spatial depth; in the halos that set off the heads; and in the representation of many of the personages, which follows an older mode. These characters, mostly of the Arabic type seen in profile, seem to interact with each other through expressive hand gestures. They appear in Arab costume, characterised by long flowing robes with *ṭirāz* bands on the upper sleeves, decorated with dotted hexagons and other geometric patterns on fabric, or patterned by folds, the shading of which is of a linear type, and, although simplified, consists of regular dark and light lines which sometimes indicate the form underneath.[103]

As mentioned, a different code is used in our painting to depict Muhammad, ʿAli and his two sons, who are placed in frontal or three-quarter poses and represent well-rounded Turkish rather than Arabic facial features, which are narrower, with rounder eyes and a large nose. Stylistically, these features, among others, recall early Arab paintings made in Mosul, which indeed has led some scholars to believe that the Freer manuscript was made there.[104] However, regarding the possible impact of Mosul on early Ilkhanid art, one should also keep in mind the gifts presented to Hülegü at Maragha in 656/1258, by the ruler of Mosul, Badr al-Din Lu'lu' (d. 657/1259).[105] These gifts could well have comprised illustrated books, making them available to the Ilkhanid court thereafter.

Finally, it might be possible to regard the clearly Shiʿite material dominating the painting as a deliberate diversion from the Orthodox view imposed – or demanded – by a patron seeking political advantage. However, the work as it is presented to the viewer's eye and intelligence appears to be the outcome of genuine persuasion.

Notes

1. *Hadith al-thaqalayn*, in ʿAllama al-Hilli, *Minhaj al-karama fi maʾrifat al-imama* (Tehran, 1296/1879), 71.

2. The other two volumes are numbered 30:21 and 47.19. I would like to thank the Freer Gallery assistant curator, Massumeh Farhad, who kindly allowed me to work on the manuscript in spring 2000.

3. Priscilla Soucek, 'The Life of the Prophet: Illustrated Versions', in *Content and Context of Visual Arts in the Islamic World*, ed. Priscilla Soucek (University Park, PA, 1988), 195–209.

4. Soucek, 'The Life of the Prophet', 197–8, fig. 3.

5. For the names of Muhammad's ancestors in other copies of Balʿami's chronicles, compare, for example, M. H. Zotenberg (tr.), *Chronique de Tabari traduite sur la version persane d'Abu ʿAli Muhammad Belʿami* (Paris, 1958), 356–80, and al-Tabari, *Taʾrikh al-rusul waʾl-muluk*, tr. Montgomery W. Watt and M. V. McDonald as *The History of al-Tabari*, vol. 6 (Albany, NY, 1988), 1–43; Ibn Ishaq, *Sirat al-Rasul*, tr. A. Guillaume as *The Life of Muhammad: A Translation of Ibn Ishaq's Sirat Rasul Allah* (London, 1955), pt 1, 3–4; Ibn Saʿd *Kitab al-tabaqat al-kabir*, tr. S. Moinul Haq (New Delhi, 1981), 1:49–54.

6. It is possible that the inscribed panel was introduced on this specific surface in order to cover an earlier stage which the patron of the *hadith al-thaqalayn* version wished for some reason to erase. Only x-raying the painting could provide us with the information needed on what exactly, if at all, was the bearing of such a layer; for it is presently set under the thick yellow wash of the inscribed panel. Unfortunately, the bound volume in which our painting appears is fragile and such a process is both difficult and risks damaging the work of art.

7. Soucek ('The Life of the Prophet', 197) believes that the title *amir al-muʾminin* attached to the name of ʿAli was added by a later hand. This, however, does not seem to be the case, since the title accords perfectly with the system applied to his three predecessors. Besides, the fact that, in ʿAli's case the title follows the name instead of preceding it may be explained by the wish to preserve the genealogical formula representing the sequence of those stemming from ʿAbd al-Muttalib. This sequence started with the names of Hamza and ʿAbbas and continued with that of ʿAli, whose *laqab* would accordingly follow rather than precede the name.

8. For a different view, see Soucek ('The Life of the Prophet,' 197), where the author argues that the names of these two, as well as the titles *amir al-muʾminin*, are a later addition. This again does not seem to be the case. The inclusion of their names is not in itself unusual in our list; for the same system also applies to the sons of Marwan and Zubayr.

9. Imam Muslim, *al-Jamiʿ sahih*, tr. ʿAbdul Hamid Siddiqi (Lahore, 1972), 1:136–7, no. 399.

10. On the restricted form of the *ahl al-bayt* in the Shiʿa vis-à-vis the Sunni interpretation, see, e.g., Moshe Sharon, 'Ahl al-Bayt – People of the House', *Jerusalem Studies in Arabic and Islam* (henceforth *JSAI*) 8 (1986), 169–84.

11. See, e.g., al-Tabrisi, al-Fadl b. al-Hasan (d. c. 1155), *Majmaʿ al-bayan fi tafsir al-Qurʾan*, vol. 7, 282–4 (Beirut, 1418/1997), 186–9; al-Hilli, Jamal al-Din Hasan b. al-Mutahhar (ʿAllama al-Hilli) (1250–1325), *Minhaj al-karama fi maʾrifat al-imama* (Tehran, 1296/1879) (henceforth *MK*), 67–68, cited in Henri Laoust, 'Les fondements de l'Imamat dans le Minhāj d'al-Hillī', *Revue des Études Islamiques* 46 (1978), 37 (*hadith* no. 1), and n. 4.

12. Cf. Zotenberg, *Chronique de Tabari*, 405.
13. Cf. Ibid., 404.
14. E.g. al-Mufid, Muhammad b. Muhammad b. al-Nuʿman al-Baghdadi al-Karkhi (d. 413/1022), *Kitāb al-irshād*, tr. I. K. A. Howard as *The Book of Guidance into the Lives of the Twelve Imams, by Shaykh al-Mufid* (Horsham and London, 1992), 123–4; al-Tabrisi, *Majmaʿ*, vol. 3, 289–91; al-Hilli, *MK*, 68, cited in Laoust, 'Les Fondements', 37–8 (*ḥadīth* no. 2), and 39, n. 1.
15. About other discrepancies between the two texts, including examples of Balʿami's supplementing of various parts of Tabari's work, see Daniel L. Elton, 'Manuscripts and Editions of Balʿami's *Tarjamah-i Tārīkh-i Tabarī*', *Journal of the Royal Asiatic Society* (1990), 282–321.
16. A. Bausani, 'Religion under the Mongols', in *The Cambridge History of Iran*, vol. 5, *The Saljuq and Mongol Periods*, ed. J. A. Boyle (Cambridge, 1968), 538–49; M. M. Mazzaoui, *The Origins of the Safawids: Shiʿism, Sufism and Ghulāt* (Wiesbaden, 1972), 22–40.
17. Cf. Soucek, 'The Life of the Prophet'.
18. Sabine Schmidtke, *The Theology of al-ʿAllāma al-Ḥillī (d. 726/1325)* (Berlin, 1991), 12–22. At Maragha, according to Schmidtke, al-Hilli also became familiar with the Sufi ideas held by a large number of Sufis staying there, e.g., Qutb al-Din al Shirazi (d. 710/1311).
19. J. A. Boyle, 'Dynastic and Political History of the Il-Khans', in *The Cambridge History of Iran*, vol. 5, *The Saljuq and Mongol Periods*, ed. J. A. Boyle (Cambridge, 1968), 391–3.
20. On Ghazan's conversion to Islam and those who influenced him in his decision, see ibid., 378–81; Bausani, 'Religion', 538–43; Charles Melville, 'Pādshāh-i Islām: The Conversion of Sultān Mahmūd Ghāzān Khan', in *Persian and Islamic Studies in Honour of P. W. Avery*, ed. Charles Melville, *Pembroke Papers* 1 (Cambridge, 1990), 159–77. An earlier attempt to Islamise the Mongols in the Ilkhanate realm was administered by Ghazan's great-uncle, Tegüder Ilkhan (r. 1282–4), who was the first member of the royal family in Iran to convert: Reuven Amitai, 'The Conversion of Tegüder Ilkhan to Islam', in *In Memoriam David Ayalon* (1914–1998), The Max Schloessinger Foundation, *JSAI* 25 (2001), 15–43.
21. Schmidtke, *Theology*, 24, n. 115. As Schmidtke shows, the plan was abandoned on the advice of Ghazan's vizier, Rashid al-Din.
22. Ibid., 12–32.
23. On Ghazan, see Melville, 'Pādshāh-i Islām'. On Uljaytu, see in particular Melville, 'The Itineraries of Sultan Oljeitü, 1304–16', *Iran* 28 (1990), 55–70.
24. Mazzaoui, *Origins*, 27–34; Bausani, 'Religion', 538–49; Scnmidtke, *Theology*, 26–7. For a different view, see Judith Pfeiffer, 'Conversion Versions: Sultan Oljeytü's Conversion to Shiism (707/1309) in Muslim Narrative Sources', *Mongolian Studies* 22 (1999), 35–67.
25. Schmidtke, *Theology*, 30.
26. See above, pp. 285–6. Cf. D. M. Donaldson, *The Shiʿite Religion* (London, 1933), 41–53; A. Tabatabaʾi, 'The Imams and the Imamate', in *Shiʿism: Doctrine, Thought and Spirituality*, ed. Seyyed Hossein Nasr (New York, 1988), 161; M. Momen, *An Introduction to Shiʿi Islam* (Yale, 1985), 147–60. A different content is recorded in Ibn Ishaq's *Sirat rasul 'llah*, according to which 'the two weighty things' are the book of God and the practice of his Prophet (the *sunna al-nabī*). According to this source, Muhammad said that the two are 'something which if you will hold fast to it you will never fall into error': Ibn Ishaq,

Muhammad (d. 150/767) in Ibn Hisham, ʿAbd al-Malik (d. 218/833), *Kitab sirat rasul Allah*, tr. A. Guillaume as *The Life of Muhammad: A Translation of Ibn Ishaq's Sirat Rasul Allah* (London, 1955), 651. For an analysis of the *ḥadīth* in its many variations, see Meir M. Bar-Asher, *Scripture and Exegesis in Early Imami Shiism* (Leyden, 1999), 79, 93–8. I wish to express my gratitude to Dr Meir Bar-Asher, who kindly offered to read my manuscript, adding some significant points.

27. Al-Khatib al-Tabrizi (d. 737/1336) (based on al-Baghawi, 516/1121), *Mishkhat al-masabih*, tr. James Robson (Lahore, 1965), 1:1352–3.

28. Howard, *Book of Guidance*, 124–5. Cf. al-Tabrisi's *Majmaʿ*, vol. 3, 289–91.

29. al-Hilli, *MK*, 71, cited in Laoust, 'Les fondements', 40, no. 10. Laoust also cites a refutation of al-Hilli's *minhaj* preserved in a copy of the austere sunni Ibn Taymiyya's *Minhaj al-sunna* (Cairo, 1321/1903) (henceforth Ibn Taymiyya, MS).

30. The sermon described in al-Hilli further contains the *ḥadīth al-safīna*, a significant image in Shiʿi writings used to emphasise the importance of the *ahl al-bayt*. See Raya Shani, 'Noah's Ark and the Ship of Faith in Fifteenth-Century Persian Painting', *JSAI* 27 (2002), 127–8, 174–81.

31. Bar-Asher, *Scripture*, 95.

32. Tabrisi, *Majmaʿ*, 1:19, and Abu Jaʿfar al-Tusi, *al-Tibyan fi tafsir al-qur'an*, 1:3, both cited in Bar-Asher, *Scripture*, 79. For earlier exegeses on the subject, see Bar-Asher, *Scripture*, 13, 17, 35, 64, 82. For more on the matter, in particular regarding the authority issue compared to that of the Prophet's successors within the Sunna, see Wilfred Madelung, 'Authority in Twelver Shiʿism in the Absence of the Imam', in *La notion d'autorité au Moyen Age: Islam, Byzance, Occident* (Paris, 1982), 163–73, repr. in Variorum (London, 1985), ch. 10. Cf. I. P. Petrushevsky, *Islam in Iran* (London, 1985), 222–6.

33. Al-Hilli, *MK*, 51–2; Ibn Taymiyya, MS, III, 270, 272, cited in Laoust, 'Les fondements', 9, nn. 3, 4; 10, n. 1.

34. E.g. al-Hilli, *al-Bab al-hadi ʿashar*, tr. William McElwee Miller as *al-Babu'l-Hadi ʿAshar: a Treatise on the Principles of Shiʿite Theology* (London, 1958) (henceforth *al-Bab*), 73, ḥadīth no. 199.

35. *al-Bab*, 70, no. 191/4.

36. Al-Hilli, *MK*, 75; Ibn Taymiyya, MS, IV, 142; *al-Bab*, 72, no. 198.

37. For the notion of ʿAli's and his descendants' knowledge, see, e.g., *al-Bab*, 71–2, ḥadīth no. 194; al-Hilli, *MK*, 75; Ibn Taymiyya, MS, IV, 135, cited in Laoust, 'Les fondements', 44, notes 2–3. For the same ideas in earlier Shiʿi exegeses, see Bar-Asher, *Scripture*, 88–9, 93–101. See also A. Tabataba'i, *Shiʿite Islam* (Albany, 1975), ch. 1, 39–57, 173–219, and Donaldson, *Shiʿite Religion*, 45–9.

38. On ʿAli and his descendants as *maʿṣūmūn*, see al-Hilli, *MK*, 3; Ibn Taymiyya, MS, III, 246, 266, cited in Laoust, 'Les fondements', 8–9, n. 1 (on p. 9); *al-Bab*, 76, no. 206. See also W. Madelung, ' ʿIṣma', *Encyclopaedia of Islam*, 2nd edn (henceforth *EI* 2); Etan Kohlberg, 'Imam and Community in the Pre-Ghayba Period', in *Authority and Political Culture in Shiʿism*, ed. A. Arjomand (New York, 1988), 25–53, repr. in *Belief and Law in Imami Shiʿism* (Aldershot, 1991), ch. 2.

39. Bar-Asher, *Scripture*, 95–6, n. 28.

40. Due to retouching done on the head of the male figure at the lower left, the hair falling along his shoulder is now only partly visible. It can be seen, though, with the help of a magnifying glass.

41. A similarity which is based on various traditions. Uri Rubin, 'Prophets and Progenitors in the Early Shīʿa Tradition', *JSAI* 1 (1979), 42–3, n. 11.

42. On this role of ʿAli, see, e.g., Etan Kohlberg, 'The Evolution of the Shīʿa', *Bulletin of the School of Oriental and African Studies* 39 (1976), 6.

43. Ron P. Buckley, 'On the Origins of Shīʿī Ḥadīth', *Muslim World* 88/2 (1998), 169–73.

44. Notable in this context is one of the ten traditions cited in al-Ṣaffār's *Baṣāʾir al-darajāt* which describes the ancient ṣuḥuf in the possession of the imams to be 'as big as a camel's thigh (*Saḥīfa mithl fakhdh al-baʿīr*)'. Andrew J. Newman, *The Formative Period of Twelver Shīʿism* (Richmond, Surrey, 2000), 75.

45. E. Mittwoch, s.v. 'Dhu 'l-Fiqār', *EI* 2, 239–40. Cf. Soucek, 'The Life of the Prophet', 194, n. 8.

46. H. Corbin, *History of Islamic Philosophy* (London, 1993), 45–56, 65.

47. See notes 34–6 above.

48. Annemarie Schimmel, *And Muhammad is His Messenger: The Veneration of the Prophet in Islamic Piety* (Chapter Hill, NC, 1985), 102.

49. V. Minorsky (tr.), *Persia in A.D. 1478–1490: An Abridged Translation of Fadullah b. Ruzbihan Khunji's* Tarikh-i ʿAlam-Ara-yi Amini (London, 1957), 62.

50. Boyle, 'Dynastic and Political History'; Mazzaoui, *Origins*.

51. Al-Hilli, *MK*, 71–2; Ibn Taymiyya, *MS*, IV, 106–7, cited in Laoust, 'Les fondements', 41, no. 11.

52. Soucek, 'The Life of the Prophet', 197, n. 38.

53. Annemarie Schimmel, *The Triumphal Sun* (London, 1993), 157–8.

54. Edward Sachau (tr.), *The Chronology of Ancient Nations: An English Version of the Arabic Text of the Athar-ul-Bakiya of Albiruni* (London, 1879), 328–9. In 204/819, on coming from Khorasan back to Baghdad, we are told that al-Maʾmun wore a green robe while his companions carried green banners of the kind displayed on the occasion of the *no-bahar* (the reawakening of nature in the spring) at Balkh. Khuda S. Bukhsh, 'The Renaissance of Islam', *Islamic Culture* 2 (1928), 418, n. 4. See also G. Le Strange, *Baghdad during the Abbasid Caliphate* (London, 1972), 301–39.

55. Qurʾan, tr. Pickthall (London, 1930), 414.

56. Momen, *Introduction*, 147–60; Sharon, 'Ahl al-Bayt', 172, n. 6.

57. See n. 38 above.

58. Idris Shah, *The Sufis* (London, 1971), 107.

59. Melville, 'Padshah-i Islam'.

60. Ibid., 166–7.

61. Henri Corbin, 'The Meaning of the Imam for Shiʿi Spirituality', in *Shiʿism: Doctrine, Thought and Spirituality*, ed. Seyyed Hossein Nasr (New York, 1988), 167–87; Corbin, *Sufi Essays* (London, 1972), 104–20 (esp. 104–11); Tabatabaʾi, 'The Imams', 156–67.

62. Bausani, 'Religion', 545–7.

63. *MK*, 76, cited in Laoust, 'Les fondements', 45, n. 5. Cf. ibid., 5.

64. Bar-Asher, *Scripture*, 12; John Cooper, 'ʿAllāma al-Hillī on the Imamate and Ijtihad', in *Authority and Political Culture in Shiʿism*, ed. Said Amir Arjomand (New York, 1988), 240–9.

65. *MK*, 51, cited in Laoust, 'Les fondements', 9, n. 2; Cooper, 'ʿAllama al-Hilli', 241–2.

66. *Al-Bab*, 79, nos 211–12.

67. The link between the *ḥadīth al-thaqalayn* and the event at Ghadir Khumm already appears in the *Kitab al-irshad* by al-Mufid: Howard, *Kitab al-irshad*, 124–5. Cf. al-Tabrisi's *Majmaʿ*, vols 3–6, 150–7.

68. For a prophet, one may refer to the Edinburgh copy of Rashid al-Din's *Jamiʿ al-tawarikh*, 1314, where the type is repeated in the figure of

'Moses in the Red Sea', and in the figure of the Christian monk Bahira, recognising the prophet in Muhammad, who was then a child accompanying his uncle's caravan (Edinburgh University Library, Arabic no. 20), D. T. Rice and Basil Gray, *The Illustrations to the World History of Rashid al-Din*, ed. Basil Gray (Edinburgh, 1976), 58 n. 10; 98 n. 30. Indicative of religious and clerical characters, such a scarf headgear frequently appears, for example, in illustrations of al-Hariri's *Maqamat*: E. Blochet, *Musulman Painting, XIIth–XVIIth century* (New York, 1975), pl. XIII.

69. Priscilla Soucek, 'An Illustrated Manuscript of al-Bīrūnī's *Chronology of Ancient Nations*', in *The Scholar and the Saint*, ed. P. J. Chelkowski (New York, 1975), 103–68, fig. 2.

70. Qur'an, tr. Pickthall, 10.

71. Al-Hilli, MK, 58, Ibn Taymiyya, MS, IV, 36, cited in Laoust, 'Les fondements', 27, n. 4. In fact, the Holy Family in the Cosmic Order is a concept presenting Fatima as the main source of the holy pedigree. The doctrine went as far as to declare that Muhammad and his Holy Family were created, before Adam, from clay which God held in his right hand, and that they returned to clay, whereupon God took some clay in his left hand and created Adam by mixing it with the clay in his right hand. Thus, the selection of the *ahl al-bayt* was predestined when the world was created, and their existence constituted the foundation of the divine cosmic order: al-Hilli, MK, 67, Ibn Taymiyya, MS, IV, 78–9, cited in Laoust, 'Les fondements', 35, n. 2.

72. E.g. Kirmani, *Kitab al-Mubin*, 1: 283, quoting al-Saffar's *Basa'ir al-Darajat*, cited in Momen, *Introduction*, 149, n. 13.

73. *Al-Bab*, 64, no. 177. For more on the subject, see E. Kohlberg, 'The Term Muhaddath in Twelver Shiʿism', in *Studia Orientalia: Memorial D. H. Banneth Edicata*, The Max Schloessinger Foundation, ed. J. Blau, S. Pines, M. J. Kister and S. Shaked (Jerusalem, 1979), 39–47. Repr. in *Belief and Law in Imāmī Shīʿism*, Variorum (Aldershot, 1991), ch. 7.

74. According to Soucek, 'The Life of the Prophet', 194, n. 9, a sword in ʿUmar's hands may also reflect traditions alleging that his conversion to Islam occurred when he had seized a sword to kill Muhammad.

75. The Freer manuscript has other depictions of the *dhu'l-fiqār* which are not directly connected with ʿAli, but express prowess in the battlefield. One example is in the battle of Badr. Here, moreover, the appearance of this sword does not conform with the tradition that it was captured by the Prophet only after the battle of Badr. For the latter, see Raya Shani, 'Pictorial representations of ʿAli b. Abu Talib in the Battlefield' (forthcoming).

76. E. Kohlberg, 'Some Imami Shiʿi Views on the Ṣaḥāba', in *Belief and Law in Imami Shi'ism*, Variorum, Aldershot, 1991, Chapter 9.

77. Bausani, 'Religion', 538–49; Mazzaoui, *The Origins*, 22–40; Annemarie Schimmel, 'The Ornament of the Saints: The Religious Situation in Iran in Pre-Safavid Times', *Iranian Studies* 7 (1974), 88–111.

78. Bausani, 'Religion', 549.

79. On both trends, see Wilfred Madelung, *Religious Trends in Early Islamic Iran* (Albany, 1988); Madelung, 'Imamism and Muʿtazilite Theology', in *Le Shiʿism Imamite*, Colloque de Strasburg, 1968 (Paris, 1970), 13–30; Petrushevsky, *Islam in Iran*, ch. X; W. Montgomery Watt, 'The Reappraisal of Abbasid Shiʿism', in *Arabic and Islamic Studies in Honour of Hamilton A. R. Gibb*, ed. George Makdisi (Leyden, 1965), 638–54; Erwin I. J. Rosenthal, 'ʿAbd al-Jabbār on the Imāmate', in *Logos Islamikos*, ed. Roger M. Savory and Dionisius A. Agius (Toronto, 1984), 207–18.

80. L. Veccia Vaglieri, 'Ibn Abī'l-Hadīd', *EI* 2, 684–7. I am grateful to Professor Wilfred Madelung, whom I consulted about this chapter during his stay in Jerusalem in October 2002. I owe the reference to Ibn Abi'l-Hadid to him. Ibn Abi'l-Hadid was in fact highly esteemed and honoured by Ibn al-ʿAlqami, the Shiʿi vizier of the last ʿAbbasid caliph, who joined forces with the Ilkhans after their conquest of Baghdad in 1258: Cf. Douglas Patton, *Badr al-Dīn Luʾluʾ, Atabeg of Mosul, 1211–1259* (Washington, 1991), 61. Cf. Muhammad b. ʿAli Ibn al-Ṭiqṭaqa, *al-Fakhri fi al-adab al-Sultaniyyat waʾl-duwal al-Isla-miyya* (Beirut), 337–8.

81. *MK*, 42, cited in Laoust, 'Les fondements', 15, n. 5.

82. Howard, *Book of Guidance*, 125.

83. Madelung, *Religious Trends*, 86. C.f. Rosenthal, 'ʿAbd al-Jabbar', 216, discussing the Muʿtazilite view on that matter vis-à-vis those of the Shiʿis and Zaydis.

84. Watt, 'The Reappraisal', 652.

85. Bar-Asher, *Scripture*, 88, n. 1.

86. Provided the inscribed panel covers an earlier version (see n. 6 above), I would dare to suggest that the latter had perhaps contained two figures representing the later of the four *khulafāʾ rāshidūn*, thus complementing the other two still extant, i.e. those supposedly of Abu Bakr and ʿUmar confronting the Prophet. This would mean that the upper part of our painting may originally have included a traditional representation of Muhammad confronted by his first four caliphs, an example of which we may find in the contemporary Persian manuscript of *Varqa va Gulshah* at the Topkapi (Hazine 841), an illustrated manuscript which was presumably made in Konya, c. 1250: Assadullah Souren Melikian-Chirvani, *Le roman de Varque et Golšâh*, special number, *Arts Asiatiques* 22 (1970); E. Atil, 'The Art of the Book', in *Turkish Art*, ed. E. Atıl (Washington and New York, 1980), 153. Provided this is so, my following conjecture would be that the patron chose to add the two edges representing the famous *dhuʾl-fiqār* to the presumably conventional sword originally held by ʿUmar.

87. Madelung (1982), 163–73.

88. Bar-Asher, *Scripture*, 100–1.

89. Cooper, 'ʿAllama al-Hilli.' The *mujtahīd* should have a solid knowledge of Arabic, as well as of the principles of theological dogmatics.

90. Ibid.

91. Erling Ladewig Petersen, *ʿAlī and Muʿāwiya in Early Arabic Tradition* (Copenhagen, 1964), 112, 134–5, 150–1; Elton, 'Manuscripts and Editions'.

92. These are the *Shūrāʾ* and battle of Siffin episodes, which is discussed by the present author in 'On the Legitimate Authority Issue in Balʿami's *Tarjuma-yi tārīkh-i Tabarī* at the Freer Gallery in Washington, DC', in *Nanni dʾErme Festschrift*, eds Michele Bernardini and Natalia Tornesello, Napoli, 2005 (under preparation).

93. See notes 88–9 above.

94. Al-Tusi, Abu Jaʿfar Muhammad b. al-Hasan (eleventh century), *al-Tibyan fi tafsir al-qurʾan* (Najaf, 1376–85/1057–65), 1:3–4, cited in Bar-Asher, *Scripture*, 96, n. 29.

95. See notes 16, 18–23 above.

96. About this argument, as reported in al-Majlisi's *Bihar al-anwar* in connection with al-Hilli's efforts to convert Uljaytu to the Shiʿa, see Judith Pfeiffer, 'Conversion Versions: Sultan Oljeytü's Conversion to Shiʿism (709/1309) in Muslim Narrative Sources,' *Mongolian Studies* 22 (1999), 41 and n. 54.

RAYA Y. SHANI

97. See also below, n. 103.

98. A similar conclusion is raised by this author with regard to a single extant example from the early Ilkhanid period of an illustrated version of the Ship of Faith depicted in the preface of Firdawsi's *Shahnama*, now in the Freer Gallery of Art, Washington DC, no. 29.26b: Shani, 'Noah's Ark', n. 152 and fig. 12.

99. See n. 23 above.

100. See notes 18–23 above.

101. See notes 59–60 above.

102. Until recently, the opinion most commonly held by scholars who have written on the manuscript is that it was produced in Shiraz during the 1330s and 1340s, when the city was under the rule of the Inju dynasty. See Marie Lukens Swietochowski 'The Metropolitan Museum of Art's Small *Shāhnāma*', in *Illustrated Poetry and Epic Images*, ed. Marie Lukens Swietochowski and Stefano Carboni (New York, 1994), 80; Marianna Shreve Simpson, 'The Illustration of an Epic: the Earliest Shahnama Manuscripts', D.Phil. dissertation (Cambridge, MA, 1978), 75–6. See also Ernst Grube, *Persian Painting in the Fourteenth Century* (Naples, 1978), 16–17. Grube recognises the similarity of the Freer manuscript to the so-called Small *Shahnama* group, the *Mu'nis al-ahrar*, and the *Shahnama* paintings in the Diez Album, pointing out, however, that their place of production is still unknown.

103. For early Ilkhanid paintings which show similar formal features linking them directly to the mature phase of the Arab tradition of book illustration, see for example the frontispiece on ff. 2b–3a of the *Kalila wa Dimna* at the British Library, Or. 13506, dated 707/1307, and the 707/1307 manuscript of al-Biruni's *Athar al-baqiya* at the University Library of Edinburgh: P. Waley and Nora M. Titley, 'An Illustrated Persian Text of Kalila and Dimna dated 704/1307–08', *British Library Journal* 1 (Spring 1975), 42–61, and Robert Hillenbrand, 'Images of Muhammad in al-Biruni's "Chronology of Ancient Nations"', in *Persian Painting from the Mongols to the Qajars: Studies in Honour of Basil W. Robinson*, ed. Robert Hillenbrand (London, 2000), 129–49. Notably, most of the aspects described above, except for the solid-red background, are completely absent on pages of the Inju school. The entire conception of Inju compositions is two-dimensional with little, if any, consideration for spatial depth or total environment. With respect to the red background used in the narrative paintings of our manuscript, indeed reminiscent of Arab paintings from Mosul, it would be interesting also to reflect on the single early extant parallel in Persian, the *Varqa va Gulsha* manuscript (Topkapi Hazine 841) (Konya, c. 1250; for the date see Atıl, 'Art of the Book', 153), where the red background is extremely common and, as in several cases found in our manuscript, is often combined with an arabesque or figural design: Melikian-Chirvani, *Varque et Golʔâh*.

104. E.g. Teresa Fitzherbert, who expressed this view in her talk at the Los Angeles Conference on Ilkhanid Art, July 2003.

105. Patton, *Badr al-Dīn Lu'lu'*, 61. Also interesting, in this context, is the emerging acceptance of Shi'ism in Mosul during the reign of Lu'lu', himself adopting moreover the *futuwwa* creed, which is consistent with moderate Shi'i ideas: ibid., 67–8. Regarding the *futuwwa* organisation established at the same period by the ʿAbbasid caliph al-Nasir al-Din Allah, see Said Amir Arjomand, *The Shadow of God and the Hidden Imam* (Chicago, 1984), 30.

CHAPTER EIGHTEEN

Style versus Substance: The Christian Iconography on Two Vessels Made for the Ayyubid Sultan al-Salih Ayyub[1]

Rachel Ward

Scenes from the life of Christ and figures of Christian saints and ecclesiastics have been identified on some seventeen inlaid brass vessels attributed to thirteenth-century Ayyubid Syria.[2] The Christian iconography is not in itself surprising: there have always been sizeable Christian communities in Syria and other areas of the Islamic world, many of them wealthy enough to commission luxury items.[3] The reason that these objects have attracted scholarly attention is that two of them, a tray in the Louvre (Figure 18.1) and a basin in the Freer Gallery (Plate 32; Figures 18.2–7), bear the name and titles of the Ayyubid Sultan al-Salih Ayyub (r. Diyar Bakr 1232–9, Damascus 1239 and 1245–9, Egypt 1240–9).

The presence of Christian iconography on objects made for a Muslim ruler has provoked several different explanations. Atil suggested that the basin was a gift for an important Crusader as a gesture of appeasement.[4] Baer suggested that the vessels symbolised the subjugation of Christians to al-Salih's authority.[5] Katzenstein and Lowry suggested that the scenes on the basin represented a conscious comparison between Christ and al-Salih at a time when Crusaders and local Christians played an important part in Muslim cultural life.[6] Most recently, Khoury has suggested that the scenes on the basin are a pictorial reflection of the *Merits of Jerusalem (Fada'il al-Quds)* texts, which featured Christ as Muslim prophet and Messiah.[7]

All of these theories have assumed that the iconography on these vessels remains Christian in substance as well as style, but Christian iconography was frequently plundered by Arab artists in the thirteenth century as the fashion for figural decoration of manuscripts and objects outstripped their repertoire.[8] Both compositions and individual figures were freely borrowed. The scene of Abu Zayd addressing a group of men in a *Maqamat* manuscript (Figure 18.8) is based on a composition of Christ washing the feet of the disciples; the men still have bare feet and one extends his leg towards the

309

Fig. 18.1 Tray made for al-Salih Ayyub, Syria or north Iraq, 1232–49.

(Louvre, Paris, MAO 360.)

Fig. 18.2 Basin made for al-Salih Ayyub, showing medallion with 'Raising of Lazarus'. Damascus, 1240–9.

(Freer Gallery of Art, Washington, DC, 55.10.)

Fig. 18.3 Basin made for al-Salih Ayyub, detail of medallion with 'Annunciation'.

Fig. 18.4 *Basin made for al-Salih Ayyub, detail of medallion with 'Virgin and Child'.*

Fig. 18.5 *Basin made for al-Salih Ayyub, detail of medallion with 'Entry into Jerusalem'.*

Fig. 18.6 Basin made for al-Salih Ayyub, detail of medallion with 'Last Supper'.

Fig. 18.7 Basin made for al-Salih Ayyub, interior with 'Christian Saints'.

Fig. 18.8 *Abu Zayd addressing a group in Najran from a* Maqamat *of al-Hariri. Probably Syria, dated 619/1222.*

(Bibliothèque Nationale, Paris, ms. arabe 6094, f. 147a.)

stooping figure of Abu Zayd. The gaunt faces, hollowed cheeks and voluminous robes are also derived from the Christian model.

Metal inlayers, working with a newly imported technique, faced an even greater challenge than painters as they had no stock of suitable designs in the same media. They sought models where they could and the result was a pot-pourri of borrowed compositions and motifs, their original meaning often lost, transformed or misunderstood. The decoration of the Blacas ewer epitomises this uninhibited plagiarism (Figure 18.9).[9] Bahram Gur, the epic hero from the Persian Shahnameh, becomes one of several huntsmen. Three of the twelve personifications of the Khurasanian zodiac cycle are randomly repeated to fill additional medallions, around the neck. Sagittarius makes a further appearance in one of the larger medallions where he is

transformed, like Bahram Gur, into an anonymous mounted hunts-man. Contemporary Iranian models are used to portray the new Turkish aristocracy with their Asian features and distinctive tunics and headgear. Scenes of everyday life: wrestlers, a lady on a camel with her servant, a masked dancer, are drawn from a classical genre tradition continued by Christian artists. Other compositions derive from religious Christian painting, although the original symbolism of the images is suppressed. The plaintiff bowing before the amir in an enthronement scene is based, like the manuscript illustration (Figure 18.8), on Christ washing the feet of the disciples: the Amir still has bare legs. It is against this background of inter-cultural borrowing that the Christian iconography on the two vessels made for al-Salih Ayyub should be viewed.

The question which this chapter will address is: how Christian are the figures and scenes on the two vessels made for al-Salih Ayyub?

The Louvre Tray[10]

The tray in the Louvre (Figure 18.1) is circular with a sunken centre and a narrow rim. The inscription naming the sultan is in the cavetto, and this dates the tray to 1232–49. Other inscriptions on the rim and around the central roundel contain traditional blessings. The main field of decoration is occupied by twelve linked medallions around a large central roundel. The medallions contain a variety of simple figural scenes: two have a galloping horseman, two have a polo player, four have a pair of soldiers fighting with swords or bows and four have a pair of standing figures in long robes.

314

The robed figures are clearly modelled on the standing saints which were a regular feature of Byzantine art.[11] But within a Christian context, the identity of holy figures was always clearly indicated by number (twelve apostles, four evangelists), attributes (wheel for Saint Catherine) and, wherever possible, inscriptions. There is nothing to identify these figures as Christian; on the contrary, any specifically Christian features have been carefully removed. They are in medallions like the other genre scenes. They do not stand or move in procession hieratically but gesticulate and talk to one another as if at a social gathering, and footed bowls in the background of three of the medallions increase the festive atmosphere. Their number (eight) is not significant, and they are identified neither by inscriptions nor by Christian attributes. Two hold staffs, which might have been tall processional crosses in the model but now have small knobs at the top and no cross bar. One of these also holds an open book but it has no script to identify it (a book carried by a similar figures on a box in Cairo is inscribed 'Qur'an' in Arabic).[12]

Despite Baer's warning that 'clothing is . . . unreliable as evidence that subject matter is Christian', it is their costume that has led to the identification of these figures as Christian.[13] Little work has been done on thirteenth-century dress, but a length of fabric worn over a tunic (sometimes covering the head) is the standard pictorial indication of a wise man or religious dignitary, Muslim and non-Muslim, in contemporary manuscript paintings from Syria, Egypt and Iraq.[14] It contrasts with the patterned tunic, boots and *sharbush* (fur hat) worn by princes and their courtiers, which reflects the costume of the culturally Turkish Ayyubid elite and was introduced into Syrian life and art only in the thirteenth century (Figure 18.10). Missing inlays make it impossible to know whether the figures wore turbans, but even they are not a certain indication of religious orientation. Muslims did not invariably wear turbans at this period. A variety of headgear is worn by the courtiers attending the amir in the Vienna *Kitab al-diryaq* frontispiece, and two figures are bare-headed (Figure 18.10). On the other hand, Christians could and did wear turbans.[15] Indeed, at certain periods Christians were forced to use coloured turbans to distinguish themselves from Muslims, which is strong evidence that their dress was otherwise very similar.[16] It is unlikely, therefore, that al-Salih Ayyub and his court would have read these figures as Christians.

The Freer Basin[17]

The basin in the Freer Gallery in Washington (Figures 18.2–7) has tall vertical sides with a flaring rim. The inlaid decoration, which is of the highest quality, covers the interior and exterior surface of the vessel. A magnificent plaited Kufic inscription containing the name and titles of al-Salih Ayyub runs around the exterior of the basin just below the rim. This is punctuated by five medallions containing

Fig. 18.10 *Frontispiece,*
Kitab al-diryaq, *north Iraq
or Syria, mid-13th century.*

(Nationalbibliothek, Vienna,
A.F.10, f. 1a.)

figural scenes which have been identified as scenes from the life of Christ. Around the middle of the basin another frieze comprises five scenes of polo players separated by medallions containing animal and grotesque heads on a ground of interlace. Below these is a narrow band of racing animals interrupted by small medallions containing a single musician. The bottom fifth is taken up by an elaborate band of arabesque interlace.

The interior of the basin (Figure 18.7) is just as finely decorated. The sultan's name and titles written in monumental *thuluth* occupy the upper third of the space, punctuated by five more medallions containing animal and grotesque heads on a ground of interlace. Below this is an arcade which circles around the interior of the basin.

Within the thirty-nine arches stand figures in long robes; these have been identified as Christian saints or ecclesiastics. Below them is a band of arabesque interlace similar to that on the exterior. The decoration of the base, which is badly rubbed and difficult to see, includes five medallions containing three figures in each. These display figures either feasting from flasks and bowls of fruit or playing flutes, drums, tambourines, lutes and zithers.

The Freer basin is usually dated after 1247, because the inscriptions include *khalīl amīr al-mu'minīn* (beloved of the Commander of the Believers), a title thought to have been bestowed on al-Salih during his investiture by the Caliph in that year.[18] But two inscriptions in al-Salih's madrasa and tomb in Cairo, both dated 641/1243, include that title.[19] It was a title used by his father, al-Kamil, and then by his younger brother, al-'Adil. Presumably al-Salih appropriated it after he replaced his deposed brother as ruler of Egypt and head of the Ayyubid empire in 1240. Therefore the basin could have been made any time between al-'Adil's death in 1240 and al-Salih's death in 1249.

The basin was probably made in Damascus. Other possible provenances include the Jazira or Cairo, both home to al-Salih for part of his reign; but he had left the Jazira by 1240, the earliest possible date of the basin, and there is no evidence that Cairo was producing inlaid metalwork before 1269.[20] Damascus, on the other hand, was home to a number of metal inlayers who had already made a series of vessels, including basins, for the Ayyubid rulers of that city.[21]

The standing figures inside the basin, like those on the Louvre tray (Figure 18.1), are clearly modelled on Christian saints, but, once again, there is nothing to identify them as such. On the contrary, their richly patterned tunics suggest that they are men of wealth and status. Physically they surround the images of feasting and music making depicted in the base of the basin and, as they are shown engaged in conversation with one another and some hold beakers, they appear to be participants in the festivities depicted there.[22]

The scenes in the medallions are also ambiguous. They are certainly modelled on pictorial images of the life of Christ. Reading from right to left, these have been identified as 'The Annunciation' (Figure 18.3), 'The Virgin and Child' (Figure 18.4), 'The Raising of Lazarus' (Figure 18.2), 'The Entry into Jerusalem' (Figure 18.5) and 'The Last Supper' (Figure 18.6). However, they are so simplified that only an intimate knowledge of Christian iconography enables their models to be identified and the source for two of the scenes remains uncertain. 'The Raising of Lazarus' (Figure 18.2) could equally be a simplification of 'The Presentation in the Temple': Lazarus is not bandaged and could be a child Christ on top of the temple altar.[23] As Katzenstein and Lowry have observed, the three standing figures of the so-called Last Supper (Figure 18.6) are too unspecific to pin to any event in Christ's life.[24]

Identification of the scenes is further obscured because they do not form a coherent cycle that can be paralleled elsewhere. The omission of the Nativity, which is almost always included in a sequence depicting the life of Christ, is especially surprising. Khoury has proposed that the scenes are based on a Muslim cycle of the life of Christ. No evidence of a pictorial Muslim cycle survives, and so it is impossible to know which scenes might have been included. However, as the Nativity was one of three Christian scenes depicted on the contemporary Freer Canteen and Christ's cradle was a pictorial image used by Muslims to represent Jerusalem on twelfth–thirteenth-century pilgrimage scrolls, it is likely to have featured in a Muslim cycle also; yet it does not appear on the basin.[25]

Like the standing figures (Figure 18.7), the scenes are distanced from their models by the omission of every specifically Christian symbol. In Christian art, Christ was invariably depicted with a cross within his halo, yet on the basin the Christ-figure is never cross-nimbed, but just bears a halo like other figures in contemporary Syrian metalwork and painting. Traditionally, in both Virgin and Child and Entry into Jerusalem iconography, Christ gives a gesture of blessing; again this has been omitted from the scenes on the basin (Figures 18.4–5). The angels in both Annunciation and Virgin and Child iconography often carry staves or croziers – here they do not (Figures 18.3–4). These omissions are unlikely to be errors as they do not occur in local Christian painting nor in the three Christian scenes on the Freer Canteen.

A thirteenth-century Muslim would not have had knowledge of Christian iconography to match a twenty-first-century art historian armed with thousands of reproductions of Christian scenes in architecture, in manuscripts and on objects. He understood the significance of a cross, the external symbol of Christianity: a halo with a cross represented Christ, a figure holding a cross was a Christian. It is unlikely that these simple scenes, which have so puzzled modern scholars, would have been read as Christian, let alone correctly identified with specific moments in the life of Christ, by al-Salih Ayyub.

They are equally unlikely to be genre scenes of the sort found on contemporary inlaid brass vessels (Figure 18.9). None of them belong to the so-called princely cycle and scenes such as three men standing or a naked man behind a brick structure are too dull to have been chosen solely for their decorative qualities. The Freer basin has an unusually elaborate programme of decoration that was carefully planned and chosen for this particular sultan. The two monumental inscriptions glorifying al-Salih (Figures 18.4–7) are exceptionally fine and must have been designed specially for the irregular panels on the basin. Al-Salih's well-known passion for polo explains the dominant images of polo players on the exterior (although polo players are frequently seen on metal objects of this period, it is unprecedented to have such large scenes around the exterior of a vessel).[26] Despite their unassuming appearance, these five medallions are placed in the most prestigious position at the top of the basin and within the titles of the Sultan (Figure 18.2). They even dictated the division into five sections of the decorative layout of the basin, which is unique at this period. They must be meaningful.

Khoury sought an 'Ayyubid-Islamic narrative account' to 'explain the enigmatic appearance of this singular repertoire' but perhaps they depict a contemporary person or event rather than a text?[27] Parallels between individuals and events and the personality and lives of Christian figures were made in Byzantine literature and painting and even on luxury vessels. For example, Maguire has revealed that scenes from the life of David reflect episodes from the life of the ruling Byzantine Emperor on an ivory box made for Basil I (d. 886) and in the frontispiece of a Psalter made for Basil II (d. 1025).[28] In thirteenth-century Europe (and possibly Acre too), historical texts were copiously illustrated with scenes from the lives of contemporary and historical figures.[29] The study of Islamic iconography is in its infancy (hence the choice of subject for this festschrift) but there is increasing evidence that the illustrations of some manuscripts had contemporary significance.[30] Attention has been focused on fourteenth-century Iran, where historical manuscripts detailing the lives of the ruling Il-Khans and their predecessors and epic tales in which the ruler's life is mirrored in that of the hero were produced, but Fitzherbert has suggested that this development may have had a period of gestation reaching back into the thirteenth century.[31] The detailed depictions of local life in thirteenth-century Arab manuscripts demonstrate an interest in the real world essential to the introduction of contemporary issues into painting. The frontispiece to the Vienna *Kitab al-Diryaq* manuscript, for example, with an amir in front of a barbeque and servants shovelling snow from the roof, all dressed in contemporary fashion, is a vivid illustration of court life in winter (Figure 18.10).

The ivory box of Basil I indicates that prestigious vessels could also bear historically significant decoration. The Freer basin, with its royal inscriptions and carefully planned decoration executed in the newly fashionable inlay technique, would certainly have been a prestigious vessel.[32] A historical interpretation of the scenes must relate to the life of al-Salih, whose titles they intersect. They cannot illustrate his achievements as he was a military man who battled both Crusaders and his cousins, therefore a celebration of his life would include fighting scenes. They are more likely to represent a single important event in his life. The problem is that various events could fit these simple images: for example they could illustrate the return of the Sultan from the hajj or a visit to a holy man. However, there is one event important enough to have been related by contemporary historians which might (and I emphasise the speculative nature of this suggestion) be represented in these scenes.

In 1239 Damascus had been seized from al-Salih Ayyub by his uncle and rival, al-Salih Isma'il, who also captured and imprisoned his oldest son and heir-apparent al-Mughith 'Umar (despite promising him safe conduct if he surrendered).[33] By 1243 the situation had settled somewhat and there was a flurry of diplomatic activity between the two men and serious hope for a peace treaty. In return for acknowledgement as ruler of Damascus and some other territories in Syria by al-Salih Isma'il, al-Salih Ayyub was to be recognised as sultan and head of the Ayyubid family in Damascus and elsewhere in Syria and his associates, including his son, were to be released from prison and allowed to return to Cairo. The release of his son was an important motivation for the peace treaty.[34]

The process advanced well. Al-Salih Ayyub was recognised as sultan by al-Salih Isma'il in September 1243 and coins were struck in Damascus in the name of al-Salih Ayyub for the first time. An inscription erected to mark the restoration of the Bab al-Salam bears his name and titles.[35] Some associates of al-Salih Ayyub were released and sent to Egypt, but his son was retained until the final oaths sealing the peace had been signed, although he was released from prison and allowed the freedom of the city. Conscious that the return of 'Umar was al-Salih Ayyub's main motivation for a peace treaty, al-Salih Isma'il wisely held on to him until the last moment. That moment never came. Letters revealing al-Salih Ayyub's plan to wage war against his uncle as soon as he had his son back were intercepted. 'Umar was returned to prison and died there in August 1244; al-Salih Isma'il was suspected of his murder. Two years later a vengeful al-Salih Ayyub had reconquered Damascus and al-Salih Isma'il had fled to Aleppo.

Is it possible that the Freer basin was commissioned by al-Salih Isma'il in 1243, when the negotiations looked extremely promising, as a diplomatic gift for his nephew? And could the five medallions illustrate the return of al-Mughith 'Umar to his father? Such a subject would have forced the artist to seek models outside his normal repertoire, and, like the illustrators of the contemporary *Maqamat* manuscripts (Figure 18.8), he would naturally have turned to the narrative tradition of Christian art for models. He may even have chosen the scenes to provoke a comparison between the life of 'Umar and that of Christ and provide an additional layer of meaning for those able to recognise it.[36] The 'Annunciation' (Figure 18.3) could represent the divine prediction of the birth of the royal heir; the scene was distanced from its model by the omission of the angel's crozier and by the exchange of the traditional domestic setting for an outdoor environment. 'The Virgin and Child' (Figure 18.4) could depict the youthful 'Umar with his mother; the cross was omitted from the child's halo and he makes no gesture of blessing. The angels in both these scenes are no problem in a royal Muslim context as angels often feature in enthronements and other ruler images. 'The Raising of Lazarus' (Figure 18.2) might represent 'Umar's release from prison; obviously he could not be swathed in bandages and emerging from a tomb, so he is shown coming out of an anonymous brick structure. 'The Entry into Jerusalem' (Figure 18.3) could depict 'Umar's journey to Cairo; again all significant Christian elements have been removed and the scene pared back to the image of a man on his mount. Finally, 'The Last Supper' (Figure 18.6) could represent the reunion of father and son in Cairo, both inclining towards the other and al-Salih Ayyub handing 'Umar a cup or gift of some kind.[37]

The functional context of a vessel adds another dimension to the interpretation of its iconography, but it is often overlooked, partly because the original setting is so difficult to reconstruct. It is likely that the context within which the Freer basin was used would have made the meaning of the medallions quite clear and justified their prominent position on the vessel. Polo and feasting, both the major features on the basin, suggest that it was used for a celebration. The figures under the arcade, some holding beakers, could be viewed as participants in the feast depicted on the base of the vessel just beneath them (Figure 18.7). If the basin had been used during the inevitable celebrations that would have marked the return of 'Umar to Cairo, the meaning of the five scenes would have been obvious. Without the context for which the basin was intended, we will probably never be sure of the meaning of these scenes, but it is hard to avoid the conclusion that they are not Christian but tell the story of a contemporary event. Perhaps the most important Christian contribution was the concept of having such a sophisticated icono-graphic programme on the basin in the first place.

The conclusion reached here, that the two objects made for the Ayyubid sultan are only Christian in style and not in substance, has important implications for other objects with decoration derived from Christian models. Hitherto they have always been treated as a single group because of their shared subject matter, on the basis that if a Muslim sultan was commissioning objects with Christian scenes, other objects might have been commissioned by Muslims within the same cultural environment. The reason why Muslims would com-mission such vessels was therefore the prime question. But the 'Christian-ness' of vessels in the group varies greatly. The Freer Canteen, with its carefully detailed images of 'The Nativity', 'The Presentation in the Temple' and 'The Entry into Jerusalem', is undeniably Christian in substance as well as style.[38] The British Museum incense-burner, on the other hand, which features nineteen robed figures modelled on Christian saints, fifteen of whom are drinking from tumblers in a very unsaintly manner, must be secu-lar.[39] Stylistic influence from Christian art does not bind the group together as convincingly as a common iconographic intention and as they are a motley collection of vessels executed in a variety of styles and techniques, there is little reason to assume that they were produced in the same workshop – or even the same city or country. The provenance, patronage and meaning of each of them should be reassessed individually.

Notes

1. An early version of this paper was presented at the XXXIII Spring Symposium of Byzantine Studies, 'Eastern Approaches to Byzantium', University of Warwick, 27–9 March 1999, organised by Antony Eastmond. My thanks to Teresa Fitzherbert for helpful comments on a final draft of the text.

2. Eva Baer, *Ayyubid Metalwork with Christian Images* (Leyden, 1989).

3. For example, a fragment of lustre pottery produced in Fatimid Egypt in the twelfth century is decorated with an unambiguous image of Christ, cross-nimbed and making a gesture of blessing which must have been intended for the local Coptic community: Cairo, Museum of Islamic Art, no. 5297, illustrated in Richard Ettinghausen and Oleg Grabar, *The Art and Architecture of Islam, 650–1250* (Harmondsworth, 1987), fig. 193.

4. Esin Atil, W. T. Chase and Paul Jett, *Islamic Metalwork in the Freer Gallery of Art* (Washington, DC,1985), 145.

5. Baer, *Christian Images*, 48.

6. Ranee Katzenstein and Glenn D. Lowry, 'Christian Themes in Thirteenth-Century Islamic Metalwork', *Muqarnas* 1 (1983), 53–68.

7. Nuha Khoury, 'Narratives of the Holy Land: Memory, Identity and Inverted Imagery in the Freer Basin and Canteen', *Orientations* (May 1998), 63–9.

8. Hugo Buchthal, 'The Painting of the Syrian Jacobites in its Relation to Byzantine and Islamic Art', *Syria* 20 (1939), 136–50 and Buchthal, 'Hellentistic Miniatures in Early Islamic Manuscripts', *Ars Islamica* 7 (1940), 125–33.

9. For illustrations of all the figural medallions on the Blacas ewer, see Rachel Ward, 'High life in Mosul: 1232 AD', *Arts of Asia* (May/June 1986), 119–24.

10. Paris, Louvre, MAO 360. This object is in very poor condition. It is most clearly reproduced in *L'Orient de Saladin, l'art des Ayyoubides*, exh. cat., Institut du Monde Arabe (Paris, 2001), 144–5.

11. Baer, *Christian Images*, 11 and fig. 24.

12. Cairo, Museum of Islamic Art, no. 15130. Baer, *Christian Images*, fig. 37.

13. Baer, *Christian Images*, 33: 'clothing is . . . unreliable as evidence that subject matter is Christian. . . . A systematic study of 13th century Muslim costume is still lacking, and there is no way of knowing whether garments . . . reflected a contemporary fashion adopted by both Christians and Muslims or the artistic model from which they derived.'

14. Richard Ettinghausen, *Arab Painting*, (Geneva, 1962), 69 (Dioscorides), 75–7 (various authors and their students), 79 (Abu Zayd dressed as a wise man), 99 (author), 106–7 (Abu Zayd dressed as wise man and the governor and Qadi whom he is addressing), 111 (Qadi), 121 (astronomer), 146 (Caliph), 150 (Qadi).

15. There are several turbaned figures in thirteenth-century Syriac lectionaries. Jules Leroy, *Les manuscrits syriaques à peintures, conservés dans les bibliothèques d'Europe et d'Orient*, 2 vols (Paris, 1964): 2:75, 86, 87.

16. Carole Hillenbrand, *The Crusades: Islamic Perspectives* (Edinburgh, 1999), 408–9, 411–15.

17. Washington, Freer Gallery of Art, no. 55.10.

18. Katzenstein and Lowry, 'Christian themes', 64; Atil et al., *Arab Metalwork*, 143.

19. E. Combe et al., *Répertoire chronologique d'épigraphie arabe* (Cairo, 1931), 11: nos 4217–9.

20. Rachel Ward, 'Tradition and Innovation: A Group of Candlesticks Made in Mamluk Egypt', in *Islamic Art in the Ashmolean Museum*, Oxford Studies in Islamic Art 10, ed. James W. Allan (Oxford, 1995), 2:147–58.

21. Such as the basin made by al-Dhaki for al-Malik al-Adil Abu Bakr, ruler of Damascus and Cairo (1238–40) (Atil et al., *Islamic Metalwork*, 145, fig. 54).

22. Their position within an arcade recalls the courtiers under arched openings that surround the throne niche at a palace in Sinjar: Hillenbrand, *Crusades*, 202–3, pls 4.11–2.

23. Compare the 'Presentation in the Temple' on the Freer Canteen: Atil et al., *Islamic Metalwork*, 127.

24. 'On the Freer basin the rendition is so summary that in at least one instance, the so-called medallion of the Last Supper, the detail is insufficient to identify the scene with a particular Christological episode': Katzenstein and Lowry, 'Christian Themes', 63.

25. Freer Canteen: Atil et al., *Islamic Metalwork*, 127. Khoury, 'Narratives', 68.

26. Al-Salih built a polo ground in Cairo in Rajab 643 and a bridge across the Nile to give easy access to it: D. S. Rice, 'Studies in Islamic Metal Work I', *Bulletin of the School of Oriental and African Studies* 14/3 (1952), 572.

27. Khoury, 'Narratives', 67. I argued recently that historical events and individuals were unlikely to have been depicted on vessels. My study of the Freer basin and awareness of Byzantine objects which do precisely that has caused me to revise this opinion (although not in relation to the Baptistère). Rachel Ward, 'The Baptistère de Saint Louis – a Mamluk Basin Made for Export to Europe', in *Islam and the Italian Renaissance*, ed. Charles Burnett and Anna Contadini (London, 1999), 115.

28. Box in the Palazzo Venezia in Rome. Psalter in the Biblioteca Marciana in Venice (Cod. Gr. 17). H. Maguire, 'The Art of Comparing in Byzantium', *The Art Bulletin* 70 (1988), 88–103. My thanks to Robin Cormack, who drew my attention to the Byzantine parallels and to Rowena Loverance for help in tracking them down.

29. Jaraslov Folda, *Crusader Manuscript Illumination at Saint-Jean d'Acre, 1275–1291* (Princeton, 1976).

30. Oleg Grabar and Sheila Blair, *Epic Images and Contemporary History: The Illustrations of the Great Mongol Shahnameh* (Chicago, 1980); P. P. Soucek, 'An Illustrated Manuscript of al-Biruni's Chronology of Ancient Nations', in *The Scholar and the Saint*, ed. Peter J. Chelkowski (New York, 1975), 103–68; Priscilla P. Soucek, 'The Life of the Prophet, Illustrated Versions', in *Content and Context of Visual Arts in the Islamic World*, ed. Priscilla P. Soucek (University Park and London, 1988), 193–209; Abolala Soudavar, 'The Saga of Abu-Sa'id Bahador Khan. The Abu-Sa'idname', in *The Court of the Il-Khans*, ed. Julian Raby and Teresa Fitzherbert, Oxford Studies in Islamic Art 12 (Oxford, 1996), 95–218; Teresa Fitzherbert, 'Portrait of a Lost Leader, Jalal al-Din Karazmshah and Juvaini', in ibid., 63–79; Teresa Fitzherbert, 'Bal'ami's Tabari. An Illustrated Manuscript of Bal'ami's *Tarjama-yi Tarikh-i*

Tabari in the Freer Gallery of Art, Washington (F59.16, 47.19 and 30.21),' unpublished Ph.D. dissertation, University of Edinburgh, 2001; Robert Hillenbrand, 'Images of Muhammad in al-Biruni's *Chronology of Ancient Nations*', in *Persian Painting from the Mongols to the Qajars: Studies in Honour of Basil W. Robinson*, ed. Robert Hillenbrand (London, 2000), 129–46. My thanks to Teresa Fitzherbert for references to topicality in Persian painting.

31. Teresa Fitzherbert, 'Portrait of a Lost Leader', 75.

32. Contemporary texts confirm that inlaid brass vessels were highly esteemed and considered appropriate gifts for foreign monarchs. Basins, the largest and finest of them, often carry the name of a high-ranking person and were used in ceremonial events such as marriage and circumcision celebrations. Basins of Damascus feature in descriptions of a wedding by the fourteenth-century Italian pilgrim Simone Sigoli, *Viaggio al Monte Sinai* (Florence, 1829, 22–4. According to al-Jazari and Maqrizi, basins were used to collect contributions at the circumcision festival of the Mamluk Sultan's brother in 692/1293): É. Quatremère, *Histoire des sultans mamlouks de l'Égypte*, 2 vols (Paris, 1845), 2:149; Jean Sauvaget, *La chronique de Damas de al-Jazari* (Paris, 1949), 28.

33. For an account of this episode, see R. Stephen Humphreys, *From Saladin to the Mongols: The Ayyubids of Damascus, 1193–1260* (New York, 1977), 250–78.

34. Ibid., 272–4.

35. *Repertoire chronolgique d'épigraphe arabe*, no. 4223.

36. Katzenstein and Lowry, 'Christian Themes', suggested that the scenes were a conscious comparison between the life of Al-Salih and that of Christ but it is difficult to identify 'The Raising of Lazarus', 'The Entry into Jerusalem' and 'The Last Supper' with episodes in al-Salih's life. Khoury, 'Narratives', pointed out that the choice of scenes emphasises the attitude to Christ and Mary shared by both Islam and Christianity, and so no problematic doctrinal issues would have been raised by the comparison.

37. A very similar composition of standing figures inclining towards one another is seen in an illustration of the arrival at Acre of John of Brienne in 1210, in a thirteenth-century chronicle illustrated within the Crusader kingdom: *The Oxford Illustrated History of the Crusades*, ed. Jonathon Riley-Smith (Oxford, 1997), 135.

38. Atil et al., *Islamic Metalwork*, 127.

39. Rachel Ward, *Islamic Metalwork* (London, 1993), figs 61, 63.

Bibliography of Robert Hillenbrand's Work

Books

1. *Imperial Images in Persian Painting* (Edinburgh, 1977).
2. *Islamic Architecture in North Africa* (London, 1976) (Co-author with Lucien Golvin; photographs by Derek Hill).
3. *Islamic Architecture: Form, Function and Meaning* (Edinburgh, 1994).
4. *Islamic Art and Architecture* (London and New York, 1999).
5. *The Architecture of Ottoman Jerusalem. An Introduction* (London, 2001).
6. *Studies in Islamic Architecture. Volume I (Collected Articles)* (London, 2001).

Books Edited

7. *Proceedings of the 10th Congress of the Union Européenne des Arabisants et Islamisants*. Edinburgh, 9–16 September 1980 (Edinburgh, 1982).
8. *The Islamic Book* (Princeton, 1984).
9. *The Art of the Saljuqs in Iran and Anatolia* (Costa Mesa, CA, 1994).
10. *The Art and Archaeology of Ancient Persia: New Light on the Parthian and Sassanian Empires*, ed. Vesta S. Curtis, Robert Hillenbrand and J. Michael Rogers (London, 1998).
11. *The 'Amiriya in Rada': The History and Restoration of a Sixteenth-Century Madrasa in the Yemen*, Oxford Studies in Islamic Art, 13, by Salma al-Radi, with contributions from Ruth Barnes, Yahya al-Nasiri and Venetia Porter (Oxford, 1998).
12. *Ottoman Jerusalem: The Islamic City, 1517–1917*, ed. Sylvia J. Auld and Robert Hillenbrand, 2 vols (London, 2000).
13. *Persian Painting from the Mongols to the Qajars* (London, 2000).
14. Shahnama. *The Visual Language of the Persian Book of Kings* (Aldershot, 2004).

Longer Contributions to Books

15. Translation of sections of *Ardabil, Grabmoschee des Schech Safi: Denkmäler persischer Baukunst* II by Friedrich Sarre (Berlin, 1924), in Martin E.Weaver, *Preliminary Study on the Conservation Problems of Five Iranian Monuments* (Paris, 1970), 73–97.
16. 'Die Kunst der Umayyaden', in *Propyläen Kunstgeschichte: Die Kunst des Islam*, ed. Bertold Spuler and Janine Sourdel-Thomine (Berlin, 1973), 145–77.
17. 'Art in the Persian Gulf', in *The Persian Gulf States: A General Survey*, ed. Alvin J. Cottrell (Baltimore, 1980), 414–84.

18. 'Islamic Art at the Crossroads: East versus West at Mshatta', in *Essays in Islamic Art and Architecture in Honor of Katharina Otto-Dorn*, ed. Abbas Daneshvari (Malibu, 1981), 63–86.

19. 'The Flanged Tomb Tower at Bastam', in *Art et société dans le monde iranien*, ed. Chahriyar Adle (Paris, 1982), 237–60.

20. 'The Islamic Art of Iran', in *A Bibliographical Guide to Iran*, ed. Laurence P. Elwell-Sutton (Brighton, 1983), 295–333.

21. Co-author of 'Architecture: Iran, Afghanistan and Central Asia', in *A Bibliography of the Architecture, Arts and Crafts of Islam. Second Supplement Jan. 1972–Dec.1980*, ed. James D. Pearson, Michael Mei-necke and George T. Scanlon (Cairo, 1984), 65–112.

22. 'The Role of Tradition in Qajar Religious Architecture', in *Qajar Iran, Political, Social and Cultural Change, 1800–1925: Studies in Honour of L. P. Elwell-Sutton*, ed. C. Edmund Bosworth and Carole Hillenbrand (Edinburgh, 1984), 352–82.

23. 'The Mosque in the Medieval Islamic World', in *Architecture in Continuity: Building in the Islamic World Today*, ed. Sherban Canta-cuzino (New York, 1985), 30–51.

24. 'Eastern Islamic Influences in Syria: Raqqa and Qal'at Ja'bar in the Later 12th Century', in *The Art of Syria and the Jazira, 1100–1250*, Oxford Studies in Islamic Art 1, ed. Julian Raby (Oxford, 1985), 21–48.

25. 'Safavid Architecture', in *The Cambridge History of Iran. 6. The Timurid and Safavid Periods*, ed. Peter Jackson and Laurence Lockhart (Cambridge, 1986), 759–842.

26. 'Aspects of Timurid Architecture in Central Asia', in *Utrecht Papers on Central Asia: Proceedings of the First European Seminar of Central Asian Studies held at Utrecht*, 16–18 December 1985, ed. Mark van Damme and Hendrik Boeschoten (Utrecht, 1987), 255–86.

27. 'Maqabir' ('Mausolea'), in *Mi'mari-yi Iran daureh-yi Islami ('Iranian Architecture of the Islamic Period')*, ed. Muhammad Yusuf Kiani (Tehran, 1344/1987), 23–51.

28. 'The Islamic Architecture of Persia', in *The Arts of Persia*, ed. Ronald W. Ferrier (New Haven and London, 1989), 80–107, 318–20.

29. ' "The Ornament of the World": Medieval Cordoba as a Cultural Centre', in *The Legacy of Muslim Spain*, Handbuch der Orientalistik, Abt.1, Bd.12, ed. Salma K. Jayyusi (Leiden, New York and Köln, 1992), 112–35.

30. 'The Uses of Space in Timurid Painting', in *Timurid Art and Culture: Iran and Central Asia in the Fifteenth Century*, ed. Lisa Golombek and Maria Subtelny (Leiden, 1992), 77–102.

31. 'Splendour and Austerity: Islamic Architectural Ornament', in *Asian Art*, ed. Jill Tilden (London, 1995), 6–27.

32. 'Images of Authority on Kashan Lustreware', in *Islamic Art in the Ashmolean Museum*, Oxford Studies in Islamic Art, 10, ed. James W. Allan (Oxford, 1995), Part I, 167–98.

33. 'The Iconography of the Shah-nama-yi Shahi', in *Safavid Persia: The History and Politics of an Islamic Society*, ed. Charles Melville (London and New York, 1996), 53–78.

34. 'The Iskandar Cycle in the Great Mongol Shahnama', in *The Proble-matics of Power: Eastern and Western Representations of Alexander the Great*, ed. Margaret Bridges and Johann-Christoph Bürgel (Bern, 1996), 203–30.

35. ' 'Anjar and Early Islamic Urbanism', in *The Idea and Ideal of the Town between Late Antiquity and the Early Middle Ages*, ed. G. P. Broglio and Bryan Ward-Perkins (Leiden, 1999), 59–98.

36. 'Islamic Architecture', in *Shogukan Encyclopaedia of World Art*, ed. Toh Sugimura et al. (Tokyo, 1999), 289–336.

37. 'Umayyad Woodwork in the Aqsa Mosque', in *Bayt al-Maqdis: Jerusalem and Early Islam*, Oxford Studies in Islamic Art 9.2, ed. Jeremy Johns (Oxford, 1999), 271–310.

38. 'The Architecture of the Ghaznavids and Ghurids', in *The Sultan's Turret: Studies in Persian and Turkish Culture in Honour of Edmund Bosworth*, ed. Carole Hillenbrand (Leiden, 2000), 124–206.

39. 'Structure, Style and Context in the Monuments of Ottoman Jerusalem', in *Ottoman Jerusalem: The Islamic City, 1517–1917*, ed. Sylvia J. Auld and Robert Hillenbrand (London, 2000) 1:1–23.

40. 'Images of Muhammad in al-Biruni's *Chronology of Ancient Nations*', in Robert Hillenbrand (ed.), *Persian Painting from the Mongols to the Qajars* (London, 2000), 129–46.

41. 'The Ghurid tomb in Herat', in Warwick Ball and Leonard Harrow (eds), *Cairo to Kabul. Afghan and Islamic Studies presented to Ralph Pinder-Wilson* (London, 2002), 123–43.

42. 'The Arts of the Book in Ilkhanid Iran', in Linda Komaroff and Stefano Carboni (eds), *The Legacy of Genghis Khan. Courtly Art and Culture in Western Asia, 1256–1353* (New York, 2002), 134–67.

43. 'The sarcophagus of Shah Isma'il at Ardabil', in Andrew J. Newman (ed.), *Society and Culture in the Early Modern Middle East. Studies on Iran in the Safavid Period* (Leiden, 2003), 165–92.

44. 'The one that got away: Ernst Herzfeld and the Islamic architecture of Iran', in *Ernst Herzfeld and the development of Near Eastern Studies, 1900–1950*, eds Ann C.Gunter and Stefan Hauser (Leiden and Boston, MA, 2004), 405–26.

Articles

45. 'Vanishing Ruins of an Empire', *Geographical Magazine* (March 1969), 456–61.

46. 'Khatchk'ar in Soviet Armenia', *Illustrated London News* (1 November 1969), 26–7.

47. 'Armenia's Vanishing Churches', *Illustrated London News* (8 August 1970), 26–7.

48. 'Islamic Monuments in Northern Iran', *Iran* 8 (1970), 204–5.

49. 'Mosques and Mausolea in Khurasan and Central Iran', *Iran* 9 (1971), 160–2.

50. 'Saljuq Monuments in Iran: I', *Oriental Art* N.S. 18/1 (1972), 64–77.

51. 'Saljuq Monuments in Iran II: The "Pir" Mausoleum at Takistan', *Iran* 10 (1972), 45–55.

52. 'The Development of Saljuq Mausolea in Iran', in *The Art of Iran and Anatolia from the 11th to the 13th century AD*, Colloquies on Art and Architecture in Asia, University of London 4 (London, 1974), 40–59.

53. 'The Paintings of Rashid al-Din's "Universal History" at Edinburgh', *University of Edinburgh Journal* 26 (1974), 331–3.

54. Entries in *A Dictionary of Architecture* by Nikolaus Pevsner, John Fleming and Hugh Honour (London, 1975): 'Bazar' (39); 'Caravanserai' (84–5); 'Iranian Architecture: Islamic Architecture' (258–62); 'Islamic Architecture' (264–70); 'Iwan' (285); 'Kaisariya' (301); 'Madrasa' (324–5); 'Maqsura' (328); 'Mihrab' (349–50); 'Minaret' (350–1); Minbar' (351); 'Mosque' (357–8); 'Musalla' (359); 'Pishtaq' (388); 'Qibla' (409); 'Turbe' (513); and 'Turkish Architecture' (513–9).

55. 'Kazwin.ii. Monuments', in *The Encylopaedia of Islam*, 2nd edn, (Leiden, 1976), 4:862–3.

56. 'Saljuq Monuments in Iran: IV. The Domed Masǧid-i Ǧami' at Suǧas', *Kunst des Orients* 10 (1976), 47–79.

57. 'Saljuq Dome Chambers in North-West Iran', *Iran* 14 (1976), 93–102.
58. 'Saljuq Monuments in Iran: IV. The Mosques of Nushabad', *Oriental Art* N.S. 22 (1976), 265–77.
59. 'A Pair of Medieval Tomb Towers in Van', *Yayla* 1 (1977), 21–4.
60. 'The Use of Glazed Tilework in Iranian Islamic Architecture', in *Akten des VII. Internationalen Kongresses für iranische Kunst und Archäologie, München, 7–10 September 1976, Archäologische Mitteilungen aus Iran. Ergänzungsband* 6, ed. Wolfram Kleiss (Berlin, 1979), 545–54.
61. 'Spatial Experiment in Medieval Islamic Architecture', in *Proceedings of the International Symposium on Islam and Science, 1–3 Muharram 1401 A.H. (10–12 November 1980)* (Islamabad, 1981), 150–5.
62. '*La dolce vita* in Early Islamic Syria: The Evidence of Later Umayyad Palaces', *Art History* 5/1 (1982), 1–35.
63. 'Abarquh.ii. Monuments', in *Encyclopaedia Iranica*, ed. Ehsan Yarshater (London, 1982) 1:65–7.
64. 'The Alhambra', in *Dictionary of the Middle Ages*, ed. Joseph R. Strayer (New York, 1982), 1:168–71.
65. 'Some Observations on the Use of Space in Medieval Islamic Buildings', in *Proceedings of the International Symposium on Islamic Architecture and Urbanism*, ed. H. Bedawi (Dammam, 1982), 17–30.
66. 'Central Asian Elements in the Tomb of Rukn-i ʿAlam, Multan', in *International Conference on Science in Islamic Polity – its Past, Present and Future*. Abstracts of papers (Islamabad, 1983), 43–4.
67. Articles in *Dictionary of the Middle Ages* 5, ed. Joseph R. Strayer (New York, 1985): 'Cordoba' (597–601); 'Granada' (651–3).
68. 'Islamic Art, Architecture and Archaeology', in *The Middle East and Islam*, ed. Paul Auchterlonie (Zug, 1986), 41–5.
69. 'Khan', in *Dictionary of the Middle Ages*, ed. Joseph R. Strayer (New York, 1986), 7:237–8.
70. 'The Classical Heritage in Islamic Art: the Case of Medieval Architecture', *The Scottish Journal of Religious Studies* 7 (1986), 123–40.
71. 'Archaeology. vi. Islamic Iran,' in *Encyclopaedia Iranica*, ed. Ehsan Yarshater (London, 1986), 2:317–22.
72. 'Architecture. vi. Islamic, Safavid to Qajar', in *Encyclopaedia Iranica*, ed. Ehsan Yarshater (London, 1986), 2:345–9.
73. 'Ardestan. ii. Monuments', in *Encyclopaedia Iranica*, ed. Ehsan Yarshater (London, 1986), 2:386–7.
74. 'The Use of Spatial Devices in the Great Mosque of Cordoba', in *Islão e Arabismo na Peninsula Iberica. Actas do XI Congresso da União Europeia de Arabistos e Islamogos*, ed. Adel Sidarus (Evora, 1986), 181–94.
75. 'Madrasa. Architecture', in *Encyclopaedia of Islam* (Leiden, 1986), 5:1136–54.
76. 'Manara', in *Encyclopaedia of Islam* (Leiden, 1987), 6:361–8.
77. 'Aštarjan', in *Encyclopaedia Iranica*, ed. Ehsan Yarshater (London, 1987), 2:846–7.
78. Articles in *Dictionary of the Middle Ages* 8, ed. Joseph R. Strayer (New York, 1987): 'Madrasa' (11–12); 'Malwiya' (68); 'Manuscript Books, Binding of: Islamic' (98–100); 'Minaret' (396–7); 'Pishtaq' (670–1).
79. 'Saljuq Monuments in Iran. V. The Imamzada Nur, Gurgan', *Iran* 25 (1987), 55–76.
80. 'Abbasid Mosques in Iran', *Rivista degli Studi Orientali* 59 (1987), 175–212.
81. 'Mazandaran', in Lisa Golombek and Donald N. Wilber, *The Timurid Architecture of Iran and Turan* (Princeton, 1988), 1:429–39, 441, 443–4.

82. 'Islamic Art and Architecture', in *The Cambridge Encyclopaedia of the Middle East and North Africa*, ed. Trevor Mostyn and Albert H. Hourani (Cambridge, 1988), 224–32.

83. 'Political Symbolism in Early Indo-Islamic Mosque Architecture: The Case of Ajmir', *Iran* 26 (1988), 128–45.

84. 'The Symbolism of the Rayed Nimbus in Early Islamic Art', *Cosmos* 2 (1988), 1–52.

85. 'Review article. Persian Lustre Ware', *Oriental Art* N.S. XXXIV (1988–9), 282–3.

86. 'Nishapur: Architecture and Decoration', *Oriental Art* N.S. XXXV/1 (1989), 44–50.

87. 'Oriental Occidental: Islamic influences in the art of Britain and America', *Oriental Art* N.S. XXXV/4 (1989), 218–25.

88. 'Qur'anic Epigraphy in Medieval Islamic Architecture', in *Mélanges Dominique Sourdel, Revue des Études Islamiques* 54, ed. Ludvik Kalus (1986, pub. 1989), 173–87.

89. 'Masjid', in *Encyclopaedia of Islam* (Leiden, 1989), 6:677–88.

90. 'Umayyad Art', in *Dictionary of the Middle Ages*, ed. Joseph R. Strayer (New York, 1989), 12:263–4.

91. 'Das Vermächtnis des Felsendoms', in *Forschungsforum. Berichte as der Otto-Friedrich-Universitat Bamberg*, Heft 2. Orientalistik (Bamberg, 1990), 64–71.

92. 'Mamluk and Ilkhanid Bestiaries: Convention and Experiment', *Ars Orientalis* 20 (1990), 149–87.

93. 'Qasr Kharanah Re-examined', *Oriental Art* N.S. XXXVII/2 (1991), 109–13.

94. 'Creswell and Contemporary Central European Scholarship', *Muqarnas* 8 (1991), 23–35.

95. 'Turco-Iranian Elements in the Medieval Architecture of Pakistan: The Case of the Tomb of Rukn-i ʿAlam at Multan', *Muqarnas* 9 (1992), 148–74.

96. Foreword to R. Lifchez (ed.), *The Dervish Lodge: Architecture, Art and Sufism in Ottoman Turkey* (Berkeley and Los Angeles, 1992), xxi–xxiv.

97. 'A Safavid Tile Mosaic Panel: The Date of the Panel', in *Sotheby's. Islamic and Indian Art: Oriental Manuscripts and Miniatures* (London, 1992), 50–1.

98. 'Musalla', in *The Encyclopaedia of Islam* (Leyden, 1992), 7:659–60.

99. 'The Qur'an Illuminated', *Art History* 17/1 (1994), 116–26.

100. 'The Architecture of the Senses', *Antique* 9/1 (1994), 666–7.

101. 'The Mausoleum of ʿAʾisha Bibi and the Central Asian Tradition of Funerary Architecture', in *Annemarie Schimmel Festschrift: Essays presented to Annemarie Schimmel on the Occasion of her Retirement from Harvard University by her Colleagues, Students and Friends (=Journal of Turkish Studies*, 18), ed. Maria E. Subtelny (Cambridge, MA, 1994), 111–20.

102. 'The Relationship between Book Painting and Luxury Ceramics in 13th-Century Iran', in *The Art of the Saljuqs in Iran and Anatolia. Proceedings of a Symposium held in Edinburgh in 1982*, ed. Robert Hillenbrand (Costa Mesa, CA, 1994), 134–45.

103. 'Saldjukids. Art and Architecture. 1. In Persia', in *Encyclopaedia of Islam* (Leiden, 1995), 8:959–64.

104. 'The Message of Misfortune', in *Asian Art* 2, ed. Jill Tilden (London, 1996), 32–45, 186–8.

105. 'Islamic Art. I.8. Subject Matter', in *The Dictionary of Art*, ed. Jane S. Turner (London, 1996), 16:127–40.

106. 'Islamic Art. II.5.(i).(c) Architecture: Afghanistan, Pakistan and Western Central Asia', ibid., 16:166–70.

107. 'Islamic Art.II.3.(i). Architecture 2. Before 661.3.661.661–c.750', ibid., 16:144–9.
108. 'Islamic Art.II.9.(i).(b) Figural Sculpture', ibid., 16:245–7.
109. 'Umayyad', ibid., 31:572–4.
110. Entries under 3,000 words in *The Dictionary of Art*, ed. Jane S. Turner (London, 1996): 'Jerusalem. (iii). The Dome of the Rock', ibid., 18:495–6; 'Jerusalem. (iv). The Aqsa Mosque', ibid., 17:496–7; 'Abbasid', ibid., 1:19–20; 'Buyid', ibid., 5:321–2; 'Damascus, Great Mosque', 8:479–80; 'Ghaznavid', ibid., 12:512–13; 'Muzaffarid', ibid., 22:391; 'Nishapur', ibid., 23:160–1; 'Saljuq', ibid., 27:630–2; 'Safavid', ibid., 27:512–13; 'Samanid', ibid., 27:667–8.
111. 'Mughal Architecture Explored', *South Asian Studies* 12 (1996), 107–25.
112. 'Literature and the Visual Arts', in *Encyclopaedia of Islamic Literature*, ed. Julie S. Meisami and Paul Starkey (London, 1998), 475–7.
113. 'Introduction', in Vesta S. Curtis, Robert Hillenbrand and J. Michael Rogers, *The Art and Archaeology of Ancient Persia: New Light on the Parthian and Sassanian Empires* (London, 1998), xiii–xiv.
114. 'Vernacular Architecture in Southern Yemen', *British Journal of Middle Eastern Studies* 25/2 (1998), 351–5.
115. 'Richard Ettinghausen and the Iconography of Islamic Art', in *Discovering Islamic Art: Scholars, Collectors and Collections*, ed. Stephen Vernoit (London, 2000), 171–81.
116. 'Introduction: The Orient of the Imagination', *Journal of the Scottish Society for Art History* 6 (2001), 6–10.
117. 'The tomb of Shah Isma'il, Ardabil', in Sheila R. Canby (ed.), *Safavid Art and Architecture* (London, 2002), 3–8.
118. 'Studying Islamic Architecture: Challenges and Perspectives', *Architectural History* 46 (2003), 1–18.
119. 'The Soul of Islamic Art', *National Art Collections Fund Quarterly* (2004), 68–72.
120. 'For God, Empire and Mammon: Some Art-Historical Aspects of the Reformed Dinars of 'Abd al-Malik', in *Al-Andalus und Europa. Zwischen Orient und Okzident*, eds Martina Müller-Wiener, Christiane Kothe, K.-H.Golzio and Joachim Gierlichs (Petersberg, 2004), 20–38.
121. 'New Perspectives in Shahnama Iconography', in *Shahnama. The Visual Language of the Persian Book of Kings*, ed. Robert Hillenbrand (Aldershot, 2004), 1–7.

Joint Articles

122. (with A. A. Bakhtiar) 'Domestic Architecture in Nineteenth-Century Iran: the Manzil-i Sartip Sidihi near Isfahan', in *Qajar Iran: Political, Social and Cultural Change, 1800–1925. Studies in Honour of L. P. Elwell-Sutton*, ed. C. Edmund Bosworth and Carole Hillenbrand (Edinburgh, 1984), 383–401.
123. (with M. Lee and C. Raso) 'Mamluk Caravansarais in Galilee', *Levant* 23 (1992), 55–92.

Index

pomegranates, 145, 147, 149–51,
    figs 9.5–7, pl. 16
Princes of the House of Timur, 90,
    pl. 11

Qadi Ahmad, 206
Qadi-yi Jahan, 207
Qairan, mosque, 154
qaqnus (swan-phoenix), 96–7,
    100n
Qarawiyyin mosque see Fez
Qasr al-Hair al-Gharbi palace, 149,
    154
Qasr al-Hair al-Sharqi, 154–5
Qayrawan, mosque of Sidi Uqba,
    23, 30
Qazwini, Aja'ib al-Makhluqat, 94
quails, 9–10
Qubbat al-Sakra 150, 154
quincunx design, 65, 69
Qusair 'Amra bath, 154, 155

Rashid al-Din
    Jami' al-tawarikh, 45, 48, 51, 56,
        241, 253, fig. 3.2, pl. 3
Ravandi, 242
Riza ('Abbasi), 263
Roger II, 61, 69, 78
Rukn al-Din Firuz, 168
Rukn al-din Khwarshah, 50, 56
rulers
    denoted by sun, 82
    holding flowers, 84–5, 90
    kneeling, 84–6, 90
    sedentary positions, 86
    wearing turquoise-green, 84, 89,
        90, pl. 7
Rumi, Jalal al-Din, Mathnawi, 7
Rustam
    and Ashkabus, fig. 15.2
    and Bizhan, fig. 15.4
    death, figs 15.1, 15.6
    and death of Suhrab, figs 15.5,
        15.7
    in leopard's mask, 256, 258,
        260–1, 266
    and lions or tigers, 253
    meets Kay Khrusraw, 46
    in Mongol dress, 253
    with Raksh and the Lion, pl. 28
    'Rustam Lassoing the King of
        Sham', 261
    in Shahnama mss: Mongol, 253:
        Inju, 253, 256: Muzaffarid,

256: Timurid, 256: Shiraz-
    Timurid, 256, 258, 260:
    Turkman, Commercial, 261:
    Safavid, 261: Isfahan, 263:
    c17, 263: c19, 263, 266: later
    Qajar, 266
'Sleeping Rustam', 261
in tiger-skin surcoat, 253, 256
and White Demon, 265, pl. 29
in youth, 261, 263

Saffah, 276
Safi al-Din Ishaq, Shaykh, 291
Sagittarius, 313
St Mary's of the Admiral church
    see Palermo
al-Salih Ayyub, 319–20
    Freer basin for, 315–21, figs
        18.2–7, pl. 32: medallions: as
        Christian symbols 317–18,
        324n: as symbols of al-
        Mughith 'Uma 320–1
    Louvre tray for, 314–15, 317,
        fig. 18.1
al-Salih Isma'il, 319–20
Sam Mirza, 207
Samarqand, mosque of madrasa of
    Ulugh Beg, 224, fig. 14.2
Sana'i, Litany of the Birds, 12
sand-casting, 13–14n
Sasan b. Babak, 272
senmurv, 16n, 119
shadawar, 94
Shah Jahan on Peacock throne, 90,
    pl. 12
Shahnama, 206
    Baysunghur b. Shah Rukh, 46
    Demotte (Great Mongol), 253,
        fig. 15.1
    Ibrahim Sultan, 11, 258
    Ismai'il II, 263
    Ismai'il, Shah, 261
    Muhammad Juki, 258
    painting styles see under
        Rustam
    Rustam in see Rustam
    Tahmasp, Shah ('Houghton'),
        202, 261
Shahr-i Sabz, masjid-i jami' of
    Ulugh Beg, 226, fig. 14.3
Shi'i 'uluma, 297–8
silver plates, Sassanid, 110, 112,
    117, 120, figs 7.15, 7.17–18,
    7.20–21

siren (musical bird), 96
sirinas
    quadruped, 94
    swan-phoenix, 93–4, 96
Solomon, 9, 12
standards see banners
strapwork design, 64, 65, 72
stupas, 127–8, 130, 138
    Guldarra, Afghanistan, 127,
        128–9, 138, 139, fig. 8.1
Suhrab, figs 15.5, 15.7
Sultan Muhammad, 261
Sultanim (sister of Shah
    Tahmasp), 204
suryanas (swan-phoenix), 95,
    98–9, pl. 14
swan-phoenix, 93, 98–9
    Abū Sayrās, 93
    arghūn, 94–5, 98, pl. 13
    qaqnus, 96–97, 100n
    sirinas, 94, 96
    suryanas, 95, 98–9, pl. 14

Tabari, 270
al-Tabrisi, 289
Tāhir, 116
Tahmasp, Shah, 202–4, 205, 206
    Khamsa for, 201
    and Twelver Shi'ism, 204
tāj, 202, 207
Taj al-Din Yildiz, 168
Tarjuma-yi tarikh-i Tabari
    and ahl al-bayt, 287–8, 290, 291,
        292, 293, 294, 299, 300,
        306n
    and 'Ali, 290, 291, 293, 295, 296,
        301, 304nn
    and angel, 290, 294–5
    and Arab school of painting,
        301, 308n
    and biblical prophet, 293–4,
        306n
    and club, 290
    and dhu'l-fiqār, 291, 295, 297,
        306n
    and divine inspiration, 294–5
    and first caliphs, 286–7, 295–6,
        307n
    and genealogy of Muhammad,
        285–6, 299
    and green clothing, 291–3
    and hadīth al-thaqalayan, 285,
        289–93, 299, pl. 31
    and Hasan, 290, 293, 294, 296